Interpreting the
Old Testament
after Christendom

AFTER CHRISTENDOM Series

Christendom was a historical era, a geographical region, a political arrangement, a sacral culture, and an ideology. For many centuries Europeans have lived in a society that was nominally Christian. Church and state have been the pillars of a remarkable civilization that can be traced back to the decision of the emperor Constantine I early in the fourth century to replace paganism with Christianity as the imperial religion.

Christendom, a brilliant but brutal culture, flourished in the Middle Ages, fragmented in the Reformation of the sixteenth century, but persisted despite the onslaught of modernity. While exporting its values and practices to other parts of the world, however, it has been slowly declining during the past three centuries. In the twenty-first century Christendom is unravelling.

What will emerge from the demise of Christendom is not yet clear, but we can now describe much of Western culture as "post-Christendom." *Post-Christendom is the culture that emerges as the Christian faith loses coherence within a society that has been definitively shaped by the Christian story and as the institutions that have been developed to express Christian convictions decline in influence.*

This definition, proposed and unpacked in *Post-Christendom*, the first book in the After Christendom series, has gained widespread acceptance. *Post-Christendom* investigated the Christendom legacy and raised numerous issues that are explored in the rest of the series. The authors of this series, who write from within the Anabaptist tradition, see the current challenges facing the church not as the loss of a golden age but as opportunities to recover a more biblical and more Christian way of being God's people in God's world.

The series addresses a wide range of issues, including theology, social and political engagement, how we read Scripture, youth work, mission, worship, relationships, and the shape and ethos of the church after Christendom.

Eleven books were published by Paternoster between 2004 and 2016:

Stuart Murray, *Post-Christendom*

Stuart Murray, *Church after Christendom*

Jonathan Bartley, *Faith and Politics after Christendom*

Jo Pimlott and Nigel Pimlott, *Youth Work after Christendom*

Alan Kreider and Eleanor Kreider, *Worship and Mission after Christendom*

Lloyd Pietersen, *Reading the Bible after Christendom*

Andrew Francis, *Hospitality and Community after Christendom*

Fran Porter, *Women and Men after Christendom*

Simon Perry, *Atheism after Christendom*

Brian Haymes and Kyle Gingerich Hiebert, *God after Christendom*

Jeremy Thomson, *Relationships and Emotions after Christendom*

Two of these (*Worship and Mission after Christendom* and *Reading the Bible after Christendom*) were also published by Herald Press.

The series is now in the hands of Wipf and Stock, who are republishing some of the existing titles, including *Post-Christendom*, and commissioning further titles, including:

Joshua Searle, *Theology after Christendom*

Andy Hardy and Dan Yarnell, *Missional Discipleship after Christendom*

John Heathershaw, *Security after Christendom*

Jeremy Thomson, *Interpreting the Old Testament after Christendom*

Andrew Francis and Janet Sutton, *Sacraments after Christendom*

Brian Haymes and Kyle Gingerich Hiebert, *God after Christendom?*

Interpreting the
Old Testament
after Christendom

A Workbook for Christian Imagination

Jeremy Thomson

CASCADE *Books* • Eugene, Oregon

INTERPRETING THE OLD TESTAMENT AFTER CHRISTENDOM
A Workbook for Christian Imagination

After Christendom Series

Copyright © 2021 Jeremy Thomson. All rights reserved. Except for brief quotations in critical publications or reviews, no part of this book may be reproduced in any manner without prior written permission from the publisher. Write: Permissions, Wipf and Stock Publishers, 199 W. 8th Ave., Suite 3, Eugene, OR 97401.

Cascade Books
An Imprint of Wipf and Stock Publishers
199 W. 8th Ave., Suite 3
Eugene, OR 97401

www.wipfandstock.com

PAPERBACK ISBN: 978-1-5326-1903-8
HARDCOVER ISBN: 978-1-4982-4505-0
EBOOK ISBN: 978-1-4982-4504-3

Cataloguing-in-Publication data:

Names: Thomson, Jeremy, author.

Title: Interpreting the Old Testament after Christendom : a workbook for Christian imagination / Jeremy Thomson.

Description: Eugene, OR: Cascade Books, 2021 | Series: After Christendom | Includes bibliographical references.

Identifiers: ISBN 978-1-5326-1903-8 (paperback) | ISBN 978-1-4982-4505-0 (hardcover) | ISBN 978-1-4982-4504-3 (ebook)

Subjects: LCSH: Bible—Old Testament—Criticism, interpretation, etc. | Bible—Hermeneutics | Bible. O.T. Joshua—Criticism, interpretations, etc. | Bible. O.T. Judges—Criticism, interpretations, etc. | Bible. O.T. Samuel—Criticism, interpretations, etc. | Bible. O.T. Kings—Criticism, interpretations, etc.

Classification: BS1171.2 T46 2021 (print) | BS1171.2 (ebook)

In gratitude to my first biblical studies teachers at Trinity College, Bristol
(1980–83):

Gervais Angel
Joyce Baldwin
John Bimson
Margaret Embry
Gordon McConville
Alec Motyer

Contents

Preface xi
Abbreviations and Reference Works xv

1. Introduction 1

PART I: Interpretative Approaches
2. The First Testament in the Second 35
3. Interpreting Whole Books 56

PART II: Reading the Former Prophets
Prelude 89
4. The Book of Joshua 93
5. The Book of Judges 118
6. The Book of Samuel 142
7. The Book of Kings 172

PART III: Interpreting the First Testament
8. Canonical Conversations 207
9. Reframing the First Testament 235
10. Facilitating Access to the First Testament 257

Bibliography 289

Preface

The writing of this book was completed during the early months (in the UK) of the Covid-19 pandemic. Some church leaders have made extravagant assertions about the protection against contracting the virus afforded by faith in Jesus.[1] I came across several claims to God's protection on the basis of Psalm 91, which declares to those who make God their refuge that "he will deliver you from the snare of the fowler and from the deadly pestilence" (v. 3). There is no doubt that this psalm exhorts people to trust God with their lives, yet it can be misunderstood and even misused. Intriguingly, a later part of this very psalm (vv. 11–12) was used by the devil to suggest Jesus might throw himself off the top of the Jerusalem temple (Matt 4:5–7; Luke 4:9–12). The response? "It is said, 'Do not put the Lord your God to the test.'" Of all people, Jesus put his life in God's hands; he would ultimately trust God to deliver him from death by going through and beyond it, having accepted this perilous path as the unavoidable outcome of his life. Yet he saw through the lure of the words of this psalm to engage in a spectacular stunt that would draw attention to himself. What was crucial about his interpretation employing a quotation from Deuteronomy 6:16? For Jews, the Torah was central to the scriptures, and Moses' words in Deuteronomy were frequently on Jesus' lips. Poor biblical interpretation may damage your physical health and harm others' as well!

Many contemporary Christians are unfamiliar with the Bible, and few churches encourage concerted Bible reading or help readers to understand how its many books work together and engage with their lives. I have spent much of the last forty years helping Christians to interpret

---

1. E.g., The BBC Radio 4 "Sunday" programme on 26th April 2020 broadcast an interview with "Pastor Audrey" from Virginia, who appealed to Psalm 91 and claimed that "God told us in his word that we are protected . . ." so that those who put their trust in such shelter would not contract the virus.

the Bible, and have facilitated learning in several adult and higher education contexts in England over the last twenty-five years. I have observed a marked decline in biblical literacy, especially regarding the Old Testament.

This is an astounding state of affairs when we consider how much the Jewish scriptures meant to Jesus and his early followers. The Gospel writers present him as intimately familiar with these sacred writings—as he taught his disciples, engaged in debate with opponents, and understood his own career and life-course. Paul and the other New Testament authors were likewise steeped in these books. It is almost incomprehensible that those who profess to love and follow Jesus should give so little time and attention to understanding them!

In my own life, I have found profound resources in the Old Testament. Its narratives shaped my identity as a child and my worldview as a young person. While training for ordained ministry in the Church of England, I wrote a dissertation on "Preaching from the Old Testament." During the challenges of Christian ministry and leadership I found companionship with Israel's prophets, and as a teacher I have found stimulus in Israel's wisdom literature. My doctoral research in ecclesiology was grounded in Israel's life as God's people in God's world. Whilst tutoring in higher education, I have seen God's Spirit at work when people wrestle with questions of biblical interpretation.

This book began to take shape when I presented a paper entitled "Reading the Deuteronomistic History after Christendom" at the Anabaptist Theological Forum in 2008. An updated version was published on the website of (what is now) the Anabaptist Mennonite Network. I am grateful to Stuart Murray Williams for accepting my proposal for a book-length treatment in the After Christendom series that provides a different perspective to Lloyd Pietersen's *Reading the Bible after Christendom*. Members of the Anabaptist Network Steering Group provided valuable feedback at an early stage. I presented a further paper to the Anabaptist Theological Forum in 2018 that focussed on literary interpretation and supersessionism's influence on hermeneutics.

I am grateful to two friends who have kindly read and commented on my first draft. I first met John Bimson in the 1970s when he was working on his doctorate on the date of the exodus and I was an engineering undergraduate; we served together on the Committee of Sheffield University Christian Union. In the 1980s he became one of my Old Testament tutors at Trinity College, Bristol, and supervised the dissertation

PREFACE

mentioned above. Now his historical and archaeological expertise and eye for detail has helped to correct a number of my mistakes and improve the manuscript. My friendship with Andrew Francis was forged while we toiled together as trustees of the London Mennonite Centre during a time of crisis and new direction in the early 2010s. He too has spotted some of my mistakes and his consideration of potential readers has encouraged me to improve presentation in some places.

I am also thankful to my editor, Robin Parry, for his careful attention to my manuscript. His expertise in the field has prompted me to sharpen my meaning in several places and to clarify my thinking in a number of others. Thanks too to the production team at Cascade who have brought my text to publication, and to the publicity team for making my book known. I am grateful to Joshua Searle, John Bimson, and Andrew Francis for writing commendations for the back cover.

As a provocation to think in new ways, I have decided to use the terms "First Testament" and "Second Testament" in place of "Old Testament" and "New Testament" as much as possible in this book (apart from quotations from other writers).[2] A number of scholars have noted that "Old Testament" fosters the dismissive attitude to the Hebrew Scriptures that is often encountered today, and some have proposed "Scripture" instead of "Old Testament," since this was the term used by Jesus and the apostles. However, the whole Christian Bible functions as scripture for the Christian community,[3] so "First" and "Second" is a better solution, when considered in comparison with common usage, such as the first and second halves of a musical performance, or even the first and second halves of a soccer match.

When making quotations from the Bible I have used the New Revised Standard Version, except in a few places, which are noted. Readers looking for a stimulating alternative might explore Robert Alter's translation.[4] I have represented God's name using the convention of YHWH (except in direct quotations from English translations and secondary authors), the English letters representing the Tetragrammaton, or four Hebrew letters used for the divine name. This has often been written in English as "Yahweh," but since the name has understandably been treated by Jewish people with such reverence that it is not spoken aloud, we do

2. As proposed by Block, in *Triumph of Grace*, xvi, among others.
3. See the discussion in Bader-Saye, *God and Israel after Christendom*, 149n7.
4. For Joshua–Kings see Alter, *Ancient Israel*.

PREFACE

not know how it was originally pronounced. Alternatively, use has been made of "Jehovah," a compound of the consonants from YHWH with the vowels from *Adonai* (Lord). The reason the Hebrew Bible places the vowels of Adonai in the name YHWH is to remind Jews when reading scripture aloud to say the word Adonai in place of speaking the divine name. The NRSV renders the name as "the LORD," distinguishing it from the generic title "Lord," but this can cause confusion and fails to register the special quality conveyed by the personal name of Israel's God (e.g., in Exod 3:13–15).[5]

I use the scholarly convention of "Common Era" and "Before the Common Era," abbreviated to CE and BCE, since it is more inclusive than the traditional AD and BC that became widely used in Christendom after 800.

In 2017 Kathy and I moved to Cilgwyn, near Newport in north Pembrokeshire, south-west Wales. She has done much to enable me to concentrate on completing this book, and I am very grateful for her love, patience, and hard work over the years since we were introduced in 1984. This book has been written with appreciation for many new friends who have made us welcome in an ancient, rugged landscape surrounded by rocky shores. So now, reader, you know a little of my story! I welcome comments and questions at jeremyhthomson@mac.com.

---

5. Again, following Block, *Triumph of Grace*, xv.

Abbreviations and Reference Works

AB	Anchor Bible
BO	BERITH OLAM: Studies in Hebrew Narrative & Poetry
CBQ	*Catholic Biblical Quarterly*
C&C	Covenant & Conversation: A Weekly Reading of the Jewish Bible
DJG	*Dictionary of Jesus and the Gospels*. Edited by Joel B. Green, Scot McKnight, and I. Howard Marshall. Downers Grove, IL: InterVarsity, 1992.
DOTHB	*Dictionary of Old Testament Historical Books*. Edited by Bill T. Arnold and H. G. M. Williamson. Downers Grove, IL: InterVarsity, 2005.
DOTP	*Dictionary of the Old Testament Prophets*. Edited by Mark J. Boda and J. Gordon McConville. Downers Grove, IL: InterVarsity, 2012.
DOTWPW	*Dictionary of Old Testament Wisdom, Poetry & Writings*. Edited by Tremper Longman III and Peter Enns. Downers Grove, IL: InterVarsity, 2008.
DSE	*Dictionary of Scripture and Ethics*. Edited by Joel B. Green, Jacqueline E. Lapsley, Rebekah Miles, and Allen Verhey. Grand Rapids: Baker Academic, 2011.
DTIB	*Dictionary for Theological Interpretation of the Bible*. Edited by Kevin J. Vanhoozer et al. Grand Rapids: Baker Academic, 2005.
EEC	*Encyclopaedia of Early Christianity*. Edited by Everett Ferguson et al. 2nd ed. London: Garland, 1998.

ABBREVIATIONS AND REFERENCE WORKS

ESV	English Standard Version
IBC	Interpretation: A Bible Commentary for Teaching and Preaching
IRUSC	Interpretation: Resources for the Use of Scripture in the Church
JBL	*Journal of Biblical Literature*
JSNTSup	Journal for the Study of the New Testament Supplement Series
JSOT	*Journal for the Study of the Old Testament*
JSOTSup	Journal for the Study of the Old Testament Supplement Series
LHBOTS	Library of Hebrew Bible/Old Testament Studies
NIB	*New Interpreters' Bible*, Vols. I–X. Edited by Leander E. Keck et al. Nashville: Abingdon, 1994–2002.
NICOT	New International Commentary on the Old Testament
NIVAC	New International Version Application Commentary
OBT	Overtures to Biblical Theology
OHBN	*Oxford Handbook of Biblical Narrative*. Edited by Danna Nolan Fewell. Oxford; Oxford University Press, 2016.
OTL	Old Testament Library
SBL	Society of Biblical Literature
SHBC	Smyth & Helwys Biblical Commentary
THOTC	Two Horizons Old Testament Commentary
TOTC	Tyndale Old Testament Commentary
WBC	Word Biblical Commentary
WKG	*What Kind of God? Collected Essays of Terence E. Fretheim*. Edited by Michael J. Chan and Brent A. Strawn. Siphrut 14. Winona Lake, IL: Eisenbrauns, 2015.*

1

Introduction

1. Interpretation after Christendom

This book is about the challenges and fascinations for Christians of interpreting the Old Testament, or as I prefer to call it, the First Testament. The focus will be on its narrative literature, though its poetry, law, and wisdom also play a part. My aim is to assist readers to encounter the books of the First Testament and discover their relevance, indeed, to hear God's Spirit speaking through them. This is not an armchair book but an aid to study, so readers may wish to have easy access to an open Bible.

There was a time in the United Kingdom when the Bible was familiar to most people because they attended church regularly, where the First Testament was read and preached from. There were references to its characters and stories in art, literature, and music, and its turns of phrase appeared in common parlance ("into the lion's den," etc.). This was the era of Christendom, when most people assumed that Christianity went hand-in-glove with the nation's culture, its politics, and its everyday life. Today some of these things linger, but they are passing out of regular usage.

During the twentieth century there was a steady decline in church-going, and a corresponding waning of influence of the churches (both established and non-conformist) in public life. There was growth in adherence to alternative religions, though the majority of the population would seem to have little interest in such things, and some would subscribe to atheism or agnosticism. In the UK, the formal links between the established church and state remain; daily business in the House of Commons is preceded by prayers, senior bishops of the Church of England sit in the House of Lords by right, the monarch is crowned by the Archbishop of Canterbury. Residents of a Church of England parish have the right to be married in its church building, have their babies baptized there, and to vote at its Annual General Meeting. State schools are supposed to have regular collective worship that is wholly or mainly of a Christian character, according to recent Education Acts, although this is rarely adhered to in practice. These are significant remnants of the past, yet they are often maintained out of tradition, inertia, or desperation rather than conviction.

Many committed Christians long for a time when this process of decline might be reversed, and we might be a "Christian country" once more. It is true that Christian traditions and values have made a significant contribution to British culture, but these were always mixed with a strong dose of Greek and Roman ideas, stories, values, and practices, together with some pagan inheritance. But it is highly questionable whether Britain was ever *truly* Christian, where the challenge of following Jesus was embraced by more than a small minority. In its origins Christianity transcended nationhood and united people across political and ethnic boundaries, since allegiance to Jesus Christ came before any other loyalty (Gal 3:28; Col 3:11, etc.). However, a process of change in Christian attitudes and practices began once Christianity was tolerated by Constantine's Edict of Milan in 313 CE and was consolidated when Theodosius banned religions other than Christianity from the Roman Empire in 381.[1] Whenever nations have formally espoused Christianity, whatever laudable motives may have been involved, it has turned into a co-opted religion, with all the iniquities of religiously sanctioned privilege, exclusion of non-conformists, oppression, and violence. There were centuries within British Christendom when certain followers of Jesus were persecuted, or at least socially disadvantaged (Lollards, Puritans, Baptists, Quakers, and Catholics).

Today, other committed Christians have accepted that Christendom lies largely in the past and that it is time to welcome living after Christendom. There are many lessons that can be learned from Christians who

---

1. For the changes in practices and mindsets that accompanied the inception of Christendom, see the complementary studies by Kreider, *Patient Ferment*, and Howard-Brook, *Empire Baptized*.

INTRODUCTION

lived during Christendom, from those who lived before Christendom began, and from those who have lived in parts of the world that have never experienced it.[2] I will not repeat the helpful historical overview of Bible reading that Lloyd Pietersen provided in his contribution to this series.[3] Like Lloyd, I recognize that Christendom lies in the past, but this book focusses more concertedly on the interpretation of the First Testament.

This chapter sets the scene by considering some of the challenges that these scriptures pose, and then sketches several approaches that have been adopted to interpret them. It considers some aspects of the interpretive approach that I seek to adopt, drawing particular attention to the impact of the long-held assumption that the Christian church has replaced God's ancient people, the Jews, in God's purposes. It closes with an overview of the chapters that follow.

2. First Testament Challenges

Readers often encounter several significant challenges; I will mention four of them.

The First Testament is frequently understood as less important than the Second. In the Protestant tradition, the letters of Paul to the Romans and Galatians have been particularly influential, and their apparently negative comments regarding "the law" have often been taken as reasons for disregarding the Torah (i.e., the Pentateuch) along with the Prophets and the Writings.[4] Judaism has been regarded as a religion of works-righteousness, and thus its scriptures have been viewed with suspicion.[5] The very use of "Old" in contrast to "New" implies that the former is out of date, superseded, and this assumption must be challenged.

Secondly, the First Testament is a large collection of books, containing many different kinds of literature. While the basic storyline can be fairly easily picked out, those who attempt to read through it from the beginning often get stuck in only the third book because Leviticus' detailed

---

2. For an extensive discussion of Christendom, its end, and what might follow, see Murray, *Post-Christendom*.

3. Pietersen, *Reading the Bible after Christendom*, chapters 2–4.

4. The Hebrew Bible consists of three parts, *Torah* (Law), *Nevi'im* (Prophets), and *Ketuvim* (Writings); together they may be referred to by the acronym *TaNaK*.

5. In Second Testament scholarship, the various "new perspectives" on Paul have seen an important re-evaluation of Paul's attitude to the law, but these have yet to filter into many church teaching programs.

regulations appear tedious. On closer inspection, the way in which God is portrayed in one book turns out to be rather different from the way the same God appears in another. For example, the standards required by this God appear to vary from one book to another; compare the regular construction of altars at various sites by the patriarchs in Genesis chapters 12–35 with the insistence upon one central shrine for worship in Deuteronomy chapter 12. How then can readers make sense of the wealth of material, but also the diversity of voices, and even competing theologies, found in the First Testament?

Thirdly, some parts of the First Testament are very contentious, and it can be tempting to avoid engaging with controversy. The debate continues in many countries about the biblical stories of creation and the scientific theory of evolution. Historians and archaeologists raise important questions about Israel's conquest of the land of Canaan, and some have doubted whether Kings Saul, David, and Solomon even existed. What interpretive perspectives might illuminate these debates, and enable readers to decide wisely concerning such issues?

Fourthly, and perhaps most troublingly, the First Testament contains several ethical challenges that alienate many readers, of which the most obvious are:

- Violence appears central to its main story; indeed, some have alleged that genocide is commanded by God on several occasions. In one of its most famous stories, God instructs Abraham to sacrifice his son, Isaac, though stops him at the last moment. If Jesus, as presented in the Second Testament, reveals a God of peace, how can this be reconciled with the violent portrayal of God in the First?
- Women are marginalized throughout the First Testament, and despite some notable exceptions in which women play significant parts, it seems an androcentric collection of books—and it has usually been interpreted that way. So, is it sexist as well as patriarchal?
- Slavery frequently appears in the pages of the First Testament, together with laws that regulate its practice; it appears to have been an institution that God is prepared to tolerate.

It is these ethical difficulties that are currently most challenging. A number of writers who are hostile to Christianity, or to any religious faith, have pointed to such ethical sore points as grounds for rejecting the Bible. Several Christian scholars have responded directly to these challenges, while others have been aware of the difficulty within their own tradition and sought to nuance their own understanding of scripture. This book cannot provide complete answers to the most challenging intellectual questions and existential challenges faced by those who seek to hear God speaking through the scriptures today, but it is hoped that it makes a constructive contribution to a pressing set of questions.

Whilst it is important to acknowledge the challenges presented by the First Testament, it is essential to give some indication of its many benefits, more of which will be discussed in the course of this book. Whilst the Second Testament discloses more about God than could be known from the First, there is much in the latter to be discovered about God, God's involvement with the world and God's dealings with God's people. Thus, several central topics of belief and behavior are at stake in the following chapters:

- *God*: how may we better understand, know, and respond to our Creator, Redeemer, and Transformer?
- *Ecclesiology*: how do God's people understand themselves in relation to God's mission to the world?
- *Ethics*: how should God's people live in the world today and how might they contribute to wider ethical discussion?
- *Scripture*: how does God communicate through a collection of ancient books to God's people today?

3. Approaches to the Interpretation of the First Testament

The challenges outlined above are complicated by the fact that many different responses to them have been developed by Christians down the centuries, and it will be helpful at this point to provide an overview of some of the interpretive options. I have identified four broad approaches to the interpretation of the First Testament, the first of which is radical rejection. The second approach finds ways round parts of scripture that are difficult to reconcile with each other, while the third faces up to the challenge of such clashing voices. The fourth approach is more conservative, but includes three alternative strategies to the challenge of violence. These approaches are not mutually exclusive, nor is this a comprehensive survey of such approaches, since that would require a book in itself, but it is intended to provide some orientation to the field.

a. Reject Entirely

This approach was first made by a second-century church leader named Marcion, at a time when no Christian Bible had yet been established. The Greek version of the Jewish scriptures (known as the Septuagint, abbreviated to LXX) was well established in the churches, and various copies of the apostolic writings circulated among them, along with numerous other documents later excluded from the canon. Marcion was born in Pontus, on the Black Sea, the son of a bishop and wealthy ship owner. He went to Rome about 140 CE, became a member of the church there, and gave it a large sum of money. Under the influence of Cerdo, a gnostic[6] teacher, he developed a novel faith, and expounded this to the church leaders, consequently being excommunicated in July 144.[7]

Marcion held that there was a radical dichotomy between the law and the gospel, and he distinguished sharply between the God of the Jewish scriptures (an inferior creator God, or *Demiurge*), and the Supreme God as revealed by Jesus Christ. However, Marcion rejected the twelve apostles as Judaizers who taught a modified Judaism that was offensive to God, believing that only Paul correctly understood the teaching of Jesus. He used Paul selectively to support his view, while rejecting as interpolations those Pauline passages that supported the Jewish scriptures. He deduced from Galatians 1:8–9 that there was only one Gospel book, identifying this as Luke, and rejected the other Gospels as contaminated with Jewish influences. Yet, while Luke was closest to the original Gospel, it too was tainted and required redaction to discard Jewish elements, such as the infancy narrative (1:1—2:52) and genealogy (3:23–38). Marcion was the first person to compile a new collection of scriptures; this consisted of an abridged Gospel of Luke, and ten expurgated letters of Paul (without 1 & 2 Timothy and Titus). It was introduced by his own

---

6. The word "gnostic" is a catch-all term used to refer to various groups that believed people could be saved from an evil world through the secret teaching of a "revealed knowledge" (*gnosis*) and thereby gain access to the true divine world beyond it, whereas all other humans were trapped in ignorance of that divine world. See Pheme Perkins, "Gnosticism."

7. For details, see Stander, "Marcion."

Antitheses, which justified his criticism of the Jewish scriptures and his formation of this canon, or authorized collection of definitive writings.

Marcion founded his own church with a similar organization and ritual as that of the Roman church, within which his own writings assumed a scripture-like status.[8] Although he died c.154, Marcion's movement spread rapidly throughout the Roman empire, flourishing for nearly a century. All the leading patristic writers denounced him, and in the second half of the fourth century, Cyril of Jerusalem thought it necessary to warn Christians not to enter a Marcionite church by mistake. Marcion was wrong, but are many contemporary Christians effectively following him in their neglect of the First Testament?

b. Employ the Concept of Divine Accommodation

The church fathers were troubled by the obvious differences between the views of God and religious practice between the Testaments. Origen responded to Marcion, Valentinus, and other gnostics by insisting that the way to interpret passages about the violent defeat of enemies, like Joshua 10:20–26, was to apply them to the personal conquest of sin.[9] Such "spiritual" or "allegorical" reading of the First Testament was widespread in the early and medieval church.[10] However, this approach fell out of favor with the Reformers, who took up an alternative approach found in many early theologians, that of divine accommodation.[11] For example, Gregory of Nazianzus (c. 329–390) had argued that God permitted animal sacrifice by Abraham and his descendants as a concession to their limited horizons of understanding and as part of a gradual process of revelation (*Orations* 5.25).

It is interesting that John Calvin, who took divine involvement in war at face value, found ways to discount other things attributed to God in the First Testament. In his *Commentary on Genesis*, he says that the account of the creation of a firmament in the sky to hold back the

---

8. For discussion of Marcion's limited influence upon the formation of the Christian canon, see McDonald, *Biblical Canon*, 324–33.

9. See the discussion in Earl, *Joshua Delusion*, 8–14, 109–11.

10. See Levy, *Medieval Biblical Interpretation*.

11. See the detailed study of Benin, *Footprints of God*.

waters above it (1:6–8) seemed "opposed to common sense, and quite incredible,"[12] and he later commented on 6:14:

> Moses wrote everywhere in homely style, to suit the capacity of the people. . . . Certainly in the first chapter he did not treat scientifically the stars, as a philosopher would; but he called them in a popular manner, according to their appearance to the uneducated rather than according to the truth.[13]

Furthermore, commenting on Genesis' striking insight into God's response to human wickedness: "the LORD was sorry that he had made humankind on the earth, and it grieved him to his heart" (6:6), Calvin writes:

> The repentance which is here ascribed to God does not properly belong to him but has reference to our understanding of him. For since we cannot comprehend him as he is, it is necessary that, for our sakes he should, in a certain sense, transform himself. That repentance cannot take place in God easily appears from this single consideration that nothing happens which is by him unexpected or unforeseen. The same reasoning, and remark, applies to what follows, that God was affected by grief. Certainly, God is not sorrowful or sad, but remains forever like himself in his celestial and happy repose: yet, because it could not otherwise be known how great is God's hatred of sin, therefore the Spirit accommodates himself to our capacity.[14]

Calvin's appeal to the concept of accommodation was a traditional way in which Jewish and Christian thinkers expressed the conviction that there were errors in scripture.

Jean Lasserre, a twentieth-century French Reformed theologian who disagreed with Calvin on the question of war,[15] faced up to the significant moral distance between God in the First and Jesus in the Second Testament, and admitted: "I can see only one satisfying answer: the systematic refusal of violence was a personal contribution by Jesus of Nazareth, His

---

12. Calvin, *Genesis 1*, 32.
13. Calvin, *Genesis 1*, 153.
14. Calvin, *Genesis 1*, 147.
15. "Calvin's fundamental error over the problem of war seems to lie precisely in the fact that he founds his ethic indifferently on the two Testaments, giving the same authority to both." Lasserre, *War and the Gospel*, 59.

original discovery."[16] The novelty of Jesus' insight is underlined by the path of his own career:

> This is part of the crucial misunderstanding between Jesus and His people. His method of non-violence was strange by comparison with the Old Testament, . . . it bewildered His contemporaries and disappointed even his friends and disciples. . . . In the crisis the crowd deserted Him at once because they were ready to use violence and could not see why He still would not use it.[17]

We might add that Jesus appears to have startled his contemporaries in several other ways, such as his unusual respect for women and children. How did Jesus come by such novel attitudes? Lassere makes some brief suggestions but does not explore this question systematically.

Kenton Sparks has recently followed the general approach of accommodation but argued carefully for acknowledging the inconsistencies and moral problems of the First and Second Testaments, by characterizing the Bible as *Sacred Word, Broken Word*. In the same way that God's creation is good yet includes evil, God's written word is good yet includes evil; in each case the flaws should not be blamed on God, but rather on the fallen, sinful state of humanity.[18] Sparks amends the traditional move of divine accommodation in three ways. Firstly, it was formerly thought that the human authors, such as Moses, colluded with the divine accommodation,[19] but Sparks proposes that the accommodation happened between God and the human author, such that God adopted Moses' ancient view of the cosmos. Secondly, accommodation was previously appealed to only at certain points where there appeared a difficulty, but Sparks argues that God adopted the human words and viewpoints of finite, fallen human authors on every page, so that the *entire* Bible is accommodated discourse. Thirdly, Sparks suggests employing the term "providential adoption" rather than "accommodation" since the latter tends to imply that God is active in communicating errant human views, whereas it is more appropriate to think that God honoured the human

---

16. Lassere, *War and the Gospel*, 62.
17. Lasserre, *War and the Gospel*, 63.
18. Sparks, *Sacred Word*, 47.
19. For example, in Calvin, *Genesis 1*, 79–80, God knew the proper scientific cosmology, *and so did Moses*, but kept it secret! Thus, both God and Moses accommodated to the Israelites' limitations.

wills of the authors, allowing them freedom to be themselves (in all their time- and culture-bound specificity).

> Such a "passive" account of the matter is particularly important in the case of biblical genocide (and similar textual terrors), else we are compelled to say that God participated in human evils to achieve a grander spiritual purpose. A better description in these cases would be that God has canonically adopted human authors as his speakers and that, in doing so, he has permitted these authors—fallen as they were—to write the sorts of things that ancient fallen people would write about their enemies. It is one of the great mysteries of faith that God's redemptive activity is carried out successfully and beautifully through the agency of fallen men and women.[20]

Such an approach means that no particular part of the Bible can be taken as straightforward communication of God's character or will for humanity, but that all must be processed through some theological framework. Sparks suggests that interpreters should attend to three voices beyond scripture's discourse when exercising such theological interpretation, each themselves with biblical grounds and enabled by the Spirit; the cosmos, the tradition, and experience.[21]

A contrasting approach to accommodation has been taken by William Webb and Gordon Oeste in their book *Bloody, Brutal and Barbaric?* They focus on holy war texts that raise ethical questions concerning genocide and war rape, and employ a composite approach to interpretation that Webb had previously developed when dealing with other controversial ethical topics.[22] This combines divine accommodation with "an incremental, redemptive-movement ethic," by which they mean that a redemptive storyline can be discerned through the Bible such that God deals with Israel in gradual steps relative to neighboring nations. From a twenty-first-century reader's perspective, God's war commands may appear barbaric (e.g., Deut 21:10–14), yet when compared with what we know about atrocious war practices in the ancient world they appear significantly restrained. For example, Amos' condemnations of various outrages committed by surrounding nations (Amos 1:2—2:3) imply that Israel would disapprove of rather than celebrate such actions.

---

20. Sparks, *Sacred Word*, 54–55.
21. Sparks, *Sacred Word*, 118–31.
22. Webb, *Slaves, Women & Homosexuals* and *Corporal Punishment*.

INTRODUCTION

In addition, Webb and Oeste make a powerful case that the language used about warfare in the First Testament is frequently hyperbolic, as is found generally in ancient Near Eastern battle records. Defending this argument against several more literal interpretations, they refute any notion of genocide in Israel's practice of warfare, and argue that Israel's larger goal was to make the land sacred space for the worship of YHWH.[23] Furthermore, these authors identify a collection of "antiwar or subversive war texts" that present YHWH as an uneasy or highly reluctant war God. For example, YHWH expresses grief over the war sufferings of Israel (e.g., Jer 9:10–11; 17–19), but also over those of other nations (e.g., Isa 15:5; 16:9–11; Jer 48:30–32; 35–36). Again, one feature of warfare in the ancient world was that the victorious king would often build a temple for his god in which the king would boast about his triumph. In contrast, when king David contemplated building a temple for his god, YHWH refused on the grounds that David had "shed much blood and waged great wars" (1 Chr 22:8; cf. 28:3). Further, Israel's temple was decorated with items that evoked the Garden of Eden rather than with depictions of war.

Webb and Oeste conclude from such restraints and reservations that, as well as God's accommodation to the use of warfare in the First Testament, God moves his people towards something better in incremental steps relative to the world around them. They go on to argue that Jesus in the Gospels does not engage in violence and Paul's letters teach a discipleship that is antithetical to violence. Finally, Jesus appears as future apocalyptic warrior, especially in the book of Revelation, but here there are several key differences between his war and conventional war practices. Indeed, the final battle is really no battle at all, since only one warrior fights with one sword, and that sword is in the mouth, not the hand (Rev 19:15). Thus, the Bible's storyline concludes by untangling the ethics of holy war; God will finally enact justice without embedded injustices.

The comparison between Israel's war texts and those from other nations in the ancient Near East succeeds in revealing significant differences, and warrants the claim that Israel's scriptures can be said to reflect certain incremental ethical advances over other societies of that time. However, Webb and Oeste squeeze too many topics into their case for subversive war texts and overplay some prophetic lamentations regarding other nations.[24] While they attend to the shift between war practices before and

23. These two points are summarized at Webb and Oeste, *Bloody, Brutal and Barbaric?* 172 and 249.

24. They refer to lamentations over certain cities without regard to the rhetorical use of this genre as a form of polemic; e.g., Ezek 27:2; 28:12; 32:2 (294).

after the adoption of monarchy, an approach that paid greater attention to changing versions of nationhood though Israel's varying polities would have strengthened their case. Nevertheless, their book demonstrates that the traditional concept of accommodation requires supplementation with further interpretive perspectives if it is to be persuasive.

c. Attend to Diversity within Scripture

Many eminent scholars have pointed to the numerous tensions and even contradictions between various parts of the First Testament; these must be acknowledged rather than denied. In order to hold together these multiple witnesses coherently, the field of biblical theology has developed, and a variety of theological approaches were proposed in the twentieth century, each appealing to different principles of integration, such as covenant (Eichrodt), salvation history (von Rad), the canon (Childs), and election (Preuss).[25]

In his *Theology of the Old Testament*, Walter Brueggemann seeks to do justice to Israel's core testimony concerning YHWH, but also to what he calls its "counter-testimony."[26] Brueggemann explores Israel's core witness in characteristic statements by attending to grammar:

- in verbal sentences—the testimony is to a God who creates, makes promises, delivers, commands, and leads.

- in adjectives—the testimony is articulated normatively at Exodus 34:6–7, "merciful, gracious, slow to anger, abounding in steadfast love and faithfulness . . . yet by no means clearing the guilty . . . ."

- in nouns—the testimony employs metaphors of governance (judge, king, warrior, father) and sustenance (artist, healer, gardener, mother, shepherd) that point substantively to God's mercy, love, and power.

This brief outline doesn't do justice to Brueggemann's detailed and subtle discussion of many texts, but it indicates his approach. He then explores Israel's counter-testimony, consisting of Israel's complaints in many

---

25. Eichrodt, *Theology of the Old Testament*; von Rad, *Old Testament Theology*; Childs, *Old Testament Theology*; Preuss, *Old Testament Theology*. For an overview of the discipline, see Bartholomew, "Biblical Theology."

26. In chapter 2 of his *Theology*, Brueggemann is sensitive to hermeneutical issues, postmodernity, and Judaism.

psalms about injustice, abandonment, and exile, as well as the questions expressed in Job and Ecclesiastes. These highlight YHWH's hiddenness, his ambiguous character (abusive? contradictory? unreliable?), and capacity for violence ("it belongs to the very fabric of this faith").[27] Brueggemann insists that lived faith moves back and forth from self-abandoning praise to self-regarding complaint, maintaining the tension between Israel's testimony and its counter-testimony.[28]

A rather more programmatic approach has been worked out in detail by Wes Howard-Brook as he traces what he identifies as two competing religious visions throughout the whole Bible, one of "creation" and the other of "empire," with Jesus fulfilling the vision of creation. He calls for people to follow the God of creation and to refuse to cooperate with the destructive forces of contemporary empires.[29]

Approaches that give due weight to the diversity of scripture call for an evaluative approach to interpretation on the part of the reader; they involve decisions as to which parts are more central or crucial than others.

d. Accept without Significant Qualification

At the opposite end of the spectrum from Marcion are those Christians who maintain that the First Testament contains no errors (of fact or morality) in what it teaches. In this approach, it is assumed that intimate divine involvement in the human process of writing guards the text from falsehoods, and especially from misrepresentation of God.[30] The strong appeal to divine inspiration can quickly become a justification of a very literal approach to interpretation, which fails to appreciate the subtlety of its language and discounts the ancient cultures within which it was written; it can flatten the variety of its books and come close to violating the very text that it seeks to honor. Yet there are many careful scholars who are alert to such subtleties of interpretation while holding a "high" view of scripture. They adhere to the authority of the First Testament while accepting some relatively minor qualifications.

---

27. Brueggemann, *Theology*, 381.
28. Brueggemann, *Theology*, 400.
29. Howard-Brook, *Come Out, My People!*
30. This view finds its basis in texts such as 2 Tim 3:16–17.

Intrinsic to this approach is the view that violence, while a regrettable aspect of the fallen human condition, is something that God is prepared to deal with. Indeed, God perpetrates violence, since it is said that God sent the flood to destroy human beings because of their spoiling of the world (Gen 6:5–8), and subsequently inflicted death by way of just punishment on many occasions; for example, upon the cities of Sodom and Gomorrah (Gen 18:20; 19:24), and upon the Egyptian firstborn (Exod 12:29). When, in response to the latter calamity, the Pharaoh permitted the people of Israel to depart from Egypt, and then changed his mind and pursued them, YHWH defeated his chariots at the Red Sea and was celebrated as a great warrior (Exod 15:1–18).

Exactly how to interpret these and later instances of divine violence has been taken in several different ways, of which I will consider three.

(i) God's use of violence is morally justified

The most offensive of such divine activity is YHWH's instruction, given through Moses, to "utterly destroy" (*ḥerem*) the inhabitants of Canaan in order that they might occupy this land, which God had promised them (Deut 7:1–6, 17–26; 20:16–18). Joshua later carries out this command at Jericho, Ai, and other cities (Josh 6:16–21; 8:18–29; 10:28–43; 11:6–23). At first glance, this utter destruction appears barbaric so that it has been condemned as genocide.[31] The killing of men, women, and children seems purely for the benefit of the chosen people. However, a closer look shows that there is a moral reason for God's instruction. This is first found in YHWH's promise to Abraham; "Know this for certain, that your offspring . . . shall come back here in the fourth generation; for the iniquity of the Amorites is not yet complete" (Gen 15:13–16). Thus the Israelites would only take possession of the promised land once the Amorites (one Canaanite tribe standing for them all) were ripe for judgment.[32] When Moses charges the Israelites to dispossess the current occupiers of the land, it is on account of their wickedness (Deut 9:4–5), which included child sacrifice (Deut 12:31) and various other transgressions (Lev 18; 20), and had the potential to corrupt the Israelites. In these

---

31. See the discussion in Copan & Flanagan, *Genocide?* chapter 1.

32. Indeed, Abraham's grandson, Jacob, rebuked his sons Simeon and Levi for their violent attack on the Canaanite city of Shechem (Gen 34:25–30; cf. 49:5–7).

ways God's command to wipe out the inhabitants of Canaan is taken as not arbitrary, but morally justified.

Yet, the reader cannot help wondering if the whole population deserved extermination, especially women and children—the use of "wickedness" as justification for mass slaughter finds echoes in genocidal activity down the centuries. A closer look reveals that the language of "blotting out" is modified somewhat to "driving out," and a process of gradual takeover is envisaged in several places (Exod 23:23–33; Num 33:51–56), even "little by little" (Deut 7:20–23), so that it can be argued that many inhabitants would have fled before Israel's army rather than been annihilated.[33]

Once settled in the land, the Israelites themselves were subject to divine punishment for their infidelity to YHWH on many occasions, often in the form of military defeat and oppressive outsider rule, and eventually were dispossessed of the land—and the suffering involved was borne by their women and children as well as by men. Thus, it can be argued that YHWH judged Israel according to the same standards, and by the same means, that had been applied to the land's previous inhabitants.

Such is the general interpretation of violence in the First Testament maintained by many Christians who stand within the Reformed traditions that are traced back to John Calvin and Martin Luther, behind whom stands the hugely influential theologian Augustine of Hippo. They uphold the ethical stance known as "just war," arguing that the Second Testament does not dispense with God's use of violence when the cause is just. They can point to God's judgment taking place when God's Spirit strikes down Ananias and Sapphira following their lie about the extent of their giving to the church, or when Paul, through the Spirit, strikes the magician Elymas blind (Acts 5:1–11; 13:6–12). Indeed, Paul uses very strong language about those who teach a false gospel (Gal 1:8–9; 5:12). Certain passages on the lips of Jesus portray a future divine judgment in which some will be condemned to hell (Matt 23:33; Mark 9:47), and saints, apostles, and prophets are exhorted to rejoice because God has pronounced violent judgment on Babylon, i.e., Rome (Rev 18:20–21).

---

33. Copan & Flannagan, *Genocide?* 76–83. Note that these authors make a concession here to the Bible's use of categorical language in certain places, that can be modified elsewhere.

(ii) God's violence is morally justified, but the role of human violence is diminished

Within the rather different "peace church" tradition, Jesus' teaching and career are interpreted as rejecting violence, both for himself and his followers.[34] The question this raises is whether Jesus definitively revealed God's character as non-violent, or revealed God's strategy to save a world in which human violence simply breeds more violence. In the latter case, it could be argued that God alone might employ violence justly in order to restrain or punish evil. Such is the view of two Mennonite scholars who sought to justify God's right to inflict violence, while distinguishing this from the human use of violence.

Millard Lind argued that the definitive character of warfare on Israel's part was that YHWH fought for his people. Supremely at the Red Sea, the people saw YHWH fight for them, while they simply had to stand still (Exod 14–15). On a number of other significant occasions, although Israelites were involved in the fighting, the key intervention came from YHWH; the battle of Jericho (Josh 6), Joshua's defeat of the Amorites at Gibeon (Josh 10), Barak's battle with the Canaanites at Mt Tabor, celebrated in Deborah's Song (Judg 4–5), Gideon's defeat of the Midianites (Judg 7), Samuel's defeat of the Philistines (1 Sam 7). It was this conviction that David expressed to Goliath before their single combat: "the LORD does not save by sword and spear; for the battle is the LORD's and he will give you into our hand" (1 Sam 17:47).[35] Such conviction was eroded by the introduction of the monarchy and its development of a standing army. Here Lind made an important observation concerning the link between holy war and political structure:

> The central issue of Israel's self-understanding therefore was Yahweh's relation to history through Torah and prophetic word, as brought into tension with Near Eastern myth where the gods were related to history through the coercive structures of kingship law and military power.[36]

Yet the prophets continued to challenge the kings to rely on YHWH for salvation rather than on political alliances, especially in Isaiah's challenge

---

34. An influential twentieth-century advocate of this view was Trocmé, *Nonviolent Revolution*.

35. Similar convictions are found in some psalms, e.g., Pss 33:16–17; 46:1–11; 147:10.

36. Lind, *Yahweh Is a Warrior*, 33.

to king Ahaz (Isa 7:1–17), and in his word to Hezekiah, following which the Assyrian host was destroyed outside Jerusalem (2 Kgs 19). The insistence of later prophets that YHWH fought against his own people through the agency of other nations showed that the biblical writers' concern with regard to warfare "was not merely another nationalism, but a profound moral conviction."[37]

John Howard Yoder insisted on reading the First Testament with respect for its own time and culture, rather than judging it according to contemporary moral norms. He built on Lind's work (at that time unpublished) to argue that what matters in understanding Israel's warfare is not its relation to the forbidding of killing in the Ten Commandments or to some theory of just war (which was developed centuries later), but Israel's trust in YHWH to deliver them from annihilation without military power or alliances. Over a long time, Israel's self-understanding as a people transitioned from a state with a homeland and monarchy, a geographical and ethnic nation, to a faithful remnant in exile without a king or temple. The prophets even developed a vision of YHWH's concern for all peoples (e.g., Isa 19:23–25; Amos 9:7) and future peace between nations and creatures (e.g., Isa 2:2–4; 11:6–9). Thus, within the First Testament itself there is a movement towards the vision of peace that is fully embodied in Jesus' teaching and career.[38] John Nugent has written a compilation and critical assessment of Yoder's many essays on the interpretation of the First Testament. He identifies Yoder's conviction that social ethics cannot be separated from ecclesiology:

> The Old Testament . . . establishes a much-needed canonical trajectory within which to interpret New Testament passages regarding the relation of God's people to the state, the nature of the powers and principalities, the meaning and role for suffering servanthood, the nature of God's reign, and what it means to live as aliens and exiles.[39]

As much as these two theologians point to nonviolence on the part of Jesus' followers, they assign violence to God. When in the early chapters of the Bible God commits himself to ongoing involvement with humanity and the world, with all its violence and injustice, it seems inevitable that

---

37. Lind, *Yahweh Is a Warrior*, 33.

38. Yoder, "If Abraham Is Our Father," in *Original Revolution*, 85–104. See also "God Will Fight for Us" in *Politics of Jesus*, 76–88.

39. Nugent, *Politics of Yahweh*, 188.

the strategy of committing Godself to one particular family and nation would entail the use of violence.

(iii) The Crucified Christ provides the key to divine violence in the First Testament

Gregory Boyd has written a major work that seeks to interpret the violent portrait of God in the First Testament by appeal to the crucified Christ, and followed this with a shorter, popular version.[40] Boyd begins with classic commitment to Jesus Christ as the ultimate revelation of God. He insists that Jesus reveals a God who is love, rejecting Augustine's definition of love as an inner attitude rather than outward behavior, which allowed Augustine to condone the imprisonment, torture, and execution of Christians that he viewed as heretics.[41] In the Second Testament, love is known by Jesus' outward behavior, his laying down of his life for us; the cross is the supreme revelation of God's love. Jesus' incarnation and ministry anticipates and culminates in the crucifixion, while his teaching about God's kingdom calls for non-violence and enemy-love on the part of his disciples. Jesus' resurrection signals God's vindication of Jesus' way of life, and thus demonstrates that the cross is both the power and the wisdom of God.[42]

Secondly, Boyd argues that, although there are glimpses in the First Testament of God as revealed by Jesus Christ, in many places we find a "fallen, culturally conditioned, ugly conception of God."[43] In such places God accommodated to the distorted understanding of God that was held by the characters and authors of the time. In that God permitted Godself to be depicted in these clouded, ill-conceived ways, they testify to God's humility, God's willingness to engage with human beings even though their grasp of God's character was imperfect. Boyd holds that when God is represented in terms that contradict what is later revealed about God in Jesus, God is stooping "to allow the sin and cultural conditioning of his

---

40. Boyd, *Crucifixion of the Warrior God*, and *Cross Vision*.
41. Argued in detail in *Crucifixion*, vol. 1 chapter 4.
42. Boyd, *Cross Vision*, 38–46.
43. Boyd, *Cross Vision*, 54, instancing Jer 13:14.

INTRODUCTION

people to *act upon him* as he bears the sin of his people."⁴⁴ Thus he calls these violent divine portraits "literary crucifixes."⁴⁵

Thirdly, Boyd works in detail to clarify portrayals of God's involvement in judgment within the First Testament. Divine judgment is often understood as God's active involvement in visiting suffering on people or nations, but Boyd advocates an Aikido-style judgment. Aikido is a non-violent school of martial arts in which practitioners, rather than use their own aggressive force, turn the actions of opponents back on the aggressors, who thus end up punishing themselves. When Jesus speaks about the coming destruction of Jerusalem (Luke 19:41–44; Matt 23:36–38) it is with grief rather than out of vengeance. Thus God longs to protect people from the destructive fall-out of their sinful choices, but when they insist on going their own way, he "hands them over" to suffer the consequences.⁴⁶

Next, Boyd distinguishes between judicial and organic forms of punishment, i.e., between punishment that is externally imposed and that in which consequences are in-built. He asserts that, "With the exception of its violent portraits of God, the Bible always describes God's judgments in terms of divine abandonment."⁴⁷ He maintains that the relationship between sin and punishment in the First Testament is organic, instancing Psalm 7:12–16, which employs standard divine warrior imagery, but sees such judgment worked out in natural self-destructive consequences.⁴⁸ Further, Boyd claims that

> whether they are crediting or blaming God when they depict him in violent ways, the very narratives in which they do this almost always contain indications that confirm that the violence they ascribe to God was actually carried out by other agents. And even when their own narratives don't provide such confirmations, other aspects of the biblical narratives do.⁴⁹

He finds evidence of this in the account of the death of the firstborn in Egypt, which begins with YHWH's speech to Moses determining to kill

---

44. Boyd, *Cross Vision*, 59.
45. Boyd, *Cross Vision*, 54 and following.
46. Boyd, *Cross Vision*, 140ff. Boyd finds confirmation of this even in some places in the First Testament; Jer 48:31; Mic 1:8; Hos 4:17; 11:8.
47. Boyd, *Cross Vision*, 149.
48. Boyd, *Cross Vision*, 153.
49. Boyd, *Cross Vision*, 163.

the firstborn people and animals (Exod 12:12), then has Moses inform the elders about the same, yet modifying it such that YHWH "would not allow the destroyer to enter your houses to strike you down" (Exod 12:23). Thus, YHWH's judgment actually took the form of refraining from preventing "the destroyer" from carrying out its desire, a point later emphasized in Hebrews 11:28.

Boyd is to be commended for addressing head-on this complex and disturbing aspect of biblical interpretation that confronts those who are convinced that "the myth of redemptive violence" must be resisted.[50] Several of his affirmations are welcome and well argued:

- The central importance of the cross in Jesus' revelation of God's character as not intrinsically violent.
- God relates to human beings in non-coercive ways.
- God's judgment as Aikido-like, and punishment as organic rather than judicial.
- The significance of evil powers, and their involvement in organic judgment.

However, there are serious flaws in his proposal, not least that he fails to define violence.[51]

Boyd's "Cruciform Hermeneutic" makes the cross central to his reading of the First Testament. At one point he explains that the cross typifies the self-sacrificial love of Jesus' whole career,[52] yet he tends to abbreviate this to Jesus' death, giving the impression that it is uniquely salvific. And although he is critical of the version of penal substitutionary atonement that sees God the Father venting his wrath on Jesus so that he would not need to vent his wrath on other human beings, he fails to explain his own understanding of the cross in atonement. Boyd emphasizes the discontinuities between the First and Second Testaments, calling the former a "shadow" revelation.[53] In particular, he denigrates the law as presented in the First Testament.[54] In *Cross Vision* there is little sense

---

50. Boyd, *Cross Vision*, 138.
51. A task well done by Paynter, *God of Violence Yesterday*, chapter 2.
52. Boyd, *Cross Vision*, 138.
53. Boyd, *Cross Vision*, 25, appealing to Col 2:16–17 and Heb 10:1.
54. Boyd, *Cross Vision*, 27, thinks that John 1:17 contrasts the law given through Moses with the grace and truth that came through Jesus Christ. On this, see chapter 2 below.

INTRODUCTION

of vitally important elements of the First Testament: its peace vision, its critique of empires, injustice, and militarism. Most seriously, Boyd commits himself to the concept of biblical infallibility, yet he treats the violent portraits of God found in the First Testament as misrepresenting God's true nature. As Helen Paynter says,

> If we follow Boyd's argument to its ultimate conclusion, we can trust nothing that the Old Testament says unless and until it is validated by the New Testament. In other words there is no authentic, reliable revelation of God prior to the coming of Jesus Christ.[55]

Despite Boyd's appeal to divine accommodation, it is difficult to avoid the conclusion that the depiction of God's character in the passages concerned *is* fallible according to Boyd's interpretation. For this reason, his view stands on the edge of those who accept the First Testament without "significant qualifications."

4. The Art of Interpretation

Given the foregoing, an explanation of the approach taken by this book is appropriate. I should point out that none of the following details are intended to displace prayers for the illumination of the Holy Spirit and openness to learn from other people, both within the church and without. It may sometimes be convenient to divide life up into compartments such as its physical, mental, and spiritual dimensions, but all aspects of life interact with each other and cannot be separated out without significant loss. Here I need to touch briefly on the specialist subject of hermeneutics, the theory of interpretation.

Hermeneutics takes account of how people read, understand, and make use of texts, especially those written in a different era or culture from our own. The idea that there are "rules" for the interpretation of texts has a long history, going back to rabbinic traditions, but since Schleiermacher in the nineteenth century and Gadamer in the later twentieth century, the notion emerged that hermeneutics was an art rather than a science; it is a practice that must be learned. This was due to their realization of the significance of the readers or communities that read or hear the text, and their role in the whole process of understanding it. Furthermore, hermeneutics "includes the second-order discipline of

---

55. Paynter, "Review," 3.

asking critically *what exactly we are doing when we read, understand, or apply* texts."[56]

Hermeneutics involves recognizing the assumptions one brings to any text as a reader—the influences of family, education, culture—books read, media absorbed, time and attention spent on particular interests, etc. When it comes to reading the Bible, hermeneutics includes reflection on sermons heard, Bible aids read, conversations had, and so on. But it is also about recognizing one's social location; I am a privileged, "white," English male who grew up in an evangelical Christian home and has lived through the second half of the twentieth century and beyond. We can become more hermeneutically aware by acknowledging such influences and the assumptions they contain, by discovering their origins and pathways, by realizing their weaknesses and prejudices as well as their strengths, and by exploring alternatives—unfamiliar and challenging, but often surprisingly illuminating.

Hermeneutics also involves recognizing the assumptions embedded in the texts we are reading—the times and cultures within which they were written—the influences upon their authors, collectors, and transmitters—and their intended audiences. We can become more hermeneutically aware of the scriptures by studying ancient languages, histories, and cultures, and realizing the subtle differences between those ancient worlds and our own, as well as the remarkable similarities.

These two aspects of hermeneutics cannot be isolated from each other, since growing awareness of the one is aided by familiarization with the other. Thus, Gadamer wrote of "the hermeneutical circle," though some recent writers prefer the use of "hermeneutical spiral" since this better reflects development over time with growing familiarization.[57]

Sensitivity to hermeneutical factors can be developed by studying how the Bible has been interpreted before, during, and after Christendom, but this is too large a subject to do it justice here. So, I have decided to sketch one of the most significant stumbling blocks for many Christians reading the First Testament, the axiomatic assumption that Christians have replaced, or superseded the Jews as God's chosen people, known as *supersessionism*.

---

56. Thiselton, *Hermeneutics*, 4.
57. See Thiselton, *Hermeneutics*, 159.

INTRODUCTION

Supersessionism in the Early Church

The roots of supersessionism lie in the so-called "parting of the ways" between the early Christian church and developing Judaism after the destruction of Jerusalem in 70 CE. Some scholars have thought that this parting had already happened by around 135 (after the Bar-Kochba revolt), while others have made the case for a more prolonged process.[58] But the model of parting ways has been seriously questioned.[59] The early Christian churches had much in common with Jewish practice and literature: weekly gatherings for prayer, regular fast days, their liturgical rites such as baptism and eucharist had their roots in Judaism, and especially reading the Jewish scriptures in the Septuagint. However, some early Christian writings, such as the Epistle of Barnabas and the epistles of Ignatius, warned against Judaizing, and during the second-century Christian apologists developed what is now known as the *Adversos Judaeos* tradition. This began with Justin Martyr, whose position has been summarized by Kendall Soulen like this;

> God's history with the carnal community of the Jews is merely a passing episode within God's more encompassing purposes for creation, which are universal and spiritual in nature. As the Hebrew Scriptures themselves testify, Christ is the climax of God's spiritual purposes for creation. Christ therefore ends God's transient relationship with Abraham's physical descendants, and initiates God's enduring relationship with the church, the spiritual community of salvation. Henceforth, the God of Israel is to be found with "the true, spiritual Israel."[60]

A generation after Justin, Irenaeus, bishop of Lyons in Gaul, wrote his great work, *Against Heresies*, combatting gnosticism and asserting the identity of genuine Christianity. By this time the apostolic writings had been largely accepted alongside the ancient Jewish scriptures in a twofold canon approximating to what we know today as the Christian Bible. Irenaeus insisted that the unity of this two-fold canon was found in the "rule of faith" (*regula fidei*), a brief summary statement of Christian

---

58. Dunn argued for the earlier date in *Parting of the Ways*. However, Boyarin has argued that the parting did not take place until the fourth century; see his *Border Lines*, and "Rethinking Jewish Christianity."
59. Becker and Reed, *Ways That Never Parted*.
60. Soulen, *God of Israel*, 37.

belief, derived from the apostles.⁶¹ In order to counter Marcion, Valentinus, and other gnostic writers of the time, Irenaeus concentrated on Genesis 1–3, but then effectively jumped straight to the Gospels and Paul. Irenaeus established a way of reading the scriptures that was so influential in the church that Israel's story is entirely missing from the Apostles' and Nicene Creeds.⁶² Soulen's verdict is that "Justin Martyr and especially Irenaeus bequeathed to the church a canonical narrative of extraordinary scope and power.... Unfortunately, however, the Irenaean solution to the unity of the canon is deeply flawed."⁶³

In his *Pascal Homily* (c.180 CE), Melito of Sardis accused the Jewish people of deicide. A long tradition of Christian invective against the Jews unfolded, heavily influenced by the rhetorical practices of the time. Tertullian vigorously combatted Marcion's position using a simple strategy; wherever Marcion had located a conflict between the law and the gospel, Tertullian diverted criticism away from the Jewish God and Jewish texts and onto the behaviors, practices, sins, and disasters of the Jews themselves (*Against Marcion*) and undermined Judaism (*Against the Jews*). According to Origen, the Jews' greatest sin of all time was their killing of Jesus, after which God had abandoned them entirely (*Apology* 26.3). Cyprian of Carthage compiled an influential anthology of proof texts to aid preachers, showing among other things, that "the Jews, as foretold, have departed from God and lost his favour ... while the Christians have succeeded to their place" (*To Quirinius* 1.5).

Scott Bader-Saye has argued that

> the church's relation to Israel and to the Gentile powers affected and was affected by the developing view of election as a private and spiritual matter and by the theological argument with the Jews concerning the visibility and presence of Christ's redemption.⁶⁴

As the centuries passed and the second coming of Jesus was delayed, Christians had to deal with a genuine challenge from Jews: "Where is this redemption that you say has occurred in Jesus Christ?" The Romans still ruled over Jerusalem, the Jews were still scattered, and violence continued to triumph over peace. Suddenly in the fourth century a new

---

61. Tertullian and Origen did likewise in the early third century.
62. The creeds contain nothing about the ministry and teachings of Jesus either!
63. Soulen, *God of Israel*, 48–49.
64. Bader-Saye, *Church and Israel*, 52.

INTRODUCTION

response to the Jews' question became possible in the light of Constantine's reign; a messianic redemption was present and visible! Eusebius' *Oration in Honor of Constantine on the Thirtieth Anniversary of His Reign* interpreted the extension of Constantine's rule as a reflection of Daniel's and Isaiah's messianic visions, and linked Christ's redemptive reign to the authority of Rome. He thereby surrendered the Jewish character of redemption to the realities of empire—it came with the sword rather than the ploughshare. Rosemary Radford Ruether comments on this way of understanding redemption:

> In the period after the establishment of the Church as the religion of the Roman Empire, this argument, that the gentile Church is a messianic fulfilment, takes on a new political tone. The universalism of the nations, gathered in the Church, is equated with the universal sway of the Christian Roman Pax. The ecumenical empire comes to be identified with the millennial reign of the messiah over the earth. . . . All nations gather into the Kingdom of Christ. The Jews alone are in exile "among their enemies." But since their enemies, the nations, now equal the elect gentile Church, the reversal of Jewish messianic hope is total. All nations are redeemed at the coming of the Messiah except the Jews![65]

As the fourth century went on, hostility to Jewish-Christian congregations grew. It is clear that many ordinary Christians were attracted to observe Jewish festivals, and sometimes took part in them, and this concerned some church leaders. John Chrysostom preached a series of defamatory sermons in Antioch, *Against Judaizing Christians* (386–87), warning the faithful against such participation.[66]

There was one Christian leader who shifted what had become the traditional invective against the Jew, Augustine of Hippo. Paula Fredricksen has shown how Augustine developed a nuanced position that amounted to a defence of the Jews, which proved influential for centuries. Indeed, on the eve of the Second Crusade in 1146, Bernard of Clairvaux preached against those who were inciting Christians in the Rhine Valley to use violence against Jews, by appeal to Psalm 59:12, "Slay them not, lest my people forget." This was a text that Augustine had employed in his argument that the Jews, alone of all the religious minorities within

---

65. Ruether, *Faith and Fratricide*, 141, quoted in Bader-Saye, *Church and Israel*, 59.
66. Wilken, *John Chrysostom and the Jews*.

the Christian state, should be tolerated (*City of God* 18.46).[67] Augustine wrote most extensively about the Jews in an anti-Manichaean work, *Against Faustus* (398–c.400), in which he developed a novel allegory from the story of Cain and Abel; Abel is a figure of Christ, while Cain is a figure of the Jews. Abel is killed by Cain, his older brother; so also Christ, the head of the younger people (i.e., the gentile Christians) is "killed by the elder people, the Jews" (12.9). God has placed upon the Jewish people the "mark of Cain" so that they should not be killed (12.12–13). Despite the originality of Augustine's usage of the biblical story and his position defending the Jews from murder, the allegory of Cain still condemned them to a cursed and wandering existence. Augustine developed his interpretation of Psalm 59:12 while composing sermons on the book of Psalms (perhaps between 410 and 415); the Jews must not be killed because they perform an essential service for the church in preserving the scriptures.[68] None of this prevented Augustine from repeating traditional condemnations or from producing a *Sermon Against the Jews*, in which he rebuked the Jews for their continuing exile and for their witless service to the church (7.9).[69] When Augustine later made his appeal to Psalm 59:12 in *City of God*, the allegory of Cain for the Jews dropped out; this was because the story of Cain's building a city (Gen 4:17) was essential to Augustine's construct of the two cities that shapes his magnum opus.[70]

The great historian of the Christian tradition Jaroslav Pelikan reviewed the appropriation of the scriptures by the early Christian apologists and theologians in this way:

> Virtually every major Christian writer of the first five centuries either composed a treatise in opposition to Judaism or made this issue a dominant theme in a treatise devoted to a different subject.... They no longer looked upon the Jewish community as a continuing participant in the holy history that had produced the church. They no longer gave serious consideration to the Jewish interpretation of the Old Testament or to the Jewish background to the New. Therefore the urgency and the poignancy about the mystery of Israel that are so vivid in the New Testament have appeared only occasionally in Christian thought, as in some passages in Augustine; but these are outweighed, even in Augustine,

---

67. Fredricksen, *Augustine*, xi–xii.
68. Fredricksen, *Augustine*, 324.
69. Fredricksen, *Augustine*, 324.
70. Fredricksen, *Augustine*, 346.

by the many others that speak of Judaism and paganism almost as though they were equally alien to the "people of God"—the church of Gentile Christians.[71]

Glimpses of Supersessionism within Christendom

Besides the mistreatment of the Jews, supersessionism entailed other racist evils. Willie James Jennings explores the outworking of supersessionist assumptions together with emerging capitalism in his profound work, *The Christian Imagination: Theology and the Origins of Race*. Because the central place of the Jewish people in God's purposes had been replaced by the Christian church, which had tied itself to the Roman Empire, and then to particular European states, it became axiomatic to think of "white" Europeans as racially superior to those of darker skins. Jennings establishes this point by exploring the detailed account of the allocation of slaves at the port of Lagos in 1444 written by Zurara, the Portuguese royal chronicler of Henry the Navigator.[72] Jennings goes on to discuss the writings of José Acosta, the Spanish Jesuit theologian working in Peru (1570–83), whose achievement was to embed colonialist attitudes within Western theology.[73]

The great English hymn writer Isaac Watts (1674–1748) sought to aid biblical literacy and wanted to enhance the worship life of Christians in particular by a Christian rendering of the Psalms in the common vernacular. Despite his dissenting commitments, some of his hymns became standards in Anglican hymnbooks down to recent times.[74] However, Jennings shows how Watts' versions of the Psalms, produced at the time when the British Empire was beginning to take shape, embedded a reading strategy in service of *nationalist* imagination. Most significantly, he substituted the name of Britain for the nations of Israel and Judah, British kings for Israelite ones, and Second Testament themes for some "dark sayings of David."[75] Jennings instances Psalm 47, the last verse of which Watts rendered:

---

71. Pelikan, *Christian Tradition*, 15, 21.
72. Jennings, *Christian Imagination*, 15–64.
73. Jennings, *Christian Imagination*, 65–116.
74. E.g., "When I survey the wondrous cross;" "Joy to the world;" "O God, our help in ages past."
75. Jennings, *Christian Imagination*, 211.

> The British islands are the Lord's,
> There Abraham's God is known;
> While powers and princes, shields and swords,
> Submit before his throne.[76]

Watts' metrical psalms connect the Christian narrative, not only with the opening up of God's election of Israel to the election of the whole world, but also assume that the Lord has claimed the British Isles and its people as his own. Jennings' conclusion is insightful;

> This is indeed a form of Israel replacement, but it captures one of the most crucial forms of replacement. The multiple biblical stories of ancient Israel's quest for land center on God. The possibility of Israel's sovereignty pivots on the divine will. God stands always between Israel and the land, Israel and its land. If land is absolutely crucial to the identity of a people, then God stood always "in the way," as it were, between Israel and its desire for land, reordering its identity first in relation to the divine word and then to the land. Israel's stories of land gained, lost, and regained disclosed the God of Israel as the creator who "owns" all land and therefore claimed all peoples. Israel's God is indeed "the King of the whole earth" (Ps 47:7). The revelation of the Creator in and through Israel is the first and foremost point of connection between Israel and all the other peoples.
>
> Watts positions Great Britain at this crucial point of revelation, turning Israel's sojourn with God into Britain's journey. He thereby destroys the trajectory of connection between Israel and the other nations. Israel simply models a connection between God and a nation. . . . Israel was the beginning point, the ethnic *arche* of a process of instantiations of a people living in communion with God. Their imperfect reality in both knowledge of and communion with God was more clearly grasped in Britain.[77]

In this reading of the First Testament, Israel simply modelled a connection between God and a nation; the trajectory connecting the people of Israel and all the other nations (through Jesus) was destroyed.[78]

There was a parallel story in the United States. Eran Shalev has charted the dominance of the Hebraic political imagination between the founding of the Republic and the Civil War.

---

76. Quoted in Jennings, *Christian Imagination*, 212.

77. Jennings, *Christian Imagination*, 213, 215.

78. Jennings, *Christian Imagination*, 275–94, discusses commonalities in the experience of Jews and "black" people at the hands of "whites."

INTRODUCTION

> The idea of America as a new Israel, founded on a Calvinist ethos that was not narrowly denominational but inclined towards the Old Testament, originated in an insular seventeenth-century outlook that singled out New England as a "chosen nation." It reverberated and expanded with the onset of the Revolution throughout the colonies-turned states as Americans repeatedly heard that they were "at present the People of Israel," or were establishing "our Israel." This image of an American people chosen for a special destiny was to remain a mainstay of American self-fashioning and the negotiation of nationhood for years.[79]

Shalev goes on to show that American thinkers of the time attempted to transcend traditional figurative exegesis; they were not simply appealing to a metaphorical Israel but presented America's very identity as a latter-day Israel. This did not stop them appealing also to other historical models, such as republican Rome, especially after 1789. However, following the Civil War, "Old Testamentism" was replaced by New Testament ideology as a result of the Great Awakening, while it was the slave community that claimed the exodus and Moses as their own.

After the Shoah

Between 1941 and 1945 Hitler's "Final Solution" succeeded in exterminating nearly six million Jews. This vile Nazi project has frequently been called "the Holocaust," but for Jews themselves this title carries overtones of wholly burnt sacrifice, as in the LXX version of Leviticus 6:16 (6:23 in NRSV and other versions). Thus "the Holocaust" carries the connotation that the attempt to eradicate the Jewish race amounted to some sort of religious devotion. This is revolting and unacceptable, so instead the Jews prefer the term "Shoah," which may be translated "catastrophe."

The horrors of the Shoah have confronted European civilization with its long history of anti-Semitism, and Christian churches have begun to realize their complicity with this history. Protestant churches have engaged in significant reflection upon the legacy of anti-Semitism within their own institutions, and in meaningful dialogue with Jews.[80] Especially since the Second Vatican Council (1962–65), there has been a growth in

---

79. Shalev, *American Zion*, 1.
80. E.g., a conference on "Mennonites and the Holocaust" was held at Bethel College in 2018.

official dialogue between the Catholic Church and Jews, and at Mainz in 1980 Pope John Paul II made a significant statement;

> The first aspect of this dialogue, namely the meeting between the people of God of the old covenant, which has never been revoked by God (Rom 11:29), and the people of God of the new covenant, is at the same time a dialogue within our church between the first and second parts of the Bible.[81]

The Catholic First Testament scholar Norbert Lohfink responded to this statement with a short book exploring the many biblical texts on the subject of the covenant, old and new. Lohfink points out significant differences in the way "covenant" is used in both Testaments; for example, in Paul's thinking expressed in Galatians 3, "Christians belong not to a 'new covenant' but to the 'Abraham covenant' which precedes and overarches the law of Sinai."[82] Taking Jeremiah's rhetoric into account in his prophecy of a new covenant (31:31–34), "the new covenant is but the earlier one, now brilliant and radiant."[83] Reflecting on the mistreatment of Jews in Christendom, Lohfink makes this provocative suggestion:

> Paul could not have known that it would come to such a darkening of the faith of the nations. Has not the situation which he describes in Rom 9–11 been reversed? Those who believe in Jesus as God's messiah have forgotten what God's gift looks like and what they are called to. They must be urged to recognize anew "the Jewishness in Christianity" . . . because perhaps today Jews are in many ways more aware of the "covenant" than Christians, . . . perhaps present day Jews are more aware that God will change the world, and so needs a "people," a society, which in contrast to other societies in the world tries to live according to God's original design for the world.[84]

Since the Second World War, the realization that for much of its existence the Christian church has assumed that Christianity replaced the Jews in God's purposes, that the church superseded Judaism, and that Jews are fair game for persecution, has been acknowledged by leading Christian theologians,[85] but it has yet to penetrate into the teaching and

---

81. Quoted in Lohfink, *Covenant*, 5.
82. Lohfink, *Covenant*, 30.
83. Lohfink, *Covenant*, 48.
84. Lohfink, *Covenant*, 80f.
85. Particularly Karl Barth and Jürgen Moltmann.

practices of many churches. We should attend to Jewish scripture scholars, like Marvin Sweeney, who have engaged in "Holocaust" theology.[86] Contemporary Jewish communicators, such as Simon Schama and Jonathan Sacks, have much to teach us about loving God after Christendom.[87]

5. Overview and Scope

Part I deals with two essential topics that set the course for the rest of the book. Chapter 2 explores some of the ways in which the scriptures were essential to Jesus and to his earliest followers who wrote the Second Testament. It has been included because its focus upon figural interpretation illuminates the way in which the First Testament feeds forward to aid interpretation of the Second. Chapter 3 makes the case for interpreting the First Testament book by book, exploring three interpretative perspectives; literary, historical, and theological, and using the book of Genesis as an example. These chapters introduce some scholarly methods of interpretation, so some readers may find them challenging and prefer to skip over them, perhaps returning to them later.

Because the First Testament is so large, it is tempting to make sweeping generalizations, and to avoid awkward details that do not conform to them. So in Part II four books are considered in some detail, Joshua, Judges, Samuel, and Kings, because together these tell a major part of Israel's story and contain some of the most ethically challenging materials.[88] A prelude introduces scholarly approaches to these books.

The drawback of this strategy is that books in which other genres are dominant (legal materials in Exodus–Deuteronomy, prophetic oracles in the Latter Prophets, poetry in the Psalms, wisdom genres in other parts of the Writings) require somewhat different approaches and cannot be

---

86. Sweeney, *After the Shoah*.

87. See especially Schama's BBC TV series, *The Story of the Jews*. He has published two out of three books so far on *The Story of the Jews*. Sacks' series of books of weekly readings of the Jewish Bible, *Covenant & Conversation*, are full of insight.

88. 1 & 2 Samuel and 1 & 2 Kings will be treated as two integrated books. Evidence from the Qumran scrolls shows that in each case the original Hebrew was a single book. Once they had been translated into Greek (LXX), their sheer length was the likely reason for division into four volumes (called 1, 2, 3, and 4 Reigns/Kingdoms). The Latin Vulgate edition divided them in the fourth century CE, but a similar division was not made in Hebrew Bibles until the late Middle Ages. While convenience may be an understandable reason for division, the whole book is required for adequate interpretation.

discussed in detail. Some of these do receive limited attention at the start of Part III, as chapter 8 considers how the various books of the First Testament work together with each other and proposes that "conversation" is a helpful model for their interrelation. Chapter 9 investigates how the First Testament story and books might be reframed in the light of Jesus by considering two theological approaches; narrative and canonical. Finally, some aspects of facilitating access to the First Testament are explored in chapter 10, and it is here that implications of the After Christendom perspective become more evident. This is a cumulative workbook that explores several aspects of the subject, but it pays off in the end!

It might be thought that a book such as this should deal with the topic of law, given what Paul says about the law in Romans and Galatians. Whilst this is an important aspect of Christian interpretation of the First Testament, I would argue that it must be set in the wider context of Israel's narrative traditions for two reasons:

- The biblical laws are given by God to the recently liberated Israelites in order that they might form a society without the injustice and oppression that they had endured in Egypt, and point to their saviour, YHWH (see Deut 4:5–8). These laws were adjusted as time went by and circumstances changed.[89] Therefore, law must be interpreted within its narrative and canonical context.

- One of the ethical limitations of laws is that they identify transgressions and stipulate penalties but cannot model the ethical goals that benefit a society; they provide an ethical *minimum*, not a maximum. Gordon Wenham has argued that the First Testament narrative texts seek "to instil both theological truths and ethical ideals into their readers."[90] Therefore laws are not the only, or even the most important, contribution to ethics; they must be understood in relation to their narrative and canonical context.[91]

This book addresses narrative and canonical aspects of interpretation; interpretation of First Testament law in light of the Second Testament is vital but must be discussed on another occasion.

---

89. Compare the laws in Deuteronomy to those in the "Book of the Law" in Exod 20–23.

90. Wenham, *Story as Torah*, 3.

91. Brown explores the relation between the biblical story of creation and moral character in *Ethos of the Cosmos*.

PART I

Interpretive Approaches

2

The First Testament in the Second

Christian interpretation of the First Testament after Christendom should take its orientation from how those scriptures were interpreted by Jesus and his earliest followers. This is not a book about Jesus or those followers, so limits must be placed on the scope of this chapter, yet attention to their attitude towards the scriptures, and to the ways in which they interpreted them should shape our approach once we turn to methods and details of contemporary interpretation in later chapters.

The Christian tradition has often placed more weight on Paul's letters than on Jesus' life, action, and teaching as portrayed in the Gospels.[1] However, I intend to give rather more weight to the Gospels than to Paul since they provide a window on Jesus and his use of scripture. Yet it makes sense to take Paul before the Gospels since he wrote before they were written, and so his letters give us our earliest glimpse of attitudes to the scriptures in the decades immediately following Jesus' life on earth.[2] His letters also indicate several ways in which the scriptures have continuing significance for the Christian church.

Jesus left no writings of his own, so we do not have direct access to the so-called "historical Jesus" but only to what some of those earliest followers remembered and wrote about his life and teachings, and what

---

1. Augustine's biblical studies focused initially on Paul (though they subsequently extended over much of the Bible) and set the trend for much of the Protestant tradition.

2. Hays, *Paul*, 31, argues that once Paul's letters were read alongside the Gospels and Acts, the urgency of Paul's relating the gospel to God's dealings with Israel was lost, and that "the Christian tradition has distorted Paul's voice or distorted its undertones."

these meant to some early churches.³ I will survey the Four Gospels, as they present details of Jesus' use of the scriptures and refer to the scriptures in presenting Jesus' story. It should become clear that the authors of the Second Testament were thoroughly immersed in those scriptures, and that the full import of their writings cannot be appreciated by contemporary readers without familiarity with the First Testament.

The subject of how the scriptures are used and understood in the apostolic writings is complex and much debated among scholars, and I have room to explore only some aspects of what is involved.⁴ The most important topic in recent discussions is *intertextuality*, the use of or reference to particular scriptural texts within the text at hand, so I will attend to this first as it will set the scene for what follows.

We must note that the evangelists and apostles were writing in Greek for Greek-reading audiences, and that their intertextual language usually resonates most strongly with the Septuagint (LXX), rather than with the original Hebrew.⁵ So in the following discussion of examples, quotations from the scriptures will usually take the form of English translations from the LXX, the first Bible of the early churches. It contains Deuterocanonical books that are unfamiliar to Protestants, such as Sirach.

1. Approaching Intertextuality

Amongst Second Testament scholars the dominant recent understanding of the use of the scriptures in the apostolic writings has been in terms of intertextuality, a field shaped by the wider study of literature and language. In biblical studies, Richard Hays has been a pioneering figure, beginning with his ground-breaking *Echoes of Scripture in the Letters of Paul* (1989), then several other publications, leading to his recent masterwork, *Echoes of Scripture in the Gospels* (2016). While previous studies

---

3. It is not necessary in this book to engage with the vast research into the so-called historical Jesus. Hays, *Gospels*, 368n13, notes the hypothetical character of such research and its tendency towards methodological circularity. He is critical of reductive accounts of Jesus, but also cautious about attempts to demonstrate that the Gospels are historically factual accounts of what Jesus said and did.

4. For a discussion of many of the issues, see Kaiser, Bock, and Enns, *Three Views*, especially Lunde's Introduction.

5. The translation process was complex, and the question of which textual forms were available to First Testament authors is complicated. See Jobes and Silva, *Invitation to the Septuagint*.

had focussed on explicit quotations of scripture, Hays drew attention to less obvious, yet just as important, allusions to and echoes of scripture.

- "Quotations" are generally introduced by a citation formula (e.g., "as it is written") or consist of a chain of words reproduced verbatim from the source text.
- "Allusions" usually involve the imbedding of several words from the source text, or at least the mention of notable characters or events that signal the intertextual link.
- "Echoes" involve the inclusion of a word or phrase that may evoke the memory of an earlier text, but only when the reader is alert and familiar with the source texts.

In each of these three forms of intertextual reference, a poetic effect may be created that is known as *metalepsis*; this occurs only when the reader recalls the original context of the source text, and then allows the two texts to engage with each other.[6] This is not an obscure authorial procedure; we can observe its use by comedians, politicians, and film-makers as well as contemporary writers and preachers.

As an example of Paul's use of allusions and echoes of scripture, Hays considers an uncontroversial passage in which Paul reflects on his imprisonment; "for I know that through your prayers and the help of the Spirit of Jesus Christ this will turn out for my deliverance" (Phil 1:19). The last part of this statement is exactly the same as in Job 13:16 (LXX): "Even this will turn out for my deliverance, for deceit will not enter in before him." There is no hint that Paul is citing Job, so readers would not realize what he is doing unless they were very familiar with the original. But once we become aware of the link, we may notice some intriguing resonances with Job's lengthy speech protesting his innocence; Job even depicts himself as a prisoner in 13:27. Paul knows of rival preachers who seem to imply that he deserves his imprisonment (Phil 1:15–17), while Job's friends were trying to persuade him that his sufferings were due to some unacknowledged sin (Job 13:7). There are important differences between Job's situation of suffering and Paul's, of course, and Paul is not claiming a typological relationship with Job. Yet careful study of Job 13 suggests that Paul's use of Job's expression in v. 16 evokes several resonances with the whole passage.

---

6. Hays writes, "The figurative effect of such an intertextual linkage lies in the unstated or suppressed points of correspondence between the two texts" (*Gospels*, 11).

> At the explicit literal level of the discourse, Paul simply borrows a phrase from Job to express confidence amidst trying circumstances. But when the source of the phrase is read in counterpoint with the new setting into which it has been transposed, a range of resonant harmonics becomes audible. None of the correspondences between Paul and Job, or between Paul's rivals and Job's interlocutors, is actually asserted; instead, they are intimated through the trope of metalepsis.[7]

Hays goes on to note that the rather formal phrase Paul uses to introduce his allusion to Job 13, "for I know that," echoes other passages in the LXX of Job (9:28, 19:25–26; 30:23), but none of these seem to carry allusive weight for Paul. Thus, Hays recognizes that limits must be placed on the pursuit of echoes and concentrates only on the most convincing cases by providing seven criteria by which to test their presence and meaning.[8]

Hays has placed great emphasis upon "figural interpretation" in the apostolic writings, an expression derived from the literary scholar Eric Auerbach, who provided the following definition:

> Figural interpretation establishes a connection between two events or persons in such a way that the first signifies not only itself but also the second, while the second involves or fulfils the first. The two poles of a figure are separated in time, but both, being real events or persons, are within temporality. They are both contained in the flowing stream which is historical life, and only the comprehension, the *intellectus spiritualis*, of their interdependence is a spiritual act.[9]

Here Hays makes an important distinction between prediction and prefiguration. Only after the second event in the "flowing stream" of time has occurred can the pattern of correspondence between the first and second events be discerned, and the first event imparts deeper significance to the second. Figural interpretation of the Bible creates a deep theological

---

7. Hays, *Paul*, 23. Metalepsis occurs when a literary echo links the text to an earlier text, placing "the reader in a field of whispered or unstated correspondences" (*Paul*, 20).

8. Hays, *Paul*, 23–33. Longenecker, in the second edition of his *Biblical Exegesis*, xiv–xvii, is critical of Hays' approach in *Paul* for lacking sufficient controls. He proposes that the primary focus should remain on explicit quotations of scripture, and only then on materials that can be shown to be allusive by several specific criteria. Yet Hays, "On the Rebound," 85, had already pointed out to critics that he had set out extensive and nuanced criteria in *Paul*, 29–33.

9. Auerbach, *Mimesis*, 73, as quoted in Hays, *Gospels*, 2.

coherence within the whole canon, demonstrating its unity as a single, cumulative, and complex pattern of meaning.[10]

Hays has made a powerful case for figural interpretation of the Bible in many places. Matthew Bates has recently argued for an alternative approach in a small number of cases, but these need not concern us here.[11]

2. Paul's Use of the Scriptures

According to the book of Acts (21:39), Paul came from Tarsus in Cilicia, in the south-east corner of modern Turkey, though he was educated at the feet of Gamaliel in Jerusalem (22:3).[12] Paul described himself as "circumcised on the eighth day, a member of the people of Israel, of the tribe of Benjamin, a Hebrew born of Hebrews; as to the law, a Pharisee" (Phil 3:5). Paul was as Jewish as could be, and the scriptures were in his life-blood. He would have been raised to read the scriptures in Hebrew, but it is clear that he was also fully versed in the Septuagint, which was commonly used in Hellenistic synagogues during his lifetime.

After his encounter with Jesus Christ *en route* to persecute followers of "the Way" in Damascus (Acts 9:1–19), Paul's life was taken up with his calling to preach the good news of Jesus as Lord, and to follow him, through suffering even to death. His Letter to the Romans begins in this way;

> Paul, a servant of Jesus Christ, called to be an apostle, set apart for the gospel of God, which he promised beforehand through his prophets *in the holy scriptures*, the gospel concerning his Son, who was descended from David according to the flesh and was declared to be Son of God with power according to the spirit of holiness by resurrection from the dead, Jesus Christ our Lord, through whom we have received grace and apostleship to bring about the obedience of faith among all the Gentiles for the sake of his name, including yourselves who are called to belong to Jesus Christ. (Rom 1:1–6, emphasis added)

---

10. Hays demonstrates how figural reading differs radically from modern historical criticism in *Gospels*, 3–4.

11. Bates argues for use of "speech in character" in Paul in *Hermeneutics,* and more widely in the Second Testament in *Birth of the Trinity.*

12. For an excellent recent biography of Paul, which takes seriously his origins in Tarsus, see Wright, *Paul: A Biography.*

INTERPRETING THE OLD TESTAMENT

Here Paul refers explicitly to God's promise of his Son in the scriptures, and readers who continue to follow this letter encounter several quotations from those scriptures (3:4, 9–18; 4:7–8; 8:36, etc.). A similar emphasis upon the scriptures can be observed when Paul introduces an early proto-creed towards the end of the First Letter to the Corinthians:

> For I handed on to you as of first importance what I in turn had received: that Christ died for our sins *in accordance with the scriptures*, and that he was buried, and that he was raised on the third day *in accordance with the scriptures*, and that he appeared to Cephas, then to the twelve. (1 Cor 15:3–5, emphasis added)

Thus, at the core of Paul's allegiance to Jesus lay the conviction that the scriptures were essential to Jesus identity and career.[13]

In the Pauline letters,[14] the scriptures are quoted some ninety-three times; mostly in Romans, First and Second Corinthians, and Galatians, with four in Ephesians and one each in First and Second Timothy.[15] Thirty-three of these quotations come from the Pentateuch, twenty-five from Isaiah, and nineteen from the Psalms.[16] Fifty-one of these citations are in complete or virtual agreement with the LXX, while twenty-two are at variance with the Hebrew. In four places Paul follows the Hebrew against the LXX, while he diverges from both in thirty-eight cases. Some quotations are combined, and these show greater variation than the others.

Paul usually introduces his quotations with a formula, such as "it is written," though sometimes with a brief "for" or "but." But Hays' work alerts us to Paul's more allusive use of the scriptures; for example, in the midst of a passage about whether or not to eat meat offered to idols, he writes;

> Indeed, even though there may be so-called gods in heaven or on earth—as in fact there are many gods and many lords—yet for us there is one God, the Father, from whom are all things and

---

13. For a thorough discussion of the two passages in this paragraph, see Bates, *Hermeneutics*, chapter 2.

14. The authenticity of some of the letters has been much debated. I tend to the view that the Pastorals are likely pseudonymous, though 2 Timothy may be authentic.

15. Figures from the appendices of Ellis' early work, *Paul's Use*, 150–87. Compare the slightly different statistics used by Hays, *Paul*, 34.

16. Plus one from Samuel, two from Kings, two from Job, one from Proverbs, two from Jeremiah, three from Hosea, one from Joel, two from Habakkuk, one from Malachi.

> for whom we exist, and one Lord, Jesus Christ, through whom are all things and through whom we exist. (1 Cor 8:5–6)

In dealing with how to behave within a pagan environment, Paul has invoked the classic Jewish confession: "Hear, O Israel: YHWH is our God, YHWH alone" (Deut 6:4). Tom Wright has argued convincingly that Paul expanded this ancient declaration in a way that is unprecedented in any other text known to us, glossing "God" with "the Father" and "Lord" with "Jesus Christ," in each case adding an explanatory clause about creation.

> Paul has placed Jesus *within* an explicit statement, drawn from the Old Testament's quarry of emphatically monotheistic texts, of the doctrine that Israel's God is the only God, the creator of the world. The *Shema* was already, at this stage of Judaism, in widespread use as *the* daily Jewish prayer. Paul has redefined it christologically, producing what we can only call a sort of Christological monotheism.[17]

Thus, Paul could creatively rework the scriptures to express his convictions regarding Jesus' divine identity.

One of the striking arguments that Hays makes is that Paul refers to the scriptures to teach about the life of the churches, more than to teach about Christ. He goes as far as to say that, in comparison with the Gospels of Matthew and John, "we rarely find Paul using Scripture to define the identity of Jesus Christ or to reflect theologically about it. . . . What Paul finds in Scripture, above all else, is a prefiguration of the *church* as the people of God . . . ."[18] This *ecclesiocentric* strategy should not really be a surprise, given that Paul's letters were written with pastoral intent to churches, not as evangelistic tracts.[19]

Hays establishes this point through his literary reading of Romans with its use of quotations "spiralling in around a common focus: the problem of God's saving righteousness in relation to Israel."[20] He discusses Paul's keynote of Rom 1:16–17 in relation to Ps 97:2, and to the lament psalms (Pss 24:2; 43:10) and later chapters of Isaiah (Isa 51:4–5; 52:10) with their overtones of shame and exile, and to Habakkuk's theodicy

---

17. Wright, *Climax of the Covenant*, 129. See also his more recent discussion of this passage in *Faithfulness of God*, 661–70.

18. Hays, *Paul*, 86.

19. Philemon and the Pastorals were addressed to individuals, but they have strong ecclesial content.

20. Hays, *Paul*, 34.

question about God's faithfulness to Israel (Hab 2:4). Hays continues to work through major passages in Romans, showing that

> Paul's argument is primarily an argument about theodicy, not about soteriology. The driving question in Romans is not "How can I find a gracious God?" but "How can we trust in this allegedly gracious God if he abandons his promises to Israel?" Christian caricatures of the Old Testament have made it difficult for belated generations of Gentile readers to grasp Paul's passion for asserting the continuity of his gospel with the message of the Law and the Prophets.[21]

Paul confronts head on the question of God's faithfulness to Israel in Romans 9–11, where the density of scriptural citation and allusion increases dramatically as he seeks to show the congruity between God's word in scripture and in his own gospel.

Leading up to the most perplexing quotation in this section of the letter in 10:5-10, Paul poses questions about how gentiles obtained the righteousness of God where Israel failed to 3the law (9:30–32), and then asserts, "Christ is the end (*telos*) of the law, for righteousness to everyone who believes" (10:4). Hays renders this; "the real aim of the law, the righteousness of God, is Jesus Christ," and appeals to previous statements in 3:21, 3:31, and 4:1–25 as establishing that the Law teaches faith-righteousness. Therefore, Paul does not play off "the righteousness from the law" (10:5) against "the righteousness of faith" (10:6); he is using these terms synonymously to support his assertion.[22] The quotation that has caused most confusion is the one from Deut 30:11–14 that includes an interpolated commentary regarding a search for Christ;

> The righteousness that comes through faith says, "Do not say in your heart, 'Who will ascend to heaven?' (that is, to bring Christ down) or 'Who will descend into the abyss?' (that is, to bring Christ up from the dead). But what does it say? "The word is near you, in your mouth and in your heart" (that is, the word of faith that we proclaim); because if you confess with your lips that Jesus is Lord and believe in your heart that God raised him from the dead, you will be saved. (Rom 10:6–9)

Here Paul makes significant changes to the original, using echoes from Deut 9:4 and the Wisdom tradition, and expands each term in

---

21. Hays, *Paul*, 53.
22. Hays, *Paul*, 76.

v. 8a—word, lips, heart—in v. 8b–9.[23] Paul echoes the idea from Deuteronomy that "the covenant depends from start to finish on grace rather than Israel's righteousness; . . . he has read Deuteronomy 30 as a metaphor for Christian proclamation."[24] The result is an intensification of the paradox of Israel's unbelief, and Paul will go on (in 11:11–14) to express his hope that such unbelief will be incorporated into God's purpose to save Israel.

Given that Paul had once been devoted to the law and opposed to Jesus' followers, and had then undergone a dramatic life reorientation around Jesus as Christ, the key question to explore is how Paul now understood the scriptures, whether, in contemporary terms, he had a coherent hermeneutic. To address these questions, Hays investigates Paul's contrast between "the letter" and "the Spirit" in the "new covenant" passage of 2 Cor 3:1—4:6. Paul defends the legitimacy of his apostolic ministry by overturning the demand for letters of recommendation through appeal to the Corinthian community itself as his letter of recommendation (3:1–3). Having coined this metaphor, Paul goes on to play with its ramifications (3:4–6); Christ is the author, Paul is the letter bearer, as well as the one recommended by it. Next, Hays notes three echoes in this passage:

- God's promise of a new covenant (2 Cor 3:6) in Jer 38:33: "I will give my laws in their mind, and upon their heart I will write them."
- God is depicted as a covenant writer in Exod 31:18: "written by the finger of God."
- The negative contrast between stone and flesh echoes Ezek 36:26: "And I will give you a new heart, and a new spirit I will give among you, and I will take away the stone heart out of your flesh, and I will give you a fleshy heart."

The effect of these intertextual hints is that in the new covenant the divine Son of God is enfleshed in the community of Paul's brothers and sisters at Corinth.[25] Hays translates the climactic statement in 3:6 in an attempt to capture the word-play linking v. 6 back to v. 3: "God has made us competent as ministers of a new covenant, a covenant not of the script

---

23. Hays, *Paul*, 73–82.
24. Hays, *Paul*, 82.
25. Hays, *Paul*, 127–29.

(*gramma*) but of the Spirit."²⁶ Paul's ministry "centers not on texts but on the Spirit-empowered transformation of human community." Unfortunately, the letter-Spirit dichotomy has been read by the Christian tradition in terms of

> an antithesis between the outward and the inward, the manifest and the latent, the body and the soul.... For Paul, the Spirit is—scandalously—identified precisely with the outward and palpable, the particular human community of the new covenant, putatively transformed by God's power so as to make Christ's message visible to all. The script, however, remains abstract and dead because it is not embodied.²⁷

When Hays comes to summarize his understanding of Paul's hermeneutics, he does so like this:

> the word of Scripture is read as the word of God to us. The text was written by some human author long ago, written to and for an ancient community of people in Israel, but original writer and readers have become types whose meaning emerges with full clarity only in the church.²⁸

Hays recognizes that Paul employs rather different ways of appealing to scripture in certain letters. In Galatians his strategy places Moses and Abraham into a dichotomous law/gospel scheme, which renders the First Testament in an antithetical typological relationship to the Second Testament. But even in that letter there are signals that Paul is uneasy with the implications of his own argument (Gal 3:21; 5:6; 6:15), so that, in the light of his return to similar issues in Romans, Galatians looks like "a preliminary heuristic probe, staking out a strong position that had to be articulated along the way to discovering a more complex hermeneutical strategy." Given Hays' work on Romans, 2 Corinthians 3, and the Israel/church typology in 1 Corinthians and Galatians, he insists that scripture retains its own voice and power to challenge and shape Paul's unfolding discourse.

> Paul's fundamental reading strategies are profoundly dialectical. The word of Scripture is not played off as a foil for the gospel,

---

26. Hays, *Paul*, 130, points out that Paul's word for scripture is *graphē*, a living and speaking presence; *gramma* does not signify scripture, but letter (NRSV) or written code (RSV), a lifeless thing.

27. Hays, *Paul*, 131.

28. Hays, *Paul*, 167.

not patronized as a primitive stage of religious development, not regarded merely as a shadow of the good things to come. Paul's urgent hermeneutical project, rather is to bring Scripture and gospel into a mutually interpretive relation, in which the righteousness of God is truly disclosed.[29]

Finally, Hays addresses the question of whether Paul's way of reading scripture should be imitated by Christians today, and proposes that, in the light of his extensive discussion, Paul's readings are normative for Christian theology and his interpretive methods are paradigmatic for Christian hermeneutics. He concludes by summarizing five facets of learning from Paul how to read scripture:

- as a narrative of election and promise
- ecclesiocentrically, or better "ecclesiotelically" (for building up the church)[30]
- in the service of proclamation or pastoral counsel
- as participants in the eschatological drama of redemption
- appreciating the metaphorical relation between the text and our own reading of it.[31]

3. The Evangelists' Use of the Scriptures

Here I summarize and compare the ways in which the evangelists make use of the scriptures, largely following Hays' *Echoes of Scripture in the Gospels*. An important aspect of Hays' work is his use of a three-fold structure to illuminate each evangelist's purpose, which demonstrates they are doing more than simply presenting Jesus' story—they are also making multiple connections with Israel's story, and throwing light on the calling of Jesus' followers. In order to grasp the full impact of Hays' work, it is necessary to read it entirely. The following summary cannot do it justice, but I will include one detailed sample from Mark's Gospel.

---

29. Hays, *Paul*, 176.

30. Hays adjusted his language regarding the churchly emphasis of Paul's reading of scripture in "On the Rebound," 77, insisting that "God's activity is directed towards the formation of a people."

31. Hays, *Paul*, 183–86.

After Jesus' dramatic action in the temple (Mark 11:15–19), he is engaged in a series of conversations with his enemies as they seek to entrap and discredit him. Finally, Jesus turns the tables on his opponents by presenting them with a riddle from Psalm 110:

> While Jesus was teaching in the temple, he said, "How can the scribes say that the Messiah is the son of David? David himself, by the Holy Spirit, declared,
> 'The LORD said to my Lord,
> "Sit at my right hand,
> until I put your enemies under your feet."'
> David himself calls him Lord; so how can he be his son?" And the large crowd was listening to him with delight.
> (Mark 12:35–7; cf. Matt 22:41–46; Luke 20:41–4)

Jesus' question is enigmatic. Surely David would not call *his own* son (the unusual Greek word order is emphatic) "*my* Lord;" or would he? Hays proposes that the answer to Jesus' conundrum lies in rethinking the categories involved. The title "Son of David" was often linked to nationalistic hopes for a military leader who would drive out the foreign powers controlling Jerusalem, and restore the sovereignty of Israel.[32] Now Psalm 110:1 speaks of the subjection of the Messiah's enemies: "until I put them under your feet," but it says nothing about the Messiah leading a revolutionary army. Instead, he is to be seated at God's right hand and wait for God to defeat his enemies. Thus Jesus does not reject expectations of the Davidic Messiah, as some have thought, but he radically redefines them in line with his earlier prophecies of his own rejection and execution (Mark 8:31; 9:30–32; 10:32–34), and his teaching about self-surrender for others (Mark 10:42–45).

Mark

Mark's Gospel opens abruptly with a quotation ascribed to the prophet Isaiah, though it actually begins with a fusion of words from Exodus and Malachi. By naming Isaiah in particular, "Mark signals his readers that the *euangelion* [good news] of Jesus Christ is to be read within the matrix of Isaiah's prophetic vision: God will return to Zion and restore Israel."[33] As Isaiah had employed the earlier exodus imagery to portray God's

---

32. Hays illustrates this expectation from the *Psalms of Solomon* 17.21–24, 26, 32.
33. Hays, *Gospels*, 21.

deliverance of Israel from the later Babylonian exile, so Mark draws on Exodus 23:20 and Isaiah 40:3 to introduce God's coming in power once more in Jesus, suggesting the promise of protection and an end to wilderness wandering. At the same time, an allusion to Malachi 3:1–5 sounds the theme of God's purifying judgment and suggests a critique of the temple establishment in Jerusalem. With this forceful opening, Mark sets up the events of his story with strong allusions to Israel's story, prompting readers to read that story *figurally*.

Mark does not draw attention to intertextual correspondences as often as does Matthew or Luke, so that some biblical scholars have thought he had little interest in the scriptures, yet careful readers may discern the Christological implications of this Gospel by attending to "the poetics of allusion embedded in Mark's distinctive narrative strategy."[34] Hays makes an arresting analogy between Mark's hermeneutical approach to reading Israel's scripture and the function of Jesus' parables, as found in Jesus' remark about the "mystery of the kingdom of God" being disclosed to some, but hidden from others (4:11–12).[35] In the middle of this parable discourse we find:

> He said to them, "Is a lamp brought in to be put under the bushel basket, or under the bed, and not on the lampstand? For there is nothing hidden, except to be disclosed; nor is anything secret, except to come to light. Let anyone with ears to hear listen!" And he said to them, "Pay attention to what you hear; the measure you give will be the measure you get, and still more will be given you. For to those who have, more will be given; and from those who have nothing, even what they have will be taken away." (4:21–25)

Mark's form of Jesus' saying in v. 22: ". . . nothing hidden, except in order to (*hina*) be disclosed . . ." when compared with the parallels in Matthew and Luke, highlights the intentionality of the hiding; ". . . nothing is veiled that will not be revealed . . ." (Matt 10:26) and ". . . nothing is hidden that will not be disclosed . . ." (Luke 8:17). The hiddenness is part of the revelatory purpose, as in apocalyptic,[36] and so Hays proposes that:

---

34. Hays, *Gospels*, 98.

35. This is not the case for all parables, since the meaning of the Parable of the Vineyard (12:1–12) is plain to all.

36. In "apocalyptic" a revelation is mediated by an otherworldly figure to a human recipient, as in the books of Daniel and Revelation. This is rather different from popular references to catastrophes.

the purpose implied here is divine intent to offer veiled self-revelation in the person of Jesus, whose identity is finally fully disclosed only at the moment of greatest obscurity, his shameful death on the cross ("Truly this man was the Son of God").[37]

Jesus' following words, ". . . listen . . . pay attention . . . the measure you give . . . ," are exhortations concerning hermeneutics. Hays presses the point about the way figurative language works: "Metaphors do not deal in direct statement: rather they intensify meaning precisely by concealing it, by speaking in an indirect mode and saying something other than what is meant."[38]

Mark holds back from explicit statements about Jesus' identity because it is a mystery, yet he presents the person of Jesus by telling his story in counterpoint with the stories and symbols of Israel's scriptures. He quotes them at key points, but more often alludes to them in ways that require discerning readership.

Matthew

Well over sixty explicit quotations from the scriptures can be found in Matthew, many more than in the other Gospels. His most obvious way of using scripture is in the so-called "fulfilment quotations," beginning with "All this took place to fulfil what had been spoken by the Lord through the prophet . . ." (1:22, cf. 2:15, 17, 23; 4:14; 8:17; 12:17; 13:35; 21:4; 27:9). Similar formulas can be found at 2:5; 3:3; 11:10; 13:14; 26:31 and there is a general fulfilment formula without a specific quotation at 26:56. Matthew's quotations and allusions are drawn from the full range of scripture—the law and the prophets, the psalms of the righteous sufferer, and the wisdom literature—but especially from Isaiah. In places he interweaves two or more texts: e.g., Mic 5:1–3 and 2 Sam 5:2 in Matt 2:6; Isa 9:1–2 and Isa 42:6–7 in Matt 4:14–16; Sir 51:27 and Jer 6:16 in Matt 11:29. Hays observes that

> For Matthew, Israel's Scripture constitutes the symbolic world in which both his characters and his readers live and move. The story of God's dealings with Israel is a comprehensive matrix out of which Matthew's Gospel narrative emerges.[39]

---

37. Hays, *Gospels*, 100.
38. Hays, *Gospels*, 101.
39. Hays, *Gospels*, 186.

Hays goes on to speak of Matthew's transfiguration of Israel's scripture, emphasizing the *figural* dimension of his interpretive vision in four ways.

Firstly, Matthew reads Israel's scripture as a story of God's dealings with Israel that can be summed up in a narrative arc of "election, kingship, unfaithfulness, exile, messianic salvation."[40] Secondly, he understands scripture as a summons to the transformation of heart (a reconfiguration of the Torah), which is characterized by radical obedience with mercy as key to the whole law—he inserts Hos 6:6 into two passages that otherwise closely follow Mark (Matt 9:12–13 and 12:1–8). While Jesus insists that the specific commandments of the law remain in place (Matt 5:17–20; 23:1–2, 23), and even radicalizes the Torah (Matt 5:21–48), Matthew provides a critical framework of love (22:34–40) and forgiveness (6:12, 14–15; 18:23–35) within which particular commandments are to be interpreted, that is derived from Israel's wisdom tradition (Sirach 27:30—28:7).

Thirdly, Matthew reads scripture as prefiguration of the Christ. His gospel

> creates a subtle and ever-shifting range of figural patterns that invite us to discern narrative correspondences between Jesus and many different Old Testament precursors: Isaac, Moses, David, Jeremiah, Wisdom, the Servant, the Righteous Sufferer, the Son of Man, and more. And underlying this kaleidoscopic variety of typologies, the most fundamental prefiguration is Matthew's astounding identification of Jesus as Emmanuel, God with us.[41]

In one way or another, all the Scriptural stories disclose something about God, and when Jesus appears on the narrative stage, we realize that he is "something greater" than all his predecessors, the messianic bearer of Israel's destiny, and the embodiment of Israel's God.

Fourthly, Matthew interprets scripture as a call for mission to the gentiles, from the gifts of the wise men (2:1–12) that call to mind Isaiah's vision of the nations coming to Israel's light (60:6), through the formula quotation in 4:12–17 referring to the gentiles (Isa 9:1–2), to the closing Great Commission (28:18–20) with its echoes of the everlasting authority given to the Son of Man in Daniel 7:14.

---

40. Hays, *Gospels*, 188.
41. Hays, *Gospels*, 189.

Luke

Where Mark's story is mysterious and elusive, and Matthew's tends to be didactic, Luke's is sweeping in scope (extending into a second volume in Acts) and measured in pace. Hays characterizes Luke's writing as a dramatic epic with a symphonic narrative that develops long melody lines and multiple variations, all coming together in a unified plan, composed by God.[42] Apart from the prologues to both Luke and Acts, the narrator rarely comments on the action; almost exclusively explicit Scriptural texts are contained in characters' speeches. From the start (1:1), the reader is prompted to consider how narrated events are linked to earlier ones, and the impression is created of strong historical continuity. Thus, "the Gospel of Luke is fraught with background, thick with Scriptural memory,"[43] sometimes through passing reference to Abraham, Moses, or Elijah, but more often by evocative echoes of scriptural stories. For example, the narrator concludes Jesus' raising of the son of the widow of Nain with "and he gave him to his mother" (7:15), which is an echo of Elijah's action in 1 Kgs 17:23. Luke uses this technique on many occasions; some are explicitly figural, encouraging readers to see scriptural characters as prefigurations of Jesus, while elsewhere they are less direct, reminding readers that the same God who was known to Israel in the past is scripting events in Jesus' life. In some cases, the intertextual links form ironic reversals between Elijah and Jesus; thus Jesus refuses to call down fire from heaven to deal with his opponents (9:54), as did Elijah (1 Kgs 18:36–39; 2 Kgs 1:10–12).[44] Luke sums up Jesus' own perspective on the scriptures in his dialogue with two disciples on the road to Emmaus; "Then beginning with Moses and all the prophets, he interpreted to them the things about himself in all the scriptures" (24:27). Later that day Jesus met the disciples and

> opened their minds to understand the scriptures, and he said to them, "Thus it is written that the Messiah is to suffer and rise from the dead on the third day, and that repentance and forgiveness of sins is to be proclaimed in his name, beginning from Jerusalem." (24:45–47)

---

42. Hays, *Gospels*, 275.
43. Hays, *Gospels*, 276; note the echo of Auerbach, *Mimesis*.
44. For details on the Elijah/Elisha cycle in Luke, see Hays, *Gospels*, 237–43.

There is no clear allusion to a specific text here (though Hos 6:2 or Isa 49:6 have been suggested), and Hays suggests that Luke is thinking of Isaiah 40–66 as a whole, read as a prophetic anticipation of the extension of God's salvation to the world.[45]

Some prominent themes in Luke are illuminated by recognizing intertextual references. God's concern for the poor and helpless is emphasized by means of scripture, especially in Jesus' Nazareth synagogue reading (4:16–19) from Isa 61:1–2 (omitting the last line of v. 2), supplemented by 58:6.[46] Suffering is a part of present experience for Jesus and his followers, since "it is written" that the Messiah must suffer (24:26–27, 46; reiterated in Acts 26:22–23), likely a reference to the Davidic psalms of lament as well as the Servant of Isaiah. The elect people of God are placed in a sharply countercultural relation to the prevailing world structures, as Peter says, "We must obey God rather than any human authority" (Acts 5:29). Reading scripture through Luke's eyes enables one to stand against the violent and coercive kingdoms of the world, as Zechariah prophecies by the Spirit (1:67–79), echoing Ps 106:10; Isa 9:1, 42:7, 59:8, 60:1–2.[47] Finally, Luke's narrative exposition of scripture leads readers to grasp that Israel's Lord visits and redeems Israel (1:68) in Christ the Lord, requiring a fundamental rethinking of our notion of "God."

Hays comments on the effect of Luke's accumulated scriptural imagery; it encourages "the formation of a certain kind of reading community. Luke is creating readers, seeking to foster the intertextual competence necessary to appreciate the nuances of the sort of narrative he is spinning."[48] He concludes that "the story does far more than instruct; it creates a world."[49]

John

There are relatively few direct scriptural citations or allusions in John's Gospel compared with the Synoptics, just as a small number of Jesus' miracles are selected and characterized as "signs." On John's narrative

---

45. Hays, *Gospels*, 413 n. 50.
46. See Hays, *Gospels*, 225–30.
47. On the background of "the dawn (*anatolē*) from on high" in Jer 23:5, Zech 3:8 & 6:12, and Isa 9:1, see Hays, *Gospels*, 230–31.
48. Hays, *Gospels*, 276.
49. Hays, *Gospels*, 277.

technique, Hays comments, "If Luke is the master of deft fleeting allusion, John is the master of the carefully framed, luminous image that shines brilliantly against a dark canvas and lingers in the imagination."[50] John's method of allusion is to evoke images and figures from Israel's scripture rather than chains of words or phrases. When he writes, "And just as Moses lifted up the serpent in the wilderness, so must the Son of Man be lifted up" (3:14), the allusion is to the incident narrated in Num 21:8-9, but the only verbal links to that passage are "Moses" and "serpent." The verb "lifted up" appears nowhere in Numbers 21, but it may faintly echo Isaiah's introduction of the mysterious suffering Servant (Isa 52:13).

John makes a significant number of direct quotations using quotation formulas, often within authorial commentary, thereby resembling Matthew rather than Mark or Luke. Throughout his account of Jesus' public ministry, quotations are introduced with "as it is written," "it is written in the prophets," "as scripture said," or something similar (1:23; 2:17; 6:31, 45; 7:38, 42; 10:34; 12:14). But once Jesus withdraws from public activity (12:36b) there is a striking change; almost all subsequent citations are introduced with a "fulfilment" formula (12:38; 13:18; 15:25; 17:12; 19:24, 28; 19:36). The only exceptions are at 12:39 and 19:37, and in both cases the quotation introduced is the second of a pair, signalled by "again." These pairs of linked quotations function to indicate the close of the two narrative blocks of the Gospel, the "book of signs" (1:19—12:50) and the "book of the passion" (13:1—19:42).[51] According to Hays, the shift to fulfilment language in these introductory formulas

> signals an *apologetic* motivation: the Evangelist is explaining that the suffering and rejection experienced by Jesus in the passion story was not some unforeseen disaster; rather, it was foreordained and played out in fulfilment of God's will, with Jesus' full knowledge and participation.[52]

John appears less interested in the story of Israel than do the Synoptic Gospels, but this is due to his intense focus on Christology; Jesus is the central figure and everything else, including Israel's past, must find its place in John's story's world in relation to him.[53] The story of Israel

---

50. Hays, *Gospels*, 284.

51. Hays, *Gospels*, 425f, discusses the implications for John's literary structure, with an argument for chapters 20–21 as a separate closing unit.

52. Hays, *Gospels*, 286.

53. Andrew Francis reminded me that the sixteenth-century Anabaptist movement

has no independent significance apart from Jesus; nevertheless, John's narrative only makes sense within the network formed by Israel's, for he regularly makes allusions to its characters.[54] Indeed, "it is impossible to understand John's Jesus apart from the story of Israel and the liturgical festivals and symbols that recall and re-present that story"; so Hays insists that Jesus *assumes* and *transforms* Israel's Torah and worship life.[55]

Israel's distinctive role in God's dealings with the world is clearly set out in Jesus' dialogue with the Samaritan woman: "You worship what you do not know; we worship what we know, for salvation is from the Jews" (4:22). Here Jesus affirms Israel's prophetic tradition (Isa 2:3; 45:14; Zech 8:23), yet he goes on to perform a hermeneutical transformation: "the hour is coming when you will worship the Father neither on this mountain nor in Jerusalem" (4:21), thus relativizing the significance of Jerusalem or any other place as the locus of God's presence.

John's understanding of the relation between Jesus and the scriptures is expressed in the key text near the end of the prologue, "The law was given through Moses: grace and truth came through Jesus Christ" (1:17). But does this mean that the law points to grace and truth, or that the grace and truth of Jesus Christ displace the law?[56] John must mean the former since, according to 1:45 and 5:45–47, Moses actually wrote about Jesus and the law bears witness to the gospel. Jesus explains the hatred that he incurs, "It was to fulfil the word that is written in their law, 'They hated me without a cause'" (15:25). Here he is quoting loosely a phrase that appears in both Ps 35:19 and Ps 69:5, and this shows that John can use the term law (*nomos*) to refer to scripture as a whole, and not simply to the Pentateuch or to passages that spell out the commandments.[57]

The best known of John's verbal echoes is found in his opening sentence, "In the beginning was the Word," which echoes and transforms Gen 1:1. John's prologue is best understood as a midrash on Genesis 1

---

treated the First Testament in a similar way because of their emphasis on *nachfolge* (passion to follow Jesus).

54. Abraham (8:51–59), Jacob (4:4–42), Moses (1:45; 3:14; 5:45–47; 6:32; 7:19; 9:28f), Elijah (1:21, 25), Isaiah (1:23; 12:38–41), David (7:42, see also 10:11ff/Ezek 34:23f.) and the Messiah/Christ (1:17, 41; 4:25; 7:31; 9:22; 11:27; 17:3; 20:31).

55. Hays, *Gospels*, 287.

56. Some readers have thought the latter, and that John's Gospel condemns the Jews, particularly in view of Jesus' words to them, "You are from your father the devil" (8:44). For a helpful discussion of this topic, see Motyer, *Your Father the Devil?*

57. Hays, *Gospels*, 297, also shows that "the law" does not refer to the Pentateuch in John 10:34 or 12:34.

that draws on traditions about creation (note the resonance with the language of Ps 33:6: "By the word of the LORD the heavens were made, and all their host by the word of his mouth") and Wisdom (Prov 8:22–31; Wisdom 10; Sir 24:1–23). Hays points out the hermeneutical implications of John's identification of Jesus as the incarnate Word who was the agent of all creation for the way that he reinterprets Israel's scripture and worship traditions; John *reads backwards*. He illustrates this from the incident of Jesus' dramatic protest in the temple (2:13–22):

> John presents both the scriptural text and the word of Jesus as enigmas that become comprehensible only *retrospectively*, only after the resurrection. . . . That is the point made emphatically in John 2:22: "After he was raised from the dead, his disciples remembered . . . and they believed *the Scripture* and *the word that Jesus had spoken*."[58]

The explicit link between the temple and Jesus' body (2:21) provides a hermeneutical key for John's symbolism in the ensuing narrative, once we bear in mind that his gospel was written likely some decades after the destruction of Jerusalem: "*Jesus takes over the temple's function as a place of mediation between God and human beings*."[59]

4. Implications for the Contemporary Interpretation

Richard Longenecker concluded one of the earlier studies of the way Second Testament writers used the scriptures by arguing that contemporary interpreters of the Bible benefit from understanding the interpretive methods employed by those first-century writers, but that we should not necessarily employ those methods ourselves since they were bound to the culture of that time and may not be appropriate today.[60] Richard Hays objected to Longenecker's distinction between the descriptive and the normative tasks in exegesis and argued from such passages as "be imitators of me" (1 Cor 4:16; 11:1; cf. Phil 3:17) that Paul's letters are a

---

58. Hays, *Gospels*, 311. See also the disciples' retrospective understanding of Jesus' entry to Jerusalem on a young donkey (12:16). Jesus tells the disciples that the Holy Spirit will help them to recall and interpret Jesus' words for the community (John 14:25–26; 16:12–15).

59. Hays, *Gospels*, 312. This symbolism is already foreshadowed in the prologue where it is said that the *Logos* "became flesh and dwelled (tabernacled) among us" (1:14), cf. Exod 25:8–9 and Ezek 37:26f.

60. Longenecker, *Biblical Exegesis*, 214–20.

hermeneutical model for Christians today.[61] He argued that it is not possible to distinguish cleanly between apostolic methods of interpretation and the theological conclusions that the apostles came to thereby.

I find this a difficult debate to decide. There are many elements of the Bible that seem culturally determined and inapplicable in other cultural contexts; for example, if this book were to be written in the languages of the Bible, it would reach a very small audience. Nevertheless, proficiency in those ancient languages may help to interpret the Bible well! Again, an understanding of the interpretive methods used by Second Testament writers may connect with contemporary interpretive methods, such as intertextuality, and better equip today's readers in our interpretive efforts. So, I incline to Hays' view overall, though Longenecker has a point about the fine details.

In the conclusion to his work on the Gospels, Hays insists that, for the Evangelists, Israel's scripture told the true story of the world, tracing out a coherent storyline that stretched from creation, through the election of Israel, to the goal of God's redemption of the world. The Evangelists' varied and imaginative uses and transformations of First Testament texts summon readers to a conversion of the imagination.

> We can hear their proclamation only if we allow their intertextual performances to retrain our sensibilities as readers and to reshape our perception of what is real. If we learn from them how to read, we will approach the reading of Scripture with a heightened awareness of *story, metaphor, prefiguration, allusion, echo, reversal, and irony*. To read Scripture well we must bid farewell to plodding literalism and rationalism in order to embrace *a complex poetic sensibility*.[62]

In the next chapter, I will extend Hays' emphasis upon metalepsis to the full context of the books that tell Israel's story, and this will shape my approach in the chapters that follow.

---

61. Hays, *Paul*, 178–92. Longenecker responded to Hays in his second edition of *Biblical Exegesis*, xxxiv–xxxix.

62. Hays, *Gospels*, 360.

3

Interpreting Whole Books

In 2017 the Bank of England introduced a new £10 note; on the reverse appeared a celebration of Jane Austen, the famous novelist, complete with a quotation, "I declare after all there is no enjoyment like reading!" At first glance, this statement, found in Austen's *Pride and Prejudice*, might seem an appropriate tribute, yet those familiar with her work would disagree. These words are uttered by the shallow character Caroline Bingley as she is trying to impress Mr Darcy, and it is clear that they are rather banal. Surely a more suitable text might have been found to celebrate the great author! The point I wish to emphasize is that there may be significant differences between the views expressed by a character within a book and those of its author. Apply this to the scriptures; a statement is not necessarily true simply because it is expressed within the pages of the Bible. Look no further than the serpent's speech in the garden of Eden (Gen 3:1–5). Yet the practice of taking short extracts out of their literary context is common amongst many who claim to revere the scriptures; "proof texting" is still prevalent in popular teaching. Long-established traditions of reading and preaching the Bible in short sections have tended to detract from the significance of the wider book.

The most important point this chapter seeks to make is that interpreters should give priority to grasping the meaning and message of whole books of the Bible. In order to achieve this, familiarity with a book's contents is necessary, so attention must be given to various components that make up the whole. But the more readers become familiar with these books as wholes, the more they realize that some statements made by certain characters within them may be deceitful, that some deeds done by "heroes" may be contrary to God's will (though not explicitly identified as such), and indeed, some views expressed by their narrators may not be all that they seem on first acquaintance.

Many believers struggle to get to this point because their churches and teachers lack the necessary skills and teaching opportunities to assist them. When I embarked on postgraduate study of biblical interpretation in the late 1980s, I remember Dick (R. T.) France, one of my tutors, telling me that his first lecture on Mark's Gospel to undergraduates consisted of reading the whole book to them out loud, because most had never read it through in one sitting.

In order to grasp the meaning of whole books, I propose that three perspectives on scripture should be explored: literary, historical, and theological.[1] I use the term "perspective" because these elements of interpretation may be isolated for the purposes of discussion, although they cannot be disentangled from each other in practice. The message of whole books is bound up with this combination of literary, historical, and theological perspectives, but it is discovered in the lives of its readers. Biblical books may convey varying messages depending on when and where they are read; the originally intended recipients, subsequent devotees, and contemporary readers.

The scriptures confront readers initially as a collection of works of literature; the many books are largely made up of stories and poems. Well translated, these are accessible to most people; they can engross us, arousing our emotions, stimulating our imaginations, shaping our worldviews, and appealing to our wills. But these stories, poems, and other literary genres originated within an ancient culture, and it is easy for today's readers to assume that they "work" just like their contemporary counterparts. Readers need to familiarize themselves with the cultures and conventions that long ago shaped the writers of these books.

Thus, as readers engage with these works from an ancient culture, historical questions arise about their relation to what is known about the past from other sources. In what sense are they reliable witnesses to the people and events of long ago? What can the study of related ancient cultures—their social systems, political organization, economic arrangements, and so on—contribute to understanding these stories and poems? Further questions can be asked about the books themselves; when were

---

1. In this, my proposal is similar to the approach taken by Dillard and Longman, *Introduction to the Old Testament*.

they written? Who were their intended recipients? How did they come to be passed down to us?

Thirdly, most of these books make frequent reference to God, link this God to a particular people, and explore the relationship between these two parties with reference to the whole of humanity and the wider world. Even the book of Esther, which does not mention God's name, has a theological dimension because it tells a story about God's people living in the diaspora rather than among the Jewish community who had returned to Jerusalem. Readers cannot escape the theological perspectives of particular books, though they may find them presented with some subtlety.

The overall message of a book, involving the art of communication, is tied up with two factors. Firstly, the rhetorical features that convey the book's message, involving the arts of composition and persuasion; such as stylistic techniques (e.g., repetition, inversion), figures of speech (metaphor, etc.), literary arrangement, narrative impact, and use of irony.[2] Secondly, consideration of the intended readership, involving the arts of relationship; originally readers would have been Jews during and after the exile, but thereafter the book's inclusion in the canon indicates such readers and hearers are God's continuing people (Christians included).

To illustrate each of these three interpretive perspectives, I have chosen examples mainly from the book of Genesis. Its place at the very beginning of the Bible means that it sets up everything else that follows. Although Part II will focus on the books of Joshua to Kings, those books cannot be rightly understood without situating them within the wider biblical narrative that begins with Genesis, indeed scholars have identified a number of ways in which these books are linked.[3] But first I will say more about my emphasis on whole books.[4]

1. The Whole-Book Approach

While many scholars now pay attention to literary features in biblical narratives, there has been less attention to whole books and what their

---

2. For overviews of this topic, see Möller, "Rhetorical Criticism," and Brown, *Scripture as Communication*, 157–63

3. See Brueggemann, *David and His Theologian*, 1–28.

4. I have been encouraged to note Ellen Davis' whole-book approach in her recent *Opening Israel's Scriptures*.

rhetorical strategy might be. Paul House has written an Old Testament Theology that works through the various books for canonical and pedagogical reasons, but he pays little attention to literary insights into these books.[5] Walter Brueggemann, who has enlivened study of the scriptures in recent decades, and from whom I have learnt much, has tended to focus on the literary features of quite short sections of text rather than their wider literary context.[6] David Cotter wrote, in his 2003 commentary on *Genesis*:

> ... among all the brilliant and provocative commentaries on Genesis, none reads the entire book as a story. This is not to say that there are not extremely important studies of individual passages within the book, or sections of the book.... However, as far as I know, there is no commentary that applies the tools of narrative analysis to the book as an integral whole.[7]

Two theoretical perspectives inform my emphasis upon whole books. Most importantly, it takes seriously the insight of modern linguistics that books are the fundamental units of meaning.[8] There are many sub-units of meaning—words, sentences, episodes, stories, cycles of stories—but finally the opening and closing parts of a book form its boundaries. Any particular part or sub-unit of the book finds its meaning in relation to the whole work. In the discipline of discourse analysis, linguists insist that the meaning of a text depends upon what they call its literary *cotext* as well as its historical *context*.[9] The author, compiler, or editor of a book sends it out into the world with some notion of coherence lest she or he be accused of confusion, contradiction, or inconsistency.[10] Two books

---

5. E.g., House's treatment of Genesis divides it into seven sections rather arbitrarily, *Old Testament Theology*, 59, and pays little attention to the links between its various sections.

6. Brueggemann has written a number of fine commentaries and an *Introduction to the Old Testament*, in which he necessarily addresses whole-book issues. But when he sets out and illustrates his method of interpretation in *A Pathway of Interpretation*, 34–39, he does not mention the significance of the wider literary context or whole book, focusing instead on rhetorical analysis of relatively short texts, coupled with key word analysis, and social analysis. This lacuna is also evident in his otherwise profound *Theology of the Old Testament*, though, he has subsequently written *Theology of the Book of Jeremiah*.

7. Cotter, *Genesis*, xxiv.

8. See Brown, *Scripture as Communication*, 212–25.

9. See Cotterell & Turner, *Linguistics & Biblical Interpretation*, 16.

10. Obviously, some publications contain sharply divergent views—collections of essays by different authors, or journals containing articles on unrelated topics—but in

may not seem to fit this requirement since they have the appearance of being anthologies or collections; the Psalter is a collection of smaller units of meaning, while Proverbs is made up of a coherent introduction (chapters 1–9) followed by several collections of brief aphorisms, each one of which could be considered a small unit of meaning. However, recent work indicates that each of these books received significant editorial shaping that underlies their collective meaning.[11]

Secondly, emphasis upon whole books takes seriously the canonical shape of the First and Second Testaments.[12] Scholars have advanced influential theories regarding the literary origins of parts of the scriptures, but these remain hypothetical and subject to revision. Whatever their origins, it is the books in their final shape, which have been preserved and read in synagogues and churches, that make up the Bible.[13]

2. Literary Perspectives

Most readers take the literary character of the scriptures for granted, yet unconscious assumptions and entrenched reading habits can obscure their meaning.[14] In order to emphasize the whole-book approach I will begin by considering the literary arrangement of books, and pursue this line of investigation to smaller-scale literary structure. A brief outline of literary genre will lead to a discussion of genealogy, of narrative, and of poetry.

---

these cases the essays or articles are individually units of meaning.

11. On Psalms, see chapter 8. On Proverbs, Heim, *Like Grapes of Gold,* has argued that most sayings in one extensive collection have been arranged into small clusters intentionally so that these clusters mean more than the sum of their individual parts.

12. Childs first emphasized the significance of the canon in his *Introduction to the Old Testament as Scripture*. Rendtorff, *Canon and Theology*, emphasizes attending to Jewish interpretation of the scriptures as well as the significance of whole books.

13. Of course, there are some debates about what those final forms are, especially over the shortened text of Jeremiah in the LXX, and the ending of Mark's Gospel. There are also differences between the Protestant, Catholic, and Orthodox canons. The standard discussion of such matters is McDonald, *Biblical Canon*.

14. There are many theoretical issues at stake in literary interpretation, but I cannot embark on them here. For one example, Sternberg, in *Poetics of Biblical Narrative*, 7–23, finds fault with "New Criticism," contrasting it with discourse-oriented analysis.

Arrangement

Many books are long and complicated, and contain several genres, so an essential aid to grasping how they work as wholes is to identify their overall literary arrangement. This may consist of an introductory section or prologue, followed by several main parts, each telling a series of stories, and a conclusion, which often carries much weight. Sometimes the arrangement is signalled in a significant way; in other cases it is less obvious, and so disagreements may arise among interpreters, over smaller details as well as the bigger picture.

It has been common to divide the book of Genesis into two unequal parts, the Primeval Stories (chapters 1–11), and the Patriarchal Stories (chapters 12–50), but in recent decades literary approaches have helped to see better how the book works as a whole. The most significant structuring device used in this book is known as the *toledot* formula. The Hebrew noun *toledot* means "generations" or "descendants" and comes from the verb *yalad*, "to bear," or "to give birth;" indeed, generativity expresses the central theme of the whole book from creation (1:28) to the overcoming of infertility and famine among the patriarchs. In the Septuagint version, the word *toledot* is translated into Greek as *genesis*, meaning "origins"—hence the book's title in the Septuagint, and then in English translations.[15]

The phrase "these are the descendants" or "this is the account," appears eleven times in the book (2:4; 5:1; 6:9; 10:1; 11:10, 27; 25:12, 19; 36:1, 9; 37:2).[16] Apart from the first case, this phrase heads a major genealogy, and this suggests that in the first case it introduces the second creation account, rather than concluding the first creation account (as has often been assumed).

This *toledot* formula points to a literary arrangement of two groups of five sections each (or pentads), introduced by a prologue. The prologue and first pentad have a universal perspective, while the second pentad deals largely with the family origins of Israel. Each pentad is made up of narratives alternating with genealogies (mainly), though the narratives in

---

15. See Wenham, *Genesis 1–15*, xxi–xxii; Janzen, *Abraham*, 2–6; Blenkinsopp, *Creation, Un-Creation, Re-Creation*, 4.

16. Its appearance in 36:9 introduces a secondary section into Esau's genealogy, and most commentators have thought it a late addition to the book, e.g., Wenham, *Genesis 16–50*, 334–36. However, Mbuvi, *Belonging in Genesis*, 52n30, argues that 5:1 is the unusual case.

the second pentad are more extensive and detailed than in the first. In the first pentad, the central story of Noah forms a new beginning in several ways (as we will see), while the central story in the second pentad forms a new beginning with the renaming of Jacob as "Israel" and the birth of his twelve sons, the ancestors of the twelve tribes. There is a significant link between the turning points of the two central sections of each pentad; "God remembered Noah" (8:1), and "God remembered Rachel" (30:22).

Genesis: Literary Arrangement

	Prologue	First creation account	1:1—2:3
Pentad 1	1)	The generations of heaven and earth	2:4—4:26
	2)	The generations of Adam (*genealogy + narrative*)	5:1—6:8
	3)	The generations of Noah	6:9—9:29
	4)	The generations of Noah's sons (*genealogy + narrative*)	10:1—11:9
	5)	The generations of Shem (*genealogy*)	11:10–26
Pentad 2	6)	The generations of Terah—mainly Abraham (*narrative*)	11:27—25:11
	7)	The generations of Ishmael (*genealogy*)	25:12–18
	8)	The generations of Isaac—mainly Jacob (*narrative*)	25:19—35:29
	9)	The generations of Esau (*genealogy*)	36:1(9)—37:1
	10)	The generations of Jacob—mainly Joseph (*narrative + poetry*)	37:2—50:26

Joseph Blenkinsopp observes of the first pentad,

> Since structure is an important way of conveying meaning, especially in ancient compositions, it seems that this fivefold arrangement was adopted to indicate the central thematic importance of the deluge by its position at the center of the pentad. What this means is that the theme of Genesis 1–11 is not just creation but something more overarching, something like creation—uncreation—re-creation.[17]

Blenkinsopp continues on the second pentad,

> The entire narrative pivots on the central unit, the story of Jacob and his 20 year exile in Mesopotamia. As a kind of destruction

17. Blenkinsopp, *Creation*, 4–5.

and re-creation, this central *peripateia* corresponds structurally and thematically to the deluge in the preceding segment. The story, vividly told, inscribes the same theme of judgement followed by passage to a new identity and a new relationship with God.[18]

Attention to the literary arrangement of the whole book helps to see connections between the primeval stories and the patriarchal stories.

Thus the overall shape of a large book can be made up of a number of parts that may vary in genre, length, and complexity, and good literary interpretation will take account of each of these factors and consider how they might hold together. In Genesis, the fifth part of the first pentad consists simply of one genealogy, while the first part of the second pentad contains a long cycle of stories about Abraham. Each one of these stories can be considered as a story in its own right, yet attention to the wider context of the Abraham cycle is essential for good interpretation.

Structure

The early Bible manuscripts did not have the chapter and verse divisions that are familiar to modern readers. But from ancient times the Hebrew manuscripts were divided into paragraphs, and the Torah was divided into 154 sections for reading in weekly worship. Modern chapter divisions are based on Archbishop Stephen Langton's system from the early thirteenth century. The division into smaller units may also go back to early times, and versifications were made with the introduction of printed English translations, corresponding mainly with existing Hebrew full stops.[19] The now long-established divisions into verses and chapters are sometimes helpful, but often unhelpful, in identifying literary structure.

Careful reading of the Bible pays attention to the particular words used and their connections across the various sentences that make up a paragraph or longer story. Many literary units may be analyzed through "close reading" of the Hebrew text. This often reveals word-plays:

- alliteration (two or more words start with similar sounds)
- rhyme (regardless of initial sounds, words sound alike)
- paronomasia (words sound similar but have different meanings).

18. Blenkinsopp, *Creation*, 5.
19. For details see Wurthwein, *Text of the Old Testament*, 30–32.

Many of these features are lost in translation,[20] though commentaries may point them out, yet it may still be possible to observe connections, repetitions, and inversions of particular words or phrases in a good translation. This structuring can work at the level of the line or sentence, but also across larger sections, and even whole books. The first creation story is a good place to begin, since its seven days are an obvious structuring device. There are repeated phrases that generate a rhythm: "God said... let there be... and it was so... and it was evening and morning." Further investigation reveals that there are eight creative acts; two acts occur on days three and six, so that there is a repeated triple day step-pattern, as follows;[21]

Patterning in the First Creation Story

Preamble	In the beginning...	1:1–2
First Day	A. Light	1:3–5
Second Day	B. Waters/Firmament	1:6–8
Third Day	C. Dry land	1:9–10
	Vegetation	1:11–13
Fourth Day	A'. Luminaries	1:14–19
Fifth Day	B'. Fish/Birds	1:20–23
Sixth Day	C'. Land animals	1:24–25
	People	1:26–28
	Vegetation for food	1:29–31
Seventh Day	D. Sabbath	2:1–3

This patterning indicates that the habitats created in the first three days participate in the creation of their inhabitants in the next three days, the Sabbath being clearly set apart.[22] A more detailed analysis of the repetitions in the whole unit reveals increasing complexity in days 3 (vegetation is created on a habitat day) and 6, and shows how day 7 links back to the Preamble.[23]

---

20. For an accessible remedy, see Schlimm, *70 Hebrew Words*.
21. See Fretheim, "Genesis," 341. See also the important discussion of recent commentators in Joerstad, *Hebrew Bible and Environmental Ethics*, 55–58.
22. See Fretheim, "Genesis," 343–45.
23. Expanded from Walsh, *Style and Structure*, 37.

Complexity in the First Creation Story

Preamble	created . . . the heavens and the earth . . . waters
A. First day	light
B. Second day	firmament, called sky, divides the waters
C1. Third day	sea and earth
C2. Third day	plants
A'. Fourth day	lights
B'. Fifth day	created . . . fish in the waters & birds in the firmament of the sky
C1'. Sixth day	animals of the earth
C+. Sixth day	humankind . . . created . . . created . . . created
C2'. Sixth day	plants for food
D. Seventh day	the heavens and the earth . . . creation

One of the most common literary structures is the concentric pattern, or *palistrophe*, in which matching elements reflect each other in reverse order. The simplest of these is known as a *chiasm*, the lines of which may be represented as ABA'. A good example of this is the conclusion of the Generations of Adam.

The Conclusion of the Generations of Adam: Genesis 6:6–7

A	*And the LORD was sorry that he had made humankind on the earth, and it grieved him to his heart.*
B	*So the LORD said, "I will blot out from the earth the human beings I have created—people together with animals and creeping things and birds of the air,*
A'	*for I am sorry that I have made them."*

For a longer palistrophic pattern, see the story of the Tower of Babel (Gen 11:1–9), while one of the longest is the account of Absalom's rebellion (2 Samuel 15–20), a concentric composition of sixteen parts.[24]

Genre

Television viewers quickly learn to recognize the difference between drama, documentary, comedy, news, and weather forecast, though some productions blur the boundaries between broadcast genres. Most Bible

---

24. According to Fokkelman, *Reading Biblical Narrative*, 215–16.

readers have some awareness that it contains a variety of kinds of literature; narratives, genealogies, collections of legal materials and of wisdom sayings; poems of various kinds—songs, psalms, prophecies. Genre competence is something that every Bible reader has to learn, not least because there are subtle differences between ancient and contemporary genres.

It is essential to devote space to the literary genre of narrative, since great swathes of the scriptures are made up of stories. It will become clear that there are narrative sub-genres, such as stories of world origins, conquest accounts, and parables, and other genres are frequently woven into narratives, especially poetry. But consideration of Genesis' literary arrangement has already indicated the significance of its genealogies, so more must be said about these first.

Genealogy

Genealogies can appear in various forms, but the most commonly distinguished are:

- Linear, in which one line of descent is traced from an ancestor, as in Genesis 5.
- Segmented, in which more than one line of descent is traced, as in Genesis 10. By describing all members of a generation, these genealogies map a social network.

A significant proportion of Genesis consists of genealogies and they make an important contribution to the literary arrangement of the book.

Westerners tend to be unfamiliar with this genre and either skip over the monotonous "begats" or insist on taking them literally as biological records of lineage. The popularity of researching one's ancestry and DNA testing have fed the dominant modern view that genealogy is a representation of "blood," that it is a biological, immutable, and objectively verifiable mode of community identity. However, oral genealogies are grounded in different conventions and regard ancestry as a product of social negotiations, so that "it is quite possible for apparently contradictory genealogies to coexist in the same society if they have different functions. The people who use genealogies do not hesitate to cite conflicting genealogies if it suits their purpose."[25]

25. Wilson, *Genealogy and History*, 203.

Obviously, the Bible can only contain written genealogies, yet Genesis 36 contains elements found in oral genealogies since there is a discrepancy between Esau's wives, Adah, of Hittite descent, Oholibamah, of Hivite descent, and Basemath, Ishmael's daughter (36:2–3), and the earlier notices of his wives Judith and Basemath, both of Hittite descent, (26:34), and later Mahalah, daughter of Ishmael (28:9). So, it seems that an ancient oral genealogical tradition has been preserved in Genesis, and Amanda Beckenstein Mbuvi argues that such genealogies should be interpreted sociologically and theologically rather than biologically.

> Biblical genealogies operate in conjunction with other family stories, orienting family members in relation to the biblical text. They also convey the fundamentals of an approach to conceptualizing both relationships and the self as a member of a community. . . . [T]he book's use of genealogy becomes a social critique and a means of nourishing a countercultural sensibility within the family, obstructing an imperial monopoly on defining identity. Instead of using oral genealogies to delineate the place of the individual in the group, Genesis uses written ones to delineate the place of the group in the world (or more specifically the cosmos).[26]

Narrative and Narrative Analysis

Biblical studies were dominated by historical-critical methods during the twentieth century. However, in its final decades, the introduction of literary approaches has provided important new perspectives (and sometimes correctives) for interpreters. I can remember the excitement of discovering Robert Alter's *The Art of Biblical Narrative* in the early 1980s.[27] Since then many studies of biblical narrative have been written, and the approach has been applied in certain commentaries. I will describe some of the key insights available from narrative approaches here, and more details will be found in later chapters.

A story relates what is happening to people, and describes objects, places, and events. However, not every description is necessarily a story. What makes a description into a story is a significant change: a bad situation is improved (e.g., when one of the characters overcomes a rival or a

---

26. Mbuvi, *Belonging in Genesis*, 46–47. The final observation is derived from noting that even the cosmos is incorporated under the rubric of the family in Gen 2:4a.

27. Alter, *Art of Biblical Narrative*.

difficult obstacle); a situation that was good at the outset grows markedly worse (e.g., due to a failure, or being hurt by a rival). In a story the main thing is the change, the event that makes the reader feel that something has occurred.[28] Some have proposed that conflict is the driver of stories, but, although conflict *is* a major driver in many stories, it is not so in every case, and so the broader category of change is preferable.

Many stories can be analyzed using a five-part plot, consisting of exposition, complication, change, unravelling, and ending,[29] however, the plot can be rather more complex and capable of more extensive analysis. As an example, I will take one of the best-known stories, the Garden of Eden. Here is one way of analyzing the plot in seven parts.

The Garden of Eden: Narrative Analysis

Setting:	The man is placed in the garden	2:4b–17
Exposition:	Character relationships are established in harmony	2:18–25
Complication:	The serpent makes statements to the woman	3:1–5
Change:	The woman and her husband eat of the tree	3:6–7
Unravelling:	YHWH God asks questions of the man and woman	3:8–13
Consequences:	Character relationships re-established in disharmony	3:14–21
Ending:	The man (and woman) is driven from the garden	3:22–24

Here the scene is set through YHWH God's actions of making, growing, and placing, with an extensive description of the garden and its locale. Next, relationships among the creatures (man and animals, man and woman) are expounded. The complication concerns YHWH God's earlier statement to the man and indicates that relationships between woman and animals are out of order. The change involves the woman following the serpent's suggestion, rather than YHWH God's command; she is followed by the man. The unravelling is initiated by YHWH God's walking, to which the man and woman respond in shame; YHWH God calls, then converses with the man and woman so that they name what they have done. YHWH God then spells out the consequences of their

---

28. Amit, *Reading Biblical Narrative*, 46.
29. Derived from Amit, *Reading Biblical Narrative*, 47.

actions to serpent, man, and woman. Finally, YHWH God considers the worst-case scenario and drives the man from the garden; it is implied that the woman is driven out with him, but use of "the man" makes a tight connection to his original placement in the garden (2:8).

Of course, this plot analysis oversimplifies in order to highlight certain symmetries as the plot unfolds; for example, character relationships already begin to be established when YHWH God first addresses the man with a command (2:16–17). However, such analysis is suggestive in drawing attention to the animal/woman complication (3:1–5), and to the change in proper order (3:6–7).

Narrative analysis of this story further identifies several features: characters (YHWH God, the man, the woman, the animals, the serpent, the cherubim), their actions (making, causing, forming, breathing, planting, growing, placing, etc.), speeches (commands, soliloquies, declarations, inquiries), and dialogues (questions, assertions, and answers). All these activities are set within certain locales (the earth outside the garden, the garden, the center of the garden). There are explicit time markers; at the start, "In the day" (2:4b), and at the unravelling, "evening" (3:8), but other suggestions of time passing can be observed in the man's naming of the animals (2:19), his later deep sleep (2:21), and elsewhere. The narrator evaluates character (the serpent as wise or crafty, 3:1) and has characters name emotions like fear (3:10), but also implies emotions like curiosity, delight, shame, disappointment, and perhaps anger and sadness. The narration is very spare and omits many things that readers would like to know, such as, why was the original prohibition given (2:16–17)? How long did the woman take before making up her mind? Why was the man so uninvolved in the decision? Such narrative "gaps" draw the reader in and provoke further reflection on the story.

Thus far narrative analysis, but this is an unusual story, with several indicators that it is not like many other biblical stories. It is a story of origins—origins of human beings, and of things wrong with the world, not least death. Two trees in the garden are unlike any other trees in the known world, and one of the animals speaks. The geographical references to the four rivers include two that are well-known and two that are not (Havilah and Gihon), and at the story's end the garden is guarded by armed cherubim. Once we compare this story with ancient stories of origins from the nearby civilizations, although containing significant differences from them, it is obvious that it belongs to this particular sub-genre.³⁰ It is extraordinarily suggestive and expresses great insight into human beings, but it does not require literal interpretation, as if the garden (or its remains) could be visited by tourists today, or that snakes once could speak.

Poetry

It is not easy to define poetry, but one place to start is with the notion of density; "Poetry is the most compact and concentrated of speech possible."³¹ Until the final decades of the twentieth century, Hebrew poetry was identified by two characteristics, meter and the parallel arrangement of lines, or cola.³² However, both these characteristics have been challenged; firstly, even experts disagree as to which, if any, syllables should be stressed or not, and thus how lines might scan (we cannot be sure how ancient Hebrew was pronounced). Secondly, it is recognized that a key feature of Hebrew poetry is parallelism; i.e., consecutive lines frequently reflect each other in some way. But Bishop Lowth's classification of parallelism as synonymous, antithetical, and complementary (or synthetic) has been shown to be clearly unsatisfactory; as James Kugel says, "Biblical parallelism is of one sort . . . , or a hundred sorts; but it is not three."³³

An important feature of the Hebrew language is that it requires fewer words than does English to express meaning. This leads to difficulties in printing the longer English versions of poetry, since one line (or colon) in Hebrew must often, once translated, spill over onto a second line. In this example, the problem only arises in the first line;

> Adah and Zillah, hear my voice; you wives of Lamech, listen to what I say:
> I have killed a man for wounding me, a boy for striking me.
> If sevenfold avenged is Cain, Lamech truly seventy-sevenfold.³⁴

30. For a discussion of these origin stories, see Brown, *Seven Pillars*, 21-32.

31. Fokkelman, *Reading Biblical Poetry*, 15.

32. A "colon" refers to a line of Hebrew poetry, often a half-verse. Alter coined the term "verset" for this in his *Art of Biblical Poetry*, 9.

33. Kugel, *Idea of Biblical Poetry*, 58. Alter produced a complementary proposal; "[Where] semantic parallelism does occur in a line, the characteristic movement is one of heightening or intensification, of focusing, specification, concretization, even what could be called dramatization" (*Art of Biblical Poetry*, 19).

34. Following, Alter, *Art of Biblical Poetry*, 5-12, I have changed "young man" to

What clearly distinguishes this passage (Gen 4:23–24) from the prose of the surrounding verses is the parallelism of meaning between each half of the three lines, the word order in one exactly mirroring that in the other. In the first line; "Adah and Zillah"/"you wives of Lamech," "hear"/"listen to," "my voice"/"what I say." In the second line, the verb does double duty for the second half (thus "ellipsis"), but otherwise the same mirroring is present. Ellipsis also appears in the third line, where the reference to "sevenfold vengeance" from the previous story of Cain (4:15) is greatly multiplied, and the word order is reversed, emphasizing the contrast between the two men and providing a sense of closure. This blood-thirsty poetic boast is the most extensive detail in the *toledot* of Adam and witnesses to the violence that goes with the other cultural achievements of Cain's descendants.

Another important feature of Hebrew poetry is the use of metaphor. For example, YHWH is said to be "the rock of Israel" in Jacob's final words (Gen 49:25), also in David's Song (2 Sam 22:2, 32, 47) and many psalms. It is important to consider how this common figure of speech works, since a number of ways of understanding it have been advanced. According to the "Ornament" theory, God is clearly not like a rock, so such language must not be taken too seriously; it is just "flowery language." According to the "It's All Metaphor" theory, all words do duty for realities for which they stand; thus "God" is a merely a sign for the ultimate being, and a particular metaphorical usage should be no surprise. In the "Surprise" theory, metaphors work by arresting our thoughts, perhaps even shocking us—who would have thought of characterizing God as a rock!

But the most perceptive and influential approach is described as the "Grounding" theory by Lakoff and Johnson, who argue that "The essence of metaphor is understanding and experiencing one kind of thing in terms of another."[35] A metaphorical statement cannot be understood literally, but some aspects of one thing can be understood in terms of some aspects of another. Thus, while God is not cold, hard, or inert, like a lump of granite, God does provide a firm foundation, or a protection for one's back, as a rock might.

"boy" in the middle line, and in the final line I have changed the NRSV word order to reflect the Hebrew.

35. Lakoff and Johnson, *Metaphors We Live By*, 5.

3. Historical Perspectives

Once the literary character of the scriptures is recognized, the question arises of what kind of literature is involved. Is biblical narrative some kind of representation of past events and people, or would fiction be a better approximation to their genre than history? If the latter, does the artistry involved obscure what actually happened, perhaps out of naiveté, partisanship, or ideology?[36] Such questions have been sharpened by increased knowledge of the history and culture of the ancient Near East, enhanced by discoveries of ancient documents and archaeological remains.

Historical perspectives draw upon a range of other disciplines that are significant for interpretation. For any reading of the First Testament, some familiarity with ancient languages supplements the use of translations. Knowledge of ancient Mesopotamian, Egyptian, and Greek cultures helps to understand the context.[37] Some aspects of ancient Israelite culture can be illuminated by historically aware anthropological and sociological studies.

Genesis, Science, and History

Genesis presents two particular challenges: the relation of its early chapters to modern science and the relation of the patriarchal stories to ancient history. In 1650 the archbishop of Armagh, James Ussher, having analyzed ancient calendars and studied ancient Egyptian and Hebrew texts, counted all the 'begats" in the First Testament and came up with a date for the creation. The result: the evening before October 23rd, 4004 BCE.[38] Since then, many have sought to reconcile a quite literal interpretation of Genesis with modern scientific discoveries, and some working in the field of creationism have, since the 1960s, sought to show that "special creation" and "flood geology" not only have scientific validity, but disprove standard views of geology, cosmology, and biological evolution, amongst other disciplines.

---

36. For a helpful discussion of these questions, see Long, *Art of Biblical History*.

37. E.g., Walton, *Ancient Near Eastern Thought*, and Greer, Hilber and Walton, *Behind the Scenes*.

38. Current estimations of the age of the earth yield approximately 4.54 billion years, referring to the formation of the earth's core or of the material out of which the earth formed. This is based on radiometric dating of meteorite material, and it is consistent with radiometric dating of lunar as well as oldest-known terrestrial samples.

Terence Fretheim recognizes that the early chapters of Genesis are "pre-scientific in the sense that they predate modern science, but not in the sense of having no interest in these types of questions." Indeed, their writers made use of knowledge of the natural world around them in their culture, since they show interest "in God's use of the earth and the waters in mediating creation (Gen 1:11–12, 20, 24), the classification of plants into certain kinds (1:11–12), and a comparable interest in animals (1:21–25)." This leads him to insist, "Despite claims to the contrary (often in the interest of combatting fundamentalism), these texts indicate that Israel's thinkers carefully pursued questions regarding the *how* of creation, and not just questions of *who* and *why*." Problems arise when it becomes clear that some features in Genesis cannot be reconciled with modern scientific knowledge. Rather than insist that everything in the Bible must correspond to reality as described by modern science, it is better to accept that its authors did not know everything about the world (such as its age). This means that "The Genesis text remains both an indispensable theological resource and an important paradigm on the way in which to integrate theological and scientific realities in a common search for truth about the world."[39]

It is significant that early church fathers like Gregory of Nyssa (331–c. 395) and Augustine of Hippo (354–430) were well aware of the problems of taking the seven days of creation literally; e.g., the fact that there is mention of day and night before the creation of the sun and moon. To read the early chapters of Genesis as if it competes with contemporary scientific fields of knowledge is a genre mistake; it makes much more sense to read it in dialogue with other ancient Near Eastern stories of origins that have been discovered from the nineteenth century onwards.[40] Creationism seems to me a mistaken attempt to refute mainstream science while swallowing the assumptions of modernity.[41]

There is no definitive answer to the question about the historicity of the patriarchal narratives. No archaeological evidence has so far come to

---

39. Fretheim, *God and World*, 28. Brown, *Seven Pillars*, reads seven biblical passages about creation in the light of current scientific knowledge and environmental concerns.

40. For a good way into these issues, see Lucas, *Can We Believe Genesis?* For in-depth exploration, see Barton & Wilkinson, *Reading Genesis after Darwin*.

41. This is not the place to enter into details of the debate, but on geology I have found convincing Young and Stearley, *The Bible, Rocks, and Time*. On science and faith more generally, see Southgate, *God, Humanity and the Cosmos*.

light that would corroborate the lives of Abraham, Isaac, Jacob, or Joseph. Yet this is not surprising, given the relative insignificance of their small clan in the world of their time. Some details of the stories appear to fit with what can be known of ancient Near Eastern culture, while others pose problems.[42] Terence Fretheim's conclusion is sensible: "While it is not possible to determine whether the women and men of Genesis were actual historical persons, it seems reasonable to claim that the narratives carry some authentic memories of Israel's pre-exodus heritage."[43] It seems likely that oral tradition preserved stories of the patriarchs, though they may have taken written form only when scribes were employed under the monarchy, with some elements reflecting traditions about David, but the Jacob and Joseph stories may reflect exilic experience.

When Were the Books Written?

There is no way to determine precisely when the books of the First Testament were written. An earliest date can be assigned to the final form of some books that refer to well-known events, e.g., 2 Kings ends in the thirty-seventh year of the exile, the first year of Evil-merodach (562/561 BCE). Genesis concludes with the death of Joseph, many years before the exodus. Traditionally its authorship was assigned to Moses, but there is no claim to that effect in the text. Historical-critical scholars have sought to explain various features and inconsistencies in the text of the Pentateuch (such as different names for the deity) by hypothesizing about documentary sources that underlie it. Although four source documents (J, E, D, P) seemed well established for much of the twentieth century, problems with that hypothesis have led to alternative proposals for the composition of the Pentateuch, and no consensus currently prevails.[44]

There is an interesting intertextual link between Genesis 1 and Jeremiah's vision of creation unmade (4:23–28; cf. 9:10).[45] It seems that the first creation story was known to Jeremiah, and that he appropriated and reversed its imagery to speak about the impending destruction of

---

42. On the difficulties of appealing to the Nuzi texts to verify patriarchal practices, see Longman, *How to Read Genesis*, 91–97.

43. Fretheim, "Genesis," 327.

44. For an overview of the issues, see Alexander, "The Authorship of the Pentateuch."

45. On Jeremiah's creation theology, see Fretheim, *Jeremiah*, 30–33.

Judah, but this is not to say that the whole book of Genesis was known to Jeremiah.[46]

We have seen that the primeval and patriarchal stories are deliberately arranged and noted the significance of Jacob's "exile" in Haran in northern Mesopotamia (28:10—31:55). This pattern can be matched with other patriarchs' sojourns;

- Abraham leaves Ur never to return, but his destination in Canaan is interrupted by sojourns in Egypt (12:10—13:1) and Gerar (20:1–18).

- Joseph is sold into Egypt by his brothers, and sojourns there until his death. His final request that his bones be carried back to Canaan from Egypt forms the conclusion of the whole book (Gen 50:24-26).[47]

These patterns must have been prominent in the mind(s) of the book's compiler(s), and point to the traumatic experience of Babylonian exile as the likely catalyst for the finalization of the book. It follows that reflection on the stories of Israel's ancestors led to the arrangement of the primeval stories.

The wider world is kept in view as the ancestors interact with various kings, exploitative relatives, and even wide populations, and not least by the inclusion of the genealogies of Ishmael and Esau (25:12–18; 36:1–43). Thus, Israel's story raised questions about how to understand the wider world. Their encounters with other cultures, not least in Babylon, meant that they were familiar with stories of origin, but these were self-regarding, polytheistic, and grounded in violence. So, to set the context of the ancestral stories, the compilers of Genesis produced their own stories of origins, parodying such myths as Marduk's defeat of Tiamat in the *Enuma Elish*, and the flood story in the Gilgamesh Epic, and including many original elements of their own. They realized that the shape of their own story reflected the wider story of the world because family and societal relationships ran through everything.

---

46. For a discussion of Jeremiah's creation language, see Lalleman, "Jeremiah, Judgement and Creation."

47. Note that Jacob's story continues alongside much of Joseph's. God's final instruction to Jacob is to go down to Egypt, and with a promise of return (46:1–4).

4. Theological Perspectives

Theological perspectives of interpretation begin by investigating what a particular book says about God, but continue to explore relations between God and the world that God has created, since it is frequently in these relations that the character of God is revealed.[48] In a broad sense, then, theological interpretation involves holding together what is said about creation, the world, and the existence of evil, as well as what is good; what may be surmised about human beings, communities, and nations; what may be deduced about God's mission, which in turn involves election, ecclesiology, and ethics. Contributions to these topics may be explicit in specific texts, but may also be implied from the wider context, from the overall thrust of a narrative, or a whole book, or from a combination of elements in harmony, contrast, or even tension.

The theological meaning of a biblical book is not discovered simply by collecting explicit statements it contains about God; it is tied up with the book's literary arrangement, structure, and genre, just as a person's spirit is expressed and conveyed through her or his body.[49] On a wider scale, theological interpretation of the First Testament involves weighing and integrating the various contributions of its numerous books, and collections of books, and for Christians it involves relating the First and Second Testaments together. These wider aspects of theological interpretation will be discussed in chapters 8 and 9.

Theology of the Book of Genesis

Because Genesis is such a long and complex book, it is difficult to do justice to its theology here.[50] One approach is to explore its theology from the perspective of a particular subject; thus, Terence Fretheim has produced a relational theology of creation in Genesis (and elsewhere in the First Testament), while Gordon McConville has written with attention to politics in Genesis (and elsewhere).[51] Here I propose some theological elements in Genesis with attention to the topic of violence, influenced by Daniel Hawk's helpful narrative treatment, because this is

---

48. See Fretheim, *God and World*.

49. See Janzen, *Abraham*, 1.

50. For a helpful, brief theology, see Wenham, "Genesis." For more extensive treatment, see Moberly, *Genesis*.

51. Fretheim, *God and World*, 29–132; McConville, *God and Earthly Power*, 30–49.

relevant to some of the questions this book seeks to address.[52] I begin with the prologue, then explore selected parts of the two pentads in some detail, before considering some elements of theological unity across the whole book.

The Prologue

A number of items are immediately evident:[53]

- There is only one God, who takes initiative and orders the whole of creation—polytheism is ruled out.
- This one God is sovereign; God simply speaks, and it is done—there is no combat with competing deities.
- One of the most striking features is the complete absence of violence—the Babylonian *Enuma Elish* tells of the god Marduk's defeat of the goddess Tiamat and his creation of the universe from her carcass.
- The sun, moon, and stars are creatures—they are not deities to be worshipped as in much of the ancient world.
- The climax is the creation of human beings in the image of God—in the Babylonian *Atrahasis* epic, the creation of humanity is an afterthought, to supply the gods with food; though the gods later regret making humans and limit human fertility.
- On the final day, God rests: the goal of creation is thus rest and peace—not ceaseless activity.

The First Pentad

Violence erupts for the first time in the "Generations of the heaven and earth" when Cain murders Abel (4:8–16), and then Lamech celebrates his vengeful victory (4:23–24). The "Generations of Adam" concludes like this:

> The LORD saw that the wickedness of man was great in the earth, and that every intention of the thoughts of his heart was only evil continually. And the LORD regretted that he had made

---

52. Hawk, *Violence*, 23–65.
53. I have drawn here on Wenham, "Genesis," 248.

man on the earth, and it grieved him to his heart. So the LORD said, "I will blot out man whom I have created from the face of the land, man and animals and creeping things and birds of the heavens, for I am sorry that I have made them." (6:5–7)

Reflecting on God's responses to the spread of human violence, Daniel Hawk comments: "Yahweh's first *act* in response to human violence, the banishment and protection of Cain, is mercy. The first *emotion* attributed to Yahweh in response to human violence is sorrow."[54] The story of Noah's Flood has struck some readers as morally appalling since God deliberately wipes out almost all humans and animals.[55] But this reflects a very superficial reading of the text. After introducing Noah and his sons, the "Generations of Noah" moves swiftly to expand on what God sees: "the earth ... corrupt ... filled with violence ... corrupt ... all flesh had corrupted its ways" (6:11–12). The triple use of "corrupt" indicates "utter ruin," the earth is no longer fit for purpose, and it is pervasive violence that has rendered it so. God announces to Noah that "because the earth is full of violence" the time for reciprocation has come; "I am about to ruin them with the earth" (6:13).[56] Sometimes when people are confronted by human atrocities, they ask why God does not do something to stop it? Well, here is what happens if God so intervenes; nothing piecemeal: almost complete devastation.

Archaeologists have unearthed a number of ancient flood stories from the wider world of ancient Israel, and the best known of these appears in tablet 11 of the *Epic of Gilgamesh*. In the light of this, Walter Moberly suggests that

> ... a good reading strategy is to take the Genesis account as a Hebrew retelling of a common story, whose details are shaped by the concern to set the well-known story in a particular light: Think about it *this* way, and one will understand more truly the situation of the world under God.[57]

Moberly goes on to point out that the biblical story's concerns "reside less in where it begins than in where it ends,"[58] and focuses on the repetition of certain weighty words in YHWH's thoughts, when the floods have subsided and Noah has come out of the ark;

54. Hawk, *Violence*, 31.
55. E.g., Dawkins, *God Delusion*, 237–38.
56. See translations in Wenham, *Genesis 1–15*, 149; Cotter, *Genesis*, 54–55.
57. Moberly, *Genesis*, 106.
58. Moberly, *Genesis*, 100.

> ... the LORD said in his heart, "I will never again curse the ground because of man, for the intention of man's heart is evil from his youth. Neither will I ever again strike down every living creature as I have done...." (8:21)

YHWH had initially decided to destroy the earth because of human evil intentions (6:5), yet here concludes that such a course of action will *not* be taken in future *because of human evil intentions*—exactly the same reason, but opposite divine resolutions. Taken as two separate statements of YHWH's thinking, these verses would present YHWH as inconsistent, but a narrative reading of the story yields something else; human beings have not changed as a result of the flood, but something about YHWH *has* changed. There is here a delicate presentation of the divine character; it is not that YHWH's character develops, but rather that YHWH adapts to developing circumstances.[59]

From a narrative perspective the first Genesis pentad shows development in numerous ways. For instance, the flood story resolves with God's renewed blessing of Noah and his sons (9:1–7), echoing 1:28, though with significant changes; this second act of creation is also an act of salvation. Again, whereas the flood story begins with YHWH *seeing* the world that humans have made, the tightly structured story of the Tower of Babel (11:1–9) involves YHWH's first *descent* into the world that humans have made, though as Hawk observes,

> It is a tentative move, as if Yahweh is only dipping a toe in troubled waters. Yahweh does not interact with any human beings. But it is a momentous entering nonetheless, and the retinue of spiritual beings that was present at the creation appears again to witness it (cf. v. 7). From this point on Yahweh will work within the world as it is. It is the first of a series of descents that will draw Yahweh deeper into the maelstrom of human violence, while simultaneously pulling humanity outward from its captivity to destructive narcissism.[60]

The Second Pentad

In the several episodes that make up the Abraham cycle, the most striking feature is the developing relationship between God and Abraham. Initially God gives instructions and promises; Abram obeys but does not reply

---

59. On the flood story and natural disasters, see Fretheim, *Creation Untamed*.
60. Hawk, *Violence*, 39.

(12:1–9). Abram receives occasional divine affirmations despite making a serious error in Egypt. Years pass; he begins to question God about his childlessness and inheritance; he receives emphatic divine reassurance, confirmed by a dramatic covenant ceremony (15:1–19). Abram and Sarai come up with a solution to their childlessness that proves unwise, then God appears again to affirm his covenantal commitment, changing the chosen couple's names to Abraham and Sarah (17:1–27).

More years pass before a fascinating encounter deepens the relationship further. It begins with Abraham offering attentive hospitality to three men; he does most of the talking and much of the preparation, until they ask after Sarah and one of them reaffirms that she will bear a son (18:1–15). The narrator then treats readers to a divine soliloquy as YHWH deliberates about whether to disclose to Abraham his impending visit to Sodom (18:16–19), an extraordinary window into the divine mind. That the decision is in the affirmative is revealed in the explicit statement to Abraham:

> How great is the outcry against Sodom and Gomorrah and how very grave their sin! I must go down and see whether they have done altogether according to the outcry that has come to me; and if not, I will know. (18:20f)

Here then is a second divine descent, specifically to investigate what humans collectively are up to in the world they have constructed. Two men (or angels, 19:1) go on to Sodom while YHWH remains to converse with Abraham, who picks up YHWH's declaration with a question: "Would you indeed sweep away the righteous with the guilty?"—and proceeds deferentially to explore how many righteous might outweigh the wicked in order to avert destruction (18:23–33).

Ellen Davis points out that in the flood story God had given a warning of the impending disaster to Noah, but that this was followed by a series of instructions, not a conversation (6:13–21). It seems that Noah did not contemplate questioning God's intention to destroy the world.

> It is notable, therefore, that now God deliberately initiates a new way of dealing with human evil, one that entails negotiation with a human moral agent: "For I have known him . . . , so that he may command his children and his house after him and they will keep the way of YHWH, by doing righteousness and justice, in order that YHWH might bring upon Abraham all that he has spoken concerning him" (18:19).[61]

---

61. Davies, *Biblical Prophecy*, 26.

Now YHWH's decision to enter into a concerted relationship with one particular human being and his descendants has progressed to a stage at which discussion and even negotiation takes place. Hawk comments; "By confiding in Abraham, Yahweh implicitly solicits the human partner's input and signals that that input may influence divine decision making. Yahweh looks to the partner for a perspective from the human side of the issue."[62]

Perhaps the most well-known story in the Abraham cycle is that of Abraham's near sacrifice of his son, Isaac (22:1–19), known in the Jewish tradition as the Aqedah ("binding"). There are many parallels between this story and the preceding one of the expulsion of Ishmael (21:12–19), and so God's instruction to Abraham in 22:2 has particular poignancy. Abraham has already departed from his father's house (12:1), separated from his nephew, Lot (13:11), and sent away his first son, Ishmael; now God is demanding his promised son, his only son, Isaac, whom he loves. The Aqedah can be analyzed, using a nine-fold narrative analysis, and paying attention to Abraham's threefold "Here I am" (*Hineni*), as follows:

The Aqedah: Narrative Analysis

Introduction	God's test	22:1a
Initiation	God's summons, Abraham's "Here I am;" God's command	22:1b–2
Exposition	Abraham's preparations and journey	22:3–6
Complication	Isaac's question; Abraham's "Here I am"; Isaac's compliance	22:7–10
Change	The Angel calls; Abraham's "Here I am"; "Do not kill the boy"	22:11–12
Unravelling	Abraham sees the ram and sacrifices it	22:13–14
Consequences	The Angel calls a second time: reaffirmation of blessing	22:15–18
Ending	Abraham and party return	22:19
Conclusion	Whom will Isaac marry? A genealogy including Rebekah	22:20–24

Abraham's initial "Here I am" is the first appearance of this expression in the Bible, and it becomes the classic response of God's servants to the divine call, signifying readiness to obey whatever God commands; Moses (Exod 3:4), Samuel (1 Sam 3:4–8), Isaiah (Isa 6:8), and Mary (Luke 1:38).

---

62. Hawk, *Violence*, 56.

Abraham's second "Here I am" is in response to Isaac's "Father!" so Abraham is as alert to his son as he is to God; thus Isaac's agency is underlined in this complicating episode. In response to his son's question, Abraham must articulate his extraordinary confidence in God's provision, a confidence that seems to carry over into Abraham's building of the altar and Isaac's compliance with being bound. The angel's sharp double call elicits Abraham's third "Here I am," and the staying of his hand.

God's command to sacrifice Isaac should be read as the climax within the development of trust between Abraham and God over their long story. Abraham has previously engaged in questionable behaviors, especially his two fear-driven pretences concerning Sarah (Gen 12:11–20 and 20:1–18). So there exists a question about Abraham's trust, and that is why the reader (but not Abraham, of course) is informed at the start that the command is a test (22:1). Terence Fretheim points out that testing must be understood, not legalistically, but relationally.

> Life in relationship inevitably brings tests of loyalty. What constitutes testing will be shaped by the nature of the relationship and the expectations the parties have for it. As a relationship matures and trust levels are built up, faithful responses to testing the relational bond will tend to become second nature. And yet, even in such a relationship, sharp moments of testing may present themselves.[63]

Theologically, the test is as real for God as it is for Abraham; it is only after Abraham has to be prevented from using the knife that God can declare, "Now I know . . ." (22:12). This incident is not about teaching Abraham some lesson; rather it establishes the fact that Abraham trusts that God has his best interests at heart, so that he will follow wherever God's command leads. Fretheim presses the points that God does not know in advance how Abraham will respond, that God places the shape of God's own future in Abraham's hands, and that Abraham's expression of trust in God to Isaac puts God's own trustworthiness on the line.[64] This story emphasizes mutuality in the relationship between God and Abraham; it is not the case that everything was planned out beforehand—for Abraham, or for today's readers.

This story requires careful handling in contemporary application. It prompts significant moral questions in the minds of readers, especially,

---

63. Fretheim, "God, Abraham," 54.
64. Fretheim, "God, Abraham," 55.

what sort of God commands someone to do such a thing? The psychoanalyst Alice Miller claimed that this passage may have contributed to an atmosphere that makes the abuse of children possible, based on numerous artistic depictions of this story.[65] Fretheim considers how many children have pondered whether their own parents would be prepared to kill them if God commanded it.[66] It should be noted that God's command to Abraham is specific to the development of their relationship; it does not have universal applicability, as do the Ten Commandments.

Another perspective can be applied to this story through considering that child sacrifice was not uncommon in the ancient world.[67] Abraham, with his pagan background, may have understood God's command in these terms. There are several subsequent repudiations of child sacrifice in Israel's legal codes (Lev 18:21; 20:2–5 and Deut 12:31; 18:10) and in the prophets (Mic 6:7 and Jer 7:31; 19:5; 32:35).[68] In the light of these emphatic repudiations in later parts of the scriptures, this story reveals, not that God may even demand child sacrifice, but that, through this episode narrating Abraham's climactic faith, God brought to an end any notion of such a demand.

The Theological Unity of Genesis

The book of Genesis is front-loaded with divine speech, but with other divine behaviors as well: actions, decisions, emotions. For example, God's attention is repeatedly characterized in terms of seeing and hearing. Ellen Davis comments on God's sevenfold seeing (1:4, 10, 12, 18, 21, 25, 31):

> The focus on God's experience of seeing is noteworthy, because biblical narrative usually confines itself to externals; it tells us what a character (including God) said or did. Only occasionally does it move inside the eyes, to tell us what and how someone saw, and when it does so, the specific perception is important. As the biblical narrative unfolds, it records three moments of human perception that echo this first report of God's seeing the world in its goodness: one when Eve, having listened to the

---

65. Miller, *The Untouched Key*, 139.
66. Fretheim, "God, Abraham," 57.
67. In Bible narratives, Jephthah sacrifices his daughter (Judg 11:34–40), and the king of Moab sacrifices his son in extreme circumstances (2 Kgs 3:27).
68. For a fascinating discussion of this tradition, see Levenson, *Death and Resurrection*.

snake, suddenly "saw *how good was* the tree [of knowledge of good and evil] for eating, and ... she took some of its fruit" (Gen 3:6); another when the "sons of God saw the daughters of humanity, *how good they were*, and they took wives for themselves" (Gen 6:2); and the third when Moses' mother first saw him, *how good he was*, and determined that this baby boy would not be thrown into the Nile (Exod 2:2). In each case we are invited to see how a moment of perception, human or divine, has lasting consequences for the characters in the narrative, and also for us who share their story.[69]

God also hears, sometimes implicitly, especially within conversations. When Adam attempts to explain, "I was afraid, because I was naked; and I hid myself," God says, "Who told you that you were naked?" (Gen 3:10). In other places, God's hearing is explicit, especially in response to human appeals. This is notable when God says to Abraham, "As for Ishmael, I have heard you; I will bless him" (Gen 17:20), and when Hagar is sent away into the wilderness;

> And God heard the voice of the boy; and the angel of God called to Hagar from heaven, and said to her, "What troubles you, Hagar? Do not be afraid; for God has heard the voice of the boy where he is." (Gen 21:17)

Here are further examples of theological continuity and development across the book of Genesis:

- God's commission to the first human pair, "Be fruitful and multiply" (1:28), finds loud echoes in God's promises to the childless Abram/Abraham (17:4–5; 20), but also in later promises to Jacob (28:3; 35:11) and Joseph (48:4).

- On three occasions in the prologue, God is said to "bless" the living creatures, the human beings, and the seventh day (1:22, 28; 2:2). The word "bless" does not appear in the first-generations story of 2:4–25; instead a garden depicts the blessedness of creation, as becomes clear when the word "curse" appears referring to the reversal of the garden's fruitfulness (3:14, 17). "Curse" is found three further times in the first pentad (4:11; 5:29; 9:25), but these five cursings are answered when the second pentad begins, when YHWH's call of

---

69. Davis, *Scripture, Culture, and Agriculture*, 46.

Abram contains a five-fold repetition of "bless/blessing" (12:2–3). As Gerald Janzen says,

> the agenda of the salvation history is to counteract the workings of evil in the world and to restore the world to its divinely intended blessedness. In this respect, then, chs. 1–11 are not the preface to the main story called salvation history; rather, the salvation history is a remedial process within the larger story of God's creation.[70]

- Janzen further points out that God's word to Abram, "I will make your name great" (12:2) is juxtaposed to the previous narrative in which the city builders construct a tower in order to "make a name for ourselves" (11:4). Their motivation is fearful defense, "lest we be scattered upon the face of the whole earth," whereas Abram's vocation is to "go from your country" (12:1).
- Again, when Abram and Lot reach the plain of the Jordan valley some time later, it is described as "well watered everywhere like the garden of YHWH . . . before YHWH had destroyed Sodom and Gomorrah" (13:10); it is assumed that readers will recall the blessings of the garden and its curse in chapters 2 and 3.[71]

The Rhetoric of Genesis

Genesis not only helps readers to frame the experiences of their lives according to the story of our ancestors in Israel's story, or according to its insights into how the world works (or doesn't). It challenges readers to consider how they handle the most intimate of family relationships, and thereby to mature in their conduct of relationships in wider society. Matthew Schlimm has written a wonderful study of anger and ethics in the book of Genesis which focusses on the narratives of conflict between Cain and Abel, Sarah and Hagar, Isaac and the herders of Gerar, Jacob and Laban, Rachel and Leah, Dinah's brothers and Shechem, Jacob and Esau, and finally Joseph and his brothers. Schlimm points to God's word to angry Cain, "If you do what is right, then a *lifting*" (4:7), and comments

---

70. Janzen, *Abraham*, 5.
71. Janzen, *Abraham*, 5–6.

that the narrator uses this word because its meaning can refer to "forgiveness" at 50:17.[72]

Cain did not do what is right, but Joseph's brothers eventually do right and experience forgiveness, just before the book closes (50:17). There is thus an interplay between Gen 4:7 and the book of Genesis as a whole, moving from fratricide to forgiveness. God's first words in a post-Edenic world lay the moral framework for all that follows.

Genesis shows the grave dangers of anger while realistically depicting ways that its worse effects can be counteracted.[73] Readers encounter not only dramatic and compelling stories. They also gain vicarious experience in handling anger, witnessing both its worst and best outcomes. They walk away from the text with a better understanding of the immense threat that anger presents for all parties involved, and they have encountered a variety of ways that anger can be handled so that it does not lead to violence. Reading Genesis is an act of moral education.[74]

---

72. See Schlimm, *From Fratricide to Forgiveness*, 137, for his translation at 4:7, and 178, for his appeal to Mikhail Bakhtin's concept of a "loophole" that allows the alteration of a word's meaning at a later point in time.

73. Interestingly, God is not said to be angry in Genesis. The first mention of YHWH's anger is at Exod 4:14.

74. Schlimm, *From Fratricide to Forgiveness*, 179.

PART II

Reading the Former Prophets

Prelude

The second part of this book turns the interpretive focus on the books of Joshua, Judges, Samuel, and Kings, which together tell the story of ancient Israel's time in the promised land, from the conquest to the exile. In the Christian Bible these are usually categorized as "historical" books, along with those that follow; Chronicles, Ezra, and Nehemiah. Ruth appears in the Christian canon after Judges, since its brief story fits into the same time-period, while Esther appears after Nehemiah because its longer story is set within the Persian diaspora. However, in the Hebrew canon the books of Joshua, Judges, Samuel, and Kings appear in the second section of the scriptures and are known as the Former Prophets. The Latter Prophets consist of the books of Isaiah, Jeremiah, Ezekiel, and the Twelve (Hosea to Malachi), while Ruth and Esther are two of the "Five Scrolls" found in the Writings. Given my aspiration to take seriously the Jewish origins of the Christian faith, I find it helpful to remember that Joshua–Kings started out with prophetic connotations since their treatment of events and people is rather different from history as it is commonly understood today; it is a prophetic reading of this part of Israel's story. This is not to deny that historical questions are vital in the interpretation of these four books, but it is a way into appreciating the commonalities between history and prophecy that scholars have explored in great detail. I will briefly summarize some key developments in their work here.

Intensive study of the First Testament developed through the nineteenth century as the methods of source criticism, and then form criticism, were refined to study the Pentateuch and its origins. In the early years of the twentieth century, source and form critics also debated how to understand the connections between the book of Deuteronomy and Joshua–Kings, and a turning point came when the German scholar

Martin Noth published his ground-breaking study in 1943.[1] Noth made the case for a single historian who had edited together a range of existing written source materials to produce an account of his people's national history in the land of Israel. This unknown "Deuteronomistic Historian" had organized this part of Israel's story into five eras around great figures; Moses, Joshua, etc. The first section, Deuteronomy, was critical to the entire composition for two reasons; firstly, the whole work was permeated with the theology of Deuteronomy; and secondly, Moses' speech that begins the History was the first of many speeches, some long, some short, that gave structure to the whole work. In addition, several narrators' comments supplied editorial reflections (Joshua 12; Judg 2:11–23; 2 Kgs 17:7–18, 20–23). Noth identified the Historian as a Judean exile writing soon after King Jehoiakin's release from Babylonian prison in 562 BCE (2 Kgs 25:27–30), whose purpose was to teach the true meaning of Israel's history.

> The meaning which he discovered was that God was recognisably at work in this history, continuously meeting the accelerating moral decline with warnings and punishments and, finally, when these proved fruitless, with total annihilation. The Deuteronomic Historian, then, perceives a just divine retribution in the history of the people. . . . He sees this as the great unifying factor in the course of events, and speaks of it not in general terms but in relation to the countless specific details reported in the extant traditions.[2]

Noth's hypothesis was initially accepted by many scholars, but then became subject to various criticisms, especially that it did not account for significant elements of grace and hope in the texts. Various modifications were proposed and there was consensus regarding the broad hypothesis, but in recent years it has come into question as the number of theories as to evidence and date of redaction has multiplied, and indications of the work of Deuteronomists have been found in many other parts of the Hebrew Bible.[3]

As an example of the recent tendency to think in terms of an extended process of development behind the Deuteronomic History (DtrH), I

---

1. An English translation, *The Deuteronomistic History*, was published in 1981.

2. Noth, *The Deuteronomistic History*, 20.

3. See the detailed discussion by Römer, *So-Called Deuteronomistic History*, 13–43. Richter provides a helpful summary in "Deuteronomistic History."

summarize Marvin Sweeney's careful argument for a series of editions behind the final form of the DtrH, working backwards as follows:[4]

- A final exilic edition of the DtrH from the mid-sixth century BCE that sought to address the problems posed by the Babylonian exile by pointing to the kings of Israel and Judah as the reason for divine punishment;
- A Josianic edition of the DtrH from the late seventh century BCE that sought to identify the sins of the northern kings of Israel as the reason for divine punishment and the reign of the righteous Josiah as the means to address that issue;
- A Hezekian edition of the DtrH from the late eighth century BCE that sought to explain the suffering of northern Israel based on its inability to produce competent and righteous rulers and to point to Hezekiah as an example of the leadership needed;
- A Jehu edition of Samuel-Kings from the early eighth century BCE that saw the rise of the house of Jehu as the means to ensure the security of the nation and to restore the past glories of the age of Solomon;
- A Solomonic edition of Samuel-Kings from the late tenth century BCE that sought to present the house of David as the key to the well-being of the united people of Israel and Judah.

Eckhart Otto is currently one of the leading Deuteronomy scholars, having written a four-volume commentary on it in recent years. He argues for a paradigm change in Pentateuchal research to interpret Deuteronomy in the context of the *Pentateuch* and as an integral part of it (as was done in the nineteenth century and earlier), rather than as a part of the *Deuteronomistic History* from Deuteronomy to 2 Kings.

> In my opinion, this is a most important paradigm change in the interpretation of the Pentateuch, because it means the end of a *captivitas babylonica* for the Book of Deuteronomy, and so also for the Pentateuch as a whole. Martin Noth and his many followers still today amputated the Pentateuch to a Tetrateuch whose

---

4. Sweeney, *I & II Kings*, 4. Few scholars have proposed the identity of the Deuteronomic Historian, but Peterson, in *Authors of the Deuteronomistic History*, has argued that Israel's literary traditions were preserved by a series of authors belonging to the priestly family at Anathoth, beginning with Abiathar, David's priest who was later banished from Jerusalem by Solomon (1 Kgs 2:26–27).

conclusions were lost, since Deuteronomy was conceptualized as part of the Deuteronomistic History and its redaction.[5]

Otto's argument supports a return to the Jewish view of the centrality of the Torah (or Pentateuch), something to which I will return in chapter 9.

If readers are unfamiliar with these books, they may find it helpful to read each one through before embarking on each of the next four chapters.

---

5. Otto, "Deuteronomy," 179. Otto also argues that the Deuteronomistic History begins with 1 Samuel 1 rather than in Deuteronomy 1–3.

4

The Book of Joshua

Joshua is currently the least popular narrative book of the Bible. It contains the stories of the Israelite conquest of Canaan, including the famous battle of Jericho, and recounts much slaughter of its indigenous peoples. The books of Judges, Samuel, and Kings contain almost as much bloodshed, but the accusation of genocide has stuck to Joshua, and so we must address the question whether this book glorifies or justifies something like "ethnic cleansing." In order to do so it is necessary first to explore some literary features of the book. It will become clear that Joshua is a book about boundaries, and thus "that there is much more at work in this book than triumphal assertions of Israelite supremacy or validations of ancestral claims."[1] Secondly, there is a historical question to consider: how reliable is the account of conquest found in Joshua? The prevailing view amongst scholars is that the archaeological record "does not support Joshua's story of a conquest by a people arriving from outside Palestine."[2] Thirdly, the most pressing theological aspect of the book will be discussed, with a view to accusations of inhumanity and genocide.

1. Literary Perspectives

I begin with the book's literary arrangement and then explore selected elements of its three main parts to identify plots and themes. This discussion

---

1. Hawk, *Joshua*, xi.
2. Nelson, *Joshua*, 3.

will begin to suggest historical and theological insights that will be taken up in subsequent sections.

Arrangement

The book is arranged in three parts. Chapters 1–12 are taken up with stories of Israelite entry into the land and encounters with its inhabitants, increasingly dominated by accounts of battles with its armies and kings. The first chapter deals with Joshua's commissioning by YHWH, following the death of Moses,[3] and his preparations for the conquest. Of particular note are his words to the tribes of Reuben and Gad and the half tribe of Manasseh, who have already taken possession of their land allocation east of the Jordan, and their commitment to send their warriors to assist the other nine-and-a-half tribes with the conquest, while their families remain behind (1:12–18).[4] A reminder of this agreement is found at the start of the list of defeated kings that brings the narrative action to a halt (12:1–6), thus forming an inclusion that signals the close of part one.

Its central chapters consist of four main campaign reports:

- A complex set of episodes culminates in the destruction of Jericho;
- A setback against Ai is resolved and reversed;
- A complication arises through Israel's alliance with Gibeon; this provokes a threat from a southern coalition of kings, who are vanquished;
- A threat from a northern coalition of kings arises and is crushed.

A table of the literary arrangement (below) helps to recognize the central place given to the ceremony at Mount Ebal and Mount Gerizim (8:30–35).

Part two consists of a description of the allocations of land to the various tribes (chapters 13–19), and the designation of special cities (chapters 20–21). Part three is signalled by the first of Joshua's three final speeches, directing the return of two-and-a-half tribes across the Jordan (chapter 22), recalling the arrangement in 1:12–18. Two farewell speeches to all Israel review the story of YHWH's faithfulness to them and challenge them to remain loyal to him in future (chapters 23–24).

---

3. Joshua had already been appointed as Moses' successor in Deut 28:7–8, 14–23.

4. See the original land allocation and military commitment of these tribes in Deut 3:12–22.

The Book of Joshua: Literary Arrangement

Part 1	The Conquest of the Land	
A	Joshua's commissioning and preparations	1:1–18
B	Destruction of Jericho	2:1—6:27
C	Destruction of Ai	7:1—8:29
D	Joshua reads the law to the people at Mt Ebal & Mt Gerizim	8:30–35
C'	Destruction of Southern kings	9:1—10:43
B'	Destruction of Northern kings & completion of conquest	11:1–23
A'	List of defeated kings east and west of the Jordan	12:1–24
Part 2	The Allocation of the Land	
A	YHWH's words: promise and command	13:1–7
B	Allocation of tribal territories	13:8—19:51
B'	Designation of special cities	20:1—21:42
A'	YHWH's acts: words fulfilled: Israel in possession	21:43–45
Part 3	The Challenge of the Future in the Land	
A	Return of the trans-Jordanian tribes: challenge of disunity	22:1–34
B	Joshua's last words	23:1–16
B'	Joshua's final challenge and the people's response	24:1–28
A'	Notices of death and burial in the Land: concluding unity	24:29–33

The Conquest of the Land

The first part of the book goes well beyond a simple account of arrival in and conquest of the land. Here I will discuss the presentation of the campaign against Jericho, and then discuss several themes that emerge through it and the following campaigns.

The Destruction of Jericho: Literary arrangement

b1	The spies saved by Rahab	2:1–24
b2	Crossing the Jordan (miracle)	3:1—4:24
b3	Camped at Gilgal: the army commander	5:1–15
b2'	Jericho destroyed (miracle)	6:1–21
b1'	Rahab saved by the spies	6:22–27

Jericho

The Jericho campaign begins with Joshua sending two spies into the land,[5] and Jericho in particular, but reaches its conclusion with Jericho's destruction only after several other important incidents. The story of Rahab and the spies is extensive and even comical since she is much smarter than the king's men (2:3–7). It centers on her remarkable confession of YHWH's sovereignty and her negotiation of safety for her extended family (2:8–14). She advises the spies about avoiding capture, and they respond by requiring a sign by which her house may be identified in the later attack, and within which her family must be gathered (2:15–21).[6] The spies go west into the hill country while their pursuers search the Jordan valley; they are then able to return and report back to Joshua.

There follows the extensive account of the crossing of the Jordan that marks Israel's physical entry into the land. Joshua and his officers issue clear commands (3:1–6), YHWH encourages Joshua, and he alerts the people (3:7–13); everything is orderly for the actual crossing, enabled by the stopping of the waters upstream when the priests' feet dip in the overflowing edge (3:14–17). This account is supplemented with another version that adds further details, especially focussing on the taking of twelve stones from the riverbed and their later setting up at Gilgal to memorialize this most significant boundary crossing (4:1–24).[7]

At the centerpoint of the literary pattern there is a pause in the advance. First, the impact of the news of this crossing of the Jordan on the Canaanite kings is noted (5:1). Then YHWH instructs Joshua to prepare

---

5. In the earlier spy story in Numbers 13–14, only two returned with a positive report of their expedition, and so this story is a reversal of that failed mission.

6. Note the echo of the Passover instructions to stay in the house, with blood on its doorway, (Exod 12:22).

7. In v. 9 Joshua sets up twelve stones in the middle of the river. Some commentators think these stones are those that are later set up at Gilgal.

and circumcise all the male Israelites, since circumcision had lapsed during the wilderness wanderings (5:2–9). Next Passover is kept and the provision of manna ceases (5:10–12). These events at Gilgal emphasize the significance of arrival in the land and the sense of a new start after past disobedience (5:6), together with new responsibility for their own sustenance (5:12). After these expressions of Israel's fidelity to YHWH, Joshua's encounter with the commander of the army of YHWH (5:13–15)[8] ensures a divine perspective on what is to follow. His words resist any attempt to tie national aspirations to YHWH's purposes—this is to be no ordinary human campaign.

The account of Jericho's destruction begins with YHWH's detailed instructions for an extraordinary seven-day ritual procession around the walled and shut-up city of Jericho, which is then implemented by Joshua (6:6–14). On the seventh day, the Israelites march in careful order round Jericho seven times; Joshua gives clear instructions about the city's devotion to destruction, the preservation of Rahab and her family, and about avoiding the temptation of booty. The people respond to Joshua's command to shout, the walls fall down, and the total slaughter is briefly told (6:15–21). A striking feature of this passage is the series of instructions given by YHWH to Joshua, then by Joshua to the priests and to the people; in each case these instructions are faithfully carried out—Israel is obedient.

Finally, Joshua instructs the two spies to bring out Rahab and her family, and they carry out their rescue mission. Although these Canaanites are "set outside the camp of Israel" (v. 23b), Rahab's extended family is said to "have lived in Israel ever since" (v. 25). Jericho is totally destroyed apart from certain valuable items that are put into the treasury of the house of YHWH. In conclusion, Joshua pronounces a curse on anyone who attempts to rebuild the city, probably so that the ruin will serve as a testimony to its devotion to YHWH. Jerome Creach discusses the concept of the ban (*herem*) in chapter 6:

> The complete destruction of the city indicates that Jericho is to be like a whole burnt offering, completely destroyed as a gift to God.... [T]he story seems to conceive the ban as a sacrifice to God, as though God required the contents of Jericho as an offering.[9]

---

8. Note the clear link to Joshua's initial commissioning, but also the echo of Moses' encounter at the burning bush (Exod 3:5).

9. Creach, *Joshua*, 63–64. Creach contrasts this sacrificial concept with

If this notion of the ban seems primitive and barbaric, it is mitigated by the deliberate presentation of Rahab as a prominent exception to the ban: each command about the devoted things is immediately followed by a reference to Rahab's salvation (6:17b, 22–23, 25). Creach continues:

> Rahab continues to be treated as a "devoted thing." She is placed outside the camp (v. 23) because, as the Lord's possession, she could not be kept as a slave, taken as a wife, or "owned" in any sense by an Israelite. Moreover, as a "devoted thing" Rahab must remain at a distance so the Israelites do not become infected with the sacred nature that required her destruction. But she is not slain. Hence the story does not focus attention on the multitude that is slaughtered. Instead it draws attention to the fact that the only Jericho resident who is named, who the reader can relate to and sympathize with, is spared annihilation.[10]

Campaign Plot and Themes

Joshua's first three campaigns, at Jericho, Ai, and Gibeon are described in some detail, and may be read as models for all the subsequent campaigns, since most of the remaining battle accounts are made up of brief summaries using formulaic language (10:28–42; 11:16–23), though there is more detail about the decisive battle with the northern kings (11:1–15). Hawk's detailed plot analysis demonstrates the similarities between the two campaigns at Jericho and Gibeon, and then contrasts them with the campaign at Ai, as shown in the following table (particular inversions are shown in bold).[11] The symmetry of structure and theme suggests that readers should attend to the issue of inclusion into and exclusion from the Israelite community. In the first and third stories Canaanites are spared from the destruction inflicted on their compatriots and are included among Israel, but in the middle story an Israelite and his family is excluded from Israel. The protracted selection process (by lot?) that

---

Deuteronomy's presentation of the ban as primarily a matter of justice (Deut 7:2, 26; 20:16–20). But Walton and Walton, *Israelite Conquest*, 169–211, argue that ḥerem concerns the destruction of Canaanite identity.

10. Creach, *Joshua*, 66.

11. This table is a modification and combination of Hawk's charts, *Joshua*, 25f and 29f.

results in the identification of Achan (7:16–21) emphasizes that he is from the tribe of Judah; he is the quintessential representative of Israel.[12]

Plot Analysis of the Campaigns at Jericho, Ai, and Gibeon

Concealment	Israelites secretly enter Jericho and are hidden by Rahab	2:1, 4
	Achan takes and hides some of the booty of Jericho	7:1, 22
	[Battle report: Israelite spies give assurance of victory]	7:2–3
	[Battle report: Israel is **routed**]	7:4–5
	Gibeonites disguise themselves, hiding their identity	9:3–6
Interrogation	The king's men interrogate Rahab concerning the spies	2:2–3
	Joshua interrogates YHWH	7:6–9
	Israelite leaders interrogate the Gibeonites	9:7–8
Diversion	Rahab sends the king's men to the fords of Jordan	2:4b–5, 7
	YHWH diverts the issue from defeat to transgression	7:10–12
	Gibeonites invite Israelite leaders to sample their provisions	9:12f
Doxology	Rahab acclaims YHWH's mighty acts at Red Sea and Jordan	2:8–11
	Achan is **admonished** to give glory to YHWH	7:19
	Gibeonites acclaim YHWH's mighty acts against Egyptians & Amorites	9:9–11
Petition	Rahab asks spies to spare her family	2:12–13
	Achan incriminates himself, offers **no plea** for deliverance	7:20f
	Gibeonites ask Joshua to make a treaty with them	9:6
Response	The spies agree to a pact with Rahab	2:14
	Achan and his family **condemned to death**	7:24f
	Joshua and leaders make a covenant of peace with Gibeonites	9:24–26
Qualification [Intensification]	Spies declare innocence and qualify pact: Rahab agrees	2:17–20
	[Joshua **curses** Achan—see below]	7:24
	Israelites grumble and leaders consign Gibeonites to menial labor: Gibeonites agree	9:16–26
Battle Report	A. YHWH assures Joshua of victory at Jericho	6:2
	YHWH promises Joshua victory at Ai	8:1f, 18
	YHWH assures Joshua of victory at Gibeon	10:8
	B. Victory achieved by miracle at Jericho	6:20
	Victory obtained through **deceit** at Ai	8:2c–21
	Victory achieved by miracle at Gibeon	10:11–14
	C. Israel massacres the people of Jericho	6:21
	Israel burns Ai and massacres its people	8:22–27
	Israel massacres the armies of the five kings	10:20

---

12. See Spina's comparison between the Rahab and Achan stories; "Given their placement in the strategic section of Joshua 2–7, these two chapters, along with the material found between them, may actually function as the hermeneutical key for understanding the theological thrust of the Book of Joshua in its entirety" (*Faith of the Outsider*, 64n).

Etiological Note	Rahab "lives within Israel to the present day"	6:25
	Achan's grave remains "to this day."	7:26
	Ai remains a pile of rubble "to the present day"	8:28
	Heap of stones over king's body remains "to this day"	8:29
	Gibeonites "cut wood and carry water to the present day"	9:27
Curse	Joshua utters a curse on those who rebuild Jericho	6:26
	Joshua **curses** Achan	7:24
	Joshua declares Gibeonites accursed	9:23

One development across these accounts is the gradual diversion of attention away from ethnic issues towards the kings of the land. The king of Jericho has only a minor part in Rahab's story (2:2–3) and the subsequent battle (6:2). The king of Ai has slightly more prominence in the next campaign (8:14, 23, 29). Several summaries of the kings' response to Israel's advances (5:1; 9:1; 10:1–2) indicate a gradual strengthening of resolve against the invaders until a coalition is formed among the kings of southern city-states (10:3–5). The narrator gives sustained attention to the fate of these five kings after their defeat, emphasizing Joshua's supremacy in the process (10:16–27). In the summaries that follow, kings feature regularly, and the final campaign is provoked by the coalition of the northern kings (11:1–5). Finally, narration gives way to listing the defeated kings of Canaan in chapter 12. Hawk points out the significance of the contrast between Joshua and the kings who "personify the continuing conflict between Israelite integrity and Canaanite plurality."[13]

Another effect created by the transition from battle accounts to summaries and then to lists of defeated kings is the impression that Joshua achieves his victories quickly and easily.[14] The repeated recording of the slaughter of every living thing in the captured cities (10:28, 32, 36, 37, 38, 39, 40; 11:11, 14) follows ancient Near Eastern conventions for the reporting of conquests.[15] In the cultural context in which these chapters were written, expressions such as "all Israel," "every person in it," "left no survivors," and "the whole land" would have been understood as *hyperbolic* and not taken literally. However, as we will see in the following section of the book, the impression of total success is modified in a number of places.

---

13. Hawk, *Joshua*, 158. Hawk notes, 176 n. 24, how each entry in the final list of kings is answered by the word "one," and thus the multiplicity of Canaan is contrasted with the unchanging integer, reflecting united Israel.

14. Although 11:18 says, "Joshua made war a long time with those kings."

15. See Younger, *Ancient Conquest Accounts*, 190–92, 241–49.

THE BOOK OF JOSHUA

The Allocation of the Land

The book's second section contains extensive geographical description of tribal land allocations, then the designation of special cities (not discussed here). It begins with a return to narrative action in the form of YHWH's instruction to the now aged Joshua to allocate the land among the tribes. Although the conquest has succeeded, "very much of the land remains to be possessed" (13:1); indeed, a significant number of inhabitants remain to be driven out by YHWH (13:2-6). This forms a striking contrast with the impression created by chapters 10-12. Several times in the subsequent chapters Israelite failure to drive out inhabitants is evident (13:13; 15:63; 16:10; 17:12, 16-18).[16] The concluding summary at 21:43-45 reverts to the declaration of complete possession and therefore "rest on every side" (cf. 22:4; 23:1). How are readers to understand the stark contrast between these two perspectives? Is the narrator employing hyperbole or irony in this summary? Hawk draws attention to the *thematic* contrast drawn with the preceding failures; the sections dealing with the apportioning of land consist mainly of Israel's actions, whereas the concluding summary emphasizes YHWH's actions (note the six-fold use of "all, every").

> By concentrating on YHWH and emphasizing these attributes, the narrator powerfully attributes Israel's successes to YHWH and accentuates divine resolve in the face of national trepidation. In contrast to Israelite inconstancy, YHWH does not waver from commitments made to the nation. Whereas Israel may fail to follow through on its part, YHWH does everything that he has promised.[17]

Allocation of Tribal Territories: Literary Arrangement

b	Lands of the eastern tribes	13:8—33
b'	Lands of the tribes in Canaan	14:1—19:51
b'1	Lands and stories connected to Judah and Joseph	14:1—17:18
b'2	Judah's possessions: *narratives of Caleb & Achsah*	14:1—15:63
b'2'	Joseph's possessions: *daughters of Zelophehad, Josephites*	16:1—17:18
b'1'	Lands of the seven remaining tribes	18:1—19:51

According to Moses' instruction, the allocation of "inheritance" east of the Jordan to the two-and-one-half tribes, is spelled out overall and

16. See also 18:3; 19:47; 20:9.
17. Hawk, *Joshua*, 225.

then by specific tribe (13:8-13, 15-32), along with notes that the tribe of Levi receives no land (13:14, 33). The remaining allocations are administered by Joshua, Eleazar the priest, and the tribal elders, employing the casting of lots (14:1-5).[18] But first the people of Judah support Caleb in the assertion of his claim on Moses' promise, and Joshua gives him the hill country of Hebron (14:6-15)—providing a reminder of past failures to trust YHWH and the requirement of wholehearted following of YHWH. Judah's allocation now takes first place among the tribes (15:1-63) and includes a second narrative concerning Caleb and his daughter Achsah (vv. 13-19).

Next follows the allocation to the Joseph tribes, overall (16:1-4), then to Ephraim (16:5-10), and Manasseh (17:1-18). The latter includes brief narratives about the five named daughters of Zelophehad (vv. 3-6),[19] and the Joseph tribes' complaint regarding their single portion (vv. 14-18). Hawk sets out the common structure of the four narratives of Caleb, Achsah, the daughters of Zelophehad, and the Josephites: confrontation—case and request—land grant—summary of results.

> These stories confuse concepts of territorial possession, kinship ties, and obedience to YHWH in various ways. Caleb represents the ideal Israelite, undaunted by Canaanite might and anxious to take the land promised to him. He is, however, an Israelite of questionable ancestry, a detail hinted at by his identification as a "Kenizzite" (14:14), the name of a clan which in other contexts is associated with the Edomites (Gen 36:11, 15, 42; 1 Chr 1:36, 53).[20] The second and third stories assail the connection between land and kinship by relating land grants awarded to women. By reporting the giving of land to women, the stories of Achsah and Zelophehad's daughters challenge the patriarchal structures which reinforce both property rights and kinship relations (structures explicitly articulated in the story of the pedigreed Achan [7:1]). Possession of land by women undermines the "male-territory" equation and subtly integrates the "other" gender into an Israelite community that traces the promise of the land only through those who are marked by circumcision (Gen 17:1-14).[21]

---

18. The exceptions of the two-and-one-half tribes and the Levites are mentioned again in 14:3f.

19. See Num 27:1-11.

20. Also see Gen 15:19.

21. Hawk, *Joshua*, 192.

The fourth story, concerning the members of Joshua's own tribe, inverts the plot established by the previous three by turning the exemplary quality of initiative on its head.

> The Josephites also request lands, but with less than noble motives. Because they are numerous, they want more than their share, declaring the hill country is insufficient but rejecting the plains because Canaanites with iron chariots live there. The Josephites thus stand in stark contrast to Caleb, who requests the kind of territory that the Josephites refuse. Given prior reports that Ephraim and Manasseh failed to take many of the cities, Joshua's command that they drive out the Canaanites concludes the episode on a note of failure.[22]

The Challenge of the Future in the Land

The final part of the book consists of a series of farewells, ending with several death and burial notices (24:29–33). It contains three challenges as to how future Israelites will behave in the land. I will focus on the often-neglected story of inter-tribal conflict in chapter 22, and then consider the more well-known final speeches of Joshua in relation to some earlier parts of the book.

Conflict over Israel's Identity

With the main business of the conquest accomplished, Joshua instructs the Reubenites, Danites, and the half tribe of Mannasseh to return across the Jordan to their allotted inheritance, as promised in 1:12–15, emphasizing faithfulness to Moses' commandments and love of YHWH (22:1–9). When these tribes reach the Jordan valley, they build a great altar, and this greatly perturbs the remaining tribes such that they prepare to make war on them (vv. 10–12). However, they send a delegation to Gilead and challenge the altar-builders; they view their act as treachery and rebellion that will bring divine wrath on the whole nation (vv. 13–20). When they suggest that their allotted land is "unclean," they imply that the Transjordanian territories are not really part of the land of Israel—only the land west of the Jordan is properly YHWH's land—and their use of the Deuteronomic expression "the whole congregation of" YHWH/Israel

---

22. Hawk, *Joshua*, 192f.

(16, 18, 20) indicates their assumption that they alone consist of the full embodiment of the nation.

The eastern tribes respond with an emphatic declaration of loyalty to YHWH and deny any thought of rebellion, bringing to the surface matters of identity and inclusion (vv. 21–29). They anticipate a future time when descendants of the other tribes will view the Jordan as the eastern boundary of the promised land, and view those beyond as outsiders (v. 25). As Hawk explains,

> They argue that the charges, innuendos, and warlike response of the Cisjordanian [i.e., west of the Jordan] tribes are symptomatic of precisely the concern that led them to build the altar, namely the fear that the tribes in Canaan would become overly preoccupied with setting boundaries. . . . The intense interchange explicitly raises many of the identity questions that have run just below the surface of the narrative. The eastern tribes appear throughout the book as implicit reminders of the ambiguities that complicate the formation of a distinctive Israelite community. . . . What, in essence, constitutes the community's internal boundaries, and how are they to be safeguarded when motives are not apparent in actions? Who, and what is Israel?[23]

The tribes west of the Jordan equate national identity with possession of the land (particularly the land west of the Jordan), whereas the eastern tribes regard bonds of kinship as more definitive for Israelite identity than the possession of specific territory. But they recognize the difference in perception between their kindred in the west and themselves, and they seek to maintain these ties for future generations through the construction of the altar. It is true that both tribal groups agree that loyalty to YHWH is a vital component of national identity, yet the whole episode demonstrates the difficulties involved in defining what obedience consists of. The easterners' explanation that they built the altar "as a witness" (v. 27) seems disingenuous since an altar is normally made for the offering of sacrifices, and the alternative of constructing a stone monument was entirely feasible, since one had been built at Gilgal (4:19–24) and Joshua would soon set up another (24:25–27). Nevertheless, their explanation satisfies the western delegation and they return "to the land of Canaan" and report back to "the Israelites" who shelve their plans for war (22:30–34). The dispute over the altar appears to be settled, yet the use of religious language and appeal to altar symbolism masks still

23. Hawk, *Joshua*, 228.

unresolved questions, especially whether unity amongst all the tribes can be maintained.

This incident is a fascinating example of how conflict may erupt among God's people, how differing assumptions find expression, how religious symbolism can be taken in different ways, and how boundary matters are crucial to identity. It highlights the issue of what Israel's identity ultimately consists in.

The Significance of the Law for Israel's Identity

The book began with God's exhortation to Joshua to lead the people across the Jordan into the land, assuring him of YHWH's presence, and urging strength and courage—note how "be strong and of good courage" appears twice in 1:5–7a, and then again at 1:9. However, these exhortations do not concern military prowess; they concern adherence to the law of Moses, since they form an inclusion around YHWH's core insistence that Joshua should be "careful to act in accordance with all the law my servant Moses commanded you . . ." (1:7b–8). Daniel Block has pointed out that these verses open "the second part of the Hebrew Bible (*Nebi'im* Prophets) with an exhortation to meditate on the Torah (i.e., Moses' speeches in Deuteronomy) . . . [just as] Psalm 1 opens the third part with a similar challenge."[24] From a canonical perspective, these words place a striking notice over the whole of Joshua, but also over Judges, Samuel, and Kings, directing the readers' attention to what has been said in Deuteronomy.

It is easy to overlook the ceremonial pause in the middle of the four campaigns, but its place at the literary center of the whole conquest account emphasizes its significance. Joshua builds an altar at Mt Ebal, sacrifices are offered, and Joshua writes a copy of the law of Moses on the stones (8:30–32), according to Moses' instructions (Deut 11:29–30; 27:1–8). Next the whole assembly of Israel is gathered for blessing around the ark between the mountains of Ebal and Gerizim (near where the town of Shechem is located, though it is not mentioned here), and then Joshua reads "all the words of the law" to them all—women, children, and resident aliens included (8:33–35). Marten Woudstra emphasizes the significance of this ceremony: "In unmistakably clear symbolism the reader is told that the right of possessing the promised land is tied to

---

24. Block, *Triumph of Grace*, 21–22.

the proclamation of, and subjection to, God's covenant claims upon his people (and upon the world)."[25]

In the final part of the book, Joshua, now an old man (23:1; cf. 13:1), summons and addresses the leaders of Israel. He reviews what has been achieved, acknowledges more remains to be accomplished, and emphasizes the importance of observing "all that is written in the book of the law of Moses" (23:8) to resist the temptation to compromise presented by the remaining nations. His concern is not with rote learning or simplistic compliance with regulations; he goes to the heart of the matter by insisting on loyalty to YHWH: "Be very careful, therefore, to love the LORD your God" (23:11). He reminds them that they are experiencing the blessings of the land and warns them of the dire consequences of perishing from the land if they transgress the covenant of YHWH their God (23:14–16).

Joshua gathers the leaders of Israel once more (24:1); this time the location of Shechem is given, recalling the reading of the law in chapter 8. He rehearses the story of Israel's ancestors and journey from Egypt to the promised land (24:2–13), and then challenges the Israelites to make a deliberate choice between YHWH and other gods. The people respond with the desired answer, but Joshua is not convinced, despite their repeated protestations (24:16–24). Finally, he makes a covenant with them, writing down his challenge and their commitment in the book of the law of God, and setting up a stone as a witness before sending them back to their inheritances (24:25–28).

At these key places in the book—at the start and at the close, as well as at the central point of the conquest account—the narrator emphasizes the importance of hearing and obeying the book of the law. The implications for the overall message of the book are well expressed by Willie James Jennings:

> This God enfolds the holy people in the truth that YHWH, not the land, is the giver of life; YHWH, not the land defines their identity; YHWH imparts into their collective life the divine *dabarim*, the divine word and demands that they live by that word . . . .[26]

---

25. Woudstra, *Joshua*, 144.
26. Jennings, *Christian Imagination*, 256.

2. Historical Perspectives

We have already seen that Joshua presents two different points of view regarding how the Israelites came to possess the land: by means of a decisive conquest under Joshua's leadership, and, by implication, through a gradual process of settlement and conflict. Can both viewpoints reflect actual events? Lawson Younger compares Joshua 9–11 with ancient Assyrian, Hittite, and Egyptian conquest accounts and shows that their common hyperbolic and totalizing rhetoric should be taken as conventional rather than literal report.[27] Jerome Creach makes comparison with more recent origin stories such as the Pilgrim Fathers' arrival in Plymouth, Massachusetts, and subsequent first harvest and celebration of Thanksgiving in 1621 CE.

> Joshua must be classified as the kind of history that was written in the ancient world to trace national origins and to support nationalistic goals.... Such accounts do not intend to deceive the audience into thinking that something happened that, in fact, did not. And in some cases, they report real events. But their concern is to create identity and teach values, not to report "what really happened." In the process of achieving those goals, stories that have a historical kernel may collapse a complex array of historical events into a simplified account (as with the American Thanksgiving story). Others may be legendary portraits of heroic figures meant to inspire (the George Washington account).[28]

So, readers must bear in mind what kind of literature Joshua is, and not insist that it measures up to modern standards of strict historical record.

Furthermore, Joshua contains a number of internal discrepancies as well as inconsistencies with the book of Judges:

- Several town lists in Joshua include the same town in different tribal allocations, e.g., is Kiriath Jearim in Judah or Benjamin (15:60; 18:28)? Are Eshtaol and Zorah in Judah or Dan (15:33; 19:41)?
- Joshua lists a number of kings as defeated, e.g., Gezer, Megiddo, Taanach (12:12, 21), but elsewhere there are reports that the tribes did not succeed in driving out those populations (Josh 16:10; 17:12; Judg 1:27–29).

---

27. Younger, *Ancient Conquest Accounts*.
28. Creach, *Joshua*, 5.

- Joshua reports the defeat of the king of Jerusalem (10:22–26; cf. 12:10), but later says that the people of Judah could not drive out the Jebusites from Jerusalem (15:63). Yet Judges states that Judah and Simeon captured and burnt Jerusalem (1:3–8), only to report a few verses later that Benjamin could not drive the Jebusites from their city (1:21).

- Joshua makes much of the defeat of Jabin, king of the dominant city of Hazor (11:1, 10–14; cf. 12:19). Yet in Judges a King Jabin reigns in Hazor and is said to oppress the Israelites cruelly for twenty years (4:2).

Such conflicting details undermine claims to complete inerrancy. They probably indicate that variant source materials lie behind the biblical text as we now have it. The editors who put these together would have realized that these conflicts existed, but did not iron them out, presumably because they were reluctant to alter their sources.[29]

Dating and Archaeology

According to 1 Kgs 6:1, King Solomon began to build the Jerusalem temple in the fourth year of his reign, 480 years after Israel's exodus from Egypt. Solomon's reign is usually dated from c. 970 BCE, so a face-value reading would indicate a date of the exodus of c. 1446 and entry into Canaan forty years later, c. 1406. However, such dating has been largely dismissed by the majority of scholars on the grounds of extensive archaeological investigation of some of the cities said in Joshua to have been conquered by the Israelites, together with examination of extrabiblical texts, including the Merneptah Stela and Amarna Letters.

During the 1930s, the archaeologist John Garstang excavated the *tell*, or ancient mound, outside the modern city of Jericho and claimed to have discovered evidence for destruction of the city walls around the date of 1400 BCE, which would cohere with the biblical dating of the exodus and conquest. Unfortunately, Garstang's field techniques were faulty, and when Kathleen Kenyon worked on Jericho during the 1950s with much improved methods, she concluded that there was evidence of

---

29. Hawk discusses the contribution of scholarship on the history of traditions and form criticism, in "Joshua," 569f.

a small unwalled settlement c. 1425–1275 BCE, with no indications of fortifications or of destruction due to an assault such as Joshua's.

A significant number of scholars are very skeptical about the historical value of biblical materials before the exile, though many others disagree with them.[30] Most of the latter take the 480 years of 1 Kgs 6:1 as a round or symbolic figure (i.e., twelve generations of forty years each), that could indicate an interval of 240–300 years (i.e., twelve generations of twenty to twenty-five years each). They also argue that the city named Rameses (Exod 1:11; 12:37) is probably the royal city Pi-Rameses founded by Pharaoh Rameses II (1279–1213 BCE), and date the exodus during his reign, thus indicating c. 1250 BCE.[31] The majority view concerning the date of Israel's entry into Canaan currently places it at the end of the Late Bronze Age (thirteenth century BCE), though there is a minority of scholars who have raised significant questions about this date.[32]

Theoretical Models

Given the apparent dissonance between the biblical materials and the archaeological evidence, several theoretical models of how the Israelites came to inhabit the land of Canaan have been developed.[33] The *conquest model* was developed in the mid-twentieth century by archaeologists, led by William Albright in the USA and Yigael Yadin in Israel, who attempted to tie the thirteenth-century destruction of cities like Bethel, Debir, Eglon, Hazor, and Lachish to the invading Israelites. In the light of further extensive archaeological discoveries, most contemporary scholars regard the conquest model as a failure. Younger observes that it "was doomed from the beginning because of its literal, simplistic reading of Joshua."[34]

---

30. See the discussion in Day, *In Search of Pre-Exilic Israel*.

31. The dates given reflect the low chronology of Kenneth Kitchen, *Reliability of the Old Testament*. Thanks to John Bimson for his assistance here.

32. Bimson, *Redating the Exodus and Conquest*, argued that many sites mentioned in Joshua appear not to have been occupied in the thirteenth century, and that the destructions of Canaanite cities cannot be correlated with Israelite invaders so neatly as was once thought. Rohl, *Test of Time*, argued for a revision of conventional Egyptian chronology, and that this would allow for an Israelite conquest in the Middle Bronze Age IIB.

33. For details of these models, see Provan, Long, and Longman, *Biblical History of Israel*, 139–47.

34. Younger, "Early Israel," 179.

Meanwhile in Europe the *peaceful infiltration model* was developed by Albrecht Alt and Martin Noth, arguing that Israel's entrance into Canaan happened gradually and largely peacefully. Originally unrelated nomadic or seminomadic peoples, the tribes formed a federation bound together by a common allegiance to YHWH with a common cult center. Noth regarded the book of Joshua as less historical than *etiological*—a story intended to explain the existence of certain features in the land or certain names, beliefs, or customs. Noth's theory of an Israelite *amphictyony* (tribal league) was based on classical Greek models, and it has been criticized as inappropriate to a rather different culture, while Alt's understanding of pastoralism has also been faulted.

The *peasant revolt model* was first proposed by George Mendenhall in 1962. He did not entirely deny the idea of conquest but saw most of the militants as of Canaanite origin. Peasant farmers grew tired of oppression by urban overlords and revolted against them under the influence of a group of slave-labourers, who had escaped from Egypt and were held together by commitment to their God, YHWH. This hypothesis was given a Marxist twist by Norman Gottwald in *The Tribes of Yahweh*. Among several criticisms of this model are; it dubiously assumes that nomads favor an egalitarian approach to leadership over a hierarchical one; it fails to reckon with the now well-attested symbiotic relationship between rural people and city-dwellers.

In recent years extensive archaeological work on ancient settlements has yielded more detailed insights into changing populations in the land during antiquity. Israel Finkelstein has proposed what may be called *a cyclic model* for Israel's origins within Canaan; Israel emerged from groups that had originally been nomads, who then settled in the highlands before reverting to a nomadic way of life at the end of the Middle Bronze Age (i.e., they were locals, not incomers like Alt's). William Dever has proposed an "agrarian frontier reform model"; the early Israelites (the same highland settlers) were mostly refugees from the Canaanite lowland towns and villages, though he allows for other groups in the mix.[35]

---

35. Finkelstein and Silberman, *Bible Unearthed*, are skeptical that any reliable historical information can be derived from the biblical text. Dever, *Who Were the Early Israelites?* has argued that the biblical text is a worthwhile resource if used appropriately and judiciously.

Conclusion

It would be unwise to insist upon a strongly literal reading of conquest as found in the first and other parts of the book. It employs the dramatic style found in other ancient conquest accounts, highlighting the involvement of YHWH in order to emphasize the divine gift of the land to Israel. Alongside this perspective must be held the rather different picture (in much of the second part) of mixed success by individual tribes in taking possession of the land, which seems to indicate a partial and gradual process of gaining control.

A number of more conservative scholars continue to maintain credence for some sort of conquest, perhaps "telescoped into a simplified, selective, focused glimpse."[36] In his theological reflections on Joshua, Stephen Williams argues that:

> It is hard to see how the claim that a significant group of people who worshipped Yahweh entered and partly occupied the land of Canaan by military force is not a core claim, even if we might wish to formulate it a bit differently or add to the core.... If this is fiction, ideology, or whatever without real basis in fact, the grounds for Israel's claim to know God, as testimony is borne to it in the Old Testament, are surely removed to a very significant degree.[37]

3. Theological Perspectives

Richard Nelson considers that readers may be disturbed by Joshua's portrayal of wholesale slaughter of the Canaanites at the behest of a crusading, nationalistic God. However, he suggests that it becomes somewhat more palatable if its relationship to actual history is not direct.

> Joshua is describing an idealistic and theoretical picture of Israel's origin in Canaan, not factual history. This romanticized epic represents an illusory invasion, conquest, and land allotment done by an idealized Israel, a unified people neatly organized into twelve tribes. Israel follows the resolute and law-abiding leadership of Joshua, the successor of Moses authorized by God. With God's help, they succeed easily.[38]

---

36. Hubbard, *Joshua*, 40.
37. Williams, in McConville and Williams, *Joshua*, 212.
38. Nelson, *Historical Books*, 81.

Nelson asserts as historical fact Israel's emergence in the land over a long time, pointing out that the Canaanites survived into the monarchy period according to 1 Kgs 9:20–21. He thinks that the book appeared "as a way of dealing with Israel's persistently weak and vulnerable position," under threat from near neighbors and later from Assyria; it was *Israel in the land* whose culture and religion were endangered by hostile outsiders. "Retelling stories of past heroes was one way of conceptualizing and strengthening Israel's title to its homeland."[39] This appears to be a psychological interpretation of Joshua, which might relieve readers of their moral and theological concerns, but does it eviscerate the book of theological worth?

In the first chapter I summarized the argument that has been made for moral justification of the conquest on account of the Canaanites' sin. However, John and Harvey Walton have disputed the translation of God's word to Abram (Gen 15:16) about the delay in his descendants' return to the land, proposing the following instead;

> It won't be until after your lifetime is over that your family will return here because the destiny of destruction that has been decreed for your friends and allies has been and continues to be deferred.[40]

Walton and Walton argue further that the depiction of the Canaanites in passages such as Leviticus 18 and Deut 9:4–5 and 12:29–31 is not a moral indictment, but a sophisticated appropriation of a common ancient Near Eastern literary device in which the enemy is depicted as the "barbarian other."[41] It is striking that such wickedness is not mentioned within the book of Joshua itself, and neither is God's wrath said to be directed against the Canaanites.[42] Lawson Stone argues that, following Israel's initial aggression against Jericho and Ai, its "southern" and "northern" campaigns were defensive responses to large-scale Canaanite threats (9:1–2; 10:1–5; 11:1–5), and suggests that war would not have been necessary had the Canaanite response been more cooperative with Israel.

---

39. Nelson, *Historical Books*, 82. Rowlett made the case for a reaction against the Assyrian experience in *Rhetoric of Violence*.

40. Walton and Walton, *Israelite Conquest*, 50–63. The Amorites appear as Abraham's friends and allies in Gen 14:13, 24.

41. Walton and Walton, *Israelite Conquest*, 137–50.

42. Fretheim, "Wrath of God," 147 n. 29.

The conquest narratives are therefore structured so as to depict the Canaanites not as morally decadent, but as increasingly resistant to the action of Yahweh. The Israelites are depicted not as a savage, unstoppable war machine blazing over Canaan, but as reacting to the Canaanite kings' opposition to Yahweh.[43]

This is a key part of Stone's argument that the book's editors sought to guide readers to a non-militaristic and non-territorial way of reading the book.

Critical Traditioning

Ellen Davis has made a strong case for evidence of what she calls "critical traditioning" in the book of Joshua, drawing on Michael Fishbane's study of "inner biblical exegesis," the process through which the Hebrew Bible reached its present form. Fishbane thinks there was an overlap between the two roles of author (or originator of a text) and scribe (as preserver and tradent), such that there was a complex interaction between the two aspects of tradition: the process of creating, changing, and passing on (*traditio*), and the literary deposit that is received as authoritative, interpreted, and passed on (*traditum*). The central concern of the tradents was the faithful transmission of the text, but they felt free to disagree with their predecessors about how God's will and word to Israel were to be interpreted. They would not throw away old materials that seemed wrong, but supplement these with other materials that put them in a different light.[44]

Read on the surface as a conventional conquest account, Joshua appears to indicate that God instructs Israel to carry out horrific violence on men, women, and children without any qualms or reservations. But read with attention to its own details and with the assistance of those who have studied comparable ancient conquest accounts, the book of Joshua nuances the depiction of conquest in a surprising number of ways.

- Joshua's sending of the spies is a strange response to YHWH's commission (1:6, 7, 9); why the secrecy? The previous spying mission had ended badly, and YHWH does not command this one. The spies are hardly heroic, hiding in a Jericho brothel. But then Rahab

---

43. Stone, "Ethical and Apologetic Tendencies," 35.
44. Davis, "Critical Traditioning," 166–70.

makes a confession that would befit an Israelite (2:9–11). Davis observes that "the conquest account begins with a sort of ethical and theological inversion. The power of Israel's God is perceived, affirmed, and even celebrated by the 'conquered.'"[45]

The ethnic distinction between Israelite and Canaanite, which might appear to drive the conquest narrative, is transcended by the contrast between Achan and Rahab, the Gibeonites, and later Caleb. It is clear that the chosen people may include outsiders and exclude insiders.

- The book insists on YHWH's role as commander (5:14) and miraculous participant in battle. This conquest is not an independent human achievement of which to be proud, but a divine gift for which to give thanks and praise. Jerome Creach says:

  > By presenting the conquest as purely the action of God, the story urges complete dependence on God. This may seem simply to shift the responsibility for violence from humans to God. But it seems rather to identify warfare as something outside human prerogative. The claim that God fights for Israel puts the responsibility for righting the world completely in God's hands.[46]

- The book repeatedly insists on obedience to YHWH's word through Moses and the book of the law. The conquest depends on human obedience to YHWH, not on human ingenuity or military expertise. While the people as a whole are largely obedient, individuals are sometimes not.[47]

- The two-and-one-half tribes who settle east of the Jordan feature at important junctures of the book (1:12–18; 12:1–6; 13:8–13, 15–32; 14:3–4; 22:1–34), though these are rarely given due weight. This feature acknowledges tensions within Israel that eventually come close to conflict and challenges the finding of identity in geography.

- Joshua is the central human of the book, though his character is hardly fleshed out, compared with later figures like David.[48] He

---

45. Davis, "Critical Traditioning," 172.
46. Creach, *Violence in Scripture*, 123.
47. Hawk, *Joshua*, 21.
48. Parallels have been drawn between Joshua and Josiah, yet Peterson, *Authors of the Deuteronomic History*, 154–56, notes numerous parallels between Joshua 6–8 and 2 Samuel 5–7 that suggest a comparison between Joshua and David, except that David

remains loyal and generally responsive to YHWH throughout, and is characterized in his death notice as "the servant of the LORD" (24:29), a description previously reserved only for Moses.

- The final part of the book looks to the future in the land, warning that transgression of the covenant will lead to its forfeiture (23:13, 16, cf. 8:34).

It is such features of Joshua that lend themselves to practical application in the life of God's people today.

Israel's Election

The questions associated with Israel's acquisition of the land, especially the violence necessary for conquest, cannot be detached from Israel's election as God's people.[49] If God chooses one particular couple and their family, and blesses them such that they become a people and nation, they must eventually be provided with a land in which to live. If they were to be perpetual nomads, they could not be a witness to other landed nations as to how to live (see Deut 4:5–8), and would likely clash with them anyway, as they did during their nomadic phase in the wilderness. We may engage in a thought experiment in which Israel found an empty land, requiring no displacement of residents, no violent conquest, yet an empty land would seem contrary to God's intentions for human dispersal to fill the earth (Gen 1:28 and 11:8); there could be no return to an empty Eden.

The election of Abraham is God's response to the iniquity and violence of humanity (Genesis 1–12).[50] It entails engagement with the world that is marred with unrighteousness and destructive conflict (e.g., Gen 18:16–33). The elect people are a work in progress, themselves guilty of fear, deception, favoritism, suspicion, betrayal, exploitation, and other relational corrosions. The book of Joshua follows the books of Exodus–Deuteronomy that include many other stories of God's violent dealings with Israel's enemies—Egypt, Amalek, and others—but also God's violent

---

fails to read the law.

49. This section was prompted by reading Williams, in McConville and Williams, *Joshua*, 146.

50. See chapter 3.

punishments of Israel itself, following the golden calf, Korah's rebellion, the idolatry at Baal Peor, and other incidents.[51]

> If God commands violence, it is part of a whole concessionary scheme of operation, an accommodation to the fact of rampant evil which he detests, but has not abolished.... In that case, the commandment expresses divine nature—particularly holiness and goodness—only in the most partial and qualified way and under universally fractured conditions of violence.[52]

Israel's Mission

Election is not the only theological perspective with which to consider Joshua. Brad Kelle has drawn attention to the difficulties of conquest when considered as part of a missional reading of the First Testament.[53] Israel was elected in the first place as central to God's mission to bring life and blessing to the whole world (Gen 12:1–3). But if such is God's mission, how would the elimination of the Canaanites bring life and blessing to the whole world? It certainly would not bring life and blessing to the Canaanites concerned, although it might be argued that through Israel's occupancy of the land, and its learning thereby, God's mission to the whole world was advanced in the long run.

The Rhetoric of Joshua

Ancient accounts of Israel's arrival in the land would have been passed on by word of mouth and written versions would have been produced sooner or later. The records of land allocation contain discrepancies and may have emerged as late as the early monarchy. A process of editing and recontextualization took place over a long time in order to address changing situations of readers. In the time of the exile (if not before) these materials were shaped into a book that questioned simplistic assumptions that Israel's conquest came about through great battles won by heroic fighters, that it was a racial matter of ethnic Israel versus ethnic Canaanite. YHWH's role in the conquest was highlighted against the limited success of tribal possession.

---

51. See Sweeney's discussion, *After the Shoah*, chapter 2.
52. Williams, in McConville and Williams, *Joshua*, 122f.
53. Kelle, *Telling the Old Testament Story*, 119–23.

Looking back from the time after the fall of Jerusalem, exiles would have known the ancient stories of Israel's ancestors, how they had been rescued from slavery in Egypt and came to occupy the land of Canaan. It seems likely that they remembered these stories through rose-tinted spectacles and wistfully hoped for a return to the good old days. We know that Jeremiah had to write a letter to the exiles in Babylon denouncing those prophets who encouraged false hope by announcing a quick end to exile (29:8–9). In our own time political leaders sometimes appeal to past fantasies of national greatness and economic prosperity—whether the British Empire of the nineteenth and early twentieth centuries or the world-wide dominance of the USA following the Second World War—ignoring the violence of colonial domination and oppressive social conditions close to home that facilitated such "success."[54]

---

54. For a fascinating conversation between the biblical narrative and the American narrative of Manifest Destiny, see Hawk, *Joshua in 3-D*.

5

The Book of Judges

Where Joshua was a book of order and accomplishment, Judges is a book of chaos and destruction. It is full of larger-than-life characters, bizarre decisions, and considerable violence, especially against women. Yet it should not be dismissed as a collection of barbaric stories from an uncivilized time; it is about the importance of human community, i.e., how to (or how not to) achieve justice and peace among human beings who are self-assertive and self-centered. More particularly, it is about how the shalom of God's people can decline over time as they lose touch with the reality of God's involvement in their lives and with the guidance of God's word. It is about God's grace in raising up leaders who may bring a measure of relief from suffering, but who may also operate with distorted notions of God or personal agendas that bring mixed results.

Judges provides glimpses of the time between the aftermath of the conquest until a generation or so before the introduction of the monarchy. During this period the Israelite tribes initially captured certain cities, but then experienced repeated domination by other people groups followed by periods of relief. Leadership would have been in the hands of tribal elders, though they are rarely mentioned (2:7; 8:14–16; 11:5–10; 21:16), but from time to time judges are raised up. The Hebrew word for "judge" conveys political and military leadership as well as a judicial function, so the term could be rendered as "bringer of justice."[1]

---

1. McCann, *Judges*, 4.

THE BOOK OF JUDGES

1. Literary Perspectives

Judges is particularly amenable to literary exploration. Along with several extended narratives presenting vivid characters, some poetry (the Song of Deborah in chapter 5), and a political fable (9:8–15), it contains a number of riddles,[2] and frequent ambiguity, humor, and irony.[3]

One of the pioneers of literary approaches to the Bible, Kenneth Gros Louis, points out that characters like Samson, Jephthah, and Deborah have appeared frequently in Western art and literature.

> At the same time, the literary potential has been detached from the narrative as a whole. Artists and readers have turned admiringly to the individual stories, culled from them, reworked them, without paying much attention to the ways in which the stories might fit together, without, in other words, considering all of Judges as a literary work with its own themes and structure.[4]

Gros Louis goes on to discuss the details of the many stories in Judges up to that of Samson, highlighting the rich diversity of its various characters and situations, its reversals of expectations, and its emphasis upon God's fidelity to his wayward people. It is a disappointment, then, that his chapter entirely omits to comment on the final part of the book, since its less well-known stories are vital for understanding the book as a whole. I will proceed to discuss the literary arrangement of the book, consider a curious detail at its beginning, focus in some detail on its final story, and reflect on its treatment of women.

Literary Arrangement

The book is arranged in three parts; a prologue sets up the pattern of failure and redemption that shapes the stories of the judges found in the central section, and an epilogue brings things to a calamitous conclusion.

The prologue is made up of two parallel sections that recount socio-political and religious decline after Joshua's death. The first of these sections begins with a note of Joshua's death, followed by an inquiry of YHWH about which tribe should be the first to fight the Canaanites, the

---

2. On the riddles, see Butler, *Judges*, 1–4.
3. On irony, see Klein, *Triumph of Irony*.
4. Gros Louis, "Judges," 141.

answer being Judah. Several Judah stories follow,[5] until Benjamin fails to drive out the Jebusites (1:1–21). The Joseph tribes are next, but fail to drive out the Canaanites, as do Zebulun, Asher, and Naphtali, while Dan is unable even to secure its allotted territory (1:22–36). An angel of YHWH explains these failures to all the Israelites in terms of disobedience; they respond with weeping and sacrifice (2:1–5).

The section on religious decline reverts to Joshua's final days,[6] but then announces a change in that subsequent generations did not know YHWH or what he had done for Israel (2:6–10). The repetitive nature of Israel's unfaithfulness to YHWH is set out (2:11–23) with the following elements:

- Israel abandons YHWH and worships other gods;
- YHWH is provoked to anger and abandons of Israel, resulting in their defeat and subsequent oppression;
- YHWH is moved to pity at Israel's groaning,[7] raising up a judge or deliverer;
- The judge dies and Israel relapses, behaving even worse.

This cycle appears to map out what will follow in the central part of the book (the pattern will gradually break down in part two). Finally, the nations that remain are listed, and it is said that they are left to test Israel (3:1–6).

The central part of the book contains accounts of six major and six minor judges, opening with Othniel from Judah and closing with Samson the Danite, reflecting the first part of the introduction which began with Judah and ended with Dan. Othniel's career exemplifies what a judge should be, and Ehud's vivid solo exploit gives a taste of some of the stories that will follow (3:7–30). The later judge stories play on the basic pattern, though they become progressively worse, so that the narrative arc can be described as a downward spiral. In chapters 4–5 Barak is the war leader, but leadership is shared with Deborah, who is said to have judged Israel (4:4–5); Jael also plays a significant role. Disunity among the tribes appears first in this cycle (5:16–17, 23). The Gideon cycle begins with an extended introduction, including an ominous prophecy (6:7–10); it

---

5. Some commentators see the invitation to Simeon as the first element of failure to obey YHWH's word; e.g., Younger, *Judges*, 65.

6. The account in 2:6–9 is close to that in Josh 24:29–31.

7. Recalling Exod 2:23.

includes dramatic military success (7:19–25) but gives way to religious disaster (8:24–27). It includes the story of Gideon's son, Abimelech, who, though the main figure in chapter 9, is not a judge at all. The land is said to have rest after several deliverances (3:11; 3:30; 5:31; 8:28), but no more after Gideon's victory.

The Jephthah cycle also begins with an extended introduction, including a dramatic interchange between the Israelites and YHWH (10:10–16). Although Jephthah succeeds in defeating the Ammonites, this leads into excruciating personal tragedy (11:34–40) and is followed by the outbreak of inter-tribal warfare (12:1–7). By Samson's time the Israelites no longer even cry out to YHWH for deliverance (13:1). The judges themselves have become increasingly implicated in the wrongdoing of the nation as a whole, with Samson epitomizing Israel's waywardness and reluctance to embrace its calling. Barry Webb expresses this well:

> As Israel had been set apart from other nations by God's covenant with her, so Samson is set apart from other men by his calling as a Nazirite. As Israel went after foreign gods, Samson goes after foreign women. Israel wanted to be as other nations; Samson wants to be as other men; and as Israel repeatedly called on Yahweh in its distress, so does Samson. In short, the sub-themes that run through the whole central section of the book (Israel's struggle against her destiny and Yahweh's perseverance with her in judgment and grace) are finally brought to a sharp focus in the story of Samson. His personal story is also the story of Israel as a whole in the judges period.[8]

The six major judge stories are arranged in careful patterns, for example:[9]

- In the first three cycles things return to the status quo that began the cycle, whereas in the last three cycles things at the end of cycle are much worse that at its start.
- The six major stories are grouped in pairs. Othniel and Ehud operate in the southern part of the country; they are the two most successful judges, their stories are the shortest, and they are the only two designated by the term "savior/deliverer" (*mosia'*). Barak and Gideon operate in the northern, Cisjordanian region; Barak responds half-heartedly to Deborah's prophecy (4:8f), while Gideon requires much persuasion before he is ready to act (6:11–24); both

---

8. Webb, *Judges*, 34f.
9. For further details see Younger, *Judges*, 34–43.

cycles contain a number of pairs, e.g., Barak and Deborah are paired against Jabin and Sisera, while Gideon faces the pairs of Oreb and Zeeb east of the Jordan, and Zebah and Zalmunna west of the Jordan. In the third pairing, Jephthah and Samson both feature agreements with leaders, vows to God and so on.

The six minor judges' stories are told quite briefly: Shamgar (3:31), Tola and Jair (10:1–5), Ibzan, Elon, and Abdon (12:8–15). Shamgar's deliverance of Israel from a Philistine incursion is extraordinary, and Tola is said to have delivered Israel, but the accounts of the others are taken up with their children and influence, implying inaction regarding deliverance, which was meant to be their role according to 2:16.

The final part of the book is made up of two sections demonstrating Israel's religious and socio-political chaos, mirroring the two sections of part one (note the similar inquiries of YHWH in 1:1–2 and 20:18). Although these stories are set in the era of the judges, no judge appears in them, and they do not follow chronologically from what has gone before. They show that Israel was more endangered by its own internal decay, morally and spiritually, than by any external attack. A repeated expression runs through these final chapters: "In those days there was no king in Israel..." (17:6; 18:1; 19:1; 21:25).

The Book of Judges: Literary Arrangement

Part 1	Prologue: From Joshua to the Judges	
A	Israel's Socio-political Decline	1:1—2:5
B	Israel's Religious Decline	2:6—3:6
Part 2	The Judges: A Downward Spiral	
C	Othniel	3:7–11
D	Ehud	3:12–30
e[10]	Shamgar	3:31
F	Barak, Deborah, and Jael	4:1—5:31
	The prose narrative	4:1–24
	The Song of Deborah and Barak	5:1–31
G	Gideon	6:1—8:35

10. Lower case has been used to signify "minor judges."

		Gideon's call and good start	6:1–32
		Gideon's victory over Midian and Amalek	6:33—8:3
		Gideon's turn for the worse	8:4–35
		Gideon's violent legacy: Abimelech	9:1–57
h, i		Tola and Jair	10:1–5
J		Jephthah	10:6—12:7
		Israel and YHWH	10:6–16
		Jephthah: from outlaw to diplomat	10:17—11:28
		Jephthath's vow and his daughter	11:29–40
		Jephthah's violent legacy	12:1–7
k, l, m		Ibzan, Elon and Abdon	12:8–15
N		Samson	13:1—16:31
		Samson's mother and father	13:1–25
		Samson's Career: from Timnah to Ramath-lehi	14:1—15:20
		Samson's Career: from Gaza to Gaza	16:1–31
Part 3	Epilogue: Internal Moral and Spiritual Chaos		
B'	Israel's Religious Chaos		17:1—18:31
		Micah's idol and his priest	17:1–13
		Migrating Danites steal Micah's idol and priest	18:1–31
A'	Israel's Socio-political Chaos		19:1—21:25
		The Levite and the abuse of his concubine	19:1–30
		Civil War	20:1–48
		Multiple abuse at Jabesh-gilead and Shiloh	21:1–25

The First Riddle

In the first section of the prologue the tribe of Judah has success in defeating Adoni-bezek at Bezek (1:5). The name of this king who dies *at* Jerusalem (1:7b) may ring a bell because Adoni-zedek was king *of* Jerusalem in Josh 10:1–5, though the names are different. A grisly detail is included here—"they cut off his thumbs and big toes"—a mutilation that Adoni-bezek himself acknowledges as divine retribution (vv. 6–7a). What is this cryptic detail and Canaanite speech doing in the very first account of tribal advance into Canaanite territory? It certainly foreshadows some macabre details of wounds inflicted later in the book (3:21–22; 4:21–22;

8:16; 9:53; 16:21; 19:29). The theme of divine retribution is essential to the whole book, as implied by the angel of YHWH at the end of this section (2:3) and set out in the second section's cycle of abandonment (2:14, 2–21). But does this detail give us a clue to reading the whole book?

Tracy Lemos has drawn attention to the effect of the mutilation inflicted upon Adoni-bezek and his victims; they were reduced to the status of dogs. She demonstrates that the treatment of people like dogs was a humiliation not uncommon in the ancient world, and notes that it appears to have been practiced in the twenty-first century by US soldiers at Abu Graib prison in Iraq. Lemos argues that:

> Physical violence was pivotal in this society to the construction of a particular type of personhood, a personhood centered on domination and subordination and one in which dominant men could abrogate the personhood of others—of other men, of women, and of children—through dehumanizing rituals of violence.[11]

Lemos goes on to discuss violence against women, including the gruesome treatment of the Levite's concubine in chapter 19, though fails to pay attention to the wider context of chapters 20–21. In view of her work, I suggest that this initial vignette may alert readers to the meaning of violence throughout the book, and thus to its offence against God's creation. Most battle accounts in the books we are exploring give very few details of the blood and injuries involved (unlike many contemporary films that seem to relish depicting them), but the occasional gruesome detail in Judges reminds readers of the reality of such violence and its dehumanizing intent.

The Final Story

The final story is introduced with the editorial observation that there was no king in Israel (19:1), which forms a deliberate envelope with 21:25. This should alert readers to take all three chapters together, and to read them as a demonstration of the consequences of individual and tribal autonomy. The fact that the main character is a Levite forms a connection with the previous story of Micah and the Danites (also punctuated by the same editorial observations, 17:6; 18:1). Micah commissions a silver idol, sets up his own shrine, and installs a wandering Levite as his priest,

---

11. Lemos, *Violence and Personhood in Ancient Israel*, 3.

another man who has links with both Bethlehem in Judah and the hill country of Ephraim (17:7-8). The double focus on Levites, who should exemplify dedication to YHWH, emphasizes the extent of Israel's moral decline. What's more, this story concludes with a reference to Shiloh (18:31), while the second ends with the abduction of "the daughters of Shiloh" (21:19-23).

The Levite and His Concubine

This Levite has taken a concubine, according her a lower status than a wife.[12] She seems to have had little choice about the relationship and he seems to regard her more as his property than his partner—perhaps that is why she became angry with him and returned to her father's home.[13] After many weeks the Levite makes the journey to win her back, and receives a positive welcome.[14] There follow several verses (vv. 4-8) describing the father's extended hospitality over five days—perhaps the father hopes to strengthen the bond with his daughter's husband (v. 3), but it is the two men who eat, while she is marginal (or is she making the meals?).[15] The question presses on the reader: when will he "speak kindly" to her?[16] Eventually the Levite is determined to leave late on day five, despite his father-in-law's repetitive pleading, and his concubine is only mentioned among his belongings (vv. 9-10).

It is late when they approach Jebus, but the Levite refuses his servant's proposal that they look there for hospitality on the grounds that it is foreign. Later still, they enter Gibeah and the Levite sits in its square, hoping that someone will take his party in (v. 15).[17] But hospitality is

---

12. For two excellent studies of this chapter, see Ansell, "This Is Her Body..." and Paynter, *Telling Terror in Judges*, 19.

13. LXX has "became angry with;" the MT "played the harlot" is suspect. See Webb, *Judges*, 455 n. 4.

14. She "brings him in" to her father's house according to the MT. See Webb, *Judges*, 455 n. 6.

15. Or is the hospitality extended by the father-in-law a means of shaming the Levite for his inhospitality to his daughter?

16. Webb, *Judges*, 458-59, points out the repeated idiomatic use of "heart" in the Hebrew of vv. 5-8 ("fortify"/ "enjoy" in NRSV) reminds us of why the Levite came to visit.

17. Extending hospitality to strangers was an important custom in the ancient Near East, but it was commanded in Israel (Exod 22:21; 23:9; Lev 19:33f), and especially towards Levites (Deut 16:14; 26:12).

lacking until an old man arrives and talks to the Levite; a conversation ensues, and they discover they have Ephraim in common. The old man responds to the Levite's request for hospitality (he makes it clear he has his own provisions), insisting that he can cover everything. No doubt relieved, the three travellers enter his house and can relax (v. 21).

But they have been spotted by the local gang of ne'er-do-wells who surround the house, threaten to break in, and demand to have sex with the Levite; this is not about the morality of homosexual relationships, but about utter humiliation. The irony of having earlier avoided a foreign city, and looked for hospitality in an Israelite one, should be obvious. The old man goes out of the house and makes the men a shocking offer, appealing to them as fellow Israelites (vv. 23–24). Readers should now recall the story of Sodom in Gen 19:4–9: that story can be understood without knowing this one in Judges, but this one demands knowledge of Lot's story in order to get its point about the inhospitality of Gibeah. Stuart Lasine exaggerates in order to highlight the ludicrous and self-defeating nature of the old man's action, compared with Lot's:

> The words and actions of the old host are almost identical to those of Lot at this point, but their effect is to invert Lot's overblown hospitality into inhospitality. The old host seems oblivious to the fact that his offer of [his guest's] concubine is "inhospitable." He follows Lot's example so precisely that it is almost as if he were following a "script." The "script" calls for two women to be offered to the mob. The host has only one virgin daughter, so he must include the guest's concubine in order to act out his role![18]

Like Lot, the old man tells the gang to "do what is good in your eyes" to the women they offer (19:24; Gen 19:8), and this is especially significant, given the refrain of 17:6 and 21:25. But he goes further than Lot in telling them to "ravish" the women (v. 24), emphasizing his callousness as a father and host. He is less courageous than Lot, who had gone outside and shut the door, risking his life, and was directly threatened.[19] Perhaps his notion of honor and hospitality means that his principal guest must be spared (he does not offer the Levite's servant). Women are reduced

---

18. Lasine, "Guest and Host," 39.

19. Lasine, "Guest and Host," 40, continues, "Taken in their total contexts in Genesis and Judges, it is clear that the narrators do not approve of these strategems ... Judges 19 uses Genesis 19 to show how hospitality is turned upside down when one's guests are not angels, and one lives in an age governed by human selfishness."

to bargaining pieces; the old man's appalling offer of his virgin daughter poignantly recalls the sacrifice of Jephthah's daughter.

When the hostile men do not respond, the Levite makes an attempt to save himself; he seizes his concubine and thrusts her out; his selfishness regarding her is complete. The response of the gang is horrific, a night-long unspeakable ordeal, briefly but brutally summarized in three verbs: they rape her, abuse her, and discard her. At dawn she collapses on the threshold. What were the Levite, his servant, and the old man doing during the night? They appear to have slept, for the Levite seems about to depart without a care in the world—except that she is not ready to do his bidding (note he is described as "her master" in v. 26 and v. 27—no longer "her husband"). His absolute failure to exhibit the least care for his concubine is staggering. The Hebrew text is unclear whether she is dead or alive, and this raises even more questions for the reader as the Levite hoists her onto his donkey and makes the journey home.[20] Could her life have been saved if she had been brought into the house after the attack? Was the journey on the donkey the last straw? What is the Levite thinking and where are his emotions? He now appears completely detached; is this due to rage at the way he has been personally treated? Does he blame her for necessitating his journey in the first place?

Once home, the Levite "grasps" (the same Hebrew word as "seized" in v. 25) the concubine, and deliberately cuts her body into twelve pieces, as one might butcher an animal (v. 29). This act of dismembering is the final, ultimate violation of her personhood; she is denied the dignity of burial. He has been callous in the extreme in his treatment of her, so his sending her body parts to all the tribes as a call to action suggests that he is acting out of his own personal affront rather than moral outrage. This act has often been compared with Saul's dismemberment of oxen in 1 Samuel 11, but it should be clear that, while the Levite's act is perverse, Saul's act is laudable. Saul divides oxen, not a woman; he does so when the spirit of God comes upon him; his message is a dramatic call to action; his action leads to the renewal of his kingship (11:14f).[21]

---

20. Recall that Achsah rode on a donkey at 1:14, full of initiative and honored by her father; this unnamed woman is nameless victim, voiceless cargo.

21. See Lasine, "Guest and Host," 42.

The Civil War

One of the problems evident in the judge narratives is that of getting the tribes to work together against outside threats: several tribes joined Barak, but others stayed away (5:14–18, 23); Gideon conflicts with the Ephraimites as well as the people of Succoth and Penuel (8:1–9, 13–17); Jephthah kills thousands of Ephraimites (12:1–6). But in this story, the grisly action of the heartless Levite is effective; all the Israelites turn out at last "as one" (20:1, 8, 11)—to deal with the tribe of Benjamin! They invite the Levite as sole witness to explain the criminal act and accept his testimony alone—they fail to investigate thoroughly (as required at Deut 13:14a). His account is a distortion of what happened according to the previous chapter's narrator:

- "A perverse lot" (19:22) become "the citizens/nobles/lords of Gibeah," implying that the crime was committed by the leading men of the city, not some "low life."
- These men had demanded sex with the Levite, but this becomes immediate intent to kill, which stresses the threat to himself and diminishes his responsibility.
- Any reference to the Levite's being in the house and putting his concubine out of the door is omitted; instead he implies that she was caught while he escaped.
- The severity of the attack on his concubine is played down, compared with the original.
- It is indicated that the woman died as a result of the multiple rape, though the time of her death is unclear in the original account.

The Levite avoids any personal culpability; in other words, he bears false witness.[22] He succeeds in stirring up his audience, but then disappears from the action. He is "at best a caricature judge who almost destroys Israel rather than saving it."[23] The tribes challenge Benjamin to hand over the perpetrators from Gibeah, but they refuse, and each side musters its large forces (20:12–17). Where is the sense of proportion? According to the Torah, punishment should be proportional to the crime (Exod 21:24). We recall that inter-tribal tension arose in Joshua 22; whereas

---

22. Younger, *Judges*, 370.
23. Webb, *Judges*, 473.

that incident was defused through consultation, the verbal exchange that takes place here is ineffective.

The account of the battle is extensive, and consists of three engagements on succeeding days, each initiated by the tribes following consultation with YHWH. There is a pattern of incremental repetition that is illustrated in the following chart.[24]

Three Battle Accounts at Gibeah in Judges 20: Plot Analysis

Preliminary Actions	Israelites' Inquiry	YHWH's Response	Result
Make plans against Gibeah and threaten the city (20:8-13a)	#1 "Who of us shall go first to fight against the Benjaminites?" (20:18a)	"Judah shall go first" (20:18b)—no promise of victory	Israelites together attack Gibeah; they are severely defeated by Benjaminites (20:19-21)
Israelites weep before YHWH (20:23a)	#2 "Shall we go up again to battle against the Benjaminites, our brothers?" (20:23b)—a hint of doubt	"Go up against them" (20:23c)	Israelites take up positions (20:22) and attack but are defeated by Benjaminites (20:24-25)
All the Israelites weep, fast, and present sacrifices (20:26)	#3 (through Phineas the high priest) "Shall we go up again to battle with Benjamin our brother, or not?" (20:28a)—uncertainty expressed	"Go, for tomorrow *I will give them into your hands*" (20:28b)	Israelites set ambush and *herem* Benjaminites, except for 600 men (20:47-48)

The account of the third engagement is complex and somewhat repetitive.[25] The use of the ambush strategy is strongly reminiscent of the second battle at Ai (Josh 8:1-23). Despite the devastating ambush, the Benjaminites fight fiercely (v. 34), so the pivot of the whole account is v. 35, where it is said that YHWH's intervention gives victory to the Israelites. There are obvious similarities to the *herem* episodes in Joshua, but here it is the *Israelite* tribe of Benjamin that is virtually wiped out, except for 600 fighting men (20:47-48).

---

24. Chart derived from Younger, *Judges*, 374. The numbers of armed men seem enormous. Perhaps the term *'elep* ("thousand") indicated a military unit such as 100, or perhaps hyperbole is involved.

25. Webb, *Judges*, 491, helpfully explains vv. 36-41 in terms of changes of perspective between the protagonists.

Multiple Abuse at Jabesh-gilead and Shiloh

Only when the battle is over does it occur to the Israelites that one tribe is "lacking," (they have slaughtered all the women and children, 20:37, 48) and they put this into a question to YHWH at Bethel (21:3). They receive no answer, even after building an altar and making offerings, and so proceed to find one of their own. At Mizpah before the battle they had made a solemn oath not give their daughters to Benjamin, and now, seized with compassion for Benjamin, they remember their other oath requiring all tribes to participate in the battle.[26] Once it is realized that Jabesh-gilead had failed to respond to the roll call, they despatch a large force to *ḥerem* that place (21:11); no discussion as to reasons why they had failed to send a contingent to Mizpah. "Ironically, it is the people who did not respond to the Levite's injustice who are murdered."[27] The reference to Shiloh in Canaan (v. 12) is also ironic—surely Israel is now like Canaan! Four hundred young, already traumatised virgins remain who become a peace offering to the Benjaminites (21:13-14). But that is still not enough! The issues are rehearsed once more, and another plan is hatched for finding wives for the remaining Benjaminites (21:19-22); forced abductions, and use of the oath against the fathers (if they don't accept the abductions, they will be accused of "giving" their daughters to the Benjaminites!). "So with consummate irony, this episode reaches its climax with the elders ... doing, in principle, the same thing as both the old man ... and the Levite had done in Gibeah."[28] The plan is executed, and all return to their homes.

The concluding editorial observation about everyone doing right in their own eyes seems appropriate in the light of the failure of Israel's leaders to respond appropriately to an appalling crime. Some scholars have argued that this refrain shows the book was intended as an apology for the adoption of the monarchy, though the later parts of the Gideon story point the other way.[29] Israel would later discover that rapes, atrocities, and civil war can occur even when there is a king such as David.

---

26. The folly of rash oath-taking picks up on Jephthah's vow.

27. Klein, *Triumph of Irony*, 188.

28. Younger, *Judges*, 383. Klein, *Triumph of Irony*, 190, points out this closing story's ironic inversion of the story of Othniel and Achsah (1:11-15) near the beginning of the book.

29. Gideon refuses to be king on the grounds that YHWH rules (8:23), and Abimelech's rule is abortive (9:22).

Women in Judges

Stories of women are more prominent in Judges than in Joshua, and it has been studied by many feminist scholars.[30] One feature of the book as a whole is the striking shift in the way that women are portrayed—from active to passive. The brief story of Achsah, found in Joshua, reappears near the start of the book (1:11-15); though she is initially treated as a trophy to be won, she seizes the initiative, and is rewarded. In the Barak narrative, he is supplanted by Deborah's prophetic summons and rebuke (4:4-10), and later by Jael's deception and resourcefulness (4:17-22). Things begin to change at the end of the Gideon narrative, when Abimelech is subdued by the deadly aim of "a certain woman" of Thebez (9:53-54).

Whereas named women are portrayed positively in the opening chapters, taking the initiative where men hang back, by the closing chapters unnamed women are portrayed as victims and objects. Jephthah's unnamed daughter suffers a tragic and horrific fate (11:34-40) in order for her father to fulfil the vow he made to YHWH before his battle with the Ammonites (11:30-31). Why does Jephthah make this vow? His extensive message to the Ammonite king demonstrates that he is well versed in the story of Israel's journey from Egypt to the occupation of Canaan (11:14-22) with YHWH's military involvement (vv. 21, 23, 24), and it concludes with an appeal to YHWH as judge (v. 27)—surely YHWH would act once more to defend Israel? Next, the spirit of YHWH comes upon Jephthah (v. 29), which is a guarantee of success when read in the context of statements to this effect elsewhere in the book (3:10; 6:34; 14:6, 19; 15:14)—but Jephthah seems unaware of this presence or what it means. He is a man out of touch with YHWH (despite all the words), and so makes a deadly, pagan deal.[31]

While there is a sense in which Jephthah's implacable seriousness about his vow might be admired, it was entirely misplaced.[32] When he sees his daughter coming out of his house, he realizes what his vow now demands, but he places the responsibility on his daughter; "*you* have brought me very low; *you* have become the cause of great trouble for me" (11:35). Extraordinarily, she responds by affirming his obligation to

---

30. E.g., Brenner, *Feminist Companion to Judges*.

31. Attempts to lessen the horror of the vow by translating "whatever" instead of "whoever" in 11:31 (as e.g., in ESV) miss the point.

32. See Webb's discussion of whether Jephthah should have broken his vow, *Judges*, 336.

fulfil his vow to YHWH, then asks for some time with her companions, before returning at the given time so that her father might make her a burnt offering.

When Phyllis Trible examined this story, she unflinchingly focussed attention on its culmination in a barbaric act of child sacrifice. She tellingly compared Jephthah's unnamed daughter with Abraham's son, Isaac, and made intriguing links between the custom of remembrance at the end of the story (11:39b–40) and the practice of remembrance in the early church (1 Cor 11:24–25).[33] When I first read Trible's book, it was a wake-up call, especially to a male reader like me, to recognize the androcentric assumptions that might be embedded in the text, let alone in traditions of reading them. Yet the problem with Trible's reading of this story is that it pays little attention to its place within the larger narrative of the book, which traces the declining state of Israel's relationship with YHWH, and its inclination to make and keep unnecessary vows, as we have seen in chapter 21.

Samson's story begins with an extended account of an angel's annunciation of conception and birth to a barren woman, who seems more sensible than her skeptical and then fearful husband, Manoah (13:1–25). When Samson grows up, he marries a Philistine woman, but she is later burned (along with her father) by the Philistines in response to Samson's revenge (14:1—15:6). He visits a Philistine prostitute and then becomes ensnared by Delilah, who stands out as the only woman named (seven times) since Jael, and whose identity is not tied to any man. Delilah has remained a figure of female betrayal in Western culture, but within the biblical story she is remarkable for initiating the action; she does not deceive Samson but asks him directly what she wants to know. In contrast, he deceives her twice and seems to be playing games with her. In some ways Delilah undoes Samson as Jael undid Sisera; the resourceful woman now works for Israel's enemies.[34]

Tammi Schneider concludes that the women in Judges do not appear as characters in their own right; they are foils for evaluating leading male figures.[35] Yet the narrator is capable of systematic minimalization of a named male figure when telling the story of Samson's parents (13:1–24). Judges has sometimes been criticized as being primarily about men's

---

33. Trible, *Texts of Terror*, 105–7.
34. See Fewell, "Judges," 74.
35. Schneider, *Judges*, 289.

concerns or interests, particularly wars, rather than women's. It is true that the penultimate chapter portrays a civil war and its utter folly, but it is flanked by chapters that portray men's multiple abuse of women.

Alice Keefe comments on what is symbolized in the most appalling stories of rape and abuse of women in chapters 19 and 21.

> These rape scenes are embedded within a gendered symbol system in which male authority is entrusted with control. But the system does not leave the feminine wholly disempowered or marginalised. The wars of men fall subject to critique and judgment through these tales of rape and the horror that is known through the eyes of these violated women. Woman's body as a sign for community, connectedness, and covenant in these Hebrew narratives offers, through images of victimization and violation, powerful rhetorical figures of witness against the realities of brokenness within the human community.[36]

While taking the individual horror of the concubine's story seriously as a matter of patriarchal violence, Dennis Olson keeps the symbolism closer to Israel, when he notes its juxtaposition with the fractious civil war "invites the reader to consider the fate of this woman who has been raped, murdered, and cut into twelve pieces, as a gruesome metaphor for the social body of the twelve-tribe union of Israel."[37]

2. Historical Perspectives

In the previous chapter we discussed some of the factors in the debate about how Israel came into the land, so will not repeat those here. As before, a number of discrepancies can be identified. In the very first section, Jerusalem is captured by Judah (1:8)—contrary to Josh 15:63, but a few verses later Benjamin is unable to drive out the Jebusites who lived in Jerusalem (1:21),[38] and Jebus is later described as a foreign city (19:12). Gaza, Ashkelon, and Ekron are said to be taken by Judah (1:18), but subsequently they are known as Philistine strongholds (16:1, 21; 14:19; 1 Sam 5:10). Hazor appears in Canaanite hands (4:2, 17) despite having

---

36. Keefe, quoted in McCann, *Judges*, 126, who comments that the no-king formula cannot be construed simply as a set up for the monarchy.
37. Olson, "Judges," 872f.
38. Jebus is among the towns allocated to Benjamin in Josh 18:28.

been previously destroyed, according to Josh 11:11, 13. The editors' concern to preserve diverse source materials may explain such discrepancies.

The song of Deborah and Barak is thought by many to be one of the earliest compositions found in the First Testament. It is likely that Othniel, Ehud, Deborah, Gideon, Jephthah, and Samson were local heroes, whose deeds were remembered, passed on orally, and embellished over the years. The details of the minor judges suggest that they too were real people. The stories would have been written down, carefully edited, and arranged in order to serve later purposes.

Archaeology

The famous Egyptian Merneptah Stela was discovered by W. M. F. Petrie in 1896. Its inscription is mainly taken up with glorifying Pharaoh Merneptah's Libyan victories in his fifth year (possibly c. 1208 BCE). Further victories are celebrated in the closing stanza, and they include the line, "Israel is laid waste, his seed is not." Although the precise significance of this assertion is debated, the reading "Israel" is rarely questioned. This is the earliest reference to Israel so far discovered, and tells us a great deal, according to William Dever:

1. There existed in Canaan by 1210 at latest a cultural and probably a political entity that called itself "Israel" and was known to the Egyptians by that name.

2. This Israel was well enough established by that time among the other peoples of Canaan to have been perceived by Egyptian intelligence as a possible challenge to Egyptian hegemony.

3. This Israel did not constitute an organized state like others in Canaan but consisted rather of loosely affiliated people, that is, an ethnic group.

4. This Israel was not located in the lowlands, under Egyptian domination, but in the more remote central hill country, on the frontier.[39]

The Philistines appear to have come to Canaan as part of a group known as the "sea peoples" who moved through the Aegean basin, destroying the Mycenaean and Minoan civilizations. These peoples came by ship via Crete and Cyprus, but also overland via Anatolia, aiming to settle

---

39. See Dever's discussion in *Beyond the Texts*, 191–94.

in Egypt. Pharaoh Rameses III claims to have repelled the attempted invasion around 1176 BCE, and the Philistines settled in the coastal towns of Gaza, Ashkelon, and Ashdod and the inland towns of Ekron and Gath. The first encounter between Israelites and Philistines appears in the brief account of Shamgar's exploit (3:31); their influence is well established in 10:6-7, and they are dominant in the Samson cycle.[40]

The Period of the Judges

There are numerous chronological markers in the book, but it is not possible to construct a timeline of events from them. In the epilogue it is said that Jonathan, the son of Gershom, son of Moses, and his sons, were priests to the tribe of Dan (18:30), and that Phineas the priest who ministered before the ark of the covenant was the son of Eleazar, son of Aaron (20:27f). However "son" does not have a single, fixed meaning in lists of ancestors, so any number of generations may have passed between the named people.[41] Chronological details are not the only structuring device in the book, since Joshua's death is noted at the start of both sections of the prologue (1:1; 2:6-8). In Jephthah's detailed account of Israel's coming into the land, sent to the Ammonite king, he claims that the Israelites have resided in the lands east of the Jordan for 300 years (11:26). Although Israel's periods of oppression are regularly spelled out (3:8, 14; 4:3; 6:1; 10:8; 13:1) and the judges are said to have operated as such for specific numbers of years (3:11, 30; 5:31; 8:28; 10:2, 3; 12:7, 9, 11, 14; 15:20; 16:31), there is a gap (3:31). There may also be overlaps between judges (suggested at 10:6-8), since many are tribal leaders operating in geographically limited areas of Israel. If all the figures are added up, they would total at least 410 years, and this cannot be reconciled with the figure of 480 years between the exodus and the founding of Solomon's temple (1 Kgs 6:1), given the prior events (at least seventy years for the wilderness wanderings until after Joshua) and subsequent events (well over 110 years for Eli until Solomon).[42] Depending on the amount of overlaps between judges' careers, either a fifteenth-century or

---

40. See Dever's discussion in *Beyond the Texts*, 87-99. The Philistines are mentioned in several places in Genesis and Exodus, though these are all anachronisms.

41. See Webb, *Judges*, 448.

42. For details and discussion, see Provan, Long, and Longman, *Biblical History of Israel*, 161-66.

thirteenth-century date for the exodus could be consistent with the numbers given.

Many scholars view the various materials in Judges as having been deliberately arranged for theological purposes by editors working hundreds of years after the events, and thus consider attempts to work out a chronology, or even to speak of "the period of the judges" as inappropriate. It is important to remember that the book consists of a collection of selected details for the purposes of conveying the book's message; it was not produced to satisfy modern standards of historical writing.

Date of Composition

There are a number of statements regarding states of affairs "to this day" (1:21, 26; 6:24; 10:4; 15:19; 18:12), but these cannot be relied on to date the book since they may have been retained from earlier sources. The way in which the Samson story is told might point to Israel's ultimate defeat and exile, in which case the book would post-date that calamity. The reference to Jonathan's descendants continuing as priests "until the time the land went into captivity" (18:30) could be taken as referring to the Assyrian deportation, indicating a date for the final form of the book no earlier than the late eighth century. However, the parallel phrase, "as long as the house of God was at Shiloh" (18:31), might mean that the "captivity" refers to the Philistine capture of the ark at Ebenezer (1 Samuel 4).[43]

It seems that the earliest date for the whole book would be some point during the late monarchy, though most scholars favor a post-exilic date, taking it as part of the Deuteronomistic History.

3. Theological Perspectives

Although the book begins with Israel's battles against the Canaanites in order to take possession of the land, it quickly becomes evident that many of these nations remained and that the Israelites mingled with them. The tribes suffer oppression, but then enjoy divinely inspired deliverance from neighboring peoples, such as the Arameans, Moabites, Midianites, Ammonites, and Philistines. Yet this book is less about Israel's privileges as YHWH's chosen people than its responsibilities and failures.

---

43. See Webb's discussion, *Judges*, 449.

The narrator registers the kindling of YHWH's anger (3:8; 10:7),[44] but YHWH's pity is less evident as the stories unfold; the reprimands in 6:7-10 and 10:11-14 reveal gathering divine exasperation.[45] The epilogue shows what chaos results both for individuals and for Israel as a whole. So, the overall perspective is one of Israel's frailty and waywardness, coupled with YHWH's gracious forgiveness and repeated efforts to move Israel towards faithfulness through a process that ultimately proves ineffective; something has to change.

However, such a summary doesn't do justice to this book's copious details; more needs to be said about its presentation of YHWH's involvement in its stories. Insights disclosed in the course of a narrative are often placed in new light by key observations at a later stage, and especially from the perspective gained once the end is reached. So, I will consider briefly YHWH's involvement in Samson's story, and then in the epilogue.

YHWH in the Samson Cycle

The angel in Samson's birth story makes clear that this child "shall begin to deliver Israel from the Philistines" (13:5). But Samson's first adult move is to ask his parents to arrange his marriage to a Philistine woman, and when they understandably object, he insists that "she pleases me," or, more literally, "she (is) right in my eyes" (14:3)—an expression that is picked up in the epilogue.[46] What are we to make of "His father and mother did not know that this was from the LORD; for he was seeking an [opportunity][47] to act against the Philistines" (14:4)? It is verses like this

---

44. Note Joshua's warning in Josh 23:6 and compare the "burning anger" of YHWH over Achan's transgression in Josh 7:1, 26.

45. The NRSV translation at 10:16b, "he could no longer bear to see Israel suffer," may be translated much less favorably; "YHWH grew exasperated with Israel's troublings." The same expression is used of Samson's impatience with Delilah at 16:16. Webb, *Judges*, 304-7, argues that 10:12b-13 "clearly imply that the putting away of foreign gods is part of a routine with which he has become all too familiar from previous experience.... Hence his refusal to save Israel any more." YHWH's exasperation could refer to Israel's misery *or* to Israel's attempts to persuade YHWH to help them. The ambiguity spurs the reader to continue in order to find out what happens.

46. A similar expression is found in Israel's earlier invitation to YHWH, "do to us what is good in your eyes" (10:15).

47. McCann, *Judges*, 102, points out that the NRSV has "pretext," but God does not need a pretext to oppose Philistine oppression and injustice; a better translation would be an "opportunity" or "occasion."

that seem to lead many Bible readers to take Samson as an unequivocal hero. After all, the narrator tells us that the spirit of YHWH is particularly active in Samson's life (13:25; 14:6, 19), that he succeeds in killing many Philistines in a number of incidents, and that when Samson prays on two occasions it is implied that he is heard (15:18; 16:28). However, when we take into account Samson's Nazirite vow (13:7), his love affairs with Philistine women compromise his effectiveness as a deliverer. At this point Clinton McCann introduces the theological concept of "incarnation," in the sense that God works with the human resources at God's disposal, flawed though they may be:

> Judges 14:4 should not be understood as an affirmation of Samson's unfaithfulness and misbehavior. . . . Even in the midst of his persistent self-assertion, Samson will be an instrument of God's purpose. A God who loves the world and who entrusts dominion to humankind (see Gen 1:26–28) can work in no other way than incarnationally. This means that for love's sake, God risks that God's purpose will not be accomplished; and . . . God's purpose is not fully accomplished by Samson. In other words, 14:4 must be heard in light of 13:5, and also in view of the larger context within and beyond the book of Judges.[48]

McCann is correct to urge readers to read particular narratorial statements about God's purpose or action in the light of wider clues in the narrative. His concept of "incarnation" is a suggestive way of holding together God's involvement in people's lives while acknowledging their failures, but it is open to misunderstanding.

YHWH in the Epilogue

When we come to the epilogue, the first story begins with Micah's mother using the name of YHWH in praise, and then almost immediately in vain (Deut 5:11), as she asks her son to commission an idol (17:2–4)! In case the irony is missed, the editor inserts a first observation about people doing what was right in their own eyes (17:6). Once Micah has installed his priest, he declares that "YHWH will prosper me" (17:13); again comes that "no king" editorial comment (18:1a). The story continues with the theft of Micah's idol, shrine, and priest by the migrating Danites, and the only mention of the divine name is when the priest replies ambiguously

---

48. McCann, *Judges*, 102.

to the spies' enquiry; "The mission you are on is under the eye of YHWH" (18:6). The narrator attributes nothing to YHWH in the whole story, so it is straightforward to conclude that YHWH has nothing to do with the whole business!

So much for what the characters say; what about the narrator's statements concerning YHWH? Commenting on the start of the civil war (20:18), McCann notes the haunting link back to the beginning of the book, and the people's enquiry of YHWH (1:1–2); now Judah is to go up against its own brothers and sisters:

> The whole sordid story belies the claim that the people were actually gathered "before the LORD" (20:1). Rather, as the framing structure of chapters 17–21 suggest . . . all the action in chapters 20–21 continues to take place under the rubric of everyone doing "what was right in their own eyes." Thus, later in chapter 20 when the text relates that the people "inquired of God" (v. 18) or "inquired of the LORD" (vv. 23, 27), the reader cannot help but be suspicious. In other words, the larger literary setting of chapter 20 subverts the claims of vv. 18, 23, 27. There is every appearance that, although the people may have thought they were inquiring of the LORD, they are actually seeking to give divine sanction to the battle plans that they *had already made on their own* in verses 1–17. The reader is made doubly suspicious by the fact that the LORD is reported to have been correct only one out of three times![49]

McCann is claiming that the overall shape of the text subverts the narrator's attributions, but what has become of his concept of "incarnation"? That would indicate that, when the narrator says of the third day's battle, "The LORD defeated Benjamin" (20:35), YHWH was indeed acting through the Israelite army to punish Benjamin,[50] albeit they overcooked it (20:36–48), giving rise to the dilemma they faced in chapter 21. This would fit with all the previous narratorial observations in Judges about YHWH punishing Israel for their unfaithfulness.

Yet McCann describes as "ridiculous" the question asked of God after the battle; "Why has it come to pass that there should be one tribe lacking in Israel?" (21:3). The Israelites themselves have done it![51] The

---

49. McCann, *Judges*, 134.

50. This is the interpretation of more conservative commentators, like Webb, *Judges*, 490, and Younger, *Judges*, 374–76.

51. McCann, *Judges*, 135.

narrator continues to attribute not simply the victory, but the catastrophe to YHWH when he says, "The people had compassion on Benjamin because the LORD had made a breach in the tribes of Israel" (21:15), as if Israel had compassion, but YHWH had not. Yet compassion is something we might associate with YHWH, and it has come upon the Israelites rather late. McCann seems to suggest that the book of Judges as a whole, particularly shaped by the editorial insertions in the epilogue, concludes by subverting its own narratorial attribution of events to YHWH. In other words, the narrator cannot be regarded as omniscient, an influential characterisation advocated by Meir Sternberg.[52]

There is better option: the narrator is being heavily ironic in his attributions of events to YHWH.[53] It is as though the narrator adopts the people's language because he *wants* readers to see how bizarre such attributions are! By the end of this book we can no longer read the narrator's attribution of events (or, at least, all of them) to YHWH as straightforward.

The Rhetoric of Judges

Many scholars have thought that Judges is an apology for the introduction of the monarchy, particularly because of the refrain in the final chapters.[54] However, there is also significant aversion to the adoption of kingship towards the end of Gideon's story (8:22f, cf. 9:7-15). It could be that "No king in Israel" refers not to human kingship, but to divine kingship—chaos results from repeatedly abandoning YHWH.[55] Alternatively, this refrain provisionally encourages readers to think of a human king as the answer, but Samuel and Kings will demonstrate this to be wrong; kings also lead to disaster—ultimately the disaster of exile. In the wider canonical context the message is that all human rulers ultimately fall short, and that only God (or his Messiah) can fit the job description.[56]

---

52. Sternberg, *Poetics of Biblical Narrative*, 84-128.

53. See Klein, *Triumph of Irony*. Also see Steussy, *David*, 95.

54. Some have argued that Judges tends to idealize Judah (i.e., David) and denigrate Benjamin (i.e., Saul), however Webb, *Judges*, 43, argues that Judah is shown in increasingly negative light as the book unfolds.

55. Beldman, *Deserting the King*, 48-59.

56. Thanks to John Bimson for passing me this interpretation.

Consideration of the depiction of YHWH's involvement in the details of events, together with the overall shape of the book requires readers to consider two things.

Firstly, God's patience and compassion for his people continues, despite their repeated disloyalty. However, a long-term decline in loyalty to YHWH has deleterious effects on adherence to YHWH's ways and confusion in hearing God's guidance; we have noted the following:

- Rash and unnecessary oath-taking that leads to child sacrifice (chapter 11) and multiple bloodshed and abuse (chapter 21)
- Inhospitality that includes appalling sexual abuse (chapter 19)
- Failures in due process and dispute resolution (chapter 20)
- Inter-tribal disunity and civil war (chapter 20)

Such societal breakdown requires a more drastic change in arrangements—in this sense the introduction of the monarchy seems a necessary change, though whether it would make any long-term difference would remain to be seen.

Secondly, God raises up a range of deliverers from various backgrounds in response to the oppression of God's people and their cries for help. Even so, such leaders may conduct themselves unwisely, inviting evaluation of their weaknesses and failures. "The Bible does not endorse an uncritical attitude toward either charismatically chosen leadership or spirit-engendered acts of power."[57]

Finally, there is an important methodological point about theological interpretation: by the end of this book full of irony, the narrator's statements about YHWH become intensely ironic. Attention to the overall shape and narrative techniques employed in this book should make the reader wary of taking statements about YHWH's involvement in events literally.

---

57. Davis, *Opening Israel's Scriptures*, 154.

6

The Book of Samuel

Some of the most famous Bible stories appear in the book of Samuel: God's call of the boy Samuel, David's victory over Goliath, David's adultery with Bathsheba. For those who dig deeper, it contains some of the most fascinating narrative and poetry in the whole Bible, with its complex portrayals of Samuel, Saul, and David, along with many other characters. Strategically within the overall story of God's people, it recounts Israel's momentous transition from a confederation of tribes to a kingdom. This book could be described as entertainment, tragedy, propaganda, or theology, but what does it seek to achieve?[1]

1. Literary Perspectives

In times gone by scholars often sought to identify various source documents behind Samuel, but in recent decades narrative approaches have increasingly been applied to read the book as a whole.[2] In addition, both literary and historical approaches have been adopted by scholars exploring the leading personalities portrayed in the book; Samuel, Saul, and especially David.[3] Such a focus is helpful when considering the narrative

---

1. An explanation of why 1 & 2 Samuel should be read as one book was given in footnote 88, near the end of chapter 1.

2. E.g., Polzin's two volumes, *Samuel and the Deuteronomist* and *David and the Deuteronomist* are part of a larger series, begun with *Moses and the Deuteronomist*.

3. E.g., Gunn, *Fate of King Saul* and *Story of King David*; Steussy, *David* and *Samuel and His God*; Halpern *David's Secret Demons*; Borgman, *David, Saul, & God*; Wright, *David, King of Israel*.

characterization of these people. However, several scholars who take a literary approach to David's story include the first two chapters of the book of Kings since they provide glimpses of David's old age and death.[4] The problem is that attention to the personality of David tends to displace attention from the literary unit of the book (which also includes parts of other characters' stories), and from the intention of those editors who shaped the book with a particular purpose.

A further methodological turn has taken place in the twenty-first century with the development of approaches that see certain narratives as making ethical evaluations of Israelite kings.[5] In particular, I have found April Westbrook's work on the David narrative, focusing attention on the stories of women, suggestive for the whole book.[6]

Arrangement

Scholars taking both historical-critical and literary approaches recognize the introductory formula marking the start of Saul's reign (1 Sam 13:1) and the concluding note of Saul's death (2 Sam 1:1), as dividing the book into three main parts grouped around the major figure in each; Samuel, Saul, and David. Within these three main parts smaller sections can be discerned, each of which may be subdivided further, so that the outline below could easily be extended.[7]

The theme of change is strong in each part: in Part 1, Eli declines while Samuel rises, only for Samuel to be displaced later by Saul. In Part 2, Saul loses divine favor and David begins to rise; a long struggle between the two leads to a crisis for David and death for Saul. In Part 3, David gradually takes control of Judah and Israel, and his reign reaches a high point in chapters 5–8, yet he stumbles and conflict between his sons results in civil war, leaving him diminished.

---

4. E.g., Borgman, *David, Saul, & God*, focuses on the use of repeated patterns in Samuel and finds these continuing into 1 Kings 1–2.

5. Smith, *Fate of Justice and Righteousness*; Lasine, *Weighing Hearts*. See also more generally, Phillips, "Commanding Faces of Biblical Stories."

6. Westbrook, "He Will Take Your Daughters."

7. In Parts 2 and 3 here I have drawn on Westbrook's detailed analysis in "*He Will Take Your Daughters,*" 231–50.

The Book of Samuel: Literary Arrangement

Part 1 Change from Eli to Samuel to Saul	Prologue: Hannah, Eli, and Samuel	1 Sam 1–4
	YHWH, the Philistines, and Samuel	1 Sam 5–7
	Samuel and the inauguration of the monarchy	1 Sam 8–12
Part 2 Change from Saul to David	Saul's reign and failures	1 Sam 13–15
	David introduced	1 Sam 16–17
	David bests Saul from inside Saul's house	1 Sam 18–20
	David bests Saul from outside Saul's house	1 Sam 21–26
	David bests Saul from without: foreign enemies	1 Sam 27–31
Part 3 Change within David's reign	David grows stronger; Saul's house declines	2 Sam 1:1—4:12
	David's power is established	2 Sam 5:1—8:15a
	David's power is displayed, but undermined	2 Sam 8:15b—14:33
	David's power is threatened	2 Sam 15–20
	Epilogue: David deconstructed	2 Sam 21–24

Jan Fokkelman has drawn attention to the structural links between the poetic pieces near the beginning, middle, and end of the whole book: Hannah's Song (1 Sam 2:1–10), David's Lament (2 Sam 1:19–27), and David's Song of Thanksgiving (2 Sam 22:1–51) together with his final Oracle (2 Sam 23:1–7): "The huge mass of prose in the middle of the so-called Deuteronomistic History, the Books of Samuel, is supported by three pillars of poetry."[8]

Hannah's song is a programmatic statement for the whole book, since the concluding mention of YHWH's king goes beyond Hannah's situation and anticipates later developments in the book. It provides a theological lens through which to understand the rise and failure of each leader it portrays. The theme of "might," "strength," and "power" (1 Sam 2:1, 4, 9, 10) eventually finds echoes in David's song of thanksgiving (2 Sam 22:33, 40), though it is important to note the contrast between Hannah's exultant celebration of Yahweh's *reversal* of normal power arrangements (despite the positive view of kingship in the final stanza) and David's triumphant celebration of Yahweh's *upholding* of his reign.[9] These

---

8. Fokkelmann, *Reading Biblical Narrative*, 186f. See also Linafelt, "Poetry and Biblical Narrative."

9. Polzin, *Samuel*, 31–35, argues that these two songs are programmatically placed at either end of the book, the triumphant tone of both serving what he sees as the

two songs of praise contrast sharply with David's tragic lament over the deaths of Saul and Jonathan at the structural center of the book. Here, the key word is "mighty," which appears in v. 21 and v. 22 as well as in the refrain "How are the mighty fallen!" (19, 25, 27).[10]

Prologue

From a literary perspective, Fokkelmann insists that the first "act" in Samuel "has been composed on the pattern ABAB, as it alternates the birth and rise of Samuel with the corruption and downfall of the priestly dynasty of the Elides."[11]

A Birth of Samuel (1:1—2:10)
   B Corruption of Eli's sons (2:11–36)
A Call of Samuel (3:1—4:1a)
   B Downfall of Eli's sons (4:1b–22)

In the final scene, Phineas' wife gives birth and names her child "Ichabod" (4:20–22); forming a counterpart to Hannah's emphatic name-giving of "Samuel" (1:20).[12]

The narrative begins with the introduction of Elkanah, but it is quickly taken over by the story of Hannah's suffering because of her lack of children.[13] Her passionate prayer for a son (1:11) forms a significant contrast with Israel's elders' later demand for a king (1 Sam 8:3); she prays earnestly to YHWH: they will abruptly challenge Samuel. Hannah's lead story alerts readers to the key role that women will play in this book, and

---

book's royal ideology. But Jobling, *1 Samuel*, 166, rightly points out the contrast between Hannah's "theology of revolution" and David's "celebration of kingship."

10. For discussion of this lament, see Fokkelman, *Reading Biblical Poetry*, 5–13.

11. Fokkelmann, *Reading Biblical Narrative*, 157. Source critics usually identify an introductory section in chapters 1–3, with a subsequent section running from 4:1b to 7:17 ("The Ark Narrative").

12. Fishbane, *Biblical Text and Texture*, 63–76, has shown how the book of Exodus begins with a prologue, chapters 1–4, that foreshadows the events and scenarios of chapters 5–19. Something similar happens in the first four chapters of 1 Samuel; note the prominence of women in both.

13. Amit's assessment of Elkanah's words to Hannah (1:8) is insightful, "Am I Not More Devoted to You Than Ten Sons?" 75:

> Elkanah's words reveal him to possess the egocentricity of a child who perceives himself as the centre of his world and is disappointed when his behavior fails to receive the attention he expects. Elkanah is revealed as one who cannot accept the fact that Hannah wants to be mother to her children and not mother to her husband.

sets the scene for all that follows, especially matters of monarchy and justice, within YHWH's judgment.

> Indeed the final words of Hannah's prayer foreshadow the exact theological ambiguity with its accompanying ethical questions, with which the reader must repeatedly grapple throughout the upcoming David narrative. That is, no man can prevail by strength alone, yet YHWH empowers the divinely chosen king (1 Sam 2:9–10). In between the two balancing realities lies the essential fulcrum—YHWH who creates all, will also judge all and respond accordingly (1 Sam 2:2–3). Thus divine empowerment comes with the caveat of a just expectation of divine evaluation concerning how such power is used.[14]

Hannah's faith-filled story is interwoven with the tragic one of Eli, whose initial judgment of her (1:14) demonstrates a tendency to "project onto others what he does not face in himself."[15] The narrator soon details the misdeeds of Eli's sons, who were treating the offerings to YHWH with contempt (1 Sam 2:12–17). They sexually exploit women servers at the tent of meeting, despite Eli's remonstrations with them (2:22–25); in contrast, Samuel grows as might be hoped (2:26). The problem of wayward sons will recur throughout the book.

Abruptly, an anonymous man of God visits Eli with a devastating indictment from God of Eli's honoring "your sons more than me," and a dire warning about his family's future (2:27–36). Thus the key theological concern of this book is raised regarding the reliability of YHWH's promises to a family, and whether they may be withdrawn in light of human transgression—this will be crucial in the later stories of Saul and of David.[16] We will see that Hannah's devotion to YHWH, expressed in the giving up of her son to serve in the house of YHWH (while also continuing to care for him), and her acute theological insight voiced in her song of praise, will contrast markedly with Saul and David. Furthermore, Polzin suggests that "these early stories about the fall of the House of Eli and the rise of Samuel, in addition to having inherent interest in themselves, form a kind of parabolic introduction to the Deuteronomic history of

---

14. Westbrook, *"He Will Take Your Daughters,"* 36.

15. Green, *King Saul's Asking*, 12.

16. David's final poetry recalls this speech; especially "those who honor me I will honor. . ." (2:30) finds a strong echo in: "With the loyal you show yourself loyal. . ." (2 Sam 22:26). Also, "I will build him a sure house" (2:35) finds an echo in: "Is not my house like this with God?" (2 Sam 23:5).

kingship."[17] Polzin points out that Eli sits on a seat/throne in 1:9 and 4:13, and finds

> an aura of ultimacy about him; he is a figure of royalty at the end of the line, old and blind, so that the oracle of the LORD reads very well not only as an introductory parable on the coming reigns of various kings throughout Israel's history, but especially as a parable about the ultimate fate of the monarchy itself.[18]

The story of the call of Samuel in chapter 3 also anticipates significant issues in the later parts of the book.[19] For instance, the scene is set using language about sight and light; no frequent *vision*, Eli's *eyesight* grew dim, so he could not *see*, the *lamp* of God had not gone out (3:1-3). The lamp will return symbolically in the book's epilogue when David's men will insist, "You shall not go out with us to battle any longer; so that you do not quench the lamp of Israel" (2 Sam 21:17b).[20] Strangely, Samuel was lying down "in the temple of YHWH," (3:3, cf. 1:9b), and "the house of YHWH," another equivalent expression, is used at 1:24 and 3:15, although the temple had not yet been built.[21] These anachronistic usages point forward to the end of the book when David purchases the future site for the temple (2 Sam 24:24; cf. 2 Sam 22:7b).

What of YHWH's message to Samuel? How culpable was Eli? Some readers think that YHWH's judgment on Eli's house is harsh, given that Eli had remonstrated with his sons,[22] but the point is that Eli had failed to *restrain* his sons (3:11-14). Eli's response when he hears Samuel's recounting of YHWH's words, "It is the LORD; let him do what seems good to him," (3:18b) appears passive, whereas his sons seem active in their evil. Samuel's growth and his establishment as a prophet is briefly described (3:19—4:1a).

Suddenly the Philistine threat impinges on Israel, battle is joined, and Israel's army defeated. The elders of Israel ask, "Why has YHWH put us to rout?" But instead of enquiring of YHWH they come up with the idea of fetching the ark of the covenant of YHWH (4:3). This arrogant

---

17. Polzin, *Samuel*, 44.
18. Polzin, *Samuel*, 44f.
19. Explained well by Polzin, *Samuel*, 49-54.
20. The lamp (*nir*) becomes symbolic of David's kingship later in Kings (1 Kgs 11:36; 15:4; 2 Kgs 8:19).
21. In contrast, "the tent of meeting" is used at 2:22, a term from the wilderness era.
22. Steussy, *Samuel*, 2-3.

reaction should be compared with Israel's abject response to defeat at Ai (Josh 7:6–9); here there is no soul-searching. As we saw at the close of Judges, YHWH's name is being used, but in vain. In contrast, when David later flees from Absalom, he refuses to use the ark as a guarantee of safe return (2 Sam 15:24–26).

When news reaches Eli of Israel's second and catastrophic defeat by the Philistines, along with the death of his sons[23] and the devastating loss of the ark of God, he falls and dies. The account could have ended there, but instead a woman's story continues, which gives events greater impact and poignancy (4:19–22). When she hears the catastrophic news, Eli's daughter-in-law gives birth, and before she dies, names her son "Ichabod," (which means "Where is the glory?"), saying, "The glory has departed from Israel, for the ark of God has gone into exile."[24] This story does not simply point up the immediate theological shock of the loss of the ark, which until this point has embodied YHWH's victorious presence amongst the Israelites, it anticipates the tragic ending of Israel's royal narrative in exile.

The ark is about to undergo a fascinating twist on earlier depictions of YHWH as warrior. Note that the Philistines remember the divine plagues against Egypt in the wilderness and realize the consequences of defeat—slavery (4:8–9). Now YHWH (symbolized by the ark) is defeated, captured, exhibited in a rival's temple—vulnerable. All this would ring loudly in the ears of Babylonian exiles if they knew that the ark had been removed to that pagan capital.[25]

The Characterization of Saul

Saul is a fascinating character. It is often assumed that he was a failure whereas David was a success. Yet many interpreters have noted positive aspects of Saul's early career and regard him as a tragic figure. To begin to understand Saul we must first explore Samuel's character since he is a key figure in the introduction of the monarchy, and it is usually presupposed that he speaks God's word authentically. But is this always the case?[26]

23. Note, Eli's sons' names are given at 1:3 but omitted at 2:12, 22. Their repeated use at 4:4, 11, 17 is for emphasis.

24. See Brueggemann, *Ichabod towards Home*, 9.

25. Did the ark go into exile? It is not included in the account of items removed from the temple in 2 Kgs 25:13–17, and thus legends have arisen about its storage in a secret location, e.g., 2 Macc 2:4–8.

26. For a helpful discussion, see Steussy, *Samuel*.

Samuel and the Introduction of the Monarchy

There is no question that the demand for a king presented to Samuel by Israel's elders was a turning point in Israel's story (1 Sam 8:5). Until this juncture Israel had not adopted a monarchy because YHWH was their king (see, e.g., Exod 15:18); it was an institutional peculiarity that distinguished them from other nations. Yet the elders' approach to Samuel must be read in the context provided by the narrator; Samuel had appointed his own sons as judges, and they became corrupt (8:1–3). The double irony is that Samuel's sons were following Eli's sons, and that monarchy tends to entrench filial corruption. It is not surprising that the elders' demand "displeased Samuel" (8:6) because it amounted to a vote of no confidence in his leadership.

YHWH's word to Samuel demonstrates insight into Samuel's self-preoccupation, whilst aligning the people's rejection to YHWH's self, and yet instructs Samuel (twice) to comply with the demand while warning of its implications (8:7–9).[27] Samuel proceeds to spell out royal ways to the people; nevertheless the people insist on having a king "to govern us and fight our battles." When YHWH instructs Samuel yet again to comply, Samuel sends the people home instead (8:10–22). It is difficult to escape the conclusion that the narrator portrays Samuel as disgruntled and obstructionist. As Robert Alter puts it, "The prophet Samuel may have God on his side, but he is also an implacable, irascible man, and often a palpably self-interested man as well."[28] There is no denying the close relationship between Samuel and YHWH, yet not everything Samuel says is "God's truth"; it is filtered through Samuel's flawed personality.

A number of scholars have read the portrayal of Saul's career as reflecting badly on YHWH, or at least on Samuel.[29] When faced with a massive Philistine army, and with some of his troops melting away (13:5–7), Saul waits seven days for Samuel to arrive, as previously instructed (10:8). But Samuel does not appear, so Saul takes it upon himself to make a burnt offering to entreat YHWH's favor before the battle; just as he does so, Samuel arrives and proceeds to berate him for his foolish disobedience, declaring that Saul will not establish a dynasty (13:8–14). Brueggemann describes Samuel here as "harsh, unresponsive, and accusatory," a "peevish" prophet who plays a "daring, brutal game with Saul's

---

27. YHWH has a history of conceding to Israel's demands on occasion; see the request for meat in Numbers 11 (cf. Ps 106:13–15).

28. Alter, *Ancient Israel*, 229.

29. Gunn finds the "dark side of God" in *Fate of King Saul*, 131.

faith, Saul's career, and eventually Saul's sanity."[30] Samuel's accusation that Saul has "not kept the commandment of the LORD your God" (13:13) is baffling because it is difficult to see what commandment Saul has broken.

Philips Long has provided a helpful explanation of Samuel's accusation, based on research into the process by which leaders in early Israel come to power, involving three stages: *designation, demonstration,* and *confirmation*.[31] Here we must back-track to Samuel's anointing of Saul in the previous section (9:1—12:25), in which source critics have tended to find multiple accession accounts. When Samuel anointed Saul and gave him his original instructions, he said,

> ... After that you shall come to Gibeath-elohim, at the place where the Philistine garrison is; there, as you come to the town, you will meet a band of prophets coming down from the shrine with harp, tambourine, flute, and lyre playing in front of them; they will be in a prophetic frenzy. Then the spirit of the LORD will possess you, and you will be in a prophetic frenzy along with them and be turned into a different person. Now when these signs meet you, do whatever you see fit to do, for God is with you. And you shall go down to Gilgal ahead of me; then I will come down to you to present burnt offerings and offer sacrifices of well-being. Seven days you shall wait, until I come to you and show you what you shall do. (10:5-8)

What is meant "do whatever you see fit to do" (v. 7)? It must have been to attack the Philistine garrison mentioned in v. 5. This would be an effective *demonstration* of Saul's recent private *designation* as king and provoke war with the Philistines. However, in the aftermath of Saul's anointing and the fulfilment of all three signs, Saul failed to do what lay to hand. The intended accession process went into abeyance (note that Saul doesn't even mention the kingship to his uncle, 10:14-16) until a number of other events occur: a second, public *designation* (10:17-27), a substitute *demonstration* (11:1-13) and a partial *confirmation* (11:14-15). The Philistine garrison is attacked later, but by Jonathan rather than Saul, and war is thereby provoked (13:3-5); only at this point is the second of Samuel's original set of instructions complied with and Samuel's seven-days delay activated (10:8b, 13:8).

Long's explanation sheds light on the apparent unfairness of Saul's rapid rejection and resolves questions about the literary coherence of

---

30. Brueggemann, *Samuel*, 99, 101.
31. Long's argument is summarized in *Samuel*, 19-20; for the details, see 113-21.

Saul's accession to the throne. Saul failed to take up the challenge of attacking the Philistine garrison when filled with the spirit of YHWH; he went on to hide himself among the baggage when Samuel summoned the tribes to publicly *designate* him as king; he was found and acclaimed, though there was some dissent (10:17-27). Saul responded decisively to the Ammonite siege of Jabesh-gilead, a *demonstration* that silenced his critics (11:1-13), following which Saul's kingship was renewed (or *confirmed*) at Gilgal, with rejoicing (11:14-15).

Nevertheless, the impression remains that Samuel is ill-disposed towards the people and their new king. He makes a long speech to all Israel, insisting on his own upright behavior (nothing is said about his sons!), rehearsing key parts of Israel's story and warning them to remain faithful to YHWH (12:1-15). He calls on YHWH to send thunder and rain to endorse his condemnation of their wickedness in asking for a king, and a storm ensues, which would have damaged their wheat harvest (12:16-18). The people ask for Samuel's intercession, and he reassures them of YHWH's commitment and his own prayers, yet retains a stern and disparaging posture regarding "your king" (12:19-25).

Saul and Moral Injury

Brad Kelle has proposed that Saul's career can be understood through the interpretive lens of moral injury, a developing field of interdisciplinary scholarly investigation and practical application. Since the Vietnam War, the unseen wounds of war have been increasingly recognized by psychologists, counsellors, caregivers, chaplains, and pastors. These unseen wounds include military sexual trauma, traumatic brain injury, and especially post-traumatic stress disorder. More recently, another unseen injury has been recognized as *moral injury*, which may be characterized as a wound resulting from the violation (by oneself or by others) of a person's core moral beliefs. Definitions abound as the field continues to develop, and three broad types of moral injury have been identified:[32]

- Acts of perpetration that may include offensive and defensive aggression, lack of restraint, acts of revenge, inflicting of collateral damage, and actions undertaken in ambiguous situations.

---

32. Adapted from Kelle, *Bible and Moral Injury*, 26f.

- Failure to act (by oneself or others) in ways that might have saved a fellow soldier, or feelings of loss of control and predictability in the world.

- Disillusionment, which may involve the perception that an authority is incompetent, unethical, or indifferent, or an individual's increasing recognition that he or she has a capacity for violence and evil.

Kelle explores the causes and effects of moral injury, including its theological dimensions, as well as discussing its healing and repair. He proposes that Saul's story may be read as that of a morally wounded warrior, and that it might contribute to our understanding of moral injury.

Kelle insists that "There is no episode in chapters 9–11 that explicitly depicts Saul perpetrating an act in a warfare context that transgresses his moral beliefs. . . . Saul (is left) with a positive sense of his person and position."[33] However, in Samuel's speech in chapter 12, "the prophet says the establishment of kingship—previously endorsed as Yhwh's will and guided by divine providence—was a rebellious act by the people outside of the covenant." Here Kalle applies the third type of moral injury to Saul, who stands offstage in this scene:

> Now . . . he hears from Yhwh's authoritative prophet that the monarchy is an abandonment of Israel's long-established covenantal way with Yhwh and that he himself is the embodiment of this violation of the very moral identity of Israel as a people. Saul now learns that by his very act of being king he has, even if unwittingly, violated part of his own moral character and identity as part of Yhwh's covenant people and served as the means for the community to do so as well.[34]

Subsequently Saul experiences two more betrayals of trust in his conflicts with Samuel over his offering sacrifice at Gilgal (13:1–15) and over his failure to destroy Agag, king of the Amelekites (15:1–33). Despite Long's explanation of Saul's failure to attack the Philistine garrison, it is difficult to resist the impression that Samuel had already written Saul off before chapter 13.

> Samuel's posturing resembles a brutal game in which Saul's real failure was failing to follow *Samuel's* personal orders and

---

33. Kelle, *Bible and Moral Injury*, 49.
34. Kelle, *Bible and Moral Injury*, 50.

colliding with the prophet's apparent resentment of the king and unwillingness to surrender his priestly power.[35]

After his capture of Agag, Saul's explanation of his actions to Samuel (15:20–21) seems reasonable rather than disobedient (he took the spoils to Gilgal, not to his home in Gibeah); however, the prophet responds with portentous poetic insistence on obedience (15:22–23), and dismisses Saul's pleas for forgiveness. How much of Saul's rejection originates from YHWH (v. 10) and how much from Samuel?

From the perspective of moral injury, Saul's hearing of Samuel's speech in chapter 12, followed by his two experiences of devastating criticism from Samuel meant that his moral world had become unreliable; he experienced betrayal of trust by his prophetic and divine authorities as they issued ambiguous commands, prejudged his guilt regardless of his motives, and interpreted his actions as negatively as possible. In subsequent chapters, Saul's behavior begins to show signs of instability, such are found among the well-recognized manifestations of moral injury, as catalogued by Kelle:

> An inability to move out of combat mode, irresponsible thrill seeking with boasting and taunting, a sense of unremitting danger, suspicion and fear of women, the need and effort to place blame, emotional numbness and loss of trust in relationships, violent rage and desire for revenge, and the potential for despair and self-harm. In Saul's story, these consequences manifest themselves as failed relationships with his daughters and son, distrust of his own men, suspicion and violent rage against innocent bystanders, persecution of a presumed usurper, and a descent into despair and isolation.[36]

The interpretive lens of moral injury does not seek to justify Saul's actions, nor does it claim authorial intention or subvert the book's larger theological purposes. It does provide a stimulating perspective on Saul's character, and it suggests ways in which the text might connect with the experience of people who have experienced moral injury in today's world.

The Characterization of David

David's name appears more times in the Hebrew Bible than that of any other human being. But who is David, and why are people (and God) so

---

35. Kelle, *Bible and Moral Injury*, 52.
36. Kelle, *Bible and Moral Injury*, 56.

drawn to him? The way in which the book of Samuel portrays this character—complex, subtle, ambiguous—is one of its greatest achievements. David is often thought of as an attractive and largely straightforward hero, who falters on one serious occasion, but is otherwise consistently faithful to YHWH, such that he can be described as "a man after his own heart" (1 Sam 13:22). Much of this perception of David comes from the book of Samuel, though other positive elements are filled in by readers who gloss over the negative elements that are present. Marti Steussy shows how this affirmative characterization of David is driven by three statements made before David's name even enters the story:

- Samuel to Saul: "The LORD has sought out a man after his own heart; and the LORD has appointed him to be ruler over his people." (1 Sam 13:14)

- Samuel to Saul: "The LORD has torn the kingdom of Israel from you this very day, and has given it to a neighbor of yours, who is better than you." (1 Sam 15:28)

- God to Samuel concerning Eliab (who is tall and good-looking, like Saul): "Do not look on his appearance or on the height of his stature, because I have rejected him; for the LORD does not see as mortals see; they look on the outward appearance, but the LORD looks on the heart." (1 Sam 16:7)

A superficial reading of these statements can lead to contrasting Saul and David like this:[37]

Saul	David
chosen by people (or Samuel)	chosen by God
on basis of appearance	on basis of heart
bad, sinful	good, virtuous

Such a contrast is misleading on three counts. First, Saul is clearly chosen by God, according to 1 Sam 9:17 and 10:24. Second, while appearance may be a factor in Saul's case (1 Sam 9:2), it is also remarked upon when David first appears (1 Sam 16:12; cf. 17:42).[38] Third, the contrast assumes that characters and relationships are static; that if Saul sins at a certain point in the story, he must never have been any good; that if God rejects

---

37. Derived from Steussy, *David*, 50.

38. Steussy's discussion of the vocabulary used to describe Saul and David, *David*, 51, shows that they are closer than translations suggest.

Saul consequently, he was never really chosen in the first place. But biblical characters do change, and the biblical God responds by making changes of God's own (see the theological section below). Indeed, the biblical narrator quite often sets the reader up to construe a character one way, only to overturn that view later.[39]

It is true that Part 2 invites readers to contrast Saul and David, usually to David's advantage. But perhaps the most striking comparison concerns their dealings with the Amalekites; Saul intends to offer his booty in sacrifice (1 Sam 15:15) yet he is condemned by Samuel, whereas David uses his booty for political bribes (1 Sam 27:9; 30:19–20) and receives no criticism whatsoever.

The Role of Women's Stories

Rather than attempt a complete survey of the way that David is characterized, I will discuss April Westbrook's ethical evaluation of David. She builds on the work of Richard Smith, who pursues an ethical evaluation of the monarchy in the narratives of David's reign, arguing carefully for a new section heading at 2 Sam 8:15b, which reads, "David administered justice and equity to all his people."[40] Smith attends to narrative details that affirm or question David's interaction with justice issues, and recognizes that several female characters serve to highlight ethical evaluation, though he does not recognize any pattern in these woman stories.

Westbrook develops Smith's proposal regarding ethical evaluation of the monarchy by attending to the vital role played by the several stories of women in the David narrative; Merab, Michal, Abigail, Rizpah, Bathsheba, Tamar, the wise woman of Tekoa, the ten concubines, and the wise woman of Abel.[41] She observes that the parallel account of King David in 1 Chronicles 11–29

> does not include any of the detailed woman stories found in the books of Samuel. . . . Thus, even a cursory comparison of these two different accounts of David makes one thing very clear— the woman stories, as a whole, are intentionally included in the

---

39. See Sternberg, *Poetics of Biblical Narrative*, 326, 348.
40. Summarized by Westbrook, "*He Will Take Your Daughters,*" 30–33.
41. Women do not receive much attention in 1 Samuel 5–17, so it seems that their regular appearance in the David narrative is a deliberate editorial strategy in the ethical evaluation of David in particular, although Saul is also implicated in his dealings with Merab and Michal (18:17–30).

books of Samuel for a purpose unique to this telling of the David story.⁴²

Alongside accounts of men's heroic deeds in the books of Samuel, the stark details of these woman stories

> consistently create very uncomfortable ambiguity for the reader who, like the Israelites within the narrative, really wants to love David and to believe that he is the noble king who will fulfil the great dream of the monarchy's potential to protect the people and ensure justice for them. In striking contrast, however, through David's interactions with women, the reader is regularly confronted with a very unlikeable person who abuses his power to violate even those loyal to him—a point made more distasteful by their typical depiction in ways that engender the sympathy of the reader toward the violated person.⁴³

These woman stories enable an ethical evaluation of the monarchy that leads the reader to consider the nature and consequences of kings and their use of power. Indeed, the women become metaphors for the kingdom itself; for example, Michal is originally possessed by Saul (as his daughter) but is eventually taken by David on account of his superior ability to capitalize on others' love and loyalty as well as to outmaneuver Saul politically (1 Sam 18:20–29).⁴⁴ Thus, when, out of political and personal expediency, Michal is used and abandoned by both Saul and David, the reader must ponder the ultimate fate of the kingdom.

Westbrook's detailed work is both convincing and inspiring. She demonstrates how the inclusion of many women's stories shows editorial awareness of their vulnerability, exploitation, and abuse within a patriarchal society, yet also of their wisdom, resilience, and bravery in some cases. I have room to incorporate only one example, Rizpah, in the following section.

Epilogue: David Deconstructed

Many commentators agree that the final chapters have been carefully organized into a concentric, three-tiered structure, centered around the

---

42. Westbrook, "He Will Take Your Daughters," 4.
43. Westbrook, "He Will Take Your Daughters," 5.
44. Westbrook, "He Will Take Your Daughters," 63.

introduction to David's second poem: "Now these are the last words of David" (23:1a), suggesting the following arrangement:[45]

Epilogue: David Deconstructed

A	David's handling of a national crisis (*narrative*)	21:1–14
B	David's decline and his exit from military affairs (*short stories*)	21:15–22
C	David's penultimate testament: a song (*long poem*)	22:1–51
C'	David's ultimate testament: an oracle (*short poem*)	23:1–7
B'	David's decline and his exit from military affairs (*longer stories*)	23:8–39
A'	David's handling of a national crisis (*narrative*)	24:1–25

Having identified these chapters as a carefully constructed unit, it should be noted that they are not detached from what precedes. The first section of the epilogue is preceded by a list of David's officials (20:23–26) that forms a link with a similar list that precedes the story of David's elevation of Mephibosheth, Jonathan's disabled son (2 Sam 8:16—9:13). It is most likely that this elevation took place after the ritual execution of Saul's other male descendants in 21:7–9.

National Crises A and A'

One way to read the account of David's handover of two of Saul's sons and five of his grandsons to the Gibeonites to be put to a gruesome death (21:1–9) is that it shows the king piously following divine guidance to resolve the national affliction of a three-year famine. Of course, the concept of bloodguilt and the impaling of Saul's descendants "before YHWH" strike contemporary readers as barbaric; David inhabited a very different world from our own. Yet some commentators are suspicious of David's motivations, given the private nature of his inquiry of YHWH and the absence of a previous account of such an attack on Gibeon by Saul.[46] Noting that David's transaction with Gibeon likely lies behind Shimei's earlier accusation about "the blood of the house of Saul" (2 Sam 16:8), they read this story as evidence of David's determination to wipe out any threat from Saul's family. Against this suspicious reading, it must be said that when David negotiates with the Gibeonites they are specific about

---

45. Adapted from Morrison, 2 *Samuel*, 276. Polzin, *David*, 210ff, identifies numerous literary connections between A and A'.

46. E.g., Brueggemann, *Samuel*, 336–38. He completely overlooks vv. 4–5.

Saul's responsibility, and ask David to hand over seven of Saul's sons for execution (vv. 3–6).

Yet David seems unusually submissive to the Gibeonites, and there are literary patterns that suggest David uses this occasion to destroy his enemies without incurring personal blood guilt (note David's promise to Saul, 1 Sam 24:21–22). Immediately prior to this story is the account of Sheba's rebellion, within which Joab assassinates Amasa, Absalom's former military commander, *in Gibeon* (20:8). After the civil war, David had made overtures to Amasa, offering to give him command instead of Joab (19:13), but Sheba's rebellion provided David with an opportunity to expose Amasa to ruthless Joab (20:4–9). This incident is itself reminiscent of Joab's assassination of Abner, Saul's military commander, *at Gibeon* (2 Sam 2:12, 13, 16, 24; 3:30), after which David made a show of outrage, yet did nothing to change Joab's position. There is an irony about the apparent show of peace in each of these cases, given the original offerings of peace and disguise that the Gibeonites employed generations earlier to deceive the invading Israelites into making a treaty (Josh 9); Gibeon stands for deceit![47]

There is one element of this story that decisively reveals the narrator's negative evaluation of David; the part played by Rizpah, the mother of Saul's two sons (21:10). This extraordinary woman spends months in the open protecting the decomposing bodies from predation day and night. As Westbrook says, Rizpah acts as a "mother in Israel," crying out for justice, although she has no power whatsoever within the monarchical system;

> The sons of Rizpah and Michal, as well as those lost in the famine, are dying because one king does not keep faith with a peace covenant and because another king needs to demonstrate power in order to keep power. In her incredibly courageous act, Rizpah, the insignificant concubine, exemplifies far greater care for justice and compassion for people than kings have ever been shown to do in this narrative.[48]

Rizpah's actions amount to a reversal of covenant curses (Deut 28:26), thereby demonstrating that they have been implemented, not by the hand of YHWH, but by the hand of David and his machinations with the Gibeonites, whose just cause has been turned into an even greater injustice. Note that David did not ask YHWH how to respond to the

---

47. Westbrook's discussion, *"He Will Take Your Daughters,"* 213–19, is illuminating.
48. Westbrook, *"He Will Take Your Daughters,"* 220.

bloodguilt issue, nor had YHWH asked for the lives of these men. Most of all, the famine did not end with the impaling, but only after Rizpah's noble rebuke and David's burial of the bones of those impaled along with those of Saul and Jonathan (21:12–14). Westbrook's conclusion is profound:

> it is not the killing of the seven descendants of Saul that resolves the issue of injustice created by the monarchy. Rather it is the requirement of the king of Israel to treat people, even his enemies, with dignity and respect—an act of humility that demonstrates faith in YHWH, rather than in the king's own power—that ultimately resolves the crisis.

Finally, this story introduces the composite epilogue that reflects on David's reign, and in it Rizpah serves as a metaphorical representation of the nation, so the reader must reflect upon the overall impact of David's reign upon Israel.

David's handling of another crisis (24:1–25) echoes the previous one, especially in its closing words (21:14b; 24:25b). It is instigated by David's holding of a census, despite Joab's protest. Conventional monarchs would conduct a census to enhance their bureaucratic and exploitative power; here counting potential recruits amounted to a failure of confidence in YHWH to protect his people, a reversal of David's confidence when confronting Goliath.[49] The puzzling element is the narrator's attribution of David's initiative to YHWH's anger, so I will return to this in the theological section below. In contrast with the Bathsheba débâcle, David's own heart strikes him, as it had long ago (1 Sam 24:5–6), and he confesses his folly (v. 10). When we consider David's response to YHWH's offer of a choice between three forms of retribution, it is revealing; "let *us* fall into the hand of YHWH, . . . but let *me* not fall into human hands" (v. 14). The people must endure pestilence rather than David endure life on the run—something he had experienced in his youth. Nevertheless, when David sees the enormity of what is happening, he confesses once more, "I have sinned," and asks for a more personal judgment "against me and against my father's house" (v. 17). The David who emerges from this episode is apparently chastened, repentant, and sincere, and he insists on paying for Araunah's threshing floor, the site of the future temple.

---

49. It also points to the more formal state arrangements that would be put in place by Solomon and subsequent kings.

Declines B and B'

The short stories in 21:15–22 are closely tied together as a literary unit, but they do much more than supplement the previous accounts of David's battles with the Philistines. Previously such an accomplished warrior, David is suddenly vulnerable and requires assistance from Abishai. As a consequence, David's men swear to him, "You shall not go out with us to battle any longer, so that you do not quench the lamp of Israel" (21:17). How ironic, given the people's original insistence on having "a king to go out before us and fight our battles" (1 Sam 8:20)![50]

The longer collection of stories in 23:8–39 is made up of the exploits of "The Three," (8–12), together with the feats of Abishai and Benaiah (18–23), and a list of "The Thirty," including Uriah the Hittite (24–39). In the central narrative (13–15), David is at the cave of Adullam (cf. 1 Sam 22:1), campaigning against Philistines based at Bethlehem. It is a testament to David's attachment to his home village, but even more to the devotion of David's men at an early stage in his career. Brueggemann comments,

> No doubt the story is preserved and told to enhance David. To that extent the narrative serves a propagandistic function. The narrator proposes a very particular kind of David, however, a David with believable innocence, with egalitarian sensitivity, who prized solidarity more than his own satisfaction. The narrative thus functions as a protest against the David of selfish arrogance and absolute ideology. In a very different context David might be perceived as "worth ten thousand of us" (18:3), but not here. David is here honored and celebrated, but not at the cost of his men.[51]

These two sections, which might appear at first glance to be collections of legendary war stories, have been carefully arranged to highlight David's declining powers on one hand and his former "common touch" on the other.

Testaments C and C'

David's Song celebrates YHWH's salvation of the king (22:2–4, 47–49), but "the *effect* of this salvation on the person of the king is at the heart

---

50. There is also an echo of 2 Sam 11:1.
51. Brueggemann, *Samuel*, 349.

of David's gratitude."⁵² Where YHWH responds to David's call by assuming the role of a dread warrior (22:7–20), David himself becomes a dread warrior (22:33–43), with the result that David is not just king of Israel, he is even "head of the nations" (22:44). By the end of the song, "God has transformed him into a miniature of himself—a quasi-god in royal garb."⁵³ David's assertion of his own righteousness, in several complementary ways (22:21–25), strikes the reader as particularly hollow following the adjacent Rizpah story. David's assertion of his loyalty to YHWH might seem more realistic if he included himself among the haughty whom YHWH brings down (22:26–28).⁵⁴

The Last Words of David continue the apotheosis of David, beginning with the opening words, "The Oracle of David" (23:1)—elsewhere in the Former Prophets such oracles are only attributed to YHWH (1 Sam 2:30; 2 Kgs 9:26; 19:33; 22:19).⁵⁵

> The effect of David's appropriation of divine language to himself is to make the king, at one and the same time, a god-like prophet of God. However much we have seen David's predecessor, Saul, maneuvering to neutralize the divine check on royal power that the prophet Samuel represented, David's speech now makes Saul's actions appear paltry and timid. David presents himself as a prophet-king whose speech can hardly be distinguished from God's: "The spirit of the LORD speaks by me, his word is upon my tongue" (23:2).⁵⁶

David goes on to use solar language of himself (23:4), something found elsewhere only of YHWH in Ps 84:12; the brightness (*nogah*) he ascribed to YHWH in 22:13 he now appropriates to himself.

When compared with Moses' final poetic words in Deuteronomy 32 and 33, David's song and final words are strikingly self-oriented. Yes, they celebrate YHWH's deliverance of his king (22:2–4, 47–49), and the fortunes of the Israelites are inevitably bound up with those of their king, so the welfare of the people is furthered through his just rule (23:3–4). But given the context of the rest of the book (let alone David's treatment

---

52. Polzin, *David*, 203.
53. Polzin, *David*, 204.
54. Note the link between 22:26–27 with Hannah's song in 1 Sam 2:30.
55. Balaam is in the same linguistic position as David in Num 24:3, 15.
56. Polzin, *David*, 204.

of Saul's family in 21:1-14), the assertion of the king's righteousness, keeping the ways of YHWH (22:21-25) appears ironic.[57]

2. Historical Perspectives

Historical questions are raised within the book itself. To take just one example, the famous story of David's single combat with Goliath (1 Sam 17) contains difficulties since Saul appears ignorant of David in the aftermath (17:55-58), yet in the previous chapter David is said to have come to Saul's court as his personal musician (16:14-23).[58] Next, according to 17:54, David took Goliath's head to Jerusalem before he put the armor in his tent, yet Jerusalem was in Jebusite hands at this time; David did not capture it until many years later (2 Sam 5:6).

Furthermore, Goliath is said to have been killed by Elhanan son of Jaare-oregim of Bethlehem in the epilogue (2 Sam 21:19). One solution might be to suppose that there were two Philistine champions named Goliath, yet the mention of the spear "like a weaver's beam" in both accounts suggests that this was one exceptional warrior whom everyone remembered. Could Elhanan be another name for David (kings might have dual names at that time, e.g., Solomon and Jedidiah in 2 Sam 12:24-25)? This explanation would entail David's father having two names, which seems unlikely. Why would David's name be given as "Elhanan" in 2 Sam 21:19 when "David" is used two verses earlier, especially given that there David's men insist he should not go out to battle any longer? It seems most likely that the book contains two conflicting accounts of Goliath's slayer. If David did kill Goliath, it would be unlikely for a writer to attribute the victory to a subordinate, but it is feasible to imagine how a subordinate's victory might be caught up into the stories about Israel's great hero.[59]

Such undeniable tensions within the Hebrew text drove the historical search to account for the origins of this literature. The dominant scholarly approach to 1 & 2 Samuel in the twentieth century was source criticism; Leonhard Rost's work on the "Succession Narrative" (2 Samuel

---

57. See Brueggemann, *Samuel*, 343.

58. Interestingly, the LXX version of 1 Samuel lacks 17:55-58 and 17:12-31, as if these verses were not in the translator's source document.

59. In 1 Chr 20:5 it is said that "Elhanan son of Jair killed Lahmi the brother of Goliath the Gittite, the shaft of whose spear was like a weaver's beam." For a discussion of the textual issues involved, see Allen, "Chronicles," 417.

9–20 + 1 Kings 1–2) has been particularly influential, but Gillian Key's critique is significant, arguing instead that 2 Samuel 10–20 is a theological biography examining sin and punishment.[60] In the earlier part of the book an underlying tension was identified in the apparently anti-monarchical and pro-monarchical passages (especially 1 Samuel 8 and 1 Samuel 9–10 respectively) that could be attributed to pre-existing source documents. Jacob Wright has recently proposed that two originally separate documents recounting the story of Saul and the story of David were later combined.[61]

It must be accepted that the book of Samuel is different from modern kinds of history writing; it contains no statement of aims; it does not assess evidence or sources employed; it includes literary features that would not be acceptable in a modern work of history. Yet Rachelle Gilmour has argued the case for Samuel as historiography:

> The use of narrative to represent the past is as old as the concept of history itself but also at the forefront of modern historical theory. A return to the centrality of narrative in history in recent years has made literary embellishment and overt ideological interpretation more acceptable in a modern concept of historiography. They are now often considered inevitable and even desirable aspects of representation. They bring the past to life, offer an interpretation of its meaning and significance, and express the complexity of human experience and national events.[62]

Gilmour goes on to discuss four aspects of Samuel's representation of the past that are important features in modern historiography, paying attention to literary devices that diverge from modern conventions and requirements: causation, ideological evaluation, meaning and significance, and coherence.

Dating and Archaeology

This book covers the last phase of Israel's tribal federation (Eli and Samuel) and its transition to a monarchy and the beginning of a state. The regnal years of Saul are incomplete at 1 Sam 13:1, so a guess at about twenty years would seem reasonable, given that David was thirty when

---

60. Rost, *Succession to the Throne of David*. Keys, *Wages of Sin*.
61. Wright, *David, King of Israel*.
62. Gilmour, *Representing the Past*, 1.

he became king at Hebron.[63] A summary list of Saul's achievements appears at 1 Sam 14:47–52, though the stories of his reign and conflicts with David continue for many more chapters, indicating where the compiler's real interests lay. David's regnal years are given as forty; seven years and six months in Hebron and thirty-three years in Jerusalem (2 Sam 5:4–5; cf. 2:11). His reign is conventionally reckoned c. 1000–960 BCE, though the biblical regnal years are rather obviously round numbers, so it is possible that David reigned around 980–950.[64]

In the late twentieth century it became fashionable amongst some scholars to deny the existence of an early state of Israel (i.e., a monarchy, court, central administration, regional officials, and standing army), and even of David himself. The debate continues between these "minimalists" and rigorous archaeologists who take a less skeptical view.[65] Among the latter is William Dever, who prioritizes archaeological evidence before examining the claims of biblical texts, and his work informs what follows.

There is little archaeological evidence for the reign of Saul, though this is not surprising, since he was a transitional figure in the introduction of the monarchy. According to 1 Sam 15:34, Saul had a house in Gibeah, usually identified with Tell el-Ful, just north of Jerusalem. Excavations there have revealed a fortress with thick walls and square towers dated to the late eleventh century, and this would fit with Saul's reign.[66] However, evidence is lacking that supports the accounts of Saul's wars with the Philistines, Amalekites, Ammonites, Moabites, Edomites, or Arameans.

It was announced in 2008 that, for the first time in the archaeology of Judah, a fortified city from the time of King David had been discovered at Khirbet Qeiyafa, identified as the biblical Shaaraim (Josh 15:36; 1 Sam 17:52; 1 Chr 4:31) in the valley of Elah, the location of David's combat with Goliath. Dever emphasizes the implications of this discovery:

1. This is essentially a short-lived, one period site whose late eleventh-early tenth-century date is secured by a ceramic repertoire that even low chronology advocates agree is very early.

---

63. Provan, Long, and Longman, *History*, 199–201

64. Dever, *Beyond the Texts*, 345.

65. For an influential rebuttal of the minimalists, see Dever, *What Did the Biblical Writers Know?*

66. Dever, *Beyond the Texts*, 344.

2. This is a strategically located fortress right on the border with Philistia that was deliberately planned, constructed, and provisioned, despite logistical difficulties.

3. This can only be understood as a government-backed barracks town, the houses incorporated into the casemate wall, just as they are at later Judahite district centers such as Beersheba, Tell Beit Mirsim, and Tell en-Naṣbeh. The notion that Khirbet Qeiyafa is simply a rural village, or a Philistine site, is absurd. Qeiyafa provides ironclad evidence of the sort of defense planning that only a centralized government was capable of achieving—in short, a nascent Judahite monarchy or, if one wishes, a kingdom.[67]

Dever concludes that in "this one case there is a striking convergence between the archaeological evidence and the biblical text. That earns the epithet *proven* or *likely* here."[68]

The Tel Dan stela, an Aramaic inscription on a broken stone was incorporated into an outer gate wall that was destroyed by the Assyrians in 732 BCE. It was found in 1993–95 and dated close to 741 BCE. It refers specifically to the "dynasty of David," and even names two kings known in the Bible: Jehoram of Israel (Ahab's son) and Amaziah of Judah.[69] This evidence confirms there was a historical David and that he founded a dynasty that was well known to neighbors.

The Aramean king Hadadezer, who appears in 2 Samuel 8 and 10, is known to have ruled Zobah and may have been a contemporary of David. However, Dever reckons that many of Samuel's battle accounts appear fantastical; David may have been able to contain the Philistines, but it is unrealistic to think he totally subdued them.[70] There is no archeological evidence that would render credible David's wars with Syria or the tribal kingdoms of Transjordan.

Date of Composition

The hypothesis of the Succession Narrative pointed towards a date for an early source document not long after the accession of Solomon to

---

67. Dever, *Beyond the Texts*, 323.
68. Dever, *Beyond the Texts*, 344.
69. Dever, *Beyond the Texts*, 348f.
70. Dever, *Beyond the Texts*, 347.

the throne, perhaps when other contenders for the throne still existed. It seems feasible that the bulk of Samuel was written during the earlier part of the monarchy, with some editorial additions added later.[71] It may have been composed for the benefit of those, either at the royal court or outside it, who could benefit from an understanding of kings and their use of power.[72] However, it is difficult to identify a definite setting or date of composition for such a narrative.

The hypothesis of the Deuteronomistic History points towards a much later date during the monarchy, or even to the exile for the final form. Personal memories of interactions with any of the characters involved would by then have long become stories, perhaps with embellishments or legendry overlays. David became a hugely important figure in Israel's memory and imagination and lay at the heart of Israel's hope for a Messiah. However, as we have explored the complexities of the narrative in its final form, we have discovered a much more disturbing portrait, subverting that exalted status.

3. Theological Perspectives

Several interrelated aspects of the divine character are apparent in this book; I will highlight sovereignty and vulnerability, repentance and covenant.

Divine Sovereignty and Vulnerability

How might we understand YHWH's anger against Israel such that "he incited David against them?" to hold a census (2 Sam 24:1)? This is a particular problem in that David later realizes that he has sinned and that his people must endure punishment; how can he be guilty if God was ultimately responsible? One way of resolving this theological conundrum is found in 1 Chr 21:1 (see chapter 8 below), but a book-wide consideration of YHWH's sovereignty might help.

Near the beginning of Samuel YHWH is twice said to have closed Hannah's womb (1 Sam 1:5, 6). Some might say that the attribution of her condition to YHWH was a good thing since Hannah was able to go to the source of her problem and entreat YHWH's favor, and that this finally

---

71. E.g., Chapman, *1 Samuel*, 223.
72. As suggested by Westbrook, *"He Will Take Your Daughters,"* 18.

led to her conception. Yet Hannah's childlessness caused her extreme distress, and so it is reasonable to ask what readers should make of such attributions of negative situations to God. Are they simply a conventional way of explaining something mysterious? Although several of Israel's matriarchs had difficulties conceiving, it is not said that YHWH had closed their wombs.[73] Hannah's seems a special case.

When an evil spirit "from YHWH" is said to torment Saul on several occasions (16:14, cf. 16:16, 23; 18:10; 19:9), is this simply a conventional explanation for otherwise strange behavior, or an instance of divine judgment, as seems to be the case in several other places?

- Eli's sons would not listen to him "for it was the will of the LORD to kill them" (1 Sam 2:25).
- As Saul pursued David, he was diverted when the spirit of God came upon him and he fell into a prophetic frenzy (1 Sam 19:23f).
- YHWH struck Nabal and he died; David understood this as judgment (1 Sam 25:38–39).
- When Uzzah touched the ark the anger of YHWH struck him (2 Sam 6:7).
- YHWH struck David's child born to Bathsheba so that he died (2 Sam 12:15).
- YHWH ordained the defeat of Ahitophel's good counsel to bring about the ruin of Absalom (2 Sam 17:14).

This regular invocation of YHWH's sovereignty coheres with the book's emphasis on giving *due weight* to YHWH, as pronounced by the man of God to Eli in 2:29-30.[74] David gives weight to YHWH during much of his early career, when settled as king in Jerusalem (2 Sam 7) and in some later stages of his reign, such as during his retreat from Jerusalem (2 Sam 15). His exclusive devotion to YHWH shows no sign of wavering throughout his life, and this must be the reason for his measure of all the kings after him in the book of Kings. In contrast, Saul set up a monument

---

73. Sarah is barren (Gen 11:30) but conceives in old age, as YHWH promised (Gen 21:1–2). Isaac prays for Rachel because she is barren, and YHWH grants his prayer (Gen 25:21). YHWH sees that Leah is unloved and opens her womb (29:31), and eventually remembers Rachel and opens her womb (Gen 30:22). Manoah's wife is also said to be barren (Judg 13:2–3).

74. See Long, *Samuel*, 27–28.

in his own honor (1 Sam 15:12) and appealed to Samuel to "honor me before the elders of my people and before Israel" (1 Sam 15:30).

While YHWH's sovereignty must be accorded due weight, YHWH's vulnerability is also evident. If Hannah's Song points forward to the monarchy (1 Sam 2:10), the last words of Phineas' wife point forward to the exile (1 Sam 4:21f). Brueggemann comments on the latter:

> This is an extraordinary piece of theology by this dying, unnamed daughter-in-law. She has grasped the point of capture of the ark and its nearly unutterable significance. After the accent on "save" in verse 3, we might have expected her to say that YHWH's capacity to save has gone. But no, she says "glory." She understands that the issue is not Israel's future, but *YHWH*'s own loss. It is YHWH who has been shamed and humiliated, and who has lost credence. . . . [She] knows that this God is exposed and vulnerable, not generically sovereign, but vulnerable to the vagaries of historical challenge. She ponders the deep disruption in the very character of YHWH, the one completely at risk in the risk of Israel.[75]

This woman's story signals the theological depth that Israel's story must acquire in light of the exile. It sets the scene for a narrative depiction of YHWH that provides theological clues for the Israelite experience of exile.

Divine Repentance and Covenant

Saul's dealings with the Amalekites (1 Sam 15) raise questions about the divine instructions to utterly destroy the enemy on account of their past opposition (Exod 17:8–15), yet since I have already explored such questions in chapter 4, I will focus instead on the divine rejection of Saul as king (15:10–35). It seems strange that God should choose Saul to be king, only to revoke that choice for what might seem a trivial reason. I have found helpful Terence Fretheim's essay which proposes that divine foreknowledge of the future is limited and finds the key to this passage in the nature of divine constancy.[76]

Fretheim begins with the important point that the stories about Saul were written from a later perspective, informed by questions about

---

75. Brueggemann, *Ichabod towards Home*, 8f.

76. Fretheim, "Divine Constancy," 267–73. This essay builds on Fretheim's previous work, *Suffering of God*, 1–78.

YHWH's commitment to David, as later expressed in the phrase ". . . but I will not take my steadfast love from him, as I took it from Saul" (2 Sam 7:15). There must have been an anxiety about the consequences of David's (and his descendants') sins subsequent to this affirmation of YHWH's commitment, given what had happened to Saul, especially when prayer and repentance were ineffective in his case (15:24-25, 30).[77] This enables Fretheim to interpret Samuel's definitive statement:

> The LORD has torn the kingdom of Israel from you this very day, and has given it to a neighbor of yours, who is better than you. Moreover the Glory of Israel will not recant or change his mind; for he is not a mortal, that he should change his mind. (15:28-29)

Samuel settles all doubts about David by insisting that God will not repent of this decision, i.e., this is not a general statement to the effect that God never has a change of mind, but rather a pronouncement of foreclosure regarding the particular promise to David.[78]

Fretheim goes on to discuss several other passages that affirm God's commitment to David, Ps 132:11 as well as the likely reference to Davidic kingship in Ps 110:4 and Num 23:19.

> 1 Samuel 15 is thus shaped by those who would deny that one can draw any conclusions regarding the Davidic dynasty on the basis of extrapolations made from God's relationship to Saul's kingship. The situation has changed. Indeed, God made an unconditional commitment to David, which means that God has given up the kind of freedom displayed in the rejection of Saul's kingship. The relinquishment of freedom in a given sphere is, of course, entailed in any statement of promise. While the kingship of Saul was explicitly conditioned by the obedience of both king and people (1 Sam 12:14-15, 25), the kingship of David was not. God placed the kingship on an entirely new footing compared to that of Saul. Why? Because God learned something from the experience (and experiment) with Saul.[79]

Those interpreters who have questioned God's fairness with regard to Saul seem to assume that God must have foreseen the outcome of

---

77. "Something very much like the situation in Psalm 89 needs to be envisaged as the context for this chapter." Fretheim, "Divine Constancy," 269.

78. "There may well be other persons and actions concerning which God will repent of a promised good (cf. Jer 18:9-10)." Fretheim, "Divine Constancy," 269.

79. Fretheim, "Divine Constancy," 270-71.

Saul's kingship, and thus should not have chosen him in the first place. However, God has so created the world that genuine human choices and responsibilities mean that God chooses self-limitations that entail foreseeing possibilities in an open future, not an eternal blueprint. Special circumstances surrounded the introduction of Israel's monarchy, given concern that the kingship would go the way of all the nations (see 1 Sam 8:7–9, 19–20; 10:25; 12:14–15, 24–25), so safeguards were necessary and ground rules established that were clear to everyone, including Saul.

In a remarkable concession to the will of the people, God acquiesced to the elders' demand, and this reveals a God who is anything but legalistic, insistent on God's own way or unwilling to compromise. A number of First Testament passages make clear that God moves into the future taking human thought and action into account (see Exod 32:11–14; Num 14:11–20). Samuel responded with anger to God's regrets over Saul (1 Sam 15:10–11) and sought to persuade God to a different course of action. The extensive narrative that follows (1 Sam 15:12–26) "may be seen as Samuel's attempt to discern the appropriateness of the divine decision and to make matters clear to Saul."[80]

It is vital to recognize that "God's primary concern in all of this is for the future of *Israel* (cf. 1 Sam 9:16; 10:1; 12:22)."[81] Chapters 13–15 chart a trend in Saul's kingship that might lead to the destruction of Israel, and so it became necessary to intervene before it reached a point where not even God could retrieve the situation. So, it may be said that Saul suffers for the sake of the people—in some sense "he is a scapegoat for Israel's insistence on trying this new way." Fretheim concludes that this narrative is

> a vivid testimony to the *historical* character of God's activity in the world, both in what God does to initiate kingship in the first place and in the changes God makes in view of new circumstances. God works with what is available at any moment, with human beings as they are, with all their foibles and flaws, and within existing societal structures and possibilities, however inadequate. But God does not only "make do" with what there is to work with; at the same time God places a high level of confidence in the human instruments chosen—in this case Saul, as well as the people. God's activity is thus conditioned and limited by such structures, which in turn are always changing, and with

---

80. Fretheim, "Divine Constancy," 272.
81. Fretheim, "Divine Constancy," 272.

which God needs to move as well, given the way in which he has chosen to relate to the world.[82]

The book of Samuel depicts God's exercise of power in the world as being self-limited; God subjects Godself to extreme vulnerability and risks reputational damage.

The Rhetoric of Samuel

Samuel is a book about the introduction of Israel's monarchy, but it is not a collection of dry facts and dates concerning such an institution. Integral to monarchy is the handing of office from fathers to sons, and Samuel is a book that invites readers to explore the complex relationships between fathers and sons—and wives and daughters have important roles as well. Eli, Samuel, and David all have sons who go astray. Saul's sons come to violent ends, and by the end of the book Mephibosheth is his only surviving grandson.[83]

If it was the case that Samuel reached its final shape towards the end of the exile, when some were hoping for a restored monarchy, then the story of Saul shouts "no more kings!" for the returning exiles, as Barbara Green says.[84] On the other hand, David shows great promise as a king at ease with the role, who is in receipt of a dynastic covenant, and who is responsive to YHWH on many occasions. Nevertheless, his behavior towards women, his treatment of Uriah, his loss of control of his sons, and his shady dealings with the Gibeonites, all confirm the follies of conventional monarchy.

---

82. Fretheim, "Divine Constancy," 273.

83. Although Saul wishes to do away with David through many chapters, he calls David "my son" on two occasions (1 Sam 24:16; 26:17, 21, 25).

84. Green, *King Saul's Asking*, xvi. Hopes were placed in Zerubbabel by the early post-exilic prophets Haggai (2:20–23) and Zechariah (4:8–13). See Rose, "Zerubbabel."

7

The Book of Kings

Some stories of Solomon are well-known; his wisdom, riches, temple-building, and the visit of the Queen of Sheba. The dramatic narratives of the prophets Elijah and Elisha dominate the center of this book. There are a couple of highlights in the reigns of Hezekiah and Josiah before things end badly with the destruction of Jerusalem and the deportation to Babylon. Is this book more than a collection of stories providing some overview of the history of the monarchy in Judah and Israel? What might its compilers and editors have wanted to convey to its readers?[1]

1. Literary Perspectives

Compared with the fascinating interactions between Samuel, Saul, David, and God in the book of Samuel, Kings seems more prosaic. Yet literary perspectives continue to provide insight into the book's arrangement, and some parts are amenable to narrative approaches. The evaluative approach that I will employ here is mainly drawn from the book of Deuteronomy, especially what it has to say about kings and prophets.

---

1. An explanation of why 1 & 2 Kings should be read as one book was given in footnote 88, near the end of chapter 1.

Arrangement

Several scholars have recognized that Kings is arranged palistrophically as in the following table:[2]

The Book of Kings: Literary Arrangement

A	The people of YHWH under a single Davidic king	1 Kgs 1:1—11:43
B	The separation of the two kingdoms	1 Kgs 12:1—14:20
C	Kings of Israel and Judah	1 Kgs 14:21—16:28
D	The house of Ahab	1 Kgs 16:29—2 Kgs 11:20
C'	Kings of Israel and Judah	2 Kgs 12:1—16:20
B'	The end of the kingdom of Israel	2 Kgs 17:1—41
A'	The people of YHWH under a single Davidic king	2 Kgs 18:1—25:30

Recognizing the literary structure helps to see that it begins and ends with YHWH's people ruled by a single Davidic king (A and A'). There is a major disruption of this order with the break-away of Northern tribes of Israel from Judah that only ends with the entire demise of the North (B and B'). The protracted outworking of this division is indicated by the interwoven sets of regnal accounts (C and C'). What is particularly striking, though, is the attention given in the central section to the house of Ahab, ruling the Northern kingdom (D). What did the final editors of the book intend readers to gather from their focus on the North at the heart of their work?

Marvin Sweeney has identified one clue in the explicit comparison between the apostasy of Manasseh of Judah and that of Ahab of Israel (2 Kgs 21:3). "Since most interpreters correctly observe that Jeroboam ben Nebat sets the pattern for apostasy among the northern kings, Ahab's mention here has attracted little attention."[3] Now Ahab was the primary monarch of the house of Omri, which was overthrown by Jehu in 2 Kgs 9–10 and all its male members killed, yet Ahab's daughter Athaliah survived because of her marriage to King Ahaziah of Judah (2 Kgs 8:18, 26). She nearly destroyed the entire house of David, but her infant son Joash survived to reclaim the throne after a coup led by the priest Jehoida (2 Kings 11).

---

2. See Walsh, "The Organization of 2 Kings 3–11," 245.
3. Sweeney, *Kings*, 11. On Jeroboam's apostasy, see 1 Kgs 12:26–33 and 13:33–34.

From the time of Joash on, the entire house of David is also descended from the house of Omri. The house of David therefore becomes subject to the judgment pronounced by Elijah against Ahab and the house of Omri (1 Kgs 21:17–29), which helps to explain the explicit parallel drawn between the actions of Ahab and those of Manasseh, who follows in the tradition of his Omride ancestral line. It also helps to explain the portrayal of the death of his righteous grandson, Josiah ben Amon, who is granted the right to die in peace by the prophet Huldah before the judgment against Jerusalem and Judah is carried out (2 Kgs 22:11–20).... The fate of the house of Omri was ultimately realized in the fate of the House of David in 1–2 Kings.[4]

A second question that is prompted by the book's literary arrangement is the sheer quantity of stories about the prophets Elijah and Elisha in the central section. A number of other named prophets appear throughout the book: Nathan (1 Kgs 1:11–45); Ahijah (1 Kgs 11:29–39; 12:15; 14:1–18; 15:29); Shemaiah (1 Kgs 12:22–24); Jehu ben Hanani (16:1–7); Micaiah (1 Kgs 22:1–28); Jonah ben Amittai (2 Kgs 14:25); Isaiah (2 Kgs 19:1—20:19); and Huldah (2 Kgs 22:14–20). In addition, there are numerous stories of, and summaries of messages from, unnamed prophets or "men of God" (e.g., 1 Kgs 13:1–32; 20:13–43; 2 Kgs 17:13, 23; 21:10–15), and it is said that "the word of YHWH came" to several kings without specifying the means, although prophets were most likely involved (1 Kgs 5:11–13; 11:11–13; 16:1–4; 2 Kgs 10:30; 15:12). Thus, while kings head the storyline, prophets also appear frequently. Yet in the central section, the stories of Elijah and Elisha outweigh those of the kings at the time. (In Elisha's case, the king is often unnamed.) These narratives convey more than their prophets' words and deeds; they provide glimpses of their characters.

To pursue these issues further I will focus attention on the initial, central, and final sections of the book.

The People of God under a Single Davidic King
(1 Kgs 1:1—11:43)

This first main section begins with the close of David's reign and the transition to Solomon's rule. This is an appropriate prologue because David, and his faithfulness to YHWH, remains a benchmark for all subsequent

---

4. Sweeney, *Kings*, 12.

kings. Yet beneath the surface of David's adherence to YHWH, there are serious causes for concern, as we have seen in Samuel, and they reappear in David's final scenes. There follows the extensive account of Solomon's reign, centered on the construction and dedication of the temple. Ostensibly the high point of Israel's monarchy, it is actually the primary exhibit in the case against Israel's kings.

Prologue: The End of David's Reign

The prologue begins with a curious little vignette concerning the aged King David and his state of health: he could not get warm. The great leader, who had united Israel and defeated its enemies, is no longer the actor; he is acted upon by his servants. What might warm up the old boy? A beautiful young virgin? But even this does not succeed; David is impotent. Were the servants smirking? Readers are certainly meant to do so! The sexual overtones are made explicit at the end of v. 4. David's loss of virility disqualifies him as king;[5] thus the question of succession is raised.

Abishag plays a minor part in the subsequent story, appearing briefly as David's attendant in 1:15[6], and she is then the subject of Adonijah's miscalculated bid (2:13-25). Although Hannah had disappeared from the book of Samuel by 2:22, she had played a major part in setting up that long narrative with her passionate prayer, her vivid song of praise, and her costly faithfulness in giving over her son to YHWH's service. Here Abishag has no prayer, no voice, only her virginity and her beauty; she is wrenched from her family and community to meet the king's needs (cf. 1 Sam 8:13). We are not told what happened to her after his death.

The function of this episode becomes evident as the struggle for succession follows, initiated by Adonijah (1:11-27). David appears passive as court intrigue goes on around him, but eventually rouses himself, when approached by Solomon's faction, Bathsheba and the prophet Nathan. Finally, David takes control and issues instructions regarding Solomon's public coronation; this goes ahead, to public acclamation (1:28-40). Adonijah realizes that he has lost and capitulates (1:41-53).

---

5. Brueggemann, *Kings*, 12.

6. This note supplies Bathsheba's point of view, as Berlin observes, *Poetics and Interpretation*, 28, "one can feel a twinge of jealousy pass through Bathsheba as she silently notes the presence of a younger, fresher woman."

David rouses himself once more to give Solomon a final "testament" (2:1–9). The first part of this charge echoes God's commission of Joshua (Josh 1:6–9), "Be strong, be courageous, and keep the charge of the LORD your God, walking in his ways and keeping his statutes." YHWH's promise of successors to David is recalled (2 Sam 7:11–16), though the condition of faithfulness was not present in the original, and so it represents "an exceedingly important turn in the royal theology of Israel."[7] He then gives Solomon specific instructions to execute his long-time general, Joab (despite Joab's unswerving loyalty), to reward the sons of Barzillai for their father's loyalty, and to bring retribution on Shimei. The language of "knowledge" and "wisdom" is striking in this speech (2:5, 6, 9, 9), yet this is a dark and deathly wisdom,[8] constituting a "warped understanding of Torah observance," according to Sweeney:

> When read in the context of the entire DtrH with its portrayal of the fall of the house of David, David's testament to Solomon indicates that the dynasty was corrupt at its very foundation. It portrays a private side to David and Solomon that contrasts with the oft-stated portrayal of David's righteousness and fidelity to YHWH and Solomon's reputation for great wisdom.[9]

The prologue concludes with a formulaic notice of David's death and burial, and a summary of his reign (2:10–11).

Although subsequent chapters will recount the reigns of many kings, the overall effect will be to question their power and significance. Women will occasionally appear, but rarely play significant roles. Prophets only become more involved at the end of Solomon's reign.

---

7. Brueggemann, *Kings*, 26.

8. One of the themes identified in 2 Samuel is that of wisdom. Provan, "Hearing the Historical Books," 265, concludes that David's mind is darkened, as he lives under divine judgment following the Bathsheba/Uriah episode.

9. Sweeney, *Kings*, 60, 61.

The Reign of Solomon: Literary Arrangement

A	Solomon eliminates threats to his security	2:12–46
	Solomon established on the throne	2:12
	Adonijah	2:13–25
	Abiathar and Joab	2:26–35
	Shimei	2:36–46
B	Solomon's wisdom, riches, and honor (i)	3:1—5:18
	Ambivalent summary: wife and devotion	3:1–3
	First divine encounter	3:4–15
	Solomon's wise judgment of prostitutes	3:16–28
	Solomon's officials and taxation districts	4:1–19
	Solomon's trade, wisdom, and reputation	4:20–34
	Solomon's negotiations with Hiram and work force	5:1–18
C	Solomon builds the temple and palace complex	6:1—7:51
	Chronological note	6:1
	Temple: main structure	6:2–10
	Second divine encounter	6:11–13
	Temple: internal decoration	6:14–38
	Palace complex	7:1–12
	Hiram brought in for bronze work	7:13–47
	Solomon completes gold work	7:48–51
C'	Solomon dedicates the temple	8:1—9:9
	Inaugural procession and speech	8:1–13
	Solomon addresses the assembly	8:14–21
	Solomon addresses YHWH, with pastoral reflection	8:22–53
	Solomon blesses the assembly	8:54–61
	Sacrifice, consecration, festival	8:62–66
	Third divine encounter	9:1–9
B'	Solomon's wisdom, riches, and honor (ii)	9:10—11:13
	Temporal formula	9:10
	Solomon's association with Hiram (and work force)	9:11–28
	Solomon's association with the Queen of Sheba	10:1–13
	Solomon's riches, wisdom, and honor	10:14–29
	Solomon's wives and apostasy	11:1–8
	Fourth divine encounter	11:9–13
A'	YHWH raises up threats to Solomon's security	11:14–43
	Hadad of Edom	11:14–22
	Rezon of Damascus	11:23–25
	Jeroboam of Israel	11:26–40
	Formulaic notice of Solomon's death	11:41–43

The Reign of Solomon

The account of Solomon's reign is arranged with strong symmetrical elements, but also significant variations.[10] At first glance it appears to proceed chronologically, however details reveal that certain elements have been collected by theme; i.e., the whole has been carefully crafted for emphasis. There are inverse parallels between the opening section in which Solomon eliminates threats to his security (2:12–46) and the closing section in which YHWH raises up threats to his security (11:14–43). The themes of Solomon's wisdom, wealth, and fame appear throughout both the longer inner sections, 3:1—5:18 and 9:10—11:13, and there are striking symmetrical parallels between their five elements. The center of the account is occupied by the temple; its construction (6:1—7:51) and dedication (8:1—9:9).

Solomon Eliminates Threats to His Security

The account of Solomon's reign begins with his ruthless consolidation of power. A solution to the threat of his half-brother is conveniently presented by Adonijah's arrogant request for a consolation prize, then those who had supported Adonijah are removed. Solomon banishes Abiathar, then has Joab executed in the cause of "peace" (2:34). Solomon sets conditions requiring Shimei to remain in Jerusalem, but later orders his execution, despite his journey to Gath not violating the prohibition of crossing the Wadi Kidron.[11] Since Abiathar is later listed as a priest along with Zadok (4:4), it seems his banishment came years into the reign, so Solomon's fulfillments of David's testament have been deliberately collected at this point.[12] The first thing we are meant to notice about Solomon's reign is that it entailed the shrewd and ruthless use of violence; there is an irony about Solomon's name.

---

10. See the discussion of Walsh, *1 Kings*, 150–56, though his analysis overplays some elements and overlooks some others.

11. A journey from Jerusalem to Gath does not require a crossing of the Wadi Kidron, according to Sweeney, *Kings*, 70–71.

12. No mention is made of rewarding the sons of Barzillai.

Solomon's Wisdom, Wealth and Fame (i)

Solomon's reign appears to begin well. When invited to ask for a gift during a dream encounter with God, he responds with humility and a request for wisdom; YHWH is pleased and grants wisdom along with riches and honor. Yet significant details add to the unease generated by Solomon's ruthless consolidation of power. Once his kingdom is established, the first thing noted concerns his marriage alliance to Pharaoh's daughter (3:1); while this reflects Solomon's international standing, it is a reminder of Israel's oppression in its exodus traditions. At this point, Solomon is loyal to YHWH, and his public piety extravagant, but why does he go to offer sacrifices at the high place in Gibeon (3:4), particularly when the ark was already located in Jerusalem?[13] YHWH appears to Solomon in a dream, and a conversation ensues (3:5–15); Solomon appears grateful, humble, responsible: pleased, YHWH grants the request for wisdom and more, but with a condition attached. This is the first of four divine encounters that will punctuate the account of the reign.

The story of Solomon's judgment between the two prostitutes (3:16–27) demonstrates his wisdom, and yet it also raises questions, since the threat of violence gives a disturbing tinge to Solomon's insight into human nature.[14]

The following section begins with a list of Solomon's high officials, concluding with Adoniram who was, shockingly, "in charge of the forced labor" (4:7). It appears from the account of Solomon's administrative districts (4:7–19) that he "ruled Judah directly as his home tribe, but ruled Israel through administrators much as one would rule a foreign or subject state."[15] The staggering extent of Solomon's realm, provisions, military forces,[16] and wisdom is celebrated, such that peace and wellbeing prevail

---

13. Sweeney, *Kings*, 72–73, reads the reference to high places and to Gibeon as both critical of Solomon. See also Walsh, *1 Kings*, 72–73.

14. Anderson, "Sword of Solomon," 79, shows how this incident follows the violent concept of wisdom established in 2 Sam 13–1 Kgs 2, in which all the violence is framed by "the sword" (2 Sam 11:25; 12:9, 10). "Thus, in addition to the shock of the mere violence of it, the 'punch' of Solomon's call to 'bring me a sword' . . .also rests in his echoing of the curse lingering over the House of David."

15. Sweeney, *Kings*, 89. The mention of one official in Judah at v. 19b does not appear in the MT, only in the LXX. According to Sweeney, *Kings*, 89–95, the introduction of administrative districts appears intended to weaken major elements within the northern tribes, especially Ephraim and Manasseh.

16. Sweeney, *Kings*, 100, notes that the number of horses appears exaggerated; it is corrected to 4,000 in 2 Chr 9:25.

(4:20–34). His combined tribal groupings of Judah and Israel fulfils God's promises to Abraham and Jacob (Gen 22:17; 32:12), while his control over the region between the Euphrates and Egypt amounts to a minor empire. The celebration of Solomon's wisdom leads into the preparations for temple construction (5:1–18). When Solomon receives an approach from Hiram, king of Tyre, who had been David's friend (2 Sam 5:11–12), he responds by setting out his intention "to build a house for the name of YHWH my God" (5:5). A treaty between the two kings provides Solomon with the timber required in return for food and oil, the produce of many farms, and a vast workforce is established to prepare materials.

It all sounds wonderful; Israel and Judah never had it so good! Yet the characterization of the workforce as "conscripted forced labor" (5:13, cf. 4:6), together with hundreds of "supervisors" (5:15) should strike readers with alarm; this sounds chillingly like Israel's founding experience in Egypt! It does not cohere with the previous description of the people of Judah and Israel as eating, drinking, and happy (4:20) and living in safety during Solomon's lifetime. The conventional expression of well-being, "all of them under their vines and fig trees" (4:25) sounds ironic.[17] When we recall David's language of knowledge and wisdom in his last testament to Solomon (2:5, 6, 9, 9), Solomon's dream request for wisdom begins to look less than innocent.[18]

Solomon's Temple Construction and Dedication

Solomon's construction of the stupendous temple and royal palace is described in sufficient detail to impress readers with the temple's glory and the care taken to ensure its sacred quality. The extensive description is interrupted by a word from YHWH that raises conditions of covenant faithfulness a notch from their initial mention in the Gibeon dream. The temple takes seven years to build, while the larger palace complex, made up of five buildings, takes *thirteen* years to complete (6:38—7:1) at great cost (7:9–12). Brueggemann's comment is perceptive: "By placing

---

17. See Brueggemann, "'Vine and Fig Tree'" in *Social Reading*, 91–110.

18. Howard-Brook, *Come Out, My People!*, 98–104, traces the theme of suspect wisdom through the flattery of David by the wise woman of Tekoa, as one who can "discern good and evil" (2 Sam 14:17), and to the temptation in the garden of Eden concerning the fruit of "the tree of the knowledge of good and evil" (Gen 2:17). He points out that "Solomon is overheard praying (in his dream) for exactly what, from the perspective of Genesis, *has been forbidden* to humanity" (102).

7:1–12 at the center of the temple report, the text skillfully shows that the temple is part of the royal complex, situated where it is to legitimate and propagandize for the monarchy."[19] The report concludes with Solomon's appointment of Hiram of Tyre[20] to make several iconic bronze fixtures for the temple, together with numerous smaller implements. Finally, Solomon himself oversees the making of numerous gold items. Walsh notes that this long and detailed account of the construction has the effect of bringing the pace of the narrative, which has been slowing gradually, to a complete halt as extended description takes over, establishing an atmosphere of enthusiasm for the glorious, extravagant, monumental edifice.[21]

Solomon holds center stage during the dedication of the temple in chapter 8. All Israel is present, the elders process, the priests carry the ark with the tent and vessels, vast sacrifices are made, and when the priests emerge from depositing the ark a cloud fills the house; readers are intended to recall the dedication of the tabernacle (Exod 40:34–35). It is easy to be dazzled by all this splendor and to miss the significance of the observation regarding the ark in v. 9, but Brueggemann notes its contrasting simplicity:

> Indeed the ark is empty... except for the Torah tablets! This low voice of presence is a vigorous reassertion of old Mosaic tradition that Yahweh's presence is known primarily as *commandment* and Israel's reception of Yahweh's presence in primarily in *obedience*.[22]

Solomon's poetic declaration (8:12–13) addresses the darkened holy of holies in which the ark resides, and which would have received the light of the sun as it rose in the east each morning.

> Insofar as darkness precedes the first act of creation, the temple symbolizes the center of the cosmos created by YHWH, but the darkened state of the holy of holies indicates that YHWH remains separate from the created world.[23]

---

19. Brueggemann, *Kings*, 104.

20. Is this the same Hiram as the king of Tyre? Ancient kings were known to be involved in the technicalities of bronze casting. See Dalley, *Hanging Garden of Babylon*, chapter 4 on Sennacherib.

21. Walsh, *1 Kings*, 108.

22. Brueggemann, *Kings*, 107.

23. Sweeney, *Kings*, 132.

In Solomon's first address to the congregation, the exodus tradition and David's dynasty are held together, including YHWH's approval of David's concept of building a house for YHWH's name (x5). The central passage is Solomon's prayer, which has two distinct parts. The first (vv. 22–26) is an appeal to YHWH, linking the incomparable, covenant keeping God of Israel to the covenant made with David and his successors, and including the element of conditionality that did not appear in 2 Samuel 7. The second part (vv. 27–53) begins with an arresting question-mark over the very concept of housing God and emphasis upon the distinct nuance of "the name," while heaven is God's proper dwelling. This leads into a series of seven advance petitions for divine response to prayers addressed "towards this place" in case of various disasters, culminating in those of repentant captives in foreign lands (vv. 46–53).

Solomon's closing blessing invokes YHWH's promise of rest given through Moses; it appeals for YHWH's presence so that Israel might practice his commandments and fulfil its purpose of witness to the nations (v. 60)—all strongly Deuteronomic emphases (see Deut 4:5–8). The narrative concludes with Solomon's further extravagant sacrifices and an all-Israel seven-day festival.

The account of YHWH's second dream appearance to Solomon is a fitting conclusion, since it is a response to his long prayer of dedication. But affirmation is accompanied by a redoubled conditionality on Solomon's adherence to YHWH, augmented by a shocking warning of disaster for Israel and the temple, for Solomon and his dynasty.

Solomon's Wisdom, Wealth and Fame (ii)

What marks this later section about Solomon's wisdom, wealth, and fame is his increased associations with foreign monarchs. First, a collection of topics in 9:10–28 underlines that Solomon became a monarch like Pharaoh. Solomon has further dealings with Hiram (9:11–15), ceding him twenty Galilean cities rather than the food promised earlier (5:20); Solomon appears to beat Hiram on the real estate deal, but surely it is a strange move to cede part of the promised land! In an account of Solomon's continued use of forced labor in further construction projects, it is asserted that non-Israelites were involved (9:15–23). Pharaoh is mentioned as giving a dowry in the form of Gezer, and his daughter appears again (9:16, 24). Solomon is further involved with Hiram in a trading arrangement with Solomon's fleet in the Red Sea (9:26–28).

The account of the visit of the Queen of Sheba follows (10:1-13), further celebrating Solomon's wisdom, opulence, and divine favor, interwoven with more details of luxury items brought from afar for the temple and House of the Forest of Lebanon (10:11-22). There is a hyperbolic claim regarding Solomon's riches, wisdom, and fame, and a further record of his chariots and horse trading (10:23-29). These passages were originally written to exalt Solomon, but in the context of the adjacent chapters, they reinforce his fascination with foreign women, military equipment, and ostentation.

It is hardly a surprise, then, to read that Solomon loved "many foreign women," and that they "turned his heart away after other gods" (11:1-8). The warning not to do so is drawn from Deuteronomy 7:3-4. Solomon actively followed a multi-religious programme of construction. Whereas YHWH was previously pleased with Solomon, here YHWH is "angry," and delivers a second prophetic word (11:9-13). There is nothing positive to say; simply a condemnation of Solomon's mind and practices, and a devastating verdict, only ameliorated out of consideration for David and Jerusalem.

YHWH Raises Up Threats to Solomon's Security

In the final section, YHWH raises up three threats to Solomon's security. The first is Hadad the Edomite, who had fled to Egypt in his youth; we hear little about his threat to Solomon, but a significant amount about his time in Egypt, where he is restrained from returning to Israel by Pharaoh. "Hadad appears as a second Moses and Solomon appears as Pharaoh in a reversal of roles that raises critical questions about Solomon and his rule."[24] The second threat, Rezon, gathered "a marauding band, after the slaughter [like] David" and eventually became king of Damascus; his rise to power is not unlike David's.

The third and most important threat is Jeroboam, and the ironies are louder in that Solomon had placed him in charge of the forced labor of the house of Joseph (11:28). He is found by the prophet Ahijah, whose pronouncement reinforces YHWH's verdict on Solomon, and consequent judgment, and holds out the promise of a dynasty of Jeroboam's own. Ahijah is from Shiloh, the old northern shrine—he "appears as a figure like Samuel; the symbolic action of the torn garment recalls the symbolism employed to express Samuel's tearing the kingdom away from

---

24. Sweeney, *Kings*, 157.

Saul (1 Sam 15:27–28)."²⁵ Solomon seeks to kill Jeroboam, forcing him to flee to Egypt, redoubling the reversal of the exodus echoes. There is an interesting contrast between two prophets: the earlier court operations of Nathan, who brought no "word of YHWH," and the subversive mission of outsider Ahijah, who brings an extensive "thus says YHWH . . ." that re-emphasizes the verdict on Solomon's reign. Prophets are now in play!

Reflections on Solomon

In the sections detailing Solomon's wisdom, wealth, and fame, his reign is portrayed as both extravagant and disturbing, especially in the light of Deuteronomy's law of the king (17:14–20). Some parts appear extraordinarily effusive (especially 4:20–34; 10:6–10, 23–25). It seems likely that Kings includes materials that may be described as propaganda. Kenton Sparks provides a helpful definition: "In its political sense, propaganda is a systematic effort to conform social opinion to the ideologies or viewpoints of those who hold or seek power."²⁶ Yet the overall effect of the account of Solomon's reign is to undermine these "golden age" passages such that their propagandist character is evident.²⁷ As we have seen before, Israelite editors preserved and added to previous compilations

---

25. Sweeney, *Kings*, 159.

26. Sparks, "Propaganda," 819. Sparks summarizes several features of the royal propaganda of the Neo-Assyrian kings that have been demonstrated from the study of ancient Assyrian documents, and these may have played a part in the Solomon account (ibid., 821):
   1. Emphasis was placed on the divine election of the king and on the legitimacy of his claim to the throne.
   2. The king was depicted as a great warrior.
   3. The king was depicted as religiously pious.
   4. The assassinations of competitors in the royal household were covered up by portraying the king as compassionate and measured in his response to those eliminated.
   5. Presentations of the king's life were uniformly positive through selective use of sources, careful omission of troublesome facts, and invention of tradition.
   6. Publication of propaganda was most prominent during periods of threat to the regime's stability—i.e., at its inception and during periods of rebellion or succession.
   7. Propaganda was disseminated to the elite classes through written texts and to the population at large through oral tradition.
   8. Because of their earthy and popular appeal, the tales produced by Neo-Assyrian propaganda sometimes persisted in recognizable form until long after they had served the regime's political purposes.

27. See further, Seibert, *Subversive Scribes*.

rather than make entire revisions of earlier versions. This reinforces the argument that contemporary readers must not read selectively but read particular parts of these accounts *in the light of the whole*.

Solomon's character is not drawn in detail, as were Saul's and David's through the many conversations and relational interactions depicted in Samuel. The significant conversations in which Solomon is involved (rather than giving orders) are few. His audience with Bathsheba concerning Adonijah's request (2:19–25) leads to decisive and brutal elimination of the competition. The dream conversation between YHWH and Solomon (3:5–14) is fascinating and positive in several ways, though YHWH's concluding condition is a significant modification of the previous unconditional commitment to David (2 Sam 7:13–16). YHWH appears a second time in response to Solomon's prayer dedicating the temple, accepting the consecration, but now with stark warnings about apostasy and consequential ruin (9:1–9). But Solomon does not respond; this is hardly a conversation. Solomon's character seems to manifest itself in his achievements and reputation, or does it disappear under his many projects and successes?

The military stability established by David enabled Solomon to organise his realm into an efficient and economically productive nation with sufficient surplus to obtain the materials to construct the temple and many other buildings. He established international relations and trade; he knew how to build an image with architecture, gold, and chariots, and so gained a considerable reputation. He became a (minor) player on the world stage (or at least, that's how he is depicted; the reality was probably not so impressive). The temptations of monarchy were subtle and crept over Solomon with progress. The wisdom that he requested (and was granted) wasn't enough to save him; it was tainted with the assumptions and aspirations of power (and violence where necessary). His "success" relied upon the exploitation of his people, especially the Northern tribes, and finally it broke the unity of the kingdom. It only remained for the arrogance and incompetence of his son Rehoboam to provoke the division between Israel and Judah (12:1–19).

The House of Ahab (1 Kgs 16:29—2 Kgs 11:20)

In the central section, extensive coverage is given to the reigns of Ahab and his second son, Jehoram, and these stories are arranged as a palistrophe:[28]

The House of Ahab: Literary Arrangement

A	Ahab accedes to the throne, introduces Baalism	1 Kgs 16:29–34
B	Ahab and the prophets, especially Elijah	1 Kgs 17:1—2 Kgs 1:18
C	Elisha succeeds Elijah	2 Kgs 2:1–25
B'	Jehoram and the prophets, especially Elisha	2 Kgs 3:1—9:13
A'	Ahab's line is destroyed, Baalism eradicated	2 Kgs 9:14—11:20

Although two northern kings are prominent in these central chapters, they are overshadowed by the most influential of the prophets, Elijah and Elisha, and so I will focus here on some of their stories.[29] Readers often admire the prophets' loyalty to YHWH, their brave announcement of YHWH's words, and their miraculous deeds in YHWH's name. Elijah and Elisha are commonly understood as heroes, compared with corrupt kings and vacillating people. Yet several of their stories are disturbing, and a number of scholars have shown that they require careful and nuanced reading. In what follows, my guides have been the close reading of Roy Heller and the interdisciplinary study of Stuart Lasine.

Heller focusses his evaluative approach to the characters of Elijah and Elisha through the two passages in Deuteronomy concerning prophecy. The first, 12:32—13:5, is part of a wider section expanding on the first commandment (12:1—13:19). It insists that the people must not follow a prophet who provides a sign or miracle and then entices them to follow other gods; indeed, such a prophet should be put to death. Heller points out that this first passage

> from beginning to end sees prophets as problematic, as people who are able, through their words and through the miracles and signs that they are able to do, to seduce and delude and thrust Israel out of the way that they should walk.[30]

---

28. For this structure and discussion, see Walsh, "Organization of 2 Kings 3–11," 245–46.

29. The final two Elisha stories, including his death and burial, occur later in 2 Kgs 13:14–21.

30. Heller, *Elijah and Elisha*, 19.

Deuteronomy contrasts YHWH's word with the words of prophets and insists that *"Israel knows YHWH's word because they can hear and read it within Deuteronomy itself."*[31]

The second passage, Deut 18:15–22, is found in the section of the law code that deals with the administrative offices within society, including judges, kings, and Levitical priests (17:2—18:22). This passage promises that a prophet will come from Israel, and will be like Moses; it explains that prophecy meets the people's request at Horeb not to hear YHWH's voice directly; it insists that prophecy should be taken seriously; it instructs that a false prophet must die; it provides a test of prophetic *in*validity. However, this test is far from clear and definitive because it does not address the question of how to know the prophetic word *is* from YHWH. It is also blatantly simplistic, since it can only be applied in retrospect, it is of no use in "real time." Thus, Heller concludes:

> Although they may be viewed as simplistic on a literal level, rhetorically the Deuteronomic laws about prophets actually press the reader to a more nuanced view of prophecy by showing the complexity and ambiguous aspects of the phenomenon of prophecy as a whole, aspects that play out in all their intricacy and difficulty in the stories of these two prophets.[32]

Lasine sets out a nuanced evaluative approach to the characters of prophets and kings by means of literary theory, psychology, and moral philosophy. He points out that the ethical implications of biblical narratives are open to various construals, and that interpreters often choose to explain the behavior of characters therein in comforting and familiar ways rather than the more precise means of understanding the role of disposition as well as the situational constraints in a character's reported behavior.[33] Lasine also addresses the complex question of difference between contemporary people and those presented in ancient Near Eastern narratives such as Samuel and Kings. While ancient literary works are different from modern ones, their "human intelligibility" allows them to seem familiar to us, and a supposedly "modern" self-structure can be found even in the serpent in the garden of Eden. The narrative rhetoric of biblical stories presents characters as readers' ancestors, and in various places urges readers to identify totally with them; this requires readers

---

31. Heller, *Elijah and Elisha*, 20, emphasis original.
32. Heller, *Elijah and Elisha*, 36.
33. Lasine, *Weighing Hearts*, 10–15.

Elijah

The formal notice of the start of Ahab's reign is followed by the narrator's extremely negative verdict (16:29-30). The note concerning the human cost of rebuilding Jericho adds to the sense of radical departure from YHWH's ways and warnings (16:31-34). Bursting into this situation comes Elijah, announcing to the king the consequences of his embrace of Baal; a contest has begun as to the very source of life—water—and Elijah does not mince his words: "As the LORD the God of Israel lives, before whom I stand, there shall be neither dew nor rain these years, except by my word" (17:1).

However, several aspects of Elijah's introduction should give the reader pause. In Joshua–Kings prophets are usually introduced with the explicit title of "prophet," yet, Elijah is simply introduced geographically. Scholars have been unable to identify Tishbe, and describing Elijah as among the "settlers" of Gilead is also strange since the Hebrew word is used elsewhere for sojourners or foreigners living in a region.[35] Heller suggests that the narrator thrusts Elijah on the reader in a way that reflects his impact upon Ahab. Since

> Elijah is, in a much larger scheme, a representative for the phenomenon of prophecy as a whole, his abrupt, cryptic introduction is exactly what we, as readers and as the original hearers or readers of the text, would have experienced: an individual who appears with little warning, with no known background, produces signs and miracles, and who also claims to declare YHWH's own intentions (Deut 13:1-5). In such a contemporary context, there would be no objective markers for who did or did not truly speak or perform YHWH's word. As such, Elijah's mysterious introduction precisely sets up a scenario aligning with what we have seen as the Deuteronomic attitude towards prophets: hesitancy and suspicion, until proven otherwise.[36]

---

34. Lasine, *Weighing Hearts*, 53–55.
35. Sweeney, *Kings*, 211.
36. Heller, *Elijah and Elisha*, 44.

The introduction of Elijah is very important for establishing his character and prophecy in general. Most commentaries read information from later parts of the story back into 17:1, and come to positive conclusions, but if readers "read forward" the characterization of Elijah is much more ambiguous.[37] His speech invokes the living YHWH, but it continues with a declaration of a drought of unspecified length, purely by Elijah's own permission and power. There is no "word of YHWH," rather Elijah asserts his own word! One of the consistent things that prophets do in Joshua–Kings is to point out apostasy and failures, yet here Elijah makes no connection between the drought and Ahab's apostasy.

However, the word of YHWH does appear in the very next verse. Dubious expectations are overturned through the episode by the Wadi Cherith (17:2–7). Elijah truly is directed by YHWH, obeys YHWH, and is provided for by YHWH. There are echoes here of Israel's experience of YHWH's provision in the wilderness, so that it would seem Elijah is truly the "prophet like Moses." This story of YHWH's provision for Elijah counters the harsh and selfish impression created by the first verse.

Then the wadi dries up; YHWH's provision is overcome by Elijah's word! So, the word of YHWH comes with another plan for Elijah's sustenance. Elijah obeys and comes to Zarephath, just a few miles from Sidon, deep inside Baal territory,[38] and finds the widow (17:8–16). When Elijah commands the widow to get him water, she complies, but when he presses her to bring bread, she objects, using an oath that reflects Elijah's in v. 1, and explains her sad predicament. Elijah responds with an exhortation not to fear, instructions, and a word of YHWH promising that her flour and oil would not cease.[39] Happily, the supply of flour and oil is unceasing, yet there is no confession of YHWH's sovereignty from the widow, as is the point of signs according to Deuteronomy.

Elijah remains in the widow's house after the famine (17:17–24). Her son gradually develops a severe sickness, so his mother understandably confronts the man of God, who takes her son upstairs to his own bed. His

---

37. Heller, *Elijah and Elisha*, 43.

38. Zarephath would have been within the previous borders of Israel, as surveyed by Joab in 2 Sam 24:6–7. It seems to have remained within that ideal, according to Obad 20.

39. Heller, *Elijah and Elisha*, 53, thinks that Elijah's requirement that the widow "give her last bit of food to him *first*, and then, with whatever might remain, to make something for herself and her son *afterwards*" further demonstrates his conflicted, ambiguous character, since this flies in the face of Deuteronomy's insistence upon care for widows and orphans (10:18, etc.).

first prayer to YHWH shows he clearly has no idea what is going on; he receives no answer, only silence. He stretches himself out on the boy, but nothing happens—three times. The mighty prophet is confronted with his own ignorance and powerlessness. From that weak position, he simply asks YHWH to intervene, and finally "YHWH listened" (17:22). This is the first time since the beginning of the chapter that a verb has been associated with YHWH. Elijah takes the boy down to his mother, simply declaring that he is alive; he does not explain that YHWH has healed her son. The widow, of course, has not seen what happened upstairs, nor is party to the narrator's explanation of YHWH's action, so her concluding confession does not involve her devotion or loyalty to YHWH (as is the concern of Deuteronomy); it centers instead on Elijah.

These opening episodes accustom readers to twists and turns in Elijah's story. He is neither a "good" nor a "bad" character; YHWH directs and listens to him, but Elijah plays things to his own advantage and in his own favor. The following, more momentous stories are similarly textured, but I can only summarize key points here. Ahab's servant Obadiah is loyal to YHWH and takes remarkable measures to protect YHWH's prophets (18:3–4), yet resists Elijah's command in what is the longest sustained speech anywhere in the Elijah–Elisha narratives (18:9–14); it is clear that Obadiah fears Elijah because Elijah is untrustworthy. On the other hand, Elijah appears most like the Deuteronomic prophet during the extended contest with the prophets of Baal at Mount Carmel, especially when he prays for Israel at its climax, using images and wording directly from Deuteronomy (18:36–37). The outcome of this contest is one of hope and relief, yet in the next story Elijah is presented as a petulant and manipulative character.

Elijah fails to take advantage of his recent victory, and takes fright when he receives Jezebel's threat, failing to grasp that she is powerless (19:1–3).[40] Having fled through the wilderness and experienced YHWH's sustenance, Elijah comes to the holy mountain of Horeb. The parallels with Moses are intended to highlight the difference between the two prophets; whereas Moses had stayed twice on Horeb without food or water for forty days and nights (Deut 9:9, 18) in order to intercede for Israel lest they be destroyed by YHWH, Elijah made the journey simply for his own sake, to express his anger and frustration. The syntax of YHWH's

---

40. Heller, *Elijah and Elisha*, 76f, points out that the king has participated in Elijah's triumph at Carmel so his consort has lost much of her support base. If Jezebel had the power to order Elijah's death, she would have already done so.

opener, "What are you doing *here*, Elijah?" (19:9) clearly questions his presence at Horeb—he should be elsewhere, teaching and leading the people in Torah obedience. Elijah's complaint separates himself from the people of Israel (what about Obadiah?), accusing them as a whole of forsaking the covenant, destroying YHWH's altars and prophets, and seeking his own life. YHWH's response is to command Elijah to stand on the mountain "before YHWH," as Elijah likes to identify himself (17:1; 18:15). There is a series of dramatic phenomena—wind, earthquake, and fire—yet YHWH is not in them (19:12). Even the silence is an empty space; this is a "non-theophany."[41] Where Moses had met YHWH face to face (Deut 34:10), Elijah wraps his face in his cloak and goes only as far as the cave entrance, seeming unwilling to have an open relationship with YHWH. Once again, he hears YHWH's question, and responds with the same complaint. It is clear that Elijah has relinquished his position as prophet, so YHWH gives him a last set of instructions that have nothing to do with rescuing Elijah from Jezebel, and finally strips him of excuses by insisting that a large number of Israelites remain loyal to YHWH (19:15–18).

Elijah leaves Horeb, but instead of anointing the two named men as kings, he finds Elisha; even so, he does not anoint him, choosing rather to throw his cloak "at him," then responds ambiguously to Elisha's request (19:19–20). The two men leave together, but they do not head for Damascus, nor search out Jehu; they are absent entirely for a chapter during which Benhadad of Aram besieges Israel. "The transition between the prophets is messy and confusing."[42]

Following the conspiracy against, and murder of, Naboth, Elijah fulfils his prophetic role (21:17–29), denouncing the actions of Ahab and Jezebel with Deuteronomic vocabulary and theology (Deut 17:14–20). Elijah's condemnation bears fruit in that Ahab repents—here Elijah's identification with the Mosaic prophet is plain. Yet in the next story concerning Ahab's son Ahaziah (2 Kgs 1:1–18), Elijah's character is ambiguous once more as his word brings violent death to over 100 Israelites, whose only fault is their attempt to bring the prophet before the king. It is difficult to escape Heller's conclusion:

---

41. Heller, *Elijah and Elisha*, 84. Dramatic manifestations cannot be trusted to point to YHWH's presence, according to Deuteronomy 13, and Elijah seems unconvinced.

42. Heller, *Elijah and Elisha*, 89.

If the stories are intended to draw Elijah with lines that resemble the Prophet like Moses, they succeed occasionally, fail often, and are equivocal throughout. If, however, Elijah's portrayal in the stories is intended to present him ambiguously, as a character who is, on the one hand, neither clearly concerned for Israel's salvation, nor, on the other, as simply a power-hungry manipulator, the stories succeed splendidly.[43]

Elisha

The assumption that Elisha authentically conveys YHWH's word and represents YHWH's will is difficult to reconcile with the drastic judgment visited on the boys from Bethel for what seems a relatively minor slight (2 Kgs 2:23–25). But if the stories of Elisha, like those of Elijah, are intended

> to portray the prophet in an ambiguous light—sometimes positive, sometimes negative, sometimes conflicted or opaque—then we should expect some stories to portray the main character negatively, just as others portray the main character positively. . . . Quite the opposite from many scholars' views, this story is not "out of the norm" among the stories of the Elijah-Elisha cycle, but is, rather, precisely in line with their narrative arc and their larger effect.[44]

Here I will focus on two juxtaposed, complementary stories, the Aramean attack on Dothan and the siege of Samaria.

War between Israel and its north-eastern neighbor, Aram, had been a regular occurrence since Ahab's reign (1 Kgs 20; 22), and the best-known Elisha story, the healing of the Aramean general Naaman (2 Kgs 5:1–19),[45] is set against that political background. The story of Elisha's involvement in the capture of the Syrian army (6:8–23) is cleverly told, focussing on different forms of sight and blindness; the narrator uses an exclamatory participle—"wow!"—to get the reader to see through the eyes of the servant (v. 15, v. 17) and then the Syrians (v. 20). It is one of the rare stories in the Elisha cycle in which the narrator explicitly states that Elisha prays to YHWH and that YHWH acts in the world of the story (6:17, 18, 20). It closes with

---

43. Heller, *Elijah and Elisha*, 109.
44. Heller, *Elijah and Elisha*, 126.
45. On Naaman see Spina, *Faith of the Outsider*, 72–93.

truly one of the most remarkable scenes of grace and goodwill in the entire Hebrew Bible.... The story is clear, the ambiguities are few, the plot is clean, the working of Elisha and of YHWH are in harmony, and at the end of the episode those who were once enemies have become, while perhaps not friends, at least respectful peers. This is Elisha at his best.[46]

Yet everything is undone in the next episode with the return of the Syrian army and their siege of Samaria (6:24—7:20). The resulting famine becomes extremely severe and the inhabitants are beyond desperate, as is revealed by a conversation on the city wall:

> The interchange between the king and the bereaved woman forms one of the most tragic scenes in the whole Bible and also establishes the framework upon which much of the ideological complexity and ambiguity of the following story will hang.[47]

The king here is Jehoram, who was not condemned outright in the regnal summary (3:1-3), and who listened to and obeyed the word of Elisha in the previous story (6:9-10, 21-23), so readers should not assume that the king is a negative or evil character. His response to the woman's initial appeal reveals that he adheres to YHWH, but then her account of a failed cannibalism pact after her own child has been eaten pushes the already agonized king to the edge of reason, such that his suppressed anger at Elisha's inaction boils over, and he orders the prophet's execution. The king's oath is threatening, and Elisha perceives that a messenger is coming to kill him, but it becomes clear that Jehoram has taken the threat back when he arrives in person to express his frustration with YHWH (6:33). Elisha does not reply directly but pronounces a word from YHWH promising almost immediate relief ... and his word comes to pass in the ensuing, somewhat comic narrative (7:1-15).

There are similarities here with story of the two prostitutes brought before Solomon (1 Kgs 3:16-28).[48] This woman is portrayed as a sympathetic character: she does not ask the king to find the hidden child so she can eat it; she simply expresses her extremity. The king does not charge her with a crime because he grasps her predicament; compared with Solomon's cool impartiality, there is no wise response to such a

---

46. Heller, *Elijah and Elisha*, 164-65.
47. Heller, *Elijah and Elisha*, 166.
48. Noted by Heller, *Elijah and Elisha*, 167, Sweeney, *Kings*, 311, and many other commentators.

horrendous state of affairs. Heller insists that this incident must be read in the light of the Deuteronomic curse that would overtake Israel if they forsake YHWH:

> In the desperate straits to which the enemy siege reduces you, you will eat the fruit of your womb, the flesh of your own sons and daughters whom the LORD your God has given you. . . . She who is the most refined and gentle among you, so gentle and refined that she does not venture to set the sole of her foot on the ground, will begrudge food to the husband whom she embraces, to her own son, and to her own daughter, begrudging even the afterbirth that comes out from between her thighs, and the children that she bears, because she is eating them in secret for lack of anything else, in the desperate straits to which the enemy siege will reduce you in your towns. (Deut 28:53–57)

Because of this intertextuality the reader should be wondering whether this incidence of cannibalism is a consequence of the sin of the king and the people? Or is the famine a crisis that could only be resolved by a miracle—none has been provided so far? The king places the blame on Elisha because he has been sitting in his house, choosing not to use his power to save the people. Indeed, he had previously advised against wiping out the Aramean threat (6:22).

The sub-plot of the fulfilment of Elisha's word to the king's skeptical captain (7:2b and 17) is heavily emphasized with repetition and reaffirmation (7:16–20)—why? Some commentators think this man dies because of his skepticism, but this seems too simple, given the questions raised about Elisha:

> It is almost as if the narrator—by providing several satisfying endings to the episode, the life-giving one mentioning the word of YHWH, and the three death dealing ones highlighting the word of Elisha—draws our attention not to the question of the officer, but to his cruel and all-too-human slaughter. . . . Bad things happen to those [who] stand up to Elisha, but this certainly does not mean that he is always a faithful representative of YHWH, or that he is unquestionably the Mosaic prophet. By no means. If prophecy, as a phenomenon, cannot stand up to honest questioning, then it may be more hazardous than beneficial.[49]

---

49. Heller, *Elijah and Elisha*, 175.

The People of God under a Single Davidic king—Revisited

The final section (2 Kgs 18:1—25:30) accounts for the reigns of the last kings of Judah before defeat, destruction, and exile. The most celebrated of these are Hezekiah and Josiah, so I will focus on them, and then comment on the book's conclusion.

Hezekiah

Hezekiah appears to be an admirable king amidst a long line of disappointments. The initial editorial summary of his reign provides a refreshing contrast with the depressing accounts of preceding kings;

> He did what was right in the sight of the LORD just as his ancestor David had done. He removed the high places, broke down the pillars.... He trusted in the LORD the God of Israel; so that there was no one like him among all the kings of Judah after him, or among those who were before him...." (2 Kgs 18:3–5)

Hezekiah's removal of the "high places" is particularly remarkable since such places were a snare for kings since the time of Solomon (1 Kgs 3:2; 11:7f, etc.), and are mentioned as a key reason for the downfall of the Northern Kingdom (2 Kgs 17:9). There follows an extensive account of Hezekiah's rebellion against Assyrian domination, his prayer in the temple for YHWH's military deliverance when that army surrounds Jerusalem (in 701 BCE), which is met by the prophet Isaiah's reassurance, and then salvation by the hand of the angel of YHWH (18:13—19:36).

However, the miraculous healing of Hezekiah (20:1–11), despite mirroring the extraordinary deliverance of Jerusalem from the Assyrian army, concludes with a disturbing counterpoint to the two stories of royal faith. The visit of a Babylonian embassy provides Hezekiah with an opportunity to show off his treasures, but Hezekiah is rebuked by Isaiah, and then responds selfishly (20:12–19). It seems that this visit occasioned an alliance between Hezekiah and Babylon to revolt against Assyria following the battlefield death of Sargon II in 705 BCE,[50] i.e., *before* the Assyrian invasion of 701. In other words, this incident has been displaced chronologically to conclude Hezekiah's deeds; it points ironically (contrast v. 6b with 17) towards the eventual loss of Jerusalem's treasures to Babylon. Robert Cohn comments;

---

50. Sweeney, *Kings*, 423.

Even the most righteous king has evinced a moral failing in his seeming capitulation to a Babylonian request, and so he must live out his extra years with the knowledge that Judah too is living on borrowed time.[51]

Josiah

The introduction to Josiah's reign is also positive, and the main body of his regnal account sets out his drastic religious reform program and national restoration, following the discovery of the book of the law during the renovation of the temple (2 Kgs 22:3—23:25). Nevertheless, when Josiah inquires of YHWH about the future, Huldah the prophetess declares that YHWH will bring disaster on Jerusalem because of the weight of previous apostasy (22:15-17); yet, because of the king's penitence, he will die in peace before the destruction occurs (22:18-20). Josiah's reforms include the destruction of the pagan "high places" to the east and south of Jerusalem that were erected by Solomon, and the destruction of Jeroboam's altar at Bethel (as prophesied long before, 1 Kgs 13:2). The narrator's emphasis upon Josiah's celebration of Passover, not kept since the days of the judges (23:21-23), also paints this king in a better light than Solomon.[52]

The evaluation of Josiah's reign (22:24-28) portrays him as uniquely righteous but goes on to remind readers of YHWH's fixed determination to destroy Judah, Jerusalem, and the temple. It comes as an enormous surprise to read the bald statement that Josiah was killed at Megiddo by Pharaoh Neco and buried in Jerusalem (22:29-30). There is no accounting for the dissonance between Josiah's violent death and Huldah's prophecy of his peaceful end.[53] However, in view of our earlier discussion of Elijah and Elisha, this final instance of a prophecy in the whole book of Kings fails to pass the Deuteronomic test of authenticity.

---

51. Cohn, *2 Kings*, 145.

52. Sweeney comments, "The Josian redaction of the DtrH has a great deal of interest in presenting a critical portrayal of Solomon because it aids in building up the righteous character of Josiah, who must correct the wrongs created by his predecessors." Sweeney, *Kings*, 81.

53. This dissonance is one of the main reasons for thinking that an edition of the book was produced towards the end of Josiah's reign, followed by a final edition produced during the exile.

The Conclusion

The accounts of the final kings follow, leading to the first Babylonian siege and exile of the most prominent and able inhabitants of Jerusalem in 596 BCE (23:31—24:26). Chapter 25 recounts Zedekiah's rebellion against Nebuchadnezzar, the siege and capture of Jerusalem in 586, and the capture and degradation of Zedekiah. The city and temple are burned, and the temple treasures are removed to Babylon. Remaining leaders are executed, and many of the people are carried off to Babylon, while the rest descend into something like anarchy.

The final verses (25:27-30) fast-forward thirty-seven years to the release from prison of King Jehoiachin, the previous king who had been taken to Babylon in the first wave of exiles, aged eighteen (24:12-15). Some commentators have interpreted this coda as a sign of hope after Judah's depressing decline and fall, but we must look beneath the surface once again.[54] Yes, Judah's king survives, and thus an ounce of hope may remain, but this closing vignette ties up the loose end of Judah's penultimate king by reinforcing his complete submission to Babylon. It seems to me to that Jehoiakin is not an actor, but acted upon; he is an impotent king, like David in 1 Kgs 1:1-4; these literary echoes bookend the whole tome.

2. Historical Perspectives

Kings covers a long time period from c. 970 to 560 BCE. The period of Solomon is controversial since the minimalists (mentioned in the previous chapter) dispute the existence of the united monarchy, so some attention must be given to the relevant archaeology.

The list of Solomon's twelve administrative districts and their centers found in 1 Kgs 4:7-19 has received partial archaeological confirmation in that more than half of them have identifiable centers (Hazor, Tirzah, Megiddo, Yoqneam, Gezer, and Beth-shemesh) that have been partially excavated and shown to have had monumental architecture consistent

---

54. King David had spared the life of Mephibosheth, Jonathan's son, and restored all Saul's lands to him, however Mephibosheth was not allowed to live independently with that provision. David required him to remain "at the king's table" (2 Sam 9:7-13), thus declaring Mephibosheth's dependence on royal favor, as well as his full subordination to the king's rule. David himself had been required by Saul to be at the king's table, and his absence prompted Saul's recognition of David's rebellion against him (1 Sam 20:24-42).

with centralized planning and administration in the tenth century. In particular, Hazor, Megiddo, and Gezer had monumental four-entryway city gates, and double or "casemate" defence walls. Megiddo and Gezer also had large multi-room palaces.[55] A network of over fifty forts strung across the northern Negev highland and the fort at Kadesh-barnea in the Sinai is further evidence of a tenth-century centralized state.[56]

One of the conventional fixed dates for the Iron I and IIA period in the southern Levant is the invasion of Pharaoh Shoshenq, which is dated circa 925, given that he died in 924.[57] This pharaoh has usually been identified with the Shishak, mentioned in 1 Kgs 11:40, who invaded Judah in the fifth year of Rehoboam, according to 1 Kgs 14:25-26, however, this identification has recently come into question.[58]

No archaeologist has been able to excavate on Jerusalem's temple mount because of the Islamic buildings that make up the holy site. It is recognized as the location of the temple built by Herod the Great, and of Solomon's temple before it. However, the remains of many Iron Age temples found throughout the southern Levant contain numerous archaeological and iconographic features that are almost exactly like those described in 1 Kings 6.[59]

After Solomon's reign, the accounts of the kings of Judah and Israel fit broadly with what is known from extra-biblical sources about the main political and military developments in the ancient Near East, although the interests of the compilers of Kings are often elsewhere.[60] For instance, an Assyrian inscription portrays Ahab as one of the more powerful kings, along with Aram, that fought against Shalmaneser at Qarqar in 853. However, this coalition must have been short-lived since the account in Kings portrays Ahab at war with Aram (1 Kings 20 and 22). There was a resurgence of Assyrian power that involved two waves of invasion into Syria and Palestine (even reaching Egypt) c. 883-824 and c. 744-660.

---

55. Dever, *Beyond the Texts*, 300-301, 323.

56. Dever, *Beyond the Texts*, 324.

57. According to Kitchen's detailed dovetailing of the biblical and Egyptian sources, *Reliability of the Old Testament*, 32-34, and against Dever, *Beyond the Texts*, 332-41. See the Review of Dever's *What Did the Biblical Writers Know?* by Peter James. Thanks to John Bimson for assisting me here.

58. See James & van der Veen, *Solomon & Shishak*.

59. Dever, *Beyond the Texts*, 350-52.

60. For discussion of this period see Provan, Long, and Longman, *Biblical History of Israel*, 267-76.

Then Assyria went into a steep decline and Babylon rose rapidly to power, while Egypt rarely went beyond its borders in this period.

Chronology of the Kings

One feature of the book is the many regnal formulae for the kings of Israel and Judah, which provide three types of data:

- The king's age at accession.
- The number of years he ruled.
- A link between the king's year of accession with a particular year in the reign of his counterpart in the other kingdom (during the divided kingdom period).

It might be thought that these data would be sufficient to enable the calculation of a relative chronology for the two kingdoms, and an absolute chronology by reference to Assyrian and Egyptian chronology. However, some difficulties are readily apparent:

- Jehoram of Israel became king "in the second year of King Jehoram son of Jehoshaphat of Judah" (2 Kgs 1:17), but his accession is later put in Jehoshaphat's eighteenth year (2 Kgs 3:1).
- Ahaz was aged twenty at the start of his reign, and he reigned sixteen years (2 Kgs 16:2), but Hezekiah, son of Ahaz was aged twenty-five when he acceded to the throne (2 Kgs 18:2). Taken together, these figures seem to imply that Ahaz was aged eleven when he fathered Hezekiah.
- Hezekiah's accession was around 727 according to 2 Kgs 18:9, but Sennacherib's invasion in 701 is placed in Hezekiah's fourteenth year according to 18:13, which implies he acceded around 714.

Kenneth Kitchen has argued that the figures in the regnal formulae must be understood on the basis of ancient Near Eastern usage, which involved a number of factors that have complicated the various figures, such as the way accession years are counted, the use of different calendars in Israel and Judah, and the practice of co-regencies.[61]

---

61. Kitchen, *Reliability of the Old Testament*, 26–32.

Composition and Date

The book names three sources: the "Book of the Acts of Solomon," the "Book of the Annals of the Kings of Israel," and the "Book of the Annals of the Kings of Judah" (1 Kgs 11:41; 14:19, etc; 14:29, etc). These three books have not survived, and we do not know if they were even available to the final editor(s). Other possible sources include the account of Solomon's succession, the narrative involving Isaiah in 2 Kings 18–20 (see Isaiah 36–39), and the traditions about Elijah and Elisha.

Kings concludes with a note about the thirty-seventh year of the first wave of exiles, which means the earliest possible date for the final form of the book would be about 560 BCE. There is no mention of any return from exile, but this does not require a date before Cyrus' edict in 538 that permitted return (as in 2 Chr 36:22–23); it could have reached its final form much later. The expression "to this day" is used with regard to states of affairs that could not have been current in the mid-sixth century (1 Kgs 8:8; 9:21; 12:19; 2 Kgs 8:22). Such "frozen references," along with the phrase "until now" (2 Kgs 13:23) probably indicate that the editor(s) is drawing on earlier sources. Other cases of "to this day" do not clearly imply a particular date of composition (2 Kgs 10:27; 14:7; 17:41).

3. Theological Perspectives

Kings emphasizes the reign of the one God of Israel and contrasts it with the habitual tendency of God's people to turn and worship other gods. This contrast may be observed especially at the denouement of Solomon's reign (1 Kings 11), in Elijah's contest with the prophets of Baal (1 Kings 18), and in the extended, sorrowful reflection upon YHWH's judgment on the northern and southern kingdoms (2 Kgs 17:7–23).[62]

For all the compromises and disappointments of Solomon's reign, God deigned to honor the temple with the cloud of YHWH's glory and the presence of YHWH's name (1 Kgs 8:10, 29).[63] When exploring Gen-

---

62. See Hess, "Kings," 422–23.

63. The temple appears occasionally through Kings when the focus is on the southern kingdom of Judah. Apart from during the reigns of Hezekiah and Josiah, note the following: King Jeroboam constructs alternative shrines at Bethel and Dan, having recognized the attraction of the Jerusalem temple (1 Kgs 12:26–33); young King Joash is hidden in the temple until old enough to be crowned, then the temple is restored to YHWH (2 Kgs 11:1–20).

esis we noted YHWH's descent to inspect Babel and Sodom; YHWH subsequently descended on Mt Sinai (Exod 19:18), and the glory of YHWH filled the tabernacle (Exod 40:34–38). Here is a further divine descent to dwell among YHWH's people. Although the construction of the temple was not from YHWH's initiative and carried its own snares, God was willing to take it into the divine purposes, as God was willing over the monarchy. Yet the patience of YHWH, extending for centuries, eventually had a limit. The reign of Manasseh is identified as the final straw, especially regarding the temple (2 Kgs 21:1–16; 23:26–27) and portends its eventual destruction.

As in Samuel, God continued to speak to kings in various ways, and especially by sending prophets. Like the kings, genuine prophets were often flawed, as is demonstrated by the man of God who came to Bethel and the old prophet who deceived him (1 Kings 13). Court prophets could adjust their messages to make them favorable to their masters, as in the story of Ahab and Micaiah (1 Kings 22). The story of Elijah marks a turning point in Israel's prophetic trajectory and, as Ellen Davis says, it draws attention to two questions: How do humans serve as channels through whom God's power of life flows? Conversely, how might they obstruct that power, bringing doom on themselves and death to others?[64]

Divine Sovereignty and Human Freedom

Terence Fretheim explores the relation between human activity on one hand and divine power and knowledge on the other. In the struggle for the accession, David sees through the human maneuverings to recognize God's will being done (1 Kgs 1:28–30, 47–48), and yet God does not act alone, but works through fallible human beings, such as Bathsheba and Nathan. "God does not perfect people before working in and through them; God can work even through human evil toward the divine purposes (see Gen 50:20)." It is easy for theologians to seize upon biblical declarations of God's purposes or control and overlook their juxtaposition with human initiative and activity within the same narrative. Fretheim continues:

> God is neither limited to human means (as if "God has no hands but our hands") nor all determining of human action (as if God micromanages the life of the world, including the human mind).

64. Davis, *Prophecy*, 57.

But between these two ditches, it is difficult to factor out the divine and human activity at work in these events.⁶⁵

To demonstrate this, Fretheim considers two subsequent divine oracles (1 Kgs 9:1–9; and 11:26–39), and I will summarize the first of these. In the second divine appearance to Solomon, YHWH holds out the possibilities of a positive and a negative future. Although we know the negative one transpired, at the time this had not been established in advance; human response to YHWH's warning genuinely mattered.

> If *both* futures are possible for God, then God has not established which future shall come to be, and God also does not *finally know* for certain which one shall occur. God knows these futures as genuine *possibilities*, though God may be said to know which future is more probable (perhaps shown in the detail given to the negative possibility). But God's knowledge of future *human* responses is not absolute. At the same time, God gives some specification regarding *what God* will do in view of the possible human responses.⁶⁶

Many biblical narratives portray the subtle interaction between divine and human activity and responsibility. God has freely chosen to engage in relationships with humans that treat them with integrity and honor, entrusting them with significance and responsibility for the future, despite their sinfulness. God calls us into partnership, not passivity, nor compulsive activity.

The Rhetoric of Kings

Marvin Sweeney contrasts two traditions influencing the historiographical viewpoints of Bible readers: the Western religious tradition that sees it as divine truth and is reluctant to analyze its truth claims; and the age of the Enlightenment with its emphasis upon empirical observation that approaches biblical narrative with rational skepticism in view of archaeological discoveries. He proposes that the reader adopt an evaluative approach that attends to the theological perspective that is worked into the text along with the historiographical perspective, and comes to this helpful conclusion:

---

65. Fretheim, "Divine Dependence on the Human," 34, 35.
66. Fretheim, "Divine Dependence on the Human," 35–36, emphasis original.

> First and Second Kings does not simply offer a historically verifiable account of the past. First and Second Kings is designed to answer the question of why Israel and Judah were exiled by arguing that the people of Israel and Judah, particularly their monarchs, failed to observe YHWH's Torah, and thereby called divine punishment upon themselves. In making such a presentation of history, 1–2 Kings is sharply critical of the kings of Israel and Judah for prompting the people to forgo observance of YHWH's expectations. First and Second Kings must therefore be recognized not simply as a work of history, but as a work of theodicy as well, insofar as it defends the notion of divine righteousness. . . . 1–2 Kings also lays a foundation for a restoration of the people to the land, based on divine Torah.[67]

It is likely that many exiles asked why YHWH had permitted Babylon's triumph; were its gods were more powerful? The rhetoric of Kings defends God's righteousness in the wake of Israel's destruction and exile. While it underlines the importance of Torah for its restoration, Kings also demonstrates that conventional monarchy is bad for Israel; its assumptions and methods involve exploitation and oppression, and it leads them astray from loyalty to YHWH.

Reflection on the Former Prophets

It would have been very easy for people in exile (or even those who returned to the land afterwards) to look back with nostalgia to the time when the original possession of the land took place, to when YHWH delivered them from numerous threats, to when the great kings David and Solomon ruled a united kingdom. These books were carefully compiled and edited from earlier sources to emphasize Israel's repeated compromises, failures, and unfaithfulness to YHWH during its time in the land, in contrast with YHWH's own patience and grace. I suggest that one of the large-scale purposes of these four books was to subvert any notion of Israel's golden age.

Nostalgia is a common human trait, and thus frequently occurs among Christian people. We cannot escape the past, since that is the meaning of time, yet we can learn from the past and discover how to move forward with God in new ways in order that the past might be redeemed. It is the details of these books that offer us opportunities to

---

67. Sweeney, *Kings*, 3.

gain insight about the workings of human relationships, the temptations of power, the tendencies towards abuse, and the remarkable interactions of YHWH with human beings.

PART III

Interpreting the First Testament

8

Canonical Conversations

Many readers of the Bible assume that it presents one story, a narrative truth that simply should be embraced, yet the details of its various books show that they present several different, even competing ways of telling that story. Having considered the interpretation of the Former Prophets in some detail, the first part of this chapter broadens horizons to take into account other parts of the First Testament. We have already seen the significance of Genesis and other parts of the Torah for interpreting these books. There are also important parallel materials especially with Samuel and Kings in 1 & 2 Chronicles, the Latter Prophets and the Psalms. There are two particular reasons for this wider exploration; literary and canonical.

Within postmodern literary theory, single narratives can become ideologically totalitarian. No single story is incomparable, and warning signals should flash whenever incomparability is claimed for a story because of the individual or group entitlement entailed in such a claim. Danna Fewell says this is "a danger that the Bible, when taken superficially as a monolithic, singular story, has perpetuated on numerous occasions."[1] Richard Bauckham responds to such concerns by arguing that the biblical story is not a modern metanarrative, and especially that Israel's story is one of resistance against the dominant narratives of the great empires from Pharaoh to Rome.[2] Yet, it is important that alternative perspectives are thrown on Israel's era of independent existence in the

---

1. Fewell, "The Work of Biblical Narrative," 18.
2. Bauckham, "Reading Scripture as a Coherent Story."

land from books other than the Former Prophets, given that all four tell their story from a similar point of view.

From a canonical point of view, the Christian church adopted the already existing collection of Jewish scriptures in their Greek translation, and then added the apostolic writings that make up the Second Testament. Norbert Lohfink explains how scholars used to think of the books of the First Testament as individual units of meaning, but that this static conception of the canon has been replaced by the realization that

> the process by which the canon came into being after the exile seems simply to have continued the process by which the individual books were composed before the exile, as far as we can understand that process. One layer of meaning was laid upon another, and new texts which were added led to an increasingly comprehensive texture of meaning; ... different versions of history are associated, complement and correct each other, and constitute together a new and higher unity of utterance. . . . The essential point in this phenomenon is that this unity of the canon was consciously sought. Those who composed and used the canon never regarded the individual "books" in the philosophical sense as books, that is, as bodies of meaning, complete in themselves. In this sense, they only regarded the canon as a whole as a book.[3]

Lohfink goes on to extend this line of thinking to include the books of the Second Testament as canonically vital in shaping the interpretation of the First Testament, and this will be taken up in the second part of this chapter as well as in the next.

If there are good reasons for having several different versions of the story, how do interpreters deal with them? Some scholars have proposed that they be understood as several voices in a conversation, a conversation that illuminates our questions, rather than providing a set of straightforward answers.[4] How, then, might that conversation take place? The field of biblical theology was briefly described in chapter 1 as a way to attend to the diversity of scripture. For all the varied ways in which Old Testament theologies have been written, there has not so far been an attempt to facilitate a conversation between the various books

---

3. Lohfink, *Inerrancy of Scripture*, 35.

4. Davis, *Opening Israel's Scriptures*, 6. For a book-length discussion, see Kuhn, *Having Words with God*. Jewish scholars have also recognized the richness of the Bible's record of ancient Israelite conversation and interaction. See Carasik, *The Bible's Many Voices*; Knohl, *Divine Symphony*.

of the First Testament.[5] Paul House has written a series of theologies of each canonical book, which concludes with a summary that picks up on his chosen centering theme (monotheism), attends to God's people, and builds bridges to the New Testament.[6] However, this approach focusses on coherence and hardly attends to difference, and thus tends to flatten the variegated witness of the books themselves.

In this chapter I make a series of suggestions as to what such a conversation might look like by considering points of similarity and difference firstly between Joshua–Kings and several other books; Chronicles, Isaiah, Micah, and Psalms. Secondly, I trace selected links between each of the Former Prophets and some books of the Second Testament; this is a reverse of the process adopted in chapter 2, adhering once more to the whole book. These two probes lay the groundwork for the following chapter in which I consider the relation between the First and Second Testament books in view of the overall scriptural frame.

1. Conversations with Other First Testament Voices

Here I provide brief overall comments on these related books and then discuss selected parts of each that parallel parts of Joshua–Kings. Some other books with connections to characters and events in the Former Prophets will not be considered for reasons of space: Ruth, Lamentations, Proverbs, Ecclesiastes, Song of Songs. The ensuing comparisons contribute to a conversation between the various voices and throw light on issues of overall interpretation.

---

5. Goldingay wrote a fascinating study of the *Theological Diversity and the Authority of the Old Testament*, in which he explored three approaches to interpret this diversity:
- A contextual or historical approach; diverse theologies of particular elements might be understood in terms of the context in which they were written.
- An evaluative or critical approach; this raises questions about which theologies might be understood as normative, and which might not, and on the basis of which criteria.
- A unifying or constructive approach; illustrated by exploring how the two large theological categories of "creation" and "salvation" may be interrelated.

6. House, *Old Testament Theology*, 539-59.

1 & 2 Chronicles

The book of Chronicles[7] begins with nine chapters of genealogies that summarize the human story from Adam and Noah to Abraham and the tribes of Israel (except Zebulun and Dan) through the time of the judges. The central section (1 Chronicles 10—2 Chronicles 9) tells the story of the united monarchy under David and Solomon, recounting in detail their great achievements while passing over some (though not all) of their faults. It begins David's story with his establishment as king of all Israel and supplements the account in Samuel with David's preparations for the temple construction and personnel (1 Chronicles 22–29). Its account of Solomon's reign places even more emphasis upon the temple construction and dedication (2 Chronicles 1–9) than does Kings. The final section (2 Chronicles 10–36) recounts the decline of the kingdom of Judah from the schism with the northern kingdom to the Babylonian exile and concludes with the decree of the Persian emperor Cyrus that permitted return to Jerusalem.

The end of the Babylonian exile prompted the renewal of Jewish worship at Jerusalem and the rebuilding of the temple, possibly with hope for the restoration of David's dynasty[8]—and this would fit with the Chronicler's focus on the previous national leadership of David and Solomon. Although Chronicles is mainly based on the earlier books of Genesis through Kings and assumes knowledge of them (e.g., 1 Chr 11:1-3 assumes David's previous military exploits and anointing by Samuel), it provides a refocused version of the story of Israel, that is centered on the Second Temple (i.e., the rebuilt temple). It addresses the situation of Jews in the Persian province of Yehud, though there is considerable debate as to whether it was written earlier or later in the Persian period.[9] But the long dominance of the Persian empire saw many Jews living permanently in the diaspora, and other features of Chronicles could indicate a time of writing after Nehemiah's reforms (c. 445 BCE).

---

7. As with Samuel and Kings, 1 & 2 Chronicles should be read as two volumes of one book.

8. For a discussion of aspirations for the restoration of the monarchy, see Rose, "Zerubbabel."

9. For a helpful discussion of date, see Duke, "Chronicles," 167f.

CANONICAL CONVERSATIONS

The Conquest Tradition

Following the initial chapters of genealogies, the Chronicler's narrative begins with the death of King Saul (1 Chr 10:1–12). This means that it makes little mention of the conquest tradition or the judges. Susan Niditch compares the Chronicler's insistence that Solomon's conscription of forced labor from the Canaanite tribes remaining in the land rather than from the people of Israel (2 Chr 8:7–9) with the equivalent passage in 1 Kgs 9:20–21, and notes that, where the latter implies that Israel had sought to exterminate all the land's inhabitants, the former "eliminates reference to the ban or Israel's volition and refers more simply to a less than complete conquest."[10] Niditch observes a similar reduction of violence in the Chronicler's account of Jehu's purge (2 Chr 22:7–9; cf. 2 Kgs 9:1—10:36), but also points to another passage during the reign of Asa that introduces the threat of violence (2 Chr 15:13; cf. 1 Kings 15). So the "crusading spirit" has not been eliminated from Chronicles, though it does offer an ideal in which violent threats need not be carried out.

It is difficult to know how much to make of Chronicles' omission of the conquest and judges traditions, since it also omits narratives of the patriarchs, exodus, and wilderness wanderings, and focusses on the monarchy and the temple. However, Niditch goes on to discuss other threads in Chronicles:

- The elimination of certain references to David's cruelty (1 Chr 28:20—29:25)
- The emphasis upon Solomon's status as a leader of peace who is allowed to build God's holy dwelling on earth (1 Chr 22:7–10; 28:3)
- The positive value of Israel's helplessness, which looks for rescue to God and emphasizes victory in war as divine miracle, the most dramatic examples of which command no human to fight (2 Chr 14:9–15; 20:1–30)

These threads enable Niditch to come to a nuanced conclusion: "The Chroniclers build upon sentiments and images available in earlier biblical tradition but combine them to make a breakthrough towards an ideology of peace."[11]

---

10. Niditch, *War*, 140.
11. Niditch, *War*, 149.

The Death of King Saul

The narration of Saul's death in battle with the Philistines follows quite closely the account in 1 Samuel 31,[12] however it is supplemented with an explicit interpretation of events that is not part of the original.

> So Saul died for his unfaithfulness; he was unfaithful to the LORD in that he did not keep the command of the LORD; moreover, he had consulted a medium, seeking guidance, and did not seek guidance from the LORD. Therefore the LORD put him to death and turned the kingdom over to David son of Jesse. (1 Chr 10:13–14)

From a literary perspective, Yairah Amit juxtaposes these two versions of the story to demonstrate that readers generally have to assume that the biblical narrator is reliable (and consistent), but they are sometimes faced with a contradiction between the perspectives of the narrators of different books. How can both narrators be trustworthy?

> The author of the Book of Samuel regards Saul with the respect due to a king of Israel and depicts his death as heroic. To make it persuasive, the author delivers the story through the authoritative, reliable narrator. In contrast, the author of the Book of Chronicles, who is a supporter of the house of David and wants to emphasize that the monarchy was justly transferred from the house of Saul to the house of David, does everything to blacken Saul's character and depict him as a great sinner. And since this author also seeks to convince the readers, the story is told through the always trustworthy narrator. Here, then, are two authors with opposing intentions, each with their own truth. The authors then and not the narrators are the source of the contradiction.[13]

Amit presses us to recognize that, however omniscient a particular narrator might appear, another narrator in a different book may present an alternative omniscient perspective. The author of each book writes at a particular time with a specific readership in mind, and so a reader in our own time seeking to take the whole canon into account must identify a

---

12. The report given to David by the young Amalekite in 2 Sam 1:4b–10 has been widely accepted as truthful, from Josephus in his *Jewish Antiquities* to contemporary scholars. However, some aspects of this account are puzzling and may not be entirely truthful, so other scholars prefer the narrator's earlier account.

13. Amit, *Reading Biblical Narratives*, 99.

framework within which to account for the several perspectives. Such a framework might be historical, ideological, or theological in perspective, or some combination of all three.

The Royal Covenant

As the Chronicler's account of David's reign unfolds, a subtle shift away from David can be discerned. In the Samuel account, once the king had settled into his new capital of Jerusalem, the prophet Nathan declared YHWH's covenant with David like this;

> Your house and your kingdom shall be made sure forever before me; your throne shall be established forever.
> (2 Sam 7:16)

In the Chronicles version of the same incident, Nathan's words to David are similar, but subtly different in that they refer, not to David, but to his future son;

> ... but I will confirm him in my house and in my kingdom forever, and his throne shall be established forever.
> (1 Chr 17:14)

Even more significant is that God's commitment is now to *God's* house and kingdom rather than David's. "We encounter here for the first time the chronicler's emphasis that the earthly kingdom was a manifestation of the kingdom of God."[14] This shift in emphasis away from David's kingdom and onto God's kingdom can be observed in several places (1 Chr 28:5; 29:23; 2 Chr 9:8; 13:8).

David's Census: God or Satan?

In chapter 6 we encountered the puzzling introduction of King David's census, which attributed it to YHWH (2 Sam 24:1). It is intriguing that a very similar account of the same events is found in Chronicles, yet with a striking difference; "Satan stood up against Israel and incited David to count the people of Israel" (1 Chr 21:1). How might readers interpret the serious theological discrepancy between these two accounts?[15]

---

14. Allen, "Chronicles," 409.
15. There are further differences of detail between the two accounts, particularly

Because the Chronicler placed great emphasis upon the temple building project, the altar-building incident from David's reign was important to include, whereas other incidents found in 2 Samuel were not. The Bathsheba débâcle and Uriah cover-up, narrated in 2 Samuel 11-12, are passed over without comment at 1 Chr 20:1. However, David's determination to hold a census is supplemented with a clause from the Bathsheba episode; "But God was displeased with this thing" (21:7), a virtual copy of 2 Sam 11:27b. The Chronicler is sometimes thought to present David without the flaws evident in Samuel, but Leslie Allen says;

> The echo in 21:7 is tantamount to saying that in his estimation this was an equivalent story. His David, too, had feet of clay. The chronicler wanted to affirm, in principle, that the Temple afforded the opportunity for the forgiveness of sins, not only in David's case, but also for all the people of God during the centuries-long dispensation launched under David and Solomon (cf. 2 Chr 7:14-16).[16]

Thus, the overall perspective (royal sin and divine grace) of these two passages is very similar, despite their different narrative placements, except for the identity of the one who incited David to hold the census.

In the Hebrew Bible *satan* appears in several places with reference to a human enemy; it is translated "adversary" in the NRSV of 1 Sam 29:4; 2 Sam 19:22; 1 Kgs 5:4; 11:14, 23, 25; and as "accuser" in Ps 109:6. On the other hand, it refers to a heavenly being in three places.

- The angel of the LORD becomes a *satan* to the prophet Balaam, who is on a mission against Israel (Num 22:22, 32).

- *The satan* appears in the opening chapters of Job (1:6-12; 2:1-6) but the definite article implies something more like a job title than a personal name.

- *The satan* appears similarly as the accuser in Zechariah's vision of the high priest, Joshua (3:1-2).

Now in 1 Chr 21:1 *satan* appears without the article, and thus it is possible to translate "an adversary" (note that it appears nowhere else in Chronicles). In which case, David's decision to hold a census could be

---

the discrepancy in the price David paid for the future site of the temple; 50 shekels of silver (2 Sam 24:24) and 600 shekels of gold (1 Chr 21:25).

16. Allen, "Chronicles," 421.

attributed to some unnamed human being;[17] this might ease somewhat the discrepancy between the two accounts. Against this solution, the LXX reads *diabolos* ("devil" in the Second Testament) in all the Hebrew Bible references to a supernatural *satan*, including 1 Chr 21:1 and at Wis 2:24, although it reads *diabolos* in reference to a human enemy at Ps 109:6; Est 7:1; 8:1 and 1 Macc 1:36. Further, the other supernatural elements in 1 Chronicles 19 (David's conversation with God through Gad in vv. 8-13; the angel of YHWH with a drawn sword and the fire from heaven in vv. 16-27) strengthen the case for the *satan* here being supernatural. Thus, there are good grounds for reading the Chronicles account as attributing the initiative to Satan.

Seeking to account for the attribution to God of David's impulse to conduct the census, I noted that bad things are said to occur at YHWH's instigation at a number of places in Samuel. Now I draw attention to the similar attributions elsewhere:

- If a prophet or dreamer urges serving other gods, this is a test from YHWH of Israel's loyalty (Deut 13:2-4).
- God sent an evil spirit between Abimelech and the lords of Shechem (Judg 9:23).
- YHWH put a lying spirit in the mouth of court prophets (1 Kgs 22:21-23).
- "Does disaster befall a city unless the LORD has done it?" (Amos 3:6).
- "I form light and create darkness, I make weal and create woe; I the LORD do all these things" (Isa 45:7).[18]

So it is not uncommon to find the attribution of evil actions to YHWH in the First Testament, and this was likely grounded in Israel's conviction that YHWH was the ultimate source and cause of all things. Indeed, the

---

17. See Tuell, *Chronicles*, 86.

18. Fretheim, "Divine Dependence on the Human," 32, comments, "The language of darkness and woe (*ra'*) in Isa 45:7 is not cosmic in orientation, but language typical in the prophets for *specific* (historical) divine judgments, whether against non-Israelites (perhaps especially in this context, see 47:5, 11) or Israel itself (commonly; e.g., Jer 32:42; see Isa 42:7). Israel's God is often the subject of verbs of judgment; "there is no other" god who is responsible. Yet, God's "creating" here is not *ex nihilo*, but action which gives specific shape to a situation of historical judgment (for other historical uses of *br'* in Isaiah 40-55, see Isa 41:20; 43:1, 7; 45:8; 48:7; 54:16)."

Chronicler does not amend other stories of God deliberately deceiving or bringing about evil ends (e.g., 2 Chr 18:18–22//1 Kgs 22:19–23). It seems as though 1 Chr 21:1 is a special case.

Whereas the texts listed above will have originated before or during the Babylonian exile, the Chronicler was writing after the exile in the Persian period, the same era in which Zechariah and Job were written. Some scholars suggest that the Chronicler's replacement of YHWH's anger with Satan corresponds to Persian religious influence.[19] There is evidence that belief in a malevolent spiritual agency developed between the Persian and Roman periods:[20]

- In the second century BCE, Jews began to speculate about the origin of demons (Jubilees 2.2; 4.22; 1 Enoch 6.1—7.6);
- The writer of Jubilees even interpreted the story of God's testing Abraham over Isaac as initiated by the Satan-like angel Mastema (Jubilees 17.15–18).[21]
- In the Qumran community it was believed everyone was ruled either by the Prince of Light or the Angel of Darkness whom God had created (1QS 3.13—4.26).

In the Second Testament Satan or the devil is a significant figure, and two passages in particular have more in common with the perspective of Chronicles than with that of Samuel.

> Therefore, to keep me from being too elated, a thorn was given me in the flesh, a messenger of Satan to torment me, to keep me from being too elated.
> (2 Cor 12:7)

> No one, when tempted, should say, "I am being tempted by God"; for God cannot be tempted by evil and he himself tempts no one.
> (Jas 1:13)

We cannot be sure, but it may be that the Chronicler replaced YHWH's anger with Satan in order to resolve the moral convolution of the passage

---

19. Crenshaw, *Defending God*, 56.

20. See Twelftree, "Demon, Devil, Satan," 163f. For a profound Jewish reflection on these matters see Levenson, *Creation and the Persistence of Evil*, 44–45.

21. This passage is helpfully discussed by Kugel, *Bible As It Was*, 171.

in an era when the attribution of evil to Satan had become theologically acceptable.

Hezekiah, Josiah, and the End of the Book

In the book of Kings Hezekiah was presented, firstly, as an exemplary king in his loyalty to YHWH, but ultimately as a somewhat negative figure. In Chronicles Hezekiah is portrayed much more positively, in line with favorable portraits of other kings of Judah. The Chronicler does not describe the full extent of Sennacherib's invasion of Judah (2 Chr 32:1–23), since he wants to attribute the Assyrian failure to capture Jerusalem to Hezekiah's purifications and Passover celebration. Indeed, he inserts four major textual units into the framework derived from Kings:

- The purification of the temple following Ahaz's death (29:3–36)
- The account of Hezekiah's great Passover (30:1–27)
- The divisions of priests and Levites in Hezekiah's time (31:2–19)
- The military and economic expansions carried out by Hezekiah (32:2–6, 27–30)

Whereas Kings emphasizes Hezekiah's struggles with Sennacherib over his religious reforms, Chronicles inverts these priorities. As Stephen Tuell, puts it,

> In Chronicles, Hezekiah is the reformer par excellence, comparable in accomplishments to David and Solomon (29:2; 30:26). For while David communicated the plan for the temple and its liturgy, and Solomon implemented the plans of his father, it was Hezekiah who reinstituted the liturgy of David, and rededicated the temple of Solomon, following the apostasy of Ahaz. Further, with his reforms centering worship on Jerusalem and his overtures to the survivors of the northern kingdom, Hezekiah recalls the glories of the united monarchy.[22]

The Chronicler suggests that Hezekiah restored some unity between the northern and southern tribes after the Assyrian conquest of Samaria. He is portrayed as a kind of second Solomon in that he invited the northern tribes to come to celebrate the Passover in the temple at Jerusalem, though only a few responded (2 Chr 30:1–12). In the post-exilic period, it seems that the Chronicler saw that everyone had a place in the reconstituted

---

22. Tuell, *Chronicles*, 211.

Israel so long as they belonged to the community of faith centered on the temple; the royal state was no longer important.

In the book of Kings, Josiah is the standout religious reformer, the only king to escape any condemnation. In Chronicles, however, Josiah is significant as the last good king, but he does not stand out. Chronicles retains Huldah's prophecy that Josiah would die in peace (34:28) and includes Josiah's death at the hands of Pharaoh Neco, but adds that Neco warns Josiah against involving himself, even claiming to speak for God (35:21). It expands that Josiah was shot by Egyptian archers despite being disguised (35:22-25), making his demise analogous to the death of wicked king Ahab who was also warned by a prophet (18:16, 33-34).

> Perhaps the most tragic aspect of Josiah's sad story is that this righteous, reforming king should end up just like the wicked apostate Ahab. The moral for the Chronicler's community is plain: if they reject the word of God, they too will be swept away, despite their former righteousness.[23]

The final kings of Judah and the destruction of Jerusalem by the Chaldeans are summarized briefly (36:1-21). But the conclusion is very different from Kings' epilogue; Chronicles notes the beginning of the Persian era together with Cyrus' famous edict that permitted exiles to return to Jerusalem and rebuild the temple (36:22-23). Thus, the Chronicler returns to his central interest; although he has spent much of his book recounting the stories of kings, his main concern has been to highlight the significance of the temple, its construction, renovation, and ongoing role at the heart of God's people under Persian rule.

Chronicles was written for a very different readership from that of Joshua-Kings. The lessons of the exile concerning Israel's time in the land, with the people's repeated failure to follow YHWH, and the kings' (general) failure to provide the humble leadership and just rule required of genuine royalty, had been clearly articulated by those earlier books (whether the lessons had been learned was another matter). It would be easy to draw pessimistic conclusions about the way the world works from Joshua-Kings. By contrast, the course of history appears to be less tightly controlled in Chronicles; even within a given reign things could change from good to bad or from worse to better—even evil Manasseh comes to acknowledge YHWH as God, according to 2 Chr 33:13, 19.

---

23. Tuell, *Chronicles*, 241.

The Latter Prophets

Here we will consider parts of the book of Isaiah since it includes narrative sections as well as oracles from the reigns of Ahaz and Hezekiah as recounted in Kings. I have also decided to consider Isaiah's near contemporary, Micah, whose prophecies contain an echo of Isaiah in his famous "peace passage" (4:1–5). If space allowed, explorations in the book of Jeremiah would be worthwhile since it includes narratives and oracles pertaining to Josiah and the final kings of Judah together with the aftermath of Jerusalem's destruction. Its final chapter duplicates 2 Kings 24–25, which serves to vindicate Jeremiah's prophecies of the destruction of Jerusalem. However, the following brief probes serve to illustrate the variety of voices among the Latter Prophets and their contribution to the First Testament conversation.

Isaiah

This book contains materials from the later part of the eighth and early years of the seventh centuries BCE, but it also appears to address exiles in Babylonia well over a century later (chapters 40–55) together with people who returned to Jerusalem after the exile (chapters 56–66). Traditionally chapters 40–66 were regarded as "long range" prophecy by the original prophet in the late eighth century, sealed up for a later readership in the sixth century BCE. Historical-critical scholarship, for much of the twentieth century, viewed the book as comprised of two or three virtually separate parts, with chapters 40–55 the product of an unnamed prophet of the exile. In the last few decades, however, scholars have recognized a more complex history of composition of the book but also realized that its various parts are interconnected, so that Isaiah's essential unity has been rediscovered.[24]

In two narrative sections of the first part of the book, the prophet Isaiah engages with King Ahaz (Isa 7:1—8:22) and with King Hezekiah (36:1—39:8). The first of these begins with a near repeat of 2 Kgs 16:5, but then recounts a clash between Isaiah and Ahaz that does not appear in Kings, though it coheres with that account (2 Kgs 16:1–20). The second passage runs parallel with 2 Kgs 18:1—20:21, though there are some differences between the two. It seems that the second passage was derived

---

24. For a helpful overview of these issues, see Williamson, "Isaiah."

from the account in Kings and that it was edited to form a transition within Isaiah from its pre-exilic to its exilic sections.[25]

> Slight modifications of the text of the Isaian version eliminate or reformulate statements that might be understood to question or criticize Hezekiah. The result is a virtual whitewash of his character in the Isaiah version to facilitate his presentation as an ideal model for piety to readers of the book.[26]

Most significantly, the portrayal of Hezekiah's submission to Sennacherib in 2 Kgs 18:14-16 has been eliminated from the Isaiah version, so removing any hint of capitulation to an arrogant, pagan monarch. Thus, Isaiah's portrayal of Hezekiah is closer to that found in Chronicles than in Kings.

There is an intriguing difference between the first and second parts of the book of Isaiah. In the first part the author(s) is deeply committed to the Davidic monarchy, even if a particular king is condemned. When King Ahaz refuses YHWH's protection offered through Isaiah in chapters 7-8, the prophet foretells the Assyrian invasion, but he does not pronounce the overthrow of the monarchy or the surrender of David's city. His hope for the future is bound up with the Davidic monarchy as he foresees that Zion will be central to all peoples (2:1-4), and the ideal king will bring peace to the whole world (11:1-10).

In the later chapters of Isaiah (40-66) there is a very different set of ideas. The previous loyalty to the Davidic dynasty has disappeared, and there is no hope for its renewal. For example, 60:17—61:1 borrows multiple terms and motifs from Isaiah 11 ("shoot," "spirit," "righteousness," "land/earth," and the theme of peace within the city), while the idea of nations coming to Zion appears in 60:5-10, as it had in 11:11. But there is no mention of a king who will bring in this new era of justice and peace in Isaiah 40-66. Terms used to describe the king's role in the early chapters are now applied to the people as a whole (compare 11:1 and 11:4-5 with 60:21).[27] The most obvious transference of royal motifs to the whole nation is found in Isa 55:3:

> Incline your ear, and come to me;
> listen, so that you may live.
> I will make with you an everlasting covenant,
> my steadfast, sure love for David

---

25. For a detailed discussion of the debates, see Seitz, *Zion's Final Destiny*.

26. Sweeney, *Kings*, 411.

27. Motifs and vocabulary from the royal Psalm 72 are employed in Isa 44:28—45:8; 49:7-23; and 60:1-21, but with references to the David dynasty removed.

The Hebrew forms of address here are in the second person plural, making it clear that the intended audience is a *group* rather than an individual. Thus, God's commitment to David's descendants found in 2 Samuel 7 and Psalm 89 is now applied to his family in the broadest sense—all Israelites, and not simply direct descendants of David or Solomon.[28]

Another indicator of the very different set of ideas in Isaiah's later chapters is the challenge to Chronicles' focus on the temple, as in: "Hear me, my brothers and my people. I had planned to build a house of rest for the ark of the covenant of the LORD, for the footstool of our God ..." (1 Chr 28:2). The very idea that YHWH needs rest or a footstool is ridiculed in Isaiah:

> Thus says the LORD:
> Heaven is my throne
>   and the earth is my footstool;
> what is the house that you would build for me,
>   and what is my resting place?
> (Isa 66:1)

The book of Isaiah is important evidence of major changes in perspectives brought about by the experience of exile, to be taken up in the following chapter.

Micah

Micah was a prophet in Judah around the same time as Isaiah in the context of the Assyrian invasion of 702/701 BCE, yet his message contrasts significantly with that of Isaiah. Where Isaiah is supportive of the Jerusalem monarchy and of Jerusalem, Micah is severe in his criticism of unjust rulers and prophesies the destruction of Jerusalem (3:9–12), such a shocking message that it was remembered over a century later in Jeremiah's time (Jer 26:18). Some passages in this book seem to envisage Babylonian exile and a return from it (2:4–13; 4:10; 7:8–20), and so it is thought that later materials were added to a collection of the original words of Micah, as appears to be the case with Isaiah. The possibility of materials from later times raises the question of whether it contains

---

28. Note that other exilic and early post-exilic passages do express hope for the renewal of the monarchy: Jer 33:14–16; Ezek 37; Zech 3:8; 4:6–10; 6:12 and Hag 1:12–15; 2:21–23.

incompatible viewpoints, but I follow Daniel Smith-Christopher in his argument for reading Micah as a coherent whole.[29]

Smith-Christopher has helpfully emphasized the location of Micah's home-town of Moresheth in the Shephelah, or lowlands of Judea, some twenty-five miles southwest of Jerusalem, and about five miles from Lachish, one of Judah's fortified cities that was besieged and captured by the Assyrians. It was also about six miles from the Philistine city of Gath, so that Moresheth was a border town. Smith-Christopher argues that

> ... the most effective way to understand Micah in his historical, geographical, and ideological context is to read his message as a regionally oriented religious and political challenge to the oppressive economic and military interests of the central elite in Jerusalem. Micah's message should be read from the "interested perspective" of Micah's own agriculturally based lowland region. Micah represents an attitude of ancient localism that sees primary loyalties to family, clan, and region, rather than identifying completely with the fate of the "national" elite in a dominant city.[30]

Commenting on Micah's famous peace passage, Smith-Christopher suspects the basis for his anti-militaristic ethos is a "populist" realization of the economic impact of warfare preparation, rather than some kind of ancient "pacifism." His imagery of weapons turned into farming tools, shows that his is an "agrarian anti-war protest."[31]

> They will hammer their swords into plows,
>   and their spears into vineyard shears.
> A nation will not lift up a sword against a nation,
>   and they will no longer train for war.
> A man will dwell under his vine and his fig tree,
>   and will no longer fear.
> (Mic 4:3–4)[32]

In Kings the traditional picture of family sufficiency—a man dwelling under his own vine and fig tree—was dangled in front of the inhabitants of Jerusalem by the invading Assyrian Rabshakeh as an invitation

---

29. Smith-Christopher, *Micah*, 43–44.
30. Smith-Christopher, *Micah*, 21.
31. Smith-Christopher, *Micah*, 145.
32. Smith-Christopher's translation, *Micah*, 24. See his extensive discussion, 139–45, of contexts and parallel passages (Isa 2:2–4 and Joel 3:10).

to surrender (2 Kgs 18:31, cf. Isa 36:16). It is fascinating that Micah attaches this same expression to his vision of peace in the impending (not utopian) future.

It is striking that Isaiah does not employ this expression in his parallel passage (Isa 2:2-4), so Smith-Christopher asks whether Micah is "advocating that the central powers should take the deal offered by Assyria. . . . Plausibly Micah has always considered Hezekiah's revolt to be the Jerusalem elite's dangerous folly."[33] This implies that Micah advocates a different approach to national security from that of Isaiah.

The Psalms

The Psalter is a collection of shorter compositions, and thus it might be thought that each psalm is best treated as a stand-alone unit of meaning.[34] Traditionally the psalms were associated with David, despite many superscriptions indicating otherwise. But in the modern era historical-critical scholars have determined that David could not have authored all the psalms, and form criticism was influential during much of the twentieth century, so that the unity of the Psalter was largely overlooked.

However, there is obvious evidence of organization in parts of the Psalter, particularly in the sub-collection of the Songs of Ascents (Psalms 120-34), and recent investigations of its shape have taken two approaches. Firstly, significant studies have been produced on limited sections of the book.[35] Secondly, there has been research on the shape of the entire book. Gerald Wilson studied the overall design of the Psalter and sought to show that it depicts the failure of the Davidic monarchy and its replacement by the rule of YHWH[36] (i.e., comparable with Chronicles). Thus in Book I, following the introductory Psalm 1, Psalm 2 powerfully endorses the Davidic ruler, then at the end of Book II, Psalm 72 is a supplication for the king to fulfil his calling, while Book III closes with Psalm 89's lament that God has removed the scepter from David's house. Book IV explores the implications of the demise of the Davidic line, while Book

---

33. Smith-Christopher, *Micah*, 24, cf. 137.

34. However, the numbering system can be misleading; Psalms 9 and 10 are generally considered to have been composed as a single acrostic psalm, and Psalm 43 seems to be a continuation of Psalm 42.

35. E.g., Howard, *Structure of Psalms 93-100*.

36. Wilson, *Editing of the Hebrew Psalter*.

V transfers the claims of David's family to the people as a whole, offering hope through the divine ruler (i.e., comparable with Isaiah). Wilson's work has had a major influence upon Psalm studies, though details of his thesis have been vulnerable to criticism.[37]

It is now recognized that, while individual psalms may be treated as stand-alone units of meaning, the placement of neighboring psalms should also be considered for thematic resonance. For example, Walter Brueggemann and William Bellinger point to microstructures within the Psalter; "Most readers of Psalm 23 . . . do not account for its position and relationship with Psalms 22 and 24."[38] Furthermore, the Psalter as a whole contains significant pointers to overall reading strategies. Indeed, it is the combination of all the psalms that provides its dual resource of comfort and challenge: note should be taken of the conversation between psalms of gratitude and praise on one hand, and those of lament and complaint on the other.[39]

References to Israel's Story in the Land

Some quite specific incidents are indicated in several psalm superscriptions, however it seems that many of these are not original but were added at a subsequent stage in the traditioning process, and so we cannot place much historical weight on them. A sizeable number of psalms have no superscription at all, but others are attributed to Moses (90), Solomon (72, 127), Ethan (89), and Asaph (50, 73–83), while eleven are associated with the Korahites, a musical guild (42–49, 84, 85, 87, 88).[40]

In psalms of thanksgiving or praise, but also of appeal for deliverance, a number of references can be found to the crossing of the Jordan in parallel with the Red Sea (66:6; 114:3–5), the conquest and land (44:1–3; 78:55; 105:44–45; 135:11–12; 136:21f), and to the time of the judges (83:9–11 refers to Midian, Jabin and Sisera, Oreb and Zeeb, Zebah, and Zalmunna; 78:60 refers to the Philistine capture of the ark near Shiloh). Psalm 99:6 is a celebration of YHWH as king, and instances Samuel along with Moses and Aaron as leaders who petitioned God on Israel's behalf,

---

37. For a recent discussion and proposal, see Ho, *Design of the Psalter.*

38. Brueggemann and Bellinger, *Psalms,* 8.

39. See especially Brueggemann, *Psalms and the Life of Faith,* and *From Whom No Secrets Are Hid.*

40. See Firth, "Asaph and the Sons of Korah."

thereby upholding the pre-monarchic era. Psalm 113:5-9 does not mention Hannah by name yet contains very strong echoes of 1 Sam 2:1-10.[41] Psalm 106:34-46 rehearses Israel's repeated infidelity in the land, and thus coheres with the perspective presented by the book of Judges.

However, the communal lament Psalm 44, having begun with a celebration of God's past victories, protests recent defeats, "Yet you have rejected and abased us, and have not gone out with our armies.... You have made us like sheep for the slaughter" (vv. 9-11). It continues;

> All this has come upon us,
>   yet we have not forgotten you,
>   or been false to your covenant.
> Our heart has not turned back,
>   nor have our steps departed from your way,
>   yet you have broken us in the haunt of jackals,
>   and covered us with deep darkness.
> If we had forgotten the name of our God,
>   or spread out our hands to a strange god,
>   would not God discover this?
> For he knows the secrets of the heart.
> Because of you we are being killed all day long,
>   and accounted as sheep for the slaughter.
> (Ps 44:11-22)

Abrupt calls for God to rise up and redeem his people form the conclusion. This is a very different reading of historical defeat from that found in Judges and Kings; it is not *Israel's* covenant failure, but *God's!* Perhaps the best way to understand the tension between the conviction of this psalm and the insistence upon Israel's unfaithfulness in the Former Prophets lies with recognizing the existence of a minority of faithful Israelites within an unfaithful majority led by apostate kings. It stands in the tradition of Isaiah 53, Job 13:15, and the Jewish martyrs.[42]

Many psalms refer to Jerusalem or Zion (2, 9, 14, 20, 48, 50, 51, 53, 65, 68, 69, 74, 76, 78, 79, 84, 87, 97, 99, 102, 110, 116, 122, 128, 129, 132, 133, 134, 135, 137, 146, 147, 149). Many refer to the temple, sanctuary, or "house of God" (5, 11, 15, 18, 20, 24, 27, 28, 29, 42-43, 48, 52, 55, 60, 63, 65, 68, 73, 74, 78, 79, 84, 92, 96, 98, 108, 114, 122, 135, 138, 150).

---

41. For a discussion of the intertextuality involved in the context of Jewish interpretation, see Grohmann, "Psalm 113 and the Song of Hannah."

42. Verse 22 is quoted by Paul in Rom 8:36, on which see Keesmaat, "The Psalms in Romans and Galatians," 149-52. This psalm should be read alongside Psalm 91!

The destruction of the temple and Jerusalem is clearly at the forefront of several psalms (74, 79, 89). Only one (137) clearly reflects the experience of Babylonian exile.

David and Royal Psalms

Many psalms are attributed to David, but the superscription "of David" may imply a loose association with Israel's greatest king (and musician), rather than actual authorship. Some indicate the author's circumstances that would make sense at particular times in David's career, such as when he was on the run from Saul, but they lack specific details that might confirm their origins. Psalm 18 is almost identical to David's song in 2 Samuel 22, and may reflect David's attainment of regional dominance, as in 2 Samuel 8. Even the great psalm of repentance (51), the superscription of which links it to David's sin with Bathsheba, concludes with a plea for the rebuilding of the walls of Jerusalem, indicating that at least this part of the psalm was written long after David's time.

David's name is used in the body of several psalms (18, 78, 89, 122, 132, 144), however it is unclear whether the implied author is David himself, one of his royal descendants, or a non-royal Israelite thinking of the Davidic king as leader and representative of the people. Several more psalms are known as royal since they refer to the king, and sometimes "YHWH's anointed," or employ other royal signifiers (2, 20, 21, 45, 61, 72, 110); enthronement is mentioned (61), and royal marriage (45). Psalm 101 is not immediately obvious as royal yet implies royal office by reflecting on the upholding of justice. These psalms show less interest in the king's personal life than in his royal role, especially as battle leader but also as bringer of justice and prosperity.[43] Psalm 89 is particularly poignant as it initially celebrates YHWH's covenantal commitment to David and his descendants, yet shockingly turns to divine rejection and abject humiliation (vv. 38–45) before a plea for restoration (vv. 46–51)—surely reflecting the Babylonian defeat and exile.

Whatever the origin of these psalms, the fact of their collection and preservation testifies to centuries of communal use with more or less literal application to immediate circumstances. With no restoration of the monarchy, the royal psalms came to be read in the light of promises of a future Davidic Messiah. James Mays explores the interrelation between

---

43. See Steussy, *David*, 158.

the David in the book of Psalms and David in the book of Samuel and argues for a genuine connection between David and the Psalms, thus directing the reader "to think of each psalm and the entire Psalter as an expression of faith in the reign of the LORD as the sphere in which individual and corporate life is lived."[44]

2. Conversations with the Second Testament

The figural relationship between the First and Second Testaments, emphasized in chapter 2, encourages interpretive movement in both directions, and it is supported by the early Christian fathers. Brevard Childs explains how the early theologians sought to interpret the apostolic writings in the light of the First Testament.

> Although it is obviously true that the Old Testament was interpreted in the light of the gospel, it is equally important to recognize that the New Testament tradition was fundamentally shaped from the side of the Old. The Old Testament was not simply a collage of texts to be manipulated, but the Jewish Scriptures were held as the authoritative voice of God, exerting a major coercion on the early church's understanding of Jesus' mission. In fact, the Jewish scriptures were the church's only scripture well into the second century. As H. von Campenhausen has forcefully stated, the problem of the early church was not what to do with the Old Testament in the light of the gospel, which was Luther's concern, but rather the reverse. In the light of the Jewish scriptures which were acknowledged to be the true oracles of God, how were Christians to understand the good news of Jesus Christ?[45]

Here I illustrate some of the ways in which the four books studied earlier contribute to understanding the Second Testament.

Joshua

Joshua is mentioned briefly in Stephen's speech before the Jerusalem council with reference to the ancestors' dispossession of the nations (Acts 7:45), and the conquest also appears briefly in Paul's speech in the

---

44. Mays, *The Lord Reigns*, 97.
45. Childs, *Biblical Theology*, 225-26.

Antioch synagogue (Acts 13:19). More significantly, the writer of the letter to the Hebrews constructs an elaborate comparison between Moses and Jesus as he appeals for his readers to hold firm in faith (3:1—4:11), emphasizing entering rest (3:11, 18; 4:3), as YHWH had once promised Israel rest in the land (Deut 12:8–12). By repeated reference to Ps 95:7b–11 (as well as to Gen 2:3), he throws forward the ongoing challenge of entering God's rest.[46]

> For if Joshua had given them rest, God would not speak later about another day. So then, a Sabbath rest still remains for the people of God; for those who enter God's rest also cease from their labours as God did from his. Let us therefore make every effort to enter that rest, so that no one may fall through such disobedience as theirs. (Heb 4:8–11)

Israel's original arrival in the land pointed forward to something that was yet to come.

We have seen that Joshua emphasizes the completeness of the occupation, yet also recognizes its incompleteness. This author leans hard on those intimations of Israel's partial occupation. Intriguingly, Joshua is not included in the catalogue of people of faith later in Hebrews, however both the destruction of Jericho's walls and the faith of Rahab are (11:30–31, cf. Jas 2:25).

In the Fourth Gospel's Upper Room discourse, Jesus prepares his disciples for impending conflicts by setting them in ultimate terms; "the ruler of this world is coming" (John 14:30). There is a strong allusion to Joshua's commission (Josh 1:6–7, 9) in Jesus' conclusion, "In the world you face persecution. But take *courage*; I have *conquered* the world" (John 16:33). This use of conquest language is applied to disciples in 1 John 5:5 and appears frequently in the book of Revelation (2:7, 11, 17, 26; 3:5, 12, 21; 12:11; cf. 11:7; 13:7; 17:14). The One seated on the throne uses the language of Joshua, saying, "Those who *conquer* will inherit (*come into possession of*) these things . . ." (21:7; cf. Josh 1:6).[47]

---

46. The idea that YHWH would give Israel rest in the land is a feature of the book of Joshua, appearing in regard to the two-and-a-half tribes at 1:13 and 15, and then to all at 21:44; 22:4 and 23:1. It is picked up in 2 Sam 7:1, 11 and 1 Kgs 5:4.

47. See Davis, *Opening Israel's Scriptures*, 140.

Matthew and the Conquest

Matthew relates how Jesus acquired his name by angelic announcement and Joseph's action (1:18–25). The name *Iēsous* is the Greek form of the Hebrew name *Yehosua* (which means "YHWH saves"), and so there is an immediate echo of God's agent in completing the people's redemption from Egypt by the conquest of Canaan; Jesus "will save his people from their sins." Of course, Jesus' name is common to all four Gospels, but only Matthew provides this explanation for his name.[48] The early Christians thought Jesus' name was significant, since Joshua's role as leader of his people when they came into their promised inheritance was a foreshadowing of Jesus' role as leader of his people, the church.[49]

Kenton Sparks has made a strong case for reading the final verses in Matthew's Gospel, known as Jesus' Great Commission, as "a serious effort . . . to interpret the Mosaic 'genocide' through the lens of Jesus' radical message of love."[50] Noting that one of the challenges facing the evangelist was that of reconciling Jesus' command to love and pray for one's enemies (5:44) with the Mosaic command to kill all of the Canaanites, Sparks surveys important elements of the Gospel that build towards this important conclusion.

Firstly, he discusses Matthew's ethnic inclusiveness in the opening genealogy, which highlights the role of four women in the lineage of Jesus the Messiah, apart from his mother Mary: Tamar, Rahab, Ruth, and "the wife of Uriah," (1:3–6). Rahab and Ruth were foreigners, and Rahab was one of those Canaanites who embraced the God of Israel. God's promise to bless the gentiles through Abraham's offspring (Gen 12:3; 18:18; 22:18) is on Matthew's agenda from the start.

Secondly, Sparks considers Jesus' encounter with the woman in the district of Tyre and Sidon who persuades him to heal her daughter (15:21–28). In Mark's Gospel, this woman is described as a Syrophoenician (7:26), but Matthew describes her, anachronistically, as a "Canaanite," emphasizing that Jesus welcomed the faith of Israel's traditional enemies.[51]

---

48. In Luke 1:31–33, the angel Gabriel tells Mary to name her son "Jesus" and makes links to his ancestor David.

49. Lactantius saw Joshua as a "figure of Christ" and Chrysostom saw the name of Joshua as "a type." See Franke, *Ancient Christian Commentary*, 2.

50. Sparks, "Gospel as Conquest," 652.

51. Sparks, "Gospel as Conquest," 654.

Next, it is well known that Matthew portrays Jesus as a new and better Moses.[52] Among the many parallels drawn between these two figures, Moses had been the intermediary through whom YHWH had given the people his law at Mt Sinai: Jesus had delivered his new law on the mountain in chapters 5–7. When Matthew concludes his Gospel with the disciples gathered around Jesus at a mountain in Galilee, readers are reminded of that first mountain on which Jesus delivered his sermon. There Jesus had taught with authority (7:29), now he declares that he has been given "all authority." This final mountain forms a parallel with the mountain in Moab up which Moses was called to die, and thus Sparks can say, "From their respective mountains, Moses and Jesus delivered their final earthly charges to the people, each in his own way exhorting them 'to obey everything I have commanded you' (Matt 28:20; cf. Deut 11:28; 31:5, 29)."[53]

Moses was not permitted to enter the promised land, however, during the transition from Moses' leadership to Joshua, YHWH had encouraged Israel and Joshua with the promise of his accompanying presence during the invasion of Canaan (Deut 31:6, 8, 23; Josh 1:5, 9, 17; 3:7). Jesus' final promise, "I am with you always, to the end of the age," is a new utterance of the divine promise made to Joshua and Israel after Moses died. But where Moses had once commanded his people to *drive out* "all the nations" (LXX Deut 11:23, cf. Josh 23:4; 24:18), Jesus charged his disciples to *make disciples of* "all the nations." Sparks concludes,

> Drawing on nonviolent themes in the Hebrew Bible and from Jesus' own ministry, Matthew employed his "fulfilment by antithesis" exegesis to show that evangelizing the nations is the appropriate fulfilment of the older Mosaic charge to kill the Gentiles. This new conception, which views the gospel as a spiritual conquest, suits Matthew's dual commitment to ethnic inclusiveness and nonviolence, and it also suits Jesus' message in his mountain sermon, namely that we should love rather than hate and kill our enemies.[54]

In this way, Matthew presents Jesus as the eschatological fulfilment of Israel's story, trumping the Mosaic covenant with the Abrahamic promise.

---

52. See Allison, *New Moses*.
53. Sparks, "Gospel as Conquest," 660.
54. Sparks, "Gospel as Conquest," 661.

Judges

The names of several judges, along with Samuel and David, are mentioned in the "heroes of faith" passage in Hebrews (11:32). How can this be squared with the reading of the book that was proposed in chapter 5? There is a much earlier summary reference to Jerubbaal, Barak, Jephthah, and Samson in Samuel's speech following the renewal of Saul's kingship (1 Sam 12:11)—the same reordered four names (in Judges, Barak precedes Jerubbaal), except that alternative names are used for Jerubbaal/Gideon. It looks as though the author of Hebrews drew on Samuel's summary of judges, rather than their detailed portrayal in Judges. Samuel raises the names of these leaders to make the point that YHWH had through them delivered the people from various oppressors. Whatever their failings, it was still true that these judges, like Samuel and David, had been the means of Israel's salvation, and they had exercised faith in YHWH along the way.

Barry Webb draws attention to the several points of correspondence between the broad outlines of Samson's career and that of Jesus:

> his annunciation by a divine messenger, his marvellous conception, his holiness as a Nazirite, his endowment with the Spirit, his rejection by his own people, his being handed over by their leaders, the mocking and scorn he suffered at their hands, and the way his calling was consummated in his death, by which he defeated the god Dagon and laid the foundation for a deliverance to be fully realized in a day to come. The correspondences are too numerous, and too germane to who Samson was, for what he achieved to be simply brushed aside as fanciful.[55]

Samuel

In the first chapter of Luke's Gospel, two women are central and bring the book of Samuel to mind; Elizabeth is barren and feels disgrace (1:7, 25), yet her husband is promised a child, and she gives birth to a son named John (1:57–66). Mary is an unmarried virgin, yet she is promised an extraordinary child. She gives voice to a song that reverberates with Hannah's prayer of praise, especially in her central perception about God's characteristic power reversals:

---

55. Webb, *Judges*, 418f.

> He has shown strength with his arm;
> > he has scattered the proud in the thoughts of their hearts.
>
> He has brought down the powerful from their thrones,
> > and lifted up the lowly;
>
> he has filled the hungry with good things,
> > and sent the rich away empty
>
> (Luke 1:31–33)

This is not the place to trace the way in which this insight into God's character is worked out in the body of Luke's Gospel, except to note that it is clearly, though unexpectedly, evident in the resurrection of Jesus in the final chapter.

Jesus' Davidic status is announced before his conception (1:27, 32, 69) as well as in his infancy narrative (2:4, 11). It appears later in the grainfield incident (6:1–6), the healing of the blind (18:35–43), and the conundrum over David's psalm (20:41–44). In addition, the accusation that Jesus claimed to be a king is central to his trial, in that Pilate asks him, "Are you the king of the Jews?" (23:2, 3), and it forms the inscription over him on the cross (23: 37, 38).

Luke includes more stories about women than the other evangelists, and Jesus' counter-cultural respect for women has often been noted, though questioned by some feminist commentators.[56] From where did this respect come? As I have reflected on Westbrook's work on the role of women's stories in the evaluation of David's character, I wonder if Jesus learnt to value women, at least in part, from the book of Samuel.

Nicholas Perrin has shown how Mark's Gospel makes a number of typological comparisons between David and Jesus during its account of the latter's final week in Jerusalem.[57] Jesus enters the Holy City in the style of Solomon at his enthronement (11:1–8, cf. 1 Kgs 1:38), is hailed as "Son of David" (11:9–10), and later is identified as David (12:10; cf. Ps 118:22–23). He is crucified as "King of the Jews" (15:26) and utters his final prayer from a Davidic psalm (22:1). "Through his shameful death on a Roman cross, Mark insists, Jesus has become Israel's king on the pattern of David."[58] Yet Perrin goes on to show how the Jesus–David analogy also extends to Mark's earlier sequencing of events. Where David was

---

56. For a nuanced discussion of the portrayal of women in Luke that engages with feminist criticism, see Spencer, *Salty Wives*.

57. In Perrin's *Jesus the Priest*, the focus is upon the "historical Jesus," yet he makes shrewd observations on the Gospels in many places.

58. Perrin, *Jesus the Priest*, 196–97.

anointed king of Israel, Jesus is anointed Davidic-messianic king (1:9–11); where David was soon thrust into combat with Israel's arch-enemy Goliath, Jesus is immediately thrust into combat with Israel's true arch-enemy Satan (1:12–13). David was pursued by the reigning pretender Saul; Jesus is embroiled in a series of conflicts (2:1—3:6), complete with the grainfield controversy (2:23–28), in which he refers to David's excursion to Nob (1 Sam 21).[59] Perrin concludes, "Whatever scriptures and traditions shaped Mark's Christology of suffering, the contribution of the Davidic narrative can hardly be denied."[60]

Kings

Matthew's opening genealogy includes the kings of Judah, from David to Jechoniah (1:6–11), placing Jesus within Israel's most celebrated dynasty. In his pronouncement of judgment on a skeptical culture, Jesus declares that the queen of the South will rise at the judgment to condemn "this generation", having travelled far to hear Solomon's wisdom. And he extends this to a personal claim: "and something greater than Solomon is here!" (Matt 12:38–42; Luke 11:29–32). In his alternative wisdom teaching about anxiety and reordering priorities, Jesus urges attention to the natural world and declares that lilies exceed the glory of Solomon (Matt 6:29; Luke 12:27).

Echoes of Elijah and Elisha are frequent in the Gospels. An angel speaks about John the Baptist before his birth in terms of Elijah (Luke 1:17), and later Jesus speaks of John in terms of Elijah (Mark 9:12–13; cf. 1:6). Richard Hays sees Luke weaving the scriptural stories of Elijah and Elisha into his narration of the identity of Jesus.[61] Jesus refers to Elijah and Elisha in his Nazareth sermon (4:25–30); his raising from the dead of the widow's son (7:11–17) recalls Elijah's raising the son of the widow of Zarephath, yet without Elijah's struggle. Later speculation about Jesus' identity includes an Elijah come again (9:8, 19), but then Jesus appears transfigured on the mountain with Moses and Elijah (9:30–31). In the

---

59. Perrin's discussion of Jesus' reference to Abiathar as high priest (2:26) shows that it was not a case of misnaming Ahimelech, given Solomon's later accession to the throne on a donkey, and his dismissal of Abiathar from the priesthood (1 Kgs 1:38; 2:26), but a deliberate challenge to the Jerusalem-based priests (*Jesus the Priest*, 198f).

60. Perrin, *Jesus the Priest*, 196.

61. Hays, *Gospels*, 237–43.

epistles both Paul and James appeal to Elijah's story (Rom 11:1–5; Jas 5:17–18).

The Temple

The temple is a key location in the Gospels and at the start of Acts. At the climax of his speech before the council, Stephen mentions Solomon and challenges the assumption God dwells in the temple by quoting Isaiah 60 (Acts 7:47–50). In all four Gospels, Jesus' action and teaching in the temple is the flash point in his confrontation with the Jewish leaders. This incident is the most obvious evidence of what was one of the most important facets of Jesus' ministry and self-understanding. Nicholas Perrin puts it this way:

> Like others before him, Jesus saw both himself and his community as a new temple. But unlike anything we meet in Second-Temple Judaism, Jesus leaves no firm boundary between his own interim temple-project and the final, eschatological temple. Quite the contrary, according to Jesus' radical understanding: the heavenly temple had already come to earth and was beginning to coalesce within his own community.[62]

Perrin goes on to argue that Jesus' healings and exorcisms, together with his meals with a variety of table companions, signal the inauguration of the kingdom of God and the creation of renewed sacred space.[63]

It is well-known that John's Gospel places Jesus' demonstration in the temple near the beginning of his narrative (2:13–22), whereas the other Gospels place it towards their close. Such placement draws attention to the significance of the temple for the whole of John's story of Jesus. Indeed, Mary Coloe has shown that temple symbolism is important throughout the Fourth Gospel, from the Prologue to the promise of life in the community of Jesus' followers (20:31).[64]

---

62. Perrin, *Jesus the Temple*, 150.
63. Perrin, *Jesus the Temple*, 152–82.
64. Coloe, *God Dwells with Us*.

9

Reframing the First Testament

Having explored the books that tell the story of Israel in the land, and considered how they may be read in conversation with several other books that tell that story from different angles, we are in a position to address the long delayed question, how might the coming of Jesus shape, or reframe our interpretation of the First Testament? The most commonly adopted way to do so is through narrative theology, so I will consider this first. However, there are some significant problems with this approach, so I will secondly explore a canonical approach.

1. The Scriptural Story as Narrative Theology

The way in which Christian Bibles have been ordered (Genesis to Esther, followed by collections of poetry and wisdom, then prophetic books) tends to encourage a meta-story, or "grand story" approach to reading these books, and this is reinforced by its simplified episodic portrayal in Children's Bibles. Several entry-level invitations to the Old Testament adopt the "time-line" approach.[1]

Stephen Crites has suggested that the appeal of stories finds its origin in the narrative quality of our lives.[2] There is something particularly appealing about an overarching story, within which sub-plots and smaller

---

1. Bartholomew and Goheen, *Drama of Scripture*; Richter, *Epic of Eden*. Drane, *Introducing the Old Testament*.

2. Crites, "Narrative Quality of Experience."

tales are to be found, and from which they derive greater significance. Many people enjoy great tomes telling epic sagas, such as *War and Peace*, *Lord of the Rings*, *Harry Potter*, or *Game of Thrones*. Perhaps it is for these reasons that narrative theology became popular towards the end of the twentieth century. In the modern period theology often took the form of rational analysis of the faith, setting out its dogmatic essentials, especially the attributes of God. But one positive aspect of postmodernity may be the realization that life is not a fixed system of constants; life moves from birth, through growth, to maturity, and to old age (though not for all); it involves changing and developing relationships; it is set within shifting social, national, and international contexts. Scriptural reflection on God's nature leads to the narrative character of theology; as John Goldingay puts it, "The 'revelation' of God's person is inextricably tied to the events in which God becomes different things, in a way any person does; it is thus inextricably tied to narrative."[3]

If the Bible can be considered as a long and complex overall narrative, important decisions must be made about how it may be held together or framed, and especially for Christians, in a way which is true to Jesus Christ. In a dictionary article on narrative theology, Joel Green suggests three approaches that, taken together, assist in identifying "the Christian narrative."[4]

- Since Aristotle, attention has been drawn to a narrative's beginning, middle, and end. These three "moments" determine the plot and structure of a narrative by identifying the narrative "need" that must be addressed and resolved.
- Narrative studies distinguish between "kernels" and "satellites," i.e., they use a logic of hierarchy. Some narrative events play a crucial or pivotal role in the overall direction ("kernels"), while others have a subsidiary role ("satellites"). Of course, there may be some disagreement as to which are "kernels," and which are "satellites."
- The hermeneutical key for a Christian reading of the scriptures is twofold: (a) its recognition that what holds the two Testaments together is the one aim of God; (b) its recognition that the character of God (and thus the nature of God's story) is paradigmatically

---

3. Goldingay, "Biblical Narrative," 131.
4. Green, "Narrative Theology," 533.

manifest in Israel's release from bondage in Egypt and decisively revealed in Jesus of Nazareth.

I will take up the first two of these proposals in order to explore the narrative approach to framing the First Testament and return to the third when exploring the overall narrative of the Two Testaments.

The Overall Narrative of the First Testament

The Bible itself contains several warrants for finding an overall narrative across its many books. Firstly, many threads tie the various books together, especially God's promises to Abraham which find fulfilment as Israel's story proceeds (e.g., Gen 15:5-6; cf. Deut 10:22), but also God's warnings through Moses (e.g., Deut 30:15-18) which came to pass at the close of Kings. Secondly, the many genealogies in Genesis, and elsewhere make family connections through the various parts of the story.[5] Thirdly, a number of passages summarize significant parts of the overall story of the First Testament, especially Neh 9:6-37 (cf. Deut 6:20-24; 26:5-9; Josh 23:2-13; Pss 78; 105; 135:8-12; 136). In the Second Testament, one passage does something similar, while another extends the story to John the Baptist and the resurrection of Jesus (Acts 7:2-50; 13:17-41). I have already concentrated on the middle part of Israel's story, in the land, so will now attend to the beginning and the end by exploring three recent studies.

Iain Provan sets out to challenge popular authors who are critical of the First Testament using a strategy of addressing a series of fundamental questions (What is the world? Who is God? Who are man and woman? etc.). He takes the book of Genesis as his starting point and then connects each theme with subsequent First Testament texts.

> This is, I think, a sound strategy, not least because the book of Genesis is where the biblical story begins and no story can be read well if the beginning is not properly understood. If we misconstrue the beginning, mistakes and misunderstandings in what follows are (nearly) inevitable.[6]

---

5. Apart from Genesis and Chronicles, genealogies are found in Exod 6:14-25; Num 3; 26; 2 Sam 3:2-5; 5:13-16; Ezra 7:1-5; 8:1-14; Ruth 4:18-22; Esth 2:5-6; cf. Matt 1:1-17; Luke 3:23-38.

6. Provan, *Seriously Dangerous Religion*, 14.

However, it is questionable whether this approach allows for plot development in the later parts of the narrative. While grasping Genesis is vital if readers are to interpret the First Testament appropriately, some of the subsequent books are just as important, though perhaps in different ways.[7] Other books that tell the end of the story may also deserve our special attention.

Mark McEntire has proposed an approach to First Testament theology that focuses on the character of God as portrayed in the books that present the overall storyline. He notes that God's character appears most vivid in the early books of the First Testament, but that God's involvement in events appears to decrease as the story progresses.[8] Interestingly, McEntire argues that more attention should be paid, and more weight given, to the "mature" God of the later books, whom he characterizes as "a restoring God." In Ezra-Nehemiah YHWH is portrayed as acting through the decisions of Cyrus, Darius, and Artaxerxes (Ezra 6:14, etc.) and through the prayers and actions of Ezra and Nehemiah. McEntire concedes that God appears to act directly at Ezra 8:31 and Neh 4:20, but maintains that the notion of God as an active, vigorous character has largely disappeared (from the present) when compared with earlier books.[9]

There is a significant weakness in McEntire's case, in that he fails to give sufficient attention to the phenomenon of divine speech through the prophets that appear in Kings, especially Isaiah.[10] Further, the miraculous defeat of Sennacherib's army (2 Kgs 19:35-37) is dismissed as making "no sense,"[11] in what looks suspiciously like a circular argument. McEntire also opts to read the change in YHWH's involvement in events

---

7. Some books may seem particularly relevant for certain situations—early liberation theologians found much inspiration in Exodus—but that is a different point.

8. McEntire, *Portraits of a Mature God*. For a comparable argument to McEntire's, but from the perspective of human experience of God, see Kugel's assemblage of an array of evidence in *The Great Shift*.

9. McEntire, *Portraits of a Mature God*, 182.

10. This is particularly notable in McEntire's use of Friedman's *Disappearance of God* (*Portraits of a Mature God*, 9), and his brief mention of the "Prophetic literature" (ibid., 16). Attention is given to Isaiah, Jeremiah, Ezekiel, and the Book of the Twelve in chapter 5, and briefly in chapter 6, yet the significance of divine speech with the prophet, and through the prophet to people and kings, is not allowed to challenge the earlier model of divine withdrawal as the story proceeds.

11. McEntire, *Portraits of a Mature God*, 144.

in terms of divine character development, when alternative explanations available.[12]

Daniel Hawk has read the long biblical narrative with attention to the question of violence.[13] From the time of Moses until the exile, YHWH covenanted with the people of Israel in a way that entailed competing on the world stage in conventional political terms: deliverance from Egyptian oppression, protection from harassment during wilderness wanderings, and military leadership in taking possession of the land. This means that YHWH is implicated in the use of violence, and sometimes even the perversion of justice. Hawk argues in detail that the reason why YHWH appears to be less involved in Israel's story towards the end of the monarchy is that YHWH had only reluctantly acceded to Israel's demand for a king, as well as to David's desire to build a temple, and eventually ceased cooperating with Israel as a nation-state according to conventional expectations in view of its repeated apostasy.

Critique

I find Hawk's insight that towards the end of the monarchy YHWH ceased cooperating with Israel as a conventional nation-state is more convincing than McEntire's argument for a shift in the divine character. However, because both McEntire and Hawk focus on the narrative literature, they tend to neglect the Latter Prophets, and so overlook YHWH's continuing involvement in Israel's life whilst in exile. Ezekiel's vision of YHWH's departure from Jerusalem culminates in an extraordinary divine reassurance to the exiles in Babylon: "Thus says the LORD God: Though I removed them far away among the nations, and though I scattered them among the countries, yet I have been a sanctuary to them for a little while in the countries where they have gone" (Ezek 11:16). YHWH disengaged from Israel as a conventional nation with territory, monarch, and temple, but not from Israel as an exiled people.

Of course, Ezekiel goes on to speak about hope for a return to the land and a restored monarchy, and his later eschatological visions (chapters 40–48) portray an ideal land, city, and temple, finally suitable as

---

12. A further observation could be made; even within the book of Genesis, God's involvement appears very high profile at the start but much lower profile in the final cycle of stories, centered on Joseph.

13. Hawk, *Violence*, 23–170.

YHWH's dwelling. Some Jews returned to the land and rebuilt the temple, but there was no return to national autonomy under a Davidic king, and the prophets' promises of a glorious return (Isa 40:1–11, etc.) were mixed with images of suffering. In many senses, exilic conditions continued and awaited resolution.

YHWH's commitment to Israel as a people, though not as a nation-state, continued to be emphasized in the Latter Prophets, while perspectives were widened to acknowledge God's superintendence of the international world as they knew it. Jeremiah had warned of Jerusalem's impending doom, but also saw YHWH's hand at work in the Babylonian invasion, calling Nebuchadnezzar "my servant" (Jer 25:9; 27:6). In the later chapters of Isaiah, Cyrus is described as YHWH's "shepherd" and "anointed" (Isa 44:28; 45:1).

The Overall Narrative of the Two Testaments

For Christians, the Second Testament not only follows the First, its portrayal of Jesus reframes the overarching story of the entire Christian Bible. The four Gospels portray Jesus in narrative genre, as the book of Acts renders the early church. The Epistles reflect on Jesus and the life of the early church in mainly didactic ways, though it has been argued that Paul's letters have an underlying narrative.[14] Yet exactly how this reframing might be decided remains to be seen. This is where Green's third proposal regarding paradigms becomes crucial.

Paradigm

Joel Green proposed that the character of God is paradigmatically manifest in Israel's release from bondage in Egypt and decisively revealed in Jesus of Nazareth. He does not explain what he means by "paradigmatically," but "paradigm" is a concept that has been used before in biblical interpretation to mean a prototypical example that illuminates scripture's meaning and allows application to other (contemporary) contexts.[15] Green has opted for the very beginning of Israel's story as a nation, arguably the defining event in Israel's story, but has he focussed too narrowly on release from bondage, and failed to include events at Sinai? The release

---

14. See the discussion in Longenecker, *Narrative Dynamics in Paul*.
15. E.g., van Iersel and Weiler, *Exodus: A Lasting Paradigm*.

is repeatedly recalled at later stages in Exodus, Leviticus, Numbers, and Deuteronomy; it is celebrated in a number of psalms, recalled in the prophets (e.g., Isa 11:16; Jer 7:25; 16:14; Ezek 20:5-6; Mic 7:15), and its imagery is employed to portray God's impending redemption of Israel in the later parts of Isaiah (43:16-21; 51:9-11; 52:11-12).[16] However, Israel's "release from bondage" was always about worshipping/serving YHWH (Exod 4:23; 5:1; 7:16; 8:1, 20; 9:1, 13; 10:3, 7), so that "the exodus" would be a better paradigm, always remembering that "the exodus" is not complete unless it includes Sinai.

In the Second Testament, Israel's release from Egypt is referenced in a number of places. On the mountain of transfiguration, Moses speaks with Jesus about his impending "exodus" (the NRSV obscures this with "departure" at Luke 9:31). Jesus' celebration of the Last Supper and his death at the festival of Passover are obviously important, and although the original Passover was one element of the exodus story, the commemorative meal includes emblems of the liberation journey from Egypt. Yet Jesus echoes Sinai (Exod 24:5-8) when he talks of a new covenant in his blood. Paul refers to the pharaoh of the exodus in Rom 9:17 and takes up the experiences of the Israelites in the exodus journey in 1 Cor 10:1-5, but most of his intertexts refer to events at Sinai (e.g., 2 Cor 3:7-18). Similarly, imagery from the second part of Exodus is important in the Letter to the Hebrews: Mt Sinai (12:18-21); the blood of the covenant (9:19-22); the construction of the tabernacle (8:5). So, can the paradigm of "the exodus" be separated from the kernel book of Exodus?

Although the exodus is certainly one of the most important paradigms in Israel's story, there are other contenders. The significance of the exile in Israel's story has been vital in historical and contemporary internal Jewish debates on identity, religion, and nationalism. It has been taken up by a number of Christian theologians and biblical scholars, and the concept of *diaspora* has been significant in cultural and postcolonialist studies.[17] I offer some elements of the exile that indicate theological shifts towards the end of the overall narrative in the First Testament.

In Joshua–Kings the land was central to Israel's story because YHWH hallowed it with his presence, especially in the specific locus of the tabernacle, and later the temple. I have already mentioned Ezekiel's assurance to the exiles that YHWH was their safe place even in Babylonian

---

16. See Fishbane, *Biblical Interpretation*, 358-68.
17. For a helpful survey, see Smith-Christopher, *Biblical Theology of Exile*, 6-21.

exile, or, we might say, YHWH has gone on pilgrimage with them and for them wherever they go. Jeremiah's letter to the exiles in Babylon extends this assurance:

> Thus says the LORD of hosts, the God of Israel, to all the exiles whom I have sent into exile from Jerusalem to Babylon: Build houses and live in them; plant gardens and eat what they produce. Take wives and have sons and daughters; take wives for your sons, and give your daughters in marriage, that they may bear sons and daughters; multiply there, and do not decrease. But seek the welfare of the city where I have sent you into exile, and pray to the LORD on its behalf, for in its welfare you will find your welfare. (Jer 29:4–7)

Although the exile is understood, in the Former Prophets, as a punishment upon Israel for its failure to love YHWH and keep Torah, here there is a glimpse of a complementary way to understand exile; as a means of bringing blessing to the nations. It is remarkable that the exiles might experience welfare (*shalom*) in Babylon, even if it was not the homeland that they longed for. Three elements of this commission—building, planting, and marrying—correspond to the exemptions from warfare in Deut 20:1–9, representing a wholeness of life that should be protected. They appear also in the vision of the new heavens and new earth in Isa 65:21–22.[18] From this point onwards, the exiled Jews began to establish viable lives outside the land, without a centralized government backed by an army, and without a centralized cult and sacrificial system in the temple. They became a people of the book, focussed on nurturing their local communities through the development of the synagogue.

These considerations led John Howard Yoder to propose that;

> More than Christians are aware, Babylon itself very soon became the cultural center of World Jewry, from the age of Jeremiah until the time we in the West call the Middle Ages. The people who re-colonized the "Land of Israel," repeatedly . . . were supported financially and educationally from Babylon, and in lesser ways from the rest of the diaspora. Our Palestinocentric reading of the story is a mistake, though a very understandable one. . . . In all the different ways represented by Sadducees, Pharisees, Maccabeans, and Essenes, Jews in Palestine had no choice but to define their identity over against the dominant Gentiles and to be divided from one another by their conflicting responses to

---

18. See Smith, *Religion of the Landless*, 132–37.

that challenge. On the other hand, the synagogues and rabbis in Babylon, and in the rest of the world where the Babylonian model was followed and Babylonian teachers were consulted, were spared that self-defeating distraction, so as to enter into creatively that Jeremianic phase of creating something qualitatively new in the history of religions.[19]

Yoder saw Jeremiah's vision of an exilic future for God's people as preferable to the approach of Ezra and Nehemiah who reconstituted a cult and a polity as a branch of the pagan imperial government.[20] In other words, while Ezra and Nehemiah were understandably seeking to work out the Deuteronomic vision of Jewish identity back in the homeland, those in the dispersion were discovering an alternative vision that was to be reignited in Jesus' ministry and in the mission of the early church. Yoder argued that, while the exile might appear less formative than the exodus because it was a defeat rather than a victory, exile is actually as significant as the exodus. In terms of God's mission to the world, whereas exodus meant the Israelites *withdrew* from Egypt, exile meant that God's people were dispersed *among* the nations.[21]

Exile might seem less prominent than exodus in the Second Testament, with the language of exile or Dispersion (*diaspora*) being picked up explicitly only in 1 Pet 1:1-2, 17 & 2:11-14 and James 1:1. However, Bruce Winter has shown that Jeremiah's vision of seeking the welfare of the city is apparent in the role and obligations of the first Christians as benefactors and citizens in several passages in the epistles (Rom 13:3-4; 16:23; 1 Cor 6:1-11; 7:17-24; 8:1—11:1; Gal 6:11-18; Phil:1:27—2:18; 1 Thess 4:11-12; 2 Thess 3:6-13; 1 Tim 5:3-16).[22] So we may understand the mission of the church in taking the life of the gospel to the world beyond Judaism as taking up the Jeremianic vision.

---

19. Yoder, "See How They Go," 57-58.
20. Yoder, "See How They Go," 74. John Goldingay, *Do We Need the New Testament?* 79, is critical of Yoder's point here, arguing that Jeremiah foresees an eventual return to the land (29:14; cf. 30:3; 31:3-25). Yet such an obvious point does not overturn Yoder's insight about the viability and vitality of the Babylonian model of Jewry. Curiously, Goldingay later (90) recognizes that "Our context is one in which God's promises have been partially fulfilled but in which nothing much seems now to be happening. We might even see ourselves as living in a situation like that of Judah in exile."
21. Yoder, "Withdrawal and Diaspora."
22. See Winter, *Seek the Welfare of the City*.

There is, therefore, a strong case for exile as a significant paradigm as well as exodus, but other important hermeneutical keys for a Christian reading of scripture should be considered. Even if Green's proposal for a paradigm is expanded to "the exodus" it begins to look rather inadequate when consideration is given to the subject of creation, to which I will return below.

2. The Scriptures as Canonical Theology

An alternative to the approach of narrative theology is to pay attention to the shape of the biblical canon, especially as it appears in the Hebrew Bible. In the prelude to Part II I noted that Eckhart Otto argues for a return to reading Deuteronomy as part of the Pentateuch rather than taking it as the beginning of a Deuteronomistic History. This has prompted me to return to a fascinating essay by Norbert Lohfink, in which he argues that there is a clear break between Deuteronomy and Joshua because the death of Moses on the frontier of the promised land constitutes a clear *literary* boundary.[23] A series of boundary markers signal the close of Deuteronomy:

- the Song of Moses (32:1-43)
- the blessing of Moses (33:1-29)
- the account of Moses' death (34:1-12).

At the beginning of Joshua, God's word comes to the new leader, "Let not this scroll of the Torah depart out of your mouth" (1:8). This expression refers back to Deut 31:24, which itself refers to the written covenant text of Deuteronomy 5-28, and yet it may ultimately have the whole Pentateuch in mind.

Lohfink makes a fundamental point about Deuteronomy's built-in fracture between the exodus story and its fulfilment in the promised land; it has significance for the whole First Testament.

> We see it in literary terms by the fact that Deuteronomy 34 is not only linked directly to Joshua 1, but in exactly the same way to the book of Isaiah, and to the Psalter, and in a somewhat less

---

23. Lohfink, "Death at the River Frontier."

clearly marked fashion to other individual building blocks of the Old Testament canon.[24]

Isaiah, the first book in the Latter Prophets, follows directly on the end of Deuteronomy since its appeal to heaven and earth (1:2) takes up Moses' Song, "Give ear, O heavens" (Deut 32:1). Isaiah soon summons the "rulers of Sodom" and "people of Gomorrah" to "Hear the Torah of our God" (1:10), and this impugning of Jerusalem refers to the impending exile that is sensed even in Deut 29:23, where those same cities are named. In the following verses, Isaiah makes clear what the Torah is concerned about:

> not sacrifices, but justice for the oppressed. In the second chapter a new and different Torah appears: the Torah for the nations, who will receive it in the eschatological pilgrimage of the nations to Zion. The tension between these two Torahs will be the content of the whole book of Isaiah.[25]

Turning to the first book in the Writings, the Psalter begins with the image of the man who

> does not follow the advice of the wicked,
>   or take the path that sinners tread,
>   or sit in the seat of scoffers;
> but his delight is in the Torah of the LORD,
>   and he murmurs his Torah day and night.
> (Ps 1:1-2)[26]

The last line here largely agrees with the formula in Josh 1:8. Next, in Psalm 2 we find the theme of the nations in the time of the Messiah, much like the second chapter of Isaiah. Granted, the key word "Torah" does not appear in Psalm 2 and it begins in the ancient imperial style,

> But then the man from Psalm 1, who now shines as the anointed king on Zion, suddenly ceases to wield his war club; instead he proclaims a message to the kings of the earth. The Torah he thus pronounces calls on them to submit themselves to the service of the God of Israel.[27]

---

24. Lohfink, "Death at the River Frontier," 5.
25. Lohfink, "Death at the River Frontier," 7.
26. Lohfink's translation, "Death at the River Frontier," 7.
27. Lohfink, "Death at the River Frontier," 7.

The kings are urged to "be wise" (2:10), and this is the same verb (in the same form and same tense) that appears twice at the beginning of Joshua (1:7, 8), where it is translated "so that you may be successful."

In pointing out these links between Deuteronomy and the Latter Prophets and the Writings as well as to the Former Prophets, Lohfink is alerting us to the "non-linear" connections between the books of the TaNaK. He explains the origin of such connections in the individual scrolls of the biblical books, that were stored upright together in small baskets; these scrolls could be accessed in a non-linear order, whereas the codices (the forerunners of modern printed books, made up of multiple leaves stitched together) that replaced the scrolls encouraged reading in linear order.[28] Thus the writing technology of that era was responsible for a kind of branching process that suggests a contemporary analogy: the books of the TaNaK are linked together like the items in a digital database, or the pages on a website.

It is well-known that among Jews the Torah has first place among the scriptures; it is "a canon within a canon." What the First Testament presents is an origin story up to the point of the crossing of the Jordan; it is a project and a promise. The remainder of the canon is a polyphonic commentary on it, with several alternatives, only one of which is Joshua–Kings. On these, Lohfink pronounces a verdict: "That was a failed experiment; at the end of it Israel is again outside the land." When we read the Latter Prophets in their final form, "the entry to the land is always still to come. Everywhere in the Old Testament canon, in one way or another, we find reflections from every possible angle on this threshold existence ... still in the wilderness." For example, in Ezekiel 20, Israel's history in the land is told from an exilic perspective, "and it all sounds as if Israel had never been in the land at all. The time in the land was still a time in the wilderness, and now Israel, by contrast, is in the 'wilderness of the peoples' (Ezek 20:35)."[29]

Lohfink's work on the canon can be supported by others, although they may not have thought in his canonical categories. Few scholars have written about the theology of the Latter Prophets as a collection of books, but Donald Gowan has summarized his important study like this:

---

28. Indeed, Lohfink thinks all the books are linked to the Torah as their fundamental textual reference. He notes that Qoheleth (Ecclesiastes) relates directly to the Torah's beginning by taking death as its central theme (Qoh 12:7; cf. Gen 3:19) ("Death at the River Frontier," 9).

29. Lohfink, "Death at the River Frontier," 10–11.

God had called a people into a special relationship with himself, giving them a land of their own, addressing them in cultic ceremonies with the assurance that he had made a covenant with them, and defining their character as his people in terms of law. He had given them priests to instruct them, kings to maintain justice, sages to guide them, and prophets to warn and exhort them when they forgot who they were. *It had not worked.* Neither Israel's worship nor daily life was truly distinct from their neighbours. They were no true witness to the nations concerning the character of their God, and the fate of the widow, orphan, immigrant, and the poor in their midst was no better than other countries. With the rise of the great empire builders in the Middle East—Assyria, followed by Babylon and Persia—God determined to do a new thing, *in effect to start over.* The little kingdoms of Israel and Judah would lose their political existence forever, but out of the death of Judah, God would raise up a new people, who would understand about God what most of their preexilic ancestors had never been able to comprehend, and who would commit themselves to obeying his will to an extent their ancestors had never done.[30]

The Second Testament as Definitive Commentary

Lohfink proposes that, as the Former and Latter Prophets and the Writings may be understood as commentaries upon the Torah, so the Second Testament is a further set of "commentaries" on the Torah, but this time the *definitive* commentary.

> In Jesus of Nazareth, God brought the Exodus to its end for Israel and also its consequences for the nations, which had long been foreseen by the prophets. To that extent the New Testament stands, great and powerful, over against the Old Testament and relativizes its own foundational text with a new one.
>
> John baptized across the Jordan, in the wilderness. But Jesus, with his first disciples, crossed over the Jordan to the west. In the land he proclaimed that the reign of God had come, and it did come in the signs and wonders in the land that Moses' epitaph could not report. That is how the gospels begin. (Even in John 3:23, [26], where the Baptizer also works in the land west of the Jordan, he only begins to do it after Jesus has crossed the Jordan ahead of him.) The gospels thus also link directly to the

---

30. Gowan, *Theology of the Prophetic Books*, 9–10, emphasis added.

situation that existed when Moses died, on the bank of the river. But since the resurrection of the dead begins at the end of the gospels, we are sure that the Exodus has reached its goal.[31]

Nevertheless, Jesus ascends after the resurrection, leaving the disciples to follow him during the in-between time before he returns. This is a striking analogy to the death of Moses and suggests that the basic text (or "canon within the canon") of the Second Testament is the fourfold set of Gospels, while the remaining books, Acts–Revelation, are commentary on it, suggesting that the Gospels can be realized in a multitude of ways.[32]

The shape of Jesus' ministry, as presented in the Gospels, suggests that he adopted the verdict of the Latter Prophets upon the project of Israel in the land, as told in the Former Prophets. Gerhard Lohfink takes up his brother's argument and discusses First Testament passages that envisage how people can live in peace and without violence (Isa 2:2–4; Mic 4:1–5; Zech 9:9–10; cf. Psalm 22), while acknowledging the frequent violence that it contains elsewhere. Commenting on Jesus' decision to renounce violence in his own career, Lohfink writes,

> Jesus did not simply reproduce and repeat the Old Testament. He certainly did not insert completely new content into it. Instead, from the immense material in his Bible, from this experience of centuries, from this heaped-up mass of wisdom and history he discerned and drew out the scarlet thread of God's will—with a sensitivity and ability to distinguish that we can only marvel at.
>
> Jesus' genius—and Jesus was a genius, if we can use such banal language of him—consisted precisely in that he brought together at its center everything Israel had already discovered, and he did so both critically and creatively . . . Jesus, by weighing the many voices with a critical ability to differentiate, allowed the new thing to arise out of what had already been known and hoped for.[33]

---

31. Lohfink, "Death at the River Frontier," 12.

32. Lohfink, "Death at the River Frontier," 12–13. Similarly, Pennington, *Reading the Gospels Wisely*, 229–58, describes the Gospels as "the archway of the canon."

33. Lohfink, *Jesus of Nazareth*, 187.

Conceptualizing the Canon

Torah	Former Prophets	Latter Prophets	Writings[34]	Gospels	Other Apostolic Writings
	First commentaries			Definitive commentary	
Genesis				Matthew	
Exodus				Mark	
Leviticus				Luke	
Numbers				John	
Deuteronomy					Acts[35]
	Joshua	Isaiah	Psalms		*Paul's Epistles*
	Judges	Jeremiah	Proverbs		*General Epistles*
	Samuel	Ezekiel	Job		Revelation
	Kings	The Twelve[36]	Ruth–Esther[37]		
			Daniel		
			Ezra & Nehemiah		
			Chronicles		

The Hermeneutical Key for a Christian Reading of the Scriptures

Whether we choose Israel's release from bondage in Egypt or the exodus as the paradigmatic manifestation of the character of God alongside the decisive revelation in Jesus of Nazareth, this paradigmatic formulation tends to prioritize salvation over creation, although Green's prior point about the "one aim of God" could hint at God's larger creation purposes. In order to throw light on this subject I will appeal to Terence Fretheim's important work on the theology of creation in *the book* of Exodus (not simply the exodus event).

---

34. There is great diversity in the order of the books of the Writings in various traditions. See Childs, *Introduction*, 502–3.

35. Acts–Revelation are commentary on the four-fold book of the Gospels.

36. "The Twelve" are Hosea–Malachi.

37. Ruth, Song of Songs, Ecclesiastes, Lamentations, and Esther are known as "The Scrolls" (*Megilloth*).

Generally, God's work in *creation provides the basic categories and interpretive clues* for what happens in redemption. God's work in creation has been shown to be life-giving, life-preserving, and life-blessing (e.g., 1:7, 12, 20). What God does in redemption is in the service of these endangered divine goals in and for the creation. The hymnic celebration of that redemptive act in Exodus 15 is permeated with creation-talk, in terms of vocabulary, structure, and theme. Not only is an *experience* of God's work as creator necessary for participation in the exodus—otherwise there would be no people to redeem, an *understanding* of God's work as creator is indispensable for the proper interpretation of what happens—there would be no exodus as we know it without it having been informed by that understanding.[38]

Fretheim describes five basic creation themes in Exodus, which can be summarized as follows:[39]

- A creation theology provides the *cosmic purpose* behind God's redemptive activity on Israel's behalf. What is at stake is God's mission to the world since "all the earth is God's" (9:29; cf. 9:14; 19:5).
- God's redemptive activity is set in terms of a *creational need*. If Pharaoh persists in his anti-life policies at the point when the creation promise has begun to be actualized (1:7), then God's purposes in creation are being subverted.
- God's redemptive activity is *cosmic in its effects*. God's defeat of the powers of chaos results, not simply in Israel's liberation, but in the reign of God over the entire cosmos (15:18).
- God's calling of Israel is given *creationwide scope*. Israel is called out from among other nations and commissioned to a task on behalf of God's earth (19:4-6).
- God's own relationship to the creation is seen in terms of an *immanental involvement*, primarily in the human form of the theophany, from the call of Moses (3:1-6) to the sea crossing (14:19) to Sinai (24:9-11). "This action bespeaks God's: (i) identity with human beings, a sharing in the human condition; (ii) willingness to undergo change, taking on a non-divine form and directly experiencing what that entails; (iii) vulnerability, risking a response in the human encounter that is other than faith or obedience. But God does not

---

38. Fretheim, "Suffering God and Sovereign God," 106-7.
39. Fretheim, "Suffering God and Sovereign God," 107-8.

thereby give up sovereignty; indeed, it is a sign of strength for God to do just this. God's sovereignty is made manifest in assuming a vulnerable form in the midst of the world."⁴⁰

God as Sovereign and Suffering in Exodus

These points set the stage for Fretheim's more extensive discussion of two central images of God in Exodus: sovereignty and suffering. Images of divine sovereignty are prominent:

- God's lordship is evident in the proclamation of the law and call to obedience.
- God's judging is experienced by the Egyptians.
- God's kingship is explicitly confirmed, though only once (15:18).

The nature of the divine sovereignty enables God to work through the natural order at will—in the plagues, the wind and the sea, the provision of food and water in the wilderness, the natural pyrotechnics at Mount Sinai. Yet this sovereignty is qualified in that it is usually in coordination with human activity, i.e., Moses, sometimes with Aaron. The divine use of nature is also congruent with what is possible for nature to become if properly used or improperly exploited—it is not arbitrary, so the plagues are congruent with the anti-creational sins of Pharaoh. Thus, the language of divine sovereignty is appropriate, yet must reckon with the complexities of divine, human, and cosmic interaction.

The order of divine rule over the human activity is rather differently conceived, especially in the opening chapters that provide a hermeneutical base. In the divine engagement with the five women in chapters 1–2, God is not the subject of any verb in their various actions, so that divine action is unobtrusive, unlikely, and vulnerable;⁴¹ God ironically uses what is low and despised in that world to shame the strong. The first word from God in the book, to Moses in 3:7–10, is programmatic (the narrator's report in 2:24–25 helps establish this) and interweaves metaphors of sovereignty and suffering. Sovereignty is evident in YHWH's initiative, YHWH's agenda-setting will to deliver Israel, and YHWH's announced ability to accomplish it. Alongside this, God declares, "I have observed

---

40. Fretheim, "Suffering God and Sovereign God," 108.

41. Pharaoh's daughter is given a notable role in that there is a direct verbal and thematic parallel between her activity (2:5–6) and that of YHWH (3:7–8).

Israel's afflictions ... and I know their sufferings." This testifies to God's intimate *experience* of this suffering; for "God to *know* suffering is, to follow the metaphorical grain, to allow suffering to enter deeply into the divine being." Yet this does not mean God is powerless in the face of this suffering; rather this suffering focusses the divine energies on the situation and works on it from the inside rather than the outside. Further, God does not act alone, and is dependent upon Moses to carry out certain tasks (14:31), which means working through Moses' frailties as well as strengths.

Divine sovereignty and suffering in subsequent interchanges with Moses and Pharaoh are discussed extensively by Fretheim, and this leads to an important reflection on the relation between these two metaphoric fields. Some metaphors for God have low revelatory capacity (e.g., "dry rot" in Hos 5:12), while others may be described as "controlling" according to their pervasiveness and distribution in the scriptures, and the nature of the genres and the traditions in which the metaphors are used, but also by how true they are to life and their capacity to capture, organize, focus, and communicate the experience of God. Study of Exodus shows that the "controlling" category of metaphors must include both sovereignty and suffering metaphoric fields, yet in the history of God-talk, sovereignty metaphors have usually been the controlling ones, and thus left largely unqualified. Once the "controlling" status of the suffering metaphors is recovered, Fretheim insists, there will be a decisive effect on common understandings of sovereignty.

> The end result is that suffering and sovereignty stand alongside each other in a metaphorical dialectic. Suffering and sovereignty are internally related to one another in God, such that the sovereign God is always suffering and the suffering God is always sovereign. Contextual factors, however, the needs of time and place, may call for one metaphoric field to achieve some ascendancy over the other. Hence, given the present common understanding of sovereignty, suffering will have a more decisive effect on sovereignty than the other way round.[42]

Fretheim then applies this approach to challenge the work of three other scholars on Exodus, and the last of these is particularly helpful in thinking about hermeneutical keys for a Christian reading of the First Testament.

---

42. Fretheim, "Suffering God and Sovereign God," 116–17.

God as Suffering and Sovereign in Second Isaiah

Erich Zenger compared the message of Isaiah 51, which is addressed to the wretched exiles in Babylon, and draws on exodus imagery, with that addressed to the oppressed Israelites in Exodus. Although the exodus revealed the kind of God YHWH is, the means by which God would act on this later occasion differs from the exodus in substantial ways. "The first exodus involved the annihilation of Israel's enemies, but this destructive aspect has now faded away." In this new exodus, "God will end Israel's suffering without the use of war and destruction." It will be a "peaceful miracle."[43] In Isa 51:9–10, Israel calls upon God to act as in the first exodus, but in 51:12–16,

> God takes up this appeal to unlimited power but gives it a new direction intended to wean Israel away from all ideas of a strong God who destroys the others; he wants Israel to discover that he is a loving God who wants to bestow new life, firstly and foremostly to Israel.[44]

God "turns to Zion like a loving mother in a personal relationship." The servant Israel "cries out for vengeance, but in reply God puts forward the picture of the Suffering Servant who by renouncing power and accepting suffering, becomes a witness to the power of reconciliation and love that can change the world."[45] The vision of Isa 2:4 captures this sense of the effects of God's new way of being the exodus God. Zenger writes of the metaphors of war and power as "transmuted into that of the caring shepherd of his people" (Isa 40:9–11), but then changes the verb to say that the Shepherd "replaces" the Warrior of Exodus.

Fretheim is critical of Zenger's depiction of what has happened to the images of God between Exodus and Isaiah. Zenger short-changes the theme of divine wrath in this part of Isaiah (e.g., 47:1–15). Fretheim insists that the old warrior image for God is not jettisoned ("YHWH goes forth like a soldier; like a warrior he stirs up his fury," 42:13)—this is necessary in order to effect Israel's salvation from oppressors (49:24–26). However, it is transformed to function as God's powerful ways of love and suffering; God's rule is now of a different order.

> Our study has uncovered a hermeneutic within Exodus itself that anticipates the Isaianic perspective. Isaiah is not a radical

---

43. Zenger, "The God of Exodus," 26.
44. Zenger, "The God of Exodus," 27.
45. Zenger, "The God of Exodus," 28.

reinterpretation of Exodus, but extends a direction of thought already present there. A suffering God is clearly in evidence in Exodus, and it remains for later witnesses such as Isaiah and the New Testament to work this out in greater depth. In other words, the transmutation of sovereignty metaphors in view of suffering ones is characteristic of both traditions.[46]

Fretheim goes on to consider the extent to which Exodus texts can serve as a paradigm for contemporary reflection and action and asks whether Christians should now read Exodus only through the eyes of Isaiah, so that Isaiah's fuller transmutation of the warrior metaphor is the definitive one.

Is the Isaianic development a matter of progress in Israel's understanding? Or, does Isaiah witness to an evolution in the divine way with the world, a change of means and methods by which to achieve the same divine goals in view of God's experience? Have all God's ways with the world been transmuted into "Love your enemies," heaping coals on their heads? Or is it a contextual matter? For the circumstances inherent in the Egyptian situation, God's warrior ways, as qualified by the suffering images of Exodus, were the only possible mode in order to accomplish Israel's liberation. For Isaiah's time, God's warrior mode is more completely transmuted. Yet there may be other times and places for God to act as warrior in a less qualified way.[47]

But I think that Fretheim has already answered these questions in a previous paragraph when he calls for metaphors of divine suffering to be given more prominence.

In New Testament terms, this means that the cross must be a primary qualifying metaphor for any doctrine of God. So often the Christological formulations of the church have been accompanied by an amazingly imperious notion of God. . . . [T]he sovereignty of God must finally be defined in terms of how it looks when nailed to a cross.[48]

Fretheim's discussion of the interaction of sovereignty and suffering as theological images in Exodus and Isaiah should make us wary of simplistic appeals to exodus or exile as paradigms. Setting these in the context of a theology of creation must also supplement a theology of salvation.

46. Fretheim, "Suffering God and Sovereign God," 121.
47. Fretheim, "Suffering God and Sovereign God," 122.
48. Fretheim, "Suffering God and Sovereign God," 121.

Looking for paradigms in the First Testament is less helpful than doing the more detailed work of grasping the theology of particular books and holding these within the canonical shape of the whole Bible.

3. Assessment

Having discussed the narrative and canonical approaches to reframing the First Testament in the light of Jesus, some assessment must be made. Firstly, some advantages of the narrative approach:

- There are textual warrants for the narrative approach in promises fulfilled, genealogies, and passages that summarize the First Testament story.
- I have emphasized the value of narrative analysis of individual books of the First Testament. Appeal to narrative on a larger scale would seem to follow for the whole library.
- The time-line approach is familiar; fitting the many and various parts of the story into the larger story is something that comes easily.
- The concept of paradigm may be useful, though it must certainly be expanded beyond the exodus to include the exile, and perhaps other alternatives.

However, there are also some significant disadvantages of this approach:

- The concept of paradigm is inadequate compared with consideration of theologies of particular books.
- I have argued that books essential to the time-line approach (Joshua–Kings), when read carefully, subvert common assumptions about the stories they tell. Exodus is about much more than Israel's release from bondage.
- Some books do not work well with a time-line approach themselves: Job stands outside Israel's story (apart from using the divine name in its prologue and epilogue). Some psalms relate to the time-line, as we have seen, but many do not. Proverbs, Ecclesiastes, and Song of Solomon may be fitted into the time-line via Solomon, but their content has little to do with it.[49]

49. Brent Strawn, *Concise Introduction*, 168–69, emphasizes that the First Testament "is actually not self-evidently a story at all. If someone says the Old Testament

Secondly, some advantages of the canonical approach advocated here:

- There are strong textual indicators of the boundary between Deuteronomy and Joshua, and of links between Deuteronomy and both Isaiah and Psalms. These point to the significance of the Torah as "the canon within the canon" of the First Testament.
- An approach that is guided by the Jewish valuing of the Torah looks to our heritage among Jesus' own people.[50] It also suggests that the Gospels form "the canon within the canon" for the whole Christian Bible.
- It allows theological insights from the books of the First Testament in which Israel's story is of small significance (i.e., Wisdom) to be given due weight.
- It delivers a positive verdict upon the project of Israel outside the land (the patriarchs as well as the exiles and the dispersion), and a negative verdict upon the project of Israel in the land, as recounted in the Former Prophets.

Two significant disadvantages of the canonical approach:

- The Christian rearrangement of the Hebrew TaNaK moved the prophets to the end, giving it a strong forward movement, pointing to Jesus and linking it to the Second Testament.[51] So, it makes sense to retain the Christian order of books, but the centrality of the Torah and its links to the other parts of the Hebrew canon should be borne in mind.
- The concept and shape of the Hebrew Bible canon is unfamiliar to most Christians, so its significance for interpreting the First Testament requires careful explanation.[52]

---

is a story, they have made it so by asserting as much. They have 'narrativized' the Old Testament, constructing or construing it as a story even when its overall form and constituent parts resist the category." Strawn goes on to suggest alternatively reading the Bible as if it were a poem or a series of poems.

50. This explains why Jesus would respond to the devil's use of Psalm 91 by resort to Deuteronomy.

51. The final book of the TaNaK is Chronicles, which summarizes much of the First Testament narrative.

52. Several scholarly introductions now largely employ the Hebrew canonical arrangement, e.g., Collins, *Introduction to the Hebrew Bible*.

10

Facilitating Access to the First Testament

In view of contemporary Christians' unfamiliarity with the First Testament, consideration of how to facilitate access to it is necessary. A common devotional strategy has been to "Find Christ in all the scriptures," but this can lead to fanciful pursuits, such as finding anything red in color, like Rahab's crimson cord (Josh 2:18, 21), to serve as an allegory for Jesus' blood.[1] Such an imposition of a Christian template suppresses the First Testament's own voice. Christians must find ways of doing justice to the First Testament in its own terms whilst also seeing Jesus as the culmination of the Bible's overall story. This may seem like an impossible task, but it may help to envisage it as an ongoing adventure of discovery, of rethinking and realignment. There are no definitive answers, only more or less helpful guidelines for the journey.

Firstly, I will seek to address the key question that teachers and churches confront in order to assist interpretation: how to express the relationship between the two Testaments. Secondly, I discuss some contemporary topics raised by the books of Joshua–Kings, and go on to suggest two further topics to which the First Testament elsewhere contributes. In conclusion, I explore how biblical literacy, especially regarding the First Testament, might be facilitated in practice.

---

1. Such an aim derives from Luke 24:27, of course, but the resort to allegory is unnecessary when there are more convincing ways in which the scriptures witness to Jesus, as we have seen, and will see in this chapter. Furthermore, things about Christ do not exhaust what may be found in the scriptures; Hays' point about the ecclesial reference of many echoes in Paul (and in the Gospels) is pertinent here.

INTERPRETING THE OLD TESTAMENT

1. The Relationship between the Testaments

For many Bible readers, the relationship between the Testaments could be summed up in terms of "prophecy and fulfilment." It is true that Jesus and the apostles often used the language of fulfilment in relation to their scriptures, although their concepts of both prophecy and fulfilment were more subtle and complex than is often recognized. Prophecy is often taken to mean prediction, and fulfilment the realization of such prediction. Much biblical prophecy concerns God's word for the immediate situation; condemnation of reprehensible behavior or exhortation to a change of attitude, as well as warning of impending disaster or encouragement by way of a promised future. These latter involve some forward look, yet they do not necessarily entail an absolute guarantee, as if all future events are fixed. Prophecy is not crystal-ball gazing; indeed, some biblical prophecies are clearly not fulfilled, despite Deuteronomy's test (18:22).[2] This may be partly because human choices are involved (the warnings or promises may be conditional) and partly because God has the freedom to adjust to a multitude of possibilities.

Fulfilment may mean the coming to pass of a prophecy from long before, as in Micah's prophecy (5:2) about the Messiah's Bethlehem birthplace, as the scribes identified, according to Matt 2:5-6. Intriguingly, Matthew does not use the word "fulfil" here, though he does elsewhere in his birth narrative (1:22; 2:15, 17, 23). But he soon comments that the Holy Family's flight to Egypt and sojourn there was "to fulfil what had been spoken by the Lord through the prophet, 'Out of Egypt I have called my son'" (2:15).[3] This is a quotation from Hos 11:1, in which YHWH reflects on the exodus centuries previously; i.e., this prophecy is a *backward* look, not a forward projection. Matthew is using the prophet's brief summary of Israel's foundational story to make a figural connection (in Hays' terms) with Jesus' childhood. Thus, for Matthew, "fulfilment" is less about ticking off predictions than understanding Jesus' story in terms set up by Israel's story.

---

2. We have noted that Huldah's prophecy regarding Josiah's death was not fulfilled (2 Kgs 22:20). Another classic example is Ezekiel's prophecy regarding Nebuchadnezzar's conquest of Tyre (26:7-14). This is followed by a later prophecy that acknowledges Nebuchadnezzar failed to conquer Tyre and promises him Egypt instead (29:17-20). The latter promise also failed to materialize. See Greenberg, *Ezekiel 21-37*, 617-18.

3. This is one place where Matthew does not follow the LXX, but a Greek translation that corresponds to the MT. See Hays, *Gospels*, 113.

Along with the continuity suggested by "prophecy and fulfilment," there is a contrasting dynamic between the Testaments that can be summed up as "discontinuity."[4] When we are comfortable with the ways in which Jesus took up and extended the First Testament story, it is easy to forget how difficult it was for his contemporaries to grasp how he could be the one that Israel was longing for; he was so radical, so extraordinary, so challenging, and so threatening to those with power that they had to do away with him. The coming of Jesus somehow changed everything. I will explore the discontinuity further before returning to the theological continuity between the two Testaments.

The Nature of the Discontinuity between the Testaments

The topic of supersessionism was introduced in chapter 1, and it is important to return to it here since misunderstandings can contribute to the neglect of the First Testament.

The Letter to the Hebrews makes an extended comparison between what was best in the old covenant and the "better" things that have replaced them with the coming of Christ. Because some readers have therefore concluded that "Jesus supersedes the Old Testament" and "the church supersedes Israel," Hebrews has often been described as "supersessionist." Church pastor and popular author Andy Stanley insists that "Jesus was sent by the Father to introduce something *entirely new*."[5] He goes on to emphasize the "obsolete" status of the old covenant, appealing to this verse: "In speaking of 'a new covenant,' he has made the first one obsolete. And what is obsolete and growing old will soon disappear" (Heb 8:13). This is an unfortunate reading of the letter since, as Dick France puts it,

> For all his dismissal of aspects of the old covenant (especially its priesthood and sacrifices) as no longer relevant, the writer of Hebrews is second to none in his love for the Old Testament

---

4. Hays, *Gospels*, 381, uses the word "reversal."

5. Stanley, *Irresistible*, 6. Stanley made headlines in 2018 for preaching from Acts 15 that Christians need to "unhitch" the Old Testament from their faith. In *Aftermath, Part 3*, Stanley said "You don't see much grace in the Old Testament . . ." (19:45), and that the early church leaders "unhitched the church from the worldview, value system, and regulations of the Jewish scriptures" (33:25).

and his desire to do justice to its role in the ongoing purpose of God.[6]

Richard Hays acknowledges that Hebrews has historically often been interpreted in a supersessionist way but shows that in recent years scholars have been realizing the complexity of processes of identity formation among distinct "Christian" and "Jewish" communities in the first Christian century. If we put aside later antagonisms between Christianity and Judaism, we notice that

> Nowhere does Hebrews suggest that the Jewish people have been replaced by a new and different people of God. Indeed, it appears that the addressees of the letter are considered part of God's "house," the same house over which Moses was faithful—that is, "the house of Israel" (3:1–6; 8:10).[7]

So, it is unhelpful to describe Hebrews' teaching as a form of "Christianity" over against "Judaism," and Hays proposes instead that it teaches a form of Jewish sectarian "New Covenantalism." This emerges from the quotation of Jeremiah's prophecy regarding a "new covenant with the house of Israel" (8:8–13, citing Jer 34:31–34). The first covenant was inadequate because it was unable to create an obedient people (cf. 10:1), and the people's failure to keep the covenant was a symptom of its shortcoming. God's solution to this problem is the creation of a new covenant in which the (same) law will be written on people's hearts and minds.

Hays arrives at 8:13a and points out that a literal translation would be, "In saying 'new' he has made the first 'old.'" He comments,

> the author of Hebrews is not interested in a blanket abolition of the Torah. Rather, his concern focuses narrowly on the cultic practice of offering sacrifices for sins under the first covenant, particularly on the Day of Atonement, as Heb. 9 will show. The new covenant instituted by Jesus provides an alternative way for purification and atonement through Jesus' once-for-all offering of his own blood. But to generalize the new covenant language of Heb. 8 into a comprehensive negation of Torah is to go far beyond anything found in the text.[8]

This suggests that the new covenant envisages the restoration of Israel, not its rejection. There is nothing in the letter about those of Jewish

---

6. France, "Relationship between the Testaments," 671.
7. Hays, "No Lasting City," 154.
8. Hays, "No Lasting City," 161.

heritage who do not recognize Jesus as the mediator of a new covenant, such as in Romans 9–11.

Hebrews was written using the imagery and thought-world of the First Testament, but Jesus was not slain like a lamb by a priest in the temple according to Levitical regulations. A victim of injustice perpetrated by the powerful, he was executed outside the city in the most sadistic and humiliating procedure by pagan soldiers. It takes a peculiar leap of the imagination to grasp how such grisly slaughter could constitute a divine transaction. Yet here is the extraordinary twist in the plot. The resurrection of Jesus declares a resounding affirmation of his person and life's work and unleashes a *transformation* of Israel's identity.

God's Spirit had been active throughout the First Testament in a great variety of ways, and yet there was a limitation to certain leaders and prophets. The classic example of this is God's response to Moses' complaint about the strain of leading so many people; "the LORD . . . took some of the spirit that was on him and put it on the seventy elders; and when the spirit rested on them, they prophesied" (Num 11:25). When Moses is informed that the Spirit rested on two other men so that they prophesied in the camp, he responds, "Would that all the LORD's people were prophets, and that the LORD would put his spirit upon them!" Moses' humble aspiration, as well as Joel's prophecy, is fulfilled in the coming of the Spirit on the early believers in Jerusalem on the Day of Pentecost (Acts 2:1–21). The empowering life of the Spirit transformed them from waiting believers (following Jesus' instructions) to active witnesses.

It took time for the earliest followers of Jesus to grasp the implications of that transformation—the book of Acts portrays these witnesses gradually (and sometimes reluctantly) spreading from Jerusalem to Rome, provoked by the Holy Spirit. Its fulcrum point is the Jerusalem Council, at which it was recognized that gentiles turning to God through the grace of the Lord Jesus should not be required to be circumcised or keep the law of Moses (15:5, 10–11, 19), except for the so-called "apostolic decree" (15:20, 29; cf. 21:25) that seems to have been derived from four Levitical laws that apply to sojourning aliens (Lev 17:8–9, 10–12, 13–14; 18:26).[9] God's ancient people, Israel, was now being radically expanded to include many gentiles on the basis of Israel's rebuilding, in accordance with Amos 9:11–12 (LXX).

---

9 See the important work of Bauckham, "James and the Gentiles," and of Beale, *The Temple*, 232–44.

Theological Continuity between the Testaments

More connects the Two Testaments than dramatic continuity and surprise. Many key theological strands run through both Testaments, and their origins in the First Testament are essential for appropriate theological interpretation of the Second Testament. Here I briefly explore several of these strands with a view to contemporary application.[10]

God and Creation

In the great civilizations of the ancient world polytheism was almost universal. Central to the First Testament is its concept of God: the one true and living God. This monotheism seems to have developed from an early henotheism (the worship of one god above all others, i.e., the existence of other deities was not denied) before becoming established after the exile, and it has been faithfully adhered to by devout Jews ever since.[11] According to Jesus, "'You shall love the Lord your God with all your heart, and with all your soul, and with all your mind.' This is the greatest and first commandment" (Matt 22:37–38, citing Deut 6:5). Jesus embodied such love in his devotion to the Father and dependence on the Spirit. As his followers began to realize Jesus' divine identity they did so from within First Testament monotheism, and the doctrine of the Trinity was built upon it; it does not subvert it.

The First Testament delivers much more about God than monotheism. Its passages about creation clearly separate God from everything else. God is not to be identified with anything in creation, as the command against idolatry makes clear (Exod 20:4–6). Yet God is not distanced from creation; rather, closely involved with it. As Fretheim shows, God, human beings, and the world are thoroughly interrelated.[12]

God's pronouncement of "very good" upon the completed creation (Gen 1:31) entails a positive evaluation of the physical world. However, the Jewish valuing and enjoyment of the world tended, in the early church, to be overcome by dualistic movements that divided reality into the physical, material world and the invisible, spiritual realm. Although the second-century church rejected gnosticism, Plato's less extreme form

---

10. See further the profound studies from a Catholic perspective of Anderson, *Christian Doctrine and the Old Testament*.
11. See Hurtado, "Monotheism."
12. Fretheim, *God and World*.

of dualism had a major influence upon Alexandrian Christianity, and Neoplatonism's influence upon Augustine has had a detrimental impact upon Protestants as well as the Catholic Church through much of history.[13] The goodness and pleasures of the physical world have been frowned upon; the body has been policed by rules lest it prove a hindrance to the cultivation of one's "spiritual" life. The enjoyment of sexual relationship within covenanted lives has been regarded as suspect, while monks and nuns, as well as priests, have been required to renounce it entirely.

However, reflection upon Jesus' Jewish worldview helps to understand that he called men and women to act responsibly and thankfully as God's servants in this earthly realm, not to escape from it. Jesus' incarnation and bodily resurrection, as well as his physical healing ministry, were emphatic endorsements of the material world. Many Christians think of life beyond the grave in disembodied, other-worldly terms. Some hope for a "rapture" from this life, leaving the world to burn, as if the promise of a new heaven and a new earth means that God will replace the world rather than redeem it. The First Testament reminds us that God's salvation is as much about the tangible world and our bodies as about the unseen world and our spiritual welfare.[14]

Thirdly, God's moral character is asserted, yet with significant shifts rather than in absolute terms. YHWH's self-proclamation to Moses, following the Golden Calf incident, is a central text of the First Testament:

> The LORD, the LORD,
> a God merciful and gracious,
> slow to anger,
> and abounding in steadfast love and faithfulness,
> keeping steadfast love for the thousandth generation,
> forgiving iniquity and transgression and sin,
> yet by no means clearing the guilty,
> but visiting the iniquity of the parents
> upon the children and the children's children,
> to the third and the fourth generation.
> (Exod 34:6–7)[15]

---

13. Although Augustine moved away from his earlier Platonism once he became a Christian and was critical of some aspects of Platonism in *City of God*, other aspects seemed to remain. See Cary, *Augustine's Invention of the Inner Self*.

14. See further, Wilson, *Our Father Abraham*, 166–90.

15. Note how, in the aftermath of the Golden Calf incident, the emphasis on mercy over punishment has shifted even within Exodus from the earlier version in 20:5–6.

To modern readers, the concluding threat of transgenerational punishment appears totally unjust, so must be explored briefly.[16] In the Former Prophets, this doctrine of divine punishment can be seen to apply in the case of the death of David's first son by Bathsheba (2 Sam 12:13–19), and especially in the attribution of Judah's destruction to the sins of Mannasseh (2 Kgs 23:26–27; 24:3–4), four generations before Jehoiachin (2 Kgs 24:19–20). However, there is evidence of questioning this transgenerational doctrine of divine punishment in Lam 5:7; "Our ancestors sinned; they are no more, and we bear their iniquities." Here the generation that endures the punishment attributes it to the sins of its ancestors, thereby insinuating its own innocence and questioning the doctrine. Whilst in Babylonia, Ezekiel wrestled with the sense of futility that this doctrine imbued in the exiles ("Our transgressions and our sins weigh upon us, and we waste away because of them; how then can we live?", 33:10). In a fascinating oracle the prophet turns the doctrine into a proverb before rejecting it and insisting on personal responsibility:

> The word of the LORD came to me: What do you mean by repeating this proverb concerning the land of Israel, "The parents have eaten sour grapes, and the children's teeth are set on edge"? As I live, says the Lord GOD, this proverb shall no more be used by you in Israel. Know that all lives are mine; the life of the parent as well as the life of the child is mine: it is only the person who sins that shall die. (Ezek 18:1–4)

Finally, the formulation of divine justice in Deuteronomy transforms the original declaration (Exod 34:6–7) like this:

> Know therefore that the LORD your God is God, the faithful God who maintains covenant loyalty with those who love him and keep his commandments, to a thousand generations, and who repays *in their own person* those who reject him. He does not delay but repays *in their own person* those who reject him. (7:9–10, emphasis added)

---

16. One way of understanding "to the third and the fourth generation" refers it to the generations that made up a family unit, often living together or nearby, who were deemed to share the guilt of the perpetrator, as can be observed in the execution of Achan along with his family (Josh 7:24–26). However, the other cases mentioned here do not fit this explanation.

The third and fourth generation are not mentioned; the transgenerational doctrine of divine punishment has been replaced by the punishment of the perpetrator.[17]

Thus, we can observe a major theological transformation between Exodus and Deuteronomy. Jesus picks up on this internal trajectory within the First Testament. It is Deuteronomy's characterization of God that illuminates Jesus' ministry of compassion, forgiveness, and suffering for Israel, yet also his combative, conflicted relationship with the Jewish leaders of his day.

Christology

Terence Fretheim argues that the First Testament provides continuing insight regarding the person of Jesus Christ:

> it is insufficient to say Jesus is important for understanding the Old Testament; the interpretive traffic going the other way is even more fundamental. We continue to need the Old Testament in our ongoing efforts to understand Jesus more fully, both historically and theologically.[18]

Fretheim goes on to demonstrate how the First Testament witnesses to God as one who is in relationship within the divine realm (Gen 1:26; Prov 8:22–31; Jer 23:18–23), and who freely enters into relationships with that which has been created. This God is present and active in the world, entering into the space and time of the world and making it God's own (Ps 104:1–3; Isa 40:22; Amos 9:6); "God—who is other than the world—works from within the world, and not on the world from without."[19] God was already doing this during the First Testament, so to suggest that God entered into time and history for the first time in the Christ event is to ignore much of the First Testament; "God's act in Jesus is an intensification of this already-existing trajectory of God's way of being present in and relating to the structures of the world."[20]

In the First Testament, God takes human form in various ways, especially in anonymous human form as a "man" or "angel/messenger" (Gen 16:7–13; 18:1—19:11; Judg 6:11–24; 13:3–23), but also likely in a

17. See Levinson, "Strategies for the Reinterpretation of Normative Texts."
18. Fretheim, "Christology," 350.
19. Fretheim, "Christology," 357.
20. Fretheim, "Christology," 358.

human form veiled in fire, cloud/smoke, or light (Exod 3:2; 24:9–11; Ezek 1:26–28). In the prophetic literature, the word of God becomes embodied in the person of the prophet (especially in Jeremiah and Ezekiel), so that they function, in effect, as ongoing theophanies; "The story of God gets caught up in the very life of the prophet."[21] And finally, the First Testament witnesses to a suffering God. We have seen how God's faithfulness to Israel through repeated failures during the eras of the judges and the kings was fraught with rejection, anger, anguish, and exasperation. God suffers with those experiencing suffering (Exod 3:7; Jer 9:17–18; 31:20), God suffers for his people (Isa 42:14; Hos 11:7–9), and God is even burdened with their sins (Isa 43:23–25). In some sense the divine life is expended for the sake of God's relationship with the people and their life together. "For this kind of God, the cross is no stranger."[22]

Ecclesiology and Mission

God's mission to bring blessing to the world that has gone wrong begins with YHWH's call of Abraham (Gen 12:1–3). The strategy of calling one particular person and his descendants is the beginning of ecclesiology; Abraham will have many descendants, a great name and a designated land. From this point onwards in Genesis and in much of the remainder of the First Testament the focus is upon God's people, yet the wider context of the world around them remains on the agenda, and from time to time their calling to be a blessing to that world is spelled out (Gen 18:17–19; Deut 4:5–8). It can be observed in Joseph's provision of food to the world (Gen 41:57) and Elisha's healing of Naaman (2 Kings 5), as well as the inclusion of outsiders into Israel, such as Rahab and Ruth.

As people rethink and develop new approaches to mission in post-Christendom, it has become common for "influencers" to say, "Christology determines missiology, and missiology determines ecclesiology."[23] But ecclesiology and missiology began together in God's purposes with Abraham, and God's coming down into the world began there also. Jesus came to fulfil and reframe all three. It is unhelpful to separate these three

21. Fretheim, "Christology," 361.
22. Fretheim, "Christology," 362.
23. E.g., Frost and Hirsch, *Shaping of Things to Come*, 16. Of course, it depends what is meant by these terms. If ecclesiology means details of church organization and activity, these can often squeeze out missional priorities, but ecclesiology means much more than this.

strands of theology out and give any one priority over another. The focus of the First Testament is upon the life and experiences of Israel; in the Gospels Jesus' mission to Israel involves the gathering of a community that harks back to the twelve tribes.[24] Ecclesiology has often been treated as a second-order doctrine in the history of theology, perhaps because denominational divisions are embarrassing. But in an era of individualism, the importance of ecclesiology must be recovered. As Stanley Hauerwas wrote, "The first social task of the church—the people capable of remembering and telling the story of the God we find in Jesus—is to be the church and thus help the world to understand itself as world."[25]

One ecclesiological topic must suffice from our earlier study of Joshua–Kings, that of unity. In the book of Joshua the tribes of Israel are strikingly presented as united, until conflict between the trans-Jordanian and cis-Jordanian tribes threatens in chapter 22, yet this is resolved. In Judges the tribes are sometimes at loggerheads and only unite to make war on one of their number in chapter 20. In Samuel, Saul is made king of all Israel, though division between Judah and the northern tribes is evident after his death. David eventually unites the kingdom, though some tensions remain, most obviously in Sheba's rebellion (2 Samuel 20). In Kings, Solomon rules a united kingdom, but because of his apostasy and oppression ten tribes are torn away; after his death Jeroboam rules the northern kingdom, setting up a rival shrine to the Jerusalem temple. No reunification occurs, though Josiah seeks to appropriate the remains of the northern territories. The prophets look to an eschatological future in which the old tribal divisions will be resolved (Jeremiah 30, 33; Ezek 37:15–28).

All this illuminates the concern for church unity in Paul's letters (e.g., 1 Cor 1:10–13; Eph 4:1–6; Phil 1:27; 2:2; 4:2). Ecclesiology and mission go hand in hand.

Analogies

How, then, can we most faithfully and helpfully put into words the relationship between the Testaments? Faithfully, in the sense of doing justice to both the Testaments: helpfully, in the sense of enabling readers to interpret the scriptures after Christendom. One way to think about the

---

24. See Lohfink, *Jesus of Nazareth*, 59–71.
25. Hauerwas, *Peaceable Kingdom*, 100.

relationship between the Testaments is in terms of analogy; i.e., comparing it with other well-known relationships. Analogies are not intended to be exact, and they may need explanation as to how far they may be helpful or unhelpful. Nevertheless, analogies, like metaphors, are essential linguistic tools that human beings employ in order to think about complex phenomena.

We have seen that those working in the field of intertextuality use the analogy of "echo." They also employ the notion of "resonance" to characterise the way in which a particular text interacts with another text. Familiarity with the texts concerned is important for resonance to occur, though sometimes "echoes are heard" or "bells ring" only when the connection is pointed out by someone else. Such analogies from the sensory world of sound are well understood but provide only limited insight into the relationship between the two Testaments, so can others be found?

The problem with analogies is that they are stepping-stones to the reality to which they are intended to lead. Analogies from human experience are usually the most helpful. Most of the analogies discussed here have been developed in relation to a salvation–history or narrative approach to the relation between First and Second Testaments. It is difficult to think of analogies for the kind of canonical approach that was discussed in the previous chapter.

Trajectory

The concept of trajectory derives from the path traced by an object projected through space under gravity, such as a golf ball driven from the tee. In literary terms, a character or theme may take particular twists and turns in the course of an extended and complex narrative.

In chapter 8 I noted that changes occur in the treatment of two key topics in the book of Isaiah, the monarchy and the temple, such that we could speak of a trajectory within that one book that came about due to the experience of Babylonian exile. In the Second Testament that trajectory continues as Jesus is portrayed as a different kind of king and his body is pictured as the temple, where God's forgiveness and healing might be obtained. This trajectory continues as the church is characterized as both a royal priesthood and the temple of the Holy Spirit. There is a theological trajectory from attributing evil events to God within earlier parts of the First Testament, through its later parts attributing evil events to Satan in a few places, to more frequent instances of the same in the Second Testament.

There is some sort of trajectory through the First Testament along a timeline that leads to Jesus and then continues in the life of the church that could be depicted as in fig. 10.1.

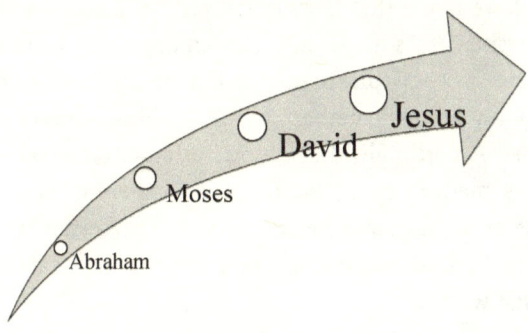

Fig 10.1

However, we must ask whether the trajectory is quite so straightforward. When Paul writes about the justice of God in relation to Israel, he leaps back behind Moses to God's promises to Abraham in order to establish that the future of God's people is grounded on the promises of God, not the keeping of the law (Rom 4:13–14; cf. Gal 3:15–18).[26] Such a trajectory requires a different way of reading the First Testament narrative. What might account for Paul's contrast between Abraham and Moses?

The analogy of trajectory may be applied even beyond the Second Testament when we consider a number of topics. The sabbath was well established as a weekly day of rest in Judaism, but as the earliest Christians celebrated Jesus' resurrection on the "eighth day" there was a shift to the first day of the week, and this soon became established.[27] Another change was more obviously generated under the impetus of Jesus' treatment of women. Paul clearly valued women highly, as can be clearly seen in the final chapter of his letter to the Romans[28] and his words to Euodia and Syntyche in his letter to the Philippians (4:2–3). There are records of women in leadership in the early church, but sadly this trajectory faltered under the influence of patriarchal society, and only began to recover in the later part of the twentieth century, under the influence of secular

---

26. See Janzen, *Abraham*, 7–12.
27. See Swartley, "Sabbath."
28. See McKnight, *Reading Romans Backwards*.

emancipatory movements, the Suffragettes and Feminists. Something similar might be argued regarding slavery.[29]

Transposition

In chapter 2 we noted that Hays employed the concept of transposition when discussing Paul's use of Job. This analogy may be drawn from the field of music, in that a tune in one particular key may be entirely shifted to a lower or higher pitch, perhaps to suit the limitations of an instrument or performer. Accordingly, the Second Testament may be understood as playing the same tune as the First, but in a different "key." For example, the practice of warfare, so common in the First Testament, is not abandoned in the Second, but transposed from the physical to the spiritual realm, in that we find:

> Put on the whole armor of God, so that you may be able to stand against the wiles of the devil. For our struggle is not against enemies of blood and flesh, but against the rulers, against the authorities, against the cosmic powers of this present darkness, against the spiritual forces of evil in the heavenly places . . . . (Eph 6:11–12)[30]

The realization that our true enemies are spiritual enables us to recognize the source of opposition from human beings and refuse to respond "in kind," i.e., without resort to violence.

Transfiguration

We also noted in chapter 2 that Hays used the word "transfigured" of Israel's scripture in Matthew's Gospel. This makes sense once the concept of figural interpretation has become familiar, however the normal use of this word among Christians is to denote the transformation of Jesus' appearance on a mountain (Matt 17:1–8; Mark 9:2–8; Luke 9:28–36). Since this unique event lies beyond normal human experience it might suggest limited comprehension value. Nevertheless, the Gospel narratives of the event convey a meaningful difference between Jesus' usual appearance

---

29. See Swartley, *Slavery, Sabbath, War & Women*.
30. Yoder Neufeld, *Put on the Armour of God*, has traced the tradition of the armor of the divine warrior back to Isaiah 59.

and the manifestation of his glory, so that it may prove a helpful analogy, given some explanation.

Drama

A number of scholars have used the language of "drama," as a way of understanding the long story of the Bible that culminates in the story of Jesus.[31] Craig Bartholomew and Michael Goheen present the biblical drama like this:[32]

Act 1: God establishes his kingdom: Creation
Act 2: Rebellion in the kingdom: Fall
Act 3: The King chooses Israel: Redemption initiated
    Scene 1: A people for the King
    Scene 2: A land for his people
Interlude: A kingdom story waiting for an ending:
    The intertestamental period
Act 4: The coming of the King: Redemption accomplished
Act 5: Spreading the news of the King: The mission of the church
    Scene 1: From Jerusalem to Rome
    Scene 2: And into all the world
Act 6: The return of the King: Redemption completed

If Jesus fulfils the story of Israel, albeit in unexpected ways, ways that were so unpredictable that no friend or foe could compute them at the time, then the First Testament may be understood as the script of the play that unfolds in the Second Testament. Those of us reading the Second Testament understand it as the second part of the script, and we seek to improvise upon the ongoing play that has extended over two thousand years (Act 5, Scene 2). Improvisation is appropriate because the multiple differences in time, place, language, and culture mean that we cannot reproduce the original play (and neither are we Jesus); rather, we

---

31. In recent biblical scholarship, N. T. Wright proposed drama as an image of salvation history in "How Can the Bible be Authoritative?" also found in *New Testament and the People of God*, 141–43.

32. Bartholomew and Goheen, *Drama of Scripture*, 25–27, adapting Wright's proposal.

are called to learn the script so well that we are able to be true to it, albeit in very different circumstances, while learning from those who have gone before us. We have a responsibility to carry it forward in consultation with one another and in dependence on the Holy Spirit.

I have found that this can be a helpful way of introducing the overall story of the Bible and to explain its role in contemporary life, though I modify how I present some parts of it. Of particular relevance to this book is that actors unfamiliar with Acts 1–3 are likely to make frequent blunders in their improvisation.

2. Connecting to the Contemporary Situation

Having explored some of the complexities of interpreting the First Testament, how might readers and churches make connections between it and contemporary life? Some scholars have pointed to the current experience of Christians in a post-Christendom society, likening it to the experience of Israelites in exile.[33] There is also much to be learned from the Jewish experience of diaspora—of living away from the land, being thoroughly embedded in another country, while having ultimate loyalties elsewhere. Here I will make a number of suggestions that arise especially from Israel's experience of exile that lies behind the four books of Joshua-Kings. I will then widen my scope to other parts of the First Testament.

The Former Prophets

I have suggested that one of the large-scale purposes of these four books was to subvert Israel's golden age, to show that YHWH's accommodation to Israel's ambition to be a conventional nation state had ended in failure. Nostalgia for the good times and the great leaders is a common human trait, and it can manifest itself among Christians who long for the time when "we were a Christian country." Reading the Former Prophets should prompt reflection upon failed attempts to construct national identity on Christian traditions, but also upon naïve Christian nostalgia for heroes of the faith. For example, Martin Luther was a courageous reformer and outstanding scholar in the Western church who had a huge influence upon German national identity, yet he expressed vitriolic antisemitic opinions, contributing to the tradition that led to Adolf

---

33. E.g., Brueggemann, *Cadences of Home*, though he prefers the term "secular."

Hitler.[34] However, it is relatively straightforward to identify fallen heroes in traditions other than one's own; spotting them closer to home is more important.

Reading the Former Prophets with awareness that Christendom has passed should mean that we make no easy equation between Israel's independent national life and conventional Christian roles and symbols. Straightforward application to contemporary situations is rarely possible and yet there are characters, relationships, and situations that prompt exploration of today's world from God's perspective.

Leaders

Leaders are vital to the well-being of churches, and they have much to learn from good models like Joshua as well as much to avoid in the careers of many judges and kings. Conflict between older and younger leaders may be illuminated by reflection on the relationship between Saul and David (though it is not an exact analogy). More important is for any leader to reflect upon their own particular responsibilities in the light of the many different leaders in Joshua–Kings with their multiple constraining circumstances as well as their various opportunities and threats, weaknesses and strengths. It is easy to overlook the role of Israel's unnamed tribal leaders and elders, but they often played significant parts in conveying leadership instructions down the line, in speaking on behalf of their people, and in decision making (e.g., Judges 20).

Priests had an important role in ancient Israel, officiating in the tabernacle and temple, and teaching the people the law. The distinction between priests and Levites is not always clear, because particular responsibilities were shared out among them (for transporting the ark, carrying out various duties in the "house of God," and so on). Occasionally priests played a significant and dangerous leadership role (Jehoiada, 2 Kings 11). Sadly, Levites could be self-regarding, callous, and bear false witness (Judges 19–20). This particular leadership role has been transformed by the coming of Jesus and the gift of the Spirit; priests are no longer needed to perform ritual sacrifices, but all believers belong to the royal priesthood (1 Pet 2:9) and are called to present our bodies as a living sacrifice to God (Rom 12:1).

---

34. Kaufman, *Luther's Jews*; Probst, *Demonizing the Jews*.

Some prophets belonged to the royal court (Micaiah, 1 Kings, 22), while others were independent. Prophets continued to have a significant role in the early church, and Paul taught that the church should weigh up what they said (1 Cor 14:26–33).[35] While many traditions have absorbed the role of God's spokesperson into that of the preacher, others have a place for contemporary words from God. In either case, prophets may speak God's word, but they may also manifest inappropriate behavior that must be challenged. Samuel, Elijah, and Elisha are often admired for their faithfulness to YHWH, yet we should also be alert to their temptations and weaknesses, for such reflections on their careers may press contemporary speakers of God's word to examine how we employ the gifts and opportunities we have been given. As we seek to name what is wrong and to convey hope when it is lacking, we may find that the prophets may become our companions.

Tabernacle, Temple, and Land

Cathedrals and church buildings are not equivalent to the tabernacle or temple of old. Jesus assumed the role of the temple in his own person, and the early church taught that the Holy Spirit dwelt among the people who gathered in Jesus' name (1 Cor 3:16–17; 2 Cor 6:16; Eph 2:21–22). Many Christians sadly still assume that churches are places to attend rather than communities to which they belong. Buildings have their place, and if buildings are to be used they should be properly maintained and appropriately furnished, yet many churches expend more money and time on buildings than upon teaching, training, and equipping people for ministry and mission.

The land itself was of great significance to ancient Israel, promised to Abraham and possessed for many generations. David made Jerusalem its capital and Solomon built the temple there. The Jewish people were displaced from the land after the Bar Kochba revolt (133–135 CE) and were only officially authorized to return in 1948. Some Christians have enthusiastically supported the modern state of Israel, believing that it fulfils ancient prophecies about a return to the land and exaltation of Israel. Others are wary of such claims of fulfilled prophecy and are concerned for the welfare of displaced and oppressed Palestinians, some of whom are Christians. To avoid supersessionism, the promise of land to

---

35. See Davis, *Biblical Prophecy*, 197–205.

Israel's descendants must be maintained, since it is central to the Torah and has always been close to the heart of Judaism, even if the argument holds that the ancient state of Israel (with a king and standing army, etc.) was a failure according to the First Testament canon.[36] The problem is that State Zionism since 1948 has owned the land exclusively, like any other modern nation state, rather than finding a way to share it with the Palestinians.[37]

Thus, the significance of place has not gone away. In his reflections upon the development of the European age of discovery and conquest, Willie James Jennings observes that it began a process of transformation of land and identity.

> The deepest theological distortion taking place is that the earth, the ground, spaces, and places are being removed as living organizers of identity and as facilitators of identity.
>
> What if your skin was inextricably bound to "the skin of the world," to borrow that marvellous phrase from Calvin Luther Martin's text *The Way of the Human Being*. What if it seemed strange, odd, and even impossible for you to conceive of your identity apart from a specific order of space—specific land, specific animals, trees, mountains, water, and arrangements of days and nights?[38]

Supposedly sophisticated Westerners need to relearn place-bound identity from others who have not neglected it.

Insiders and Outsiders

We have seen that assumptions about race are subverted in Joshua, with the inclusion of outsiders into Israel like Rahab, the Gibeonites, and Caleb, and the exclusion of the disobedient Achan. The faith of an outsider such as Naaman, the Syrian general (2 Kings 5), is a striking fulfilment

---

36. Most Christian literature that argues against the centrality of land tends towards supersessionism; e.g., Burge, *Jesus and the Land*.

37. This is the argument of Phillip Ben-Shmuel, a native Israeli Messianic Jew, who draws on the alternative Zionism of Martin Buber. See his essay, "Hagshamah. A Theology for an Alternative Messianic Jewish Zionism" in a collection of viewpoints from across the spectrum of convictions, Munayer & Loden, eds., *The Land Cries Out*, 142–73. For a recent theological discussion of the Palestinian-Israeli conflict by a Western Christian who has lived and worked among Palestinians for many years, see Alain Epp Weaver, *Inhabiting the Land*.

38. Jennings, *Christian Imagination*, 39–40.

of Israel's calling as God's witness. David Firth has traced the theme of insiders and outsiders through the Former Prophets and shown that ethnicity itself was not the issue. In the chapter recounting David's sin over Bathsheba, her husband is actually given much more attention than she. Uriah is immediately noticeable as a foreigner, a Hittite (2 Sam 11:3).[39] His only speech shows that he has a clear understanding of and commitment to Israel's faith (11:11). Even when David gets him drunk, Uriah does not go home to sleep with his wife. Thus, the integrity of this descendant of the Canaanite population is contrasted with David's sexually transgressive, manipulative and ultimately heinous behavior.

The implications of such reflections are significant for understanding the extension of God's people to the gentiles in the Second Testament. But they are enormous for contemporary attitudes regarding "the other" within societies that are marred by historic racism (see below) and many other forms of discrimination. Christians and churches must find ways to reach out to "the other" with respect, hospitality (and acceptance of hospitality), and in a spirit of discovery.

Relationship with God

In view of the frequent assumption that the God of the Old Testament is judgmental and vengeful, the Former Prophets emphasize YHWH's willingness to persevere with the Israelites through their many cycles of apostasy and repentance both before and after the introduction of the monarchy, as recounted in Judges and Kings; look again at the sorrowful litany of repeated covenant betrayal in 2 Kgs 17:7-23. Yes, in the context of conventional politics, the discipline of military defeat and external oppression was employed in the attempt to convince Israel of its obligation to be loyal to YHWH (as had been the case under the leadership of Joshua and David). The issue of loyalty might appear a matter of dictatorial partisanship on YHWH's part were it not for the Creator's blessings being integral with YHWH's righteousness and justice and that these required a reciprocal way of life among YHWH's people. Although these matters are abundantly expounded in the Torah and appealed to repeatedly by the Latter Prophets (e.g., Jer 4:19-22), they appear explicitly in fewer places

---

39. "Uriah" indicates that his parents believed in YHWH, although probably descendants of Heth (Gen 10:15) rather than the better-known Anatolian Hittites. See Firth, *Including the Stranger*, 121f.

in the Former Prophets, such as Elijah's condemnation of Ahab over the judicial murder of Naboth (1 Kings 21). Yet the book of Judges shows that Israel's decline into religious chaos went hand in hand with in appalling inhospitality, civil war, and multiple abuse of women, all under the banner of YHWH! (Judges 19–21).

One of the most disturbing themes of these books is the way in which the very people who bear YHWH's name, and on whose lips YHWH's name frequently appears, behave outrageously towards their fellow Israelites (indigenous and incomers). Even the great King David, one of the Bible's most celebrated figures, is revealed by the book of Samuel as seriously flawed, especially in his relations with women, and notoriously in his surreptitious slaying of Uriah. In what ways, then, might God's people today be taking Jesus' name in vain?

More Widely

The First Testament has much to contribute to many important contemporary topics of concern once we take its ancient cultural context into account and recognize our own cultural inheritance. I have selected just two here: racism and the environment.

Racism

Racism is based on a biological notion of race, an assumption that physical, mental, and moral characteristics (real or imagined) are transmitted genetically and are therefore permanent. "Racism assumes the hierarchical ordering and rejection of other races and the ideas, customs, and practices associated with them."[40] In particular, racism is often a matter of skin color, and some of the worst forms of prejudice and discrimination have been perpetrated by so-called "white" against "black" people, though Hispanics and Asians often experience something similar.

There is nothing about skin color in the Genesis story of Noah, however, it has become entwined with interpretations of his curse of Canaan after the flood (Gen 9:20–27). From the early centuries of the Common Era the name of Ham, Canaan's father, was understood to be related to the Hebrew word for "black" or "brown," and thus indicated associations with the black African. However, recent research has shown conclusively

---

40. Sechrest, "Racism," 655.

that there is no etymological relationship between "Ham" and the meanings "black," "dark," or "hot" (as in, coming from a hot country).[41] David Goldenberg has traced in detail the historical origins and applications of the distinct but entangled concepts of blackness and slavery. Studies of explanations of unusual skin color in traditional cultures in Africa, the Americas, and the Mediterranean have led to a striking conclusion:

> In both light-skinned and dark-skinned societies, ethnocentric-driven folktales saw the origin of "non-normal" skin color in divine punishment for disobedience. Only the colors are reversed. These value judgments are ethnocentric expressions of conformism to the dominant aesthetic taste, what social scientists call "somatic norm preference," that is, a bias for the society's normal pigmentation.[42]

In Bible-oriented societies these etiologies are commonly attributed to the misdeeds of a biblical personality. In one rabbinic tale, Ham had sexual intercourse with his wife whilst they were inside the ark, something that God had forbidden, so God punished him by turning his skin black[43]. We should note that this story says nothing about slavery; the etiology of slavery comes in the later Genesis account of Noah's curse of Canaan.

The etiology of black skin as Ham's punishment for observing Noah's nakedness is found across the Muslim world from the seventh century and into modern times, yet without mention of slavery. However, with the Muslim conquests in Africa and the resulting increase of black slaves in the Near East, black skin became incorporated into Noah's curse of Ham across much Islamic literature such that black slavery developed in the form of an insidious dual curse tying blackness to servitude.[44] A similar development of the dual curse of Ham occurred in the Christian West as it was influenced by Muslim cultural and commercial engagement. Here, the adoption of the dual curse coincided with the expansion of black slavery from the sixteenth century, and the consequent disparagement of the black African. It then moved from Europe to British colonial America and, by extension, to all the black peoples listed in the so-called

---

41. See Goldenberg, *Black and Slave*, 141–56.
42. Goldenberg, *Black and Slave*, 32.
43. See Goldenberg, *Black and Slave*, 19.
44. See Goldenberg, *Black and Slave*, 199–200.

"Table of Nations" in Genesis 10. It was often used to defend slavery and "white" supremacy in the USA, and to justify apartheid in South Africa.

To assist repentance from racism we should turn more concertedly to Genesis and note that, according to the text, Noah does not curse Ham, but curses Ham's son Canaan to slavery. Because the Canaanites were Israel's perennial enemies, it seems reasonable to interpret the curse of slavery as racist. But does the book of Genesis approve of Noah's curse, just because he was previously described as righteous and blameless (6:9)? This curse marks an important turning point in the biblical story since it embeds a hierarchical relationship among Noah's descendants that eventually leads to empire in the Tower of Babel (11:1–9). Amanda Beckenstein Mbuvi argues that the racist use of the story of the curse of Ham owes more to the attempt to find authority for ideas about race that originated elsewhere than to Genesis.

> Indeed, until the passage is placed within the framework of modern racial thinking, the biblical text simply does not provide enough information to construct all the details of the story as it has become popularized. Although Cain (possibly) receives some sort of identifying mark (Gen 4:15), Gen 9 never names skin color (or any other feature) as a physical manifestation of Noah's curse. That aspect of the curse of Ham legend comes from the association between the Hamites and Africa derived from Gen 10 and from the assumption that the descendants of Ham were racially distinct from those of his brothers. Filtering the biblical text through the lens of conventional understandings of social reality, people already inclined to associate dark skin with debasement easily found in Noah's curse a basis for such an assumption. Moderns merged their racial typologies into the biblical text and then read from the Bible the origin and legitimating basis of those typologies.[45]

Genesis 10 has often been treated as if it were a modern classification of early races.[46] Yet commentators on this passage express frustration when seeking to identify an ordered classificatory system within it.[47] This is be-

---

45. Mbuvi, *Belonging in Genesis*, 72. She goes on to illustrate such assumptions in Matthew Henry's *Commentary on the Whole Bible* (1708–10) and the *Treasury of Scriptural Knowledge* (c. 1830).

46. Mbuvi, *Belonging in Genesis*, 78, 87–88, 119, points to the influence of colonial censuses on conceptions of ethnic identity.

47. Mbuvi, *Belonging in Genesis*, 88–91, discusses the Genesis commentaries of Skinner, Speiser, and Westermann.

cause it attaches equal weight to multiple levels of belonging: residential kinship group, language, land, and nation (vv. 5, 20, 31). Furthermore, Genesis 10 is *not* a table, but a genealogy, a family tree.

> The genealogical format not only classifies and groups, but also conveys relatedness across the entire system.... [S]ituating a story about interactions between groups within the experience of a single nuclear family transforms it, coloring it with the intimacy and intensity of family life. Behavior that might come across as ordinary in intergroup relations looks quite different when considered in relation to members of a single family.... It is striking that the portion of the Bible most concerned with human diversity adopts such an intimate approach to the subject, tracing all the world's peoples to three brothers from a dysfunctional family.... Above all, the rubric of family infuses the relationships in Genesis with an urgency that dealings between relative strangers would lack. It implies a certain permanence to relationships, a commitment that does not depend on the willingness of the participants. One's family constitutes those with whom one has to deal whether one wants to or not; brothers remain brothers even if they choose never to interact.[48]

Finally, there is a correspondence between the seventy descendants of Noah in Genesis 10 and the seventy descendants of Jacob in Gen 46:27, and this implies that the internal differences among the descendants of Jacob are as many as those among the whole of humanity.

Few people willingly admit to racism. It is easy to identify racism in other people and countries while making allowances for it in one's own cultural world. Racism has been a significant aspect of many societies for centuries and subtly influences language, family attitudes, institutions, news media, and culture in general. It has been tied up with the history of slavery, capitalism, and colonialism—and Christian missions.[49] "White" Christians must wake up and identify discrimination wherever it occurs, take active steps to challenge and eradicate it, and consult as to how to make redress for past wrongs. More than this, Christian "white" folks must begin to cast down our "white" idols, as Hezekiah and Josiah tore down long-established idolatrous shrines (2 Kgs 18:1–6; 23:13–15). So argues Andrew Draper (who self-identifies as "white"), and then

---

48. Mbuvi, *Belonging in Genesis*, 90–93.
49. See Sechrest et al., *Can "White" People Be Saved?*

proposes five practices in which "white" folks must engage to resist the socio-political order of whiteness:[50]

- Repentance for complicity in systemic sin.
- Learning from non-white theological resources.
- Locating our lives in places and structures not our own.
- Tangible submission to non-white ecclesial leadership.
- Hearing and speaking the glory of God in unfamiliar cadences.

The Environment

We live in an era when public concern about climate change and pollution of the environment have risen up the political agenda, and yet a huge amount of inertia inhibits radical change of lifestyles within the richest nations. Is it possible that reading the First Testament might assist in a change of mind? A number of books have been written that explore this topic, and I will introduce one that has the potential to shift our way of looking at the world.[51]

Mari Joerstad explores the usually overlooked attribution in the First Testament of activity and affect to trees, fields, soil, and mountains.[52] Such activity is evident in the Genesis prologue when the earth "brings forth vegetation . . ." in obedience to God's command (1:12). Here the earth is an *active agent* alongside God, as Fretheim has said, "God makes a decision to create in community rather than alone; at the divine initiative, the creation plays an active role in God's creative work."[53] God goes on to give tasks to each creature and blesses the sea, air and land creatures with fertility. The psalms are full of non-human voices: the pastures of the wilderness, the hills, and the floods (Ps 65:12–13; 93:3), but especially,

> The heavens are telling the glory of God;
> and the firmament proclaims his handiwork.
> Day to day pours forth speech,

---

50. See Draper, "The End of 'Mission': Christian Whiteness and the Decentering of White Identity."

51. E.g., Bauckham, *Bible and Ecology*; Davis, *Scripture, Culture and Agriculture*; Tull, *Inhabiting Eden*.

52. Joerstad, *Hebrew Bible and Environmental Ethics*.

53. Fretheim, *Creation Untamed*, 11.

and night to night declares knowledge.
There is no speech, nor are there words;
  their voice is not heard;
yet their voice goes out through all the earth,
  and their words to the end of the world.
(Ps 19:1–4)

YHWH and YHWH's prophets repeatedly summon the heavens and the earth to listen to oracles of judgment and consolation; "'Be appalled, O heavens, at this, be shocked, be utterly desolate,' says the LORD . . ." (Jer 2:19). This feature of prophetic literature is usually described as the literary device known as "apostrophe" and the addressees are not regarded as capable of real response. But this cannot be assumed about ancient cultures, especially as many traditional societies continue to treat the non-human world in a similar way. Joerstad draws attention to recent anthropological studies of animism, a worldview in which the category of "person" is not confined to human beings (or God); she quotes anthropologist Graham Harvey:

> Animists are people who recognize that the world is full of persons, only some of whom are human, and that life is always lived in relationship with others. Animism is lived out in various ways that are all about learning to act respectfully (carefully and constructively) towards and among other persons.[54]

Joerstad goes on to say,

> The ontologies of animists and the writers of the Hebrew Bible share a family resemblance. Personhood is not a human characteristic, but a concept that "is anterior and logically superior to the concept of the human." The concept of personhood encompasses humans, but is not limited to us. In addition to human persons, there are also mountain persons, river persons, wind persons, etc.[55]

The problem is that "We are deeply habituated to the Cartesian split, to mind/body dualism, and struggle to think of creatures without brains as persons."[56] If we were to read the First Testament carefully, we might learn that the world is full of persons, some of whom are not human;

---

54. Harvey, *Animism*, xi.

55. Joerstad, *Hebrew Bible and Environmental Ethics*, 22, quoting Eduardo Vivieros de Castro.

56. Joerstad, *Hebrew Bible and Environmental Ethics*, 208.

we might attend to these persons so that we might develop interaction, friendship, and even conversation with them.

Having read Joerstad's work, I was struck by Joshua's final words to Israel:

> Joshua wrote these words in the book of the law of God; and he took a large stone, and set it up there under the oak in the sanctuary of the LORD. "See, this stone shall be a witness against us; for it has heard all the words of the LORD that he spoke to us; therefore it shall be a witness against you, if you deal falsely with your God." (Josh 24:26–27)

3. Facilitating Biblical Literacy

The first followers of Jesus were Jewish and knew their scriptures well. In the early years of the Christian church, people were drawn in from pagan backgrounds, yet leaders like Paul wrote to them as if they were inheritors of those Jewish stories (e.g., 1 Cor 10:1–11; the Galatian churches were gentile, yet Paul assumes they know the stories of Abraham, Sarah, and Mt Sinai). It is likely that Luke's Gospel was a teaching tool in the early church, with teachers explaining some of the intertextual complexities for communities of gentiles converts.[57] James Sanders has argued that there must have been a concerted programme of developing biblical literacy in the early church.

> I am convinced that early Christians underwent rather intensive programs of instruction in the faith upon conversion, and that at the center of such programs was the "churches' book," the Septuagint, or whatever scrolls of it they had access to.... The Septuagint had the advantage of already being accepted in the Hellenistic world generally as worthy literature, and in some non-Jewish quarters as being somewhat authoritative.[58]

There is a strong case for contemporary Christian churches engaging in concerted catechetical practices (here we have much to learn from the early churches), central to which should be familiarization with the First as well as the Second Testament, together with exploration of questions of interpretation.

---

57. Sanders, *From Sacred Story*, xl.
58. Sanders, *From Sacred Story*, xi.

We should consider that we live in the "Age of the Image" and many people simply do not read literature. In a culture that is dominated by short media debates and tweets of no more than 140 characters, there is often impatience with an extensive and nuanced presentation of a point of view. Having acknowledged this, there are other aspects of culture that counter the trend towards the brief, the controversial, and the attention-grabbing. Long TV series and box sets are popular and indicate that people enjoy extended dramas and even documentaries (such as *Blue Planet*). People are prepared to give time and attention to arresting visual content.

What can be done to work with people who are familiar with the electronic media? Some helpful teaching material is available on the internet (as well as much that is unhelpful), though most consists simply of talking heads.[59] A good place to begin may be the graphic approach of *The Bible Project*, especially in that some of its videos provide an overview of individual books of the Bible.[60] These use professional graphics and seek to convey how the books work as books. They tend to oversimplify and skate over the more difficult issues; and they have particular theological perspectives that are rather simplistic.[61] These limitations are understandable in a project seeking to make complex literature accessible to beginners.

It is important to remember that the written word has not been eclipsed by visual images: novels continue to be popular, in physical book form as well as in electronic format. There is no substitute for reading the biblical text, and reading it with regard to its literary, historical, and theological dimensions. Developing biblical literacy must include helping people to understand how these texts and stories fit together, and ultimately form whole books of the Bible, with overarching plots and rhetorical strategies that may nuance particular parts. Teachers and preachers should aim to model such interpretation and encourage people to discover appropriate reading aids.

---

59. This book was completed during the time of worldwide protests following the Minneapolis Police killing of George Floyd on May 25th, 2020. On the subject of racism, see the four-part Bible teaching series by Jordan Ryan and Matthew Schlimm, "Shedding Light: Conversation Starters for Churches."

60. www.thebibleproject.com

61. The claim (*What Is BibleProject?*) that the Bible is "one unified story" does not do justice to its variety and complexity.

Conventional ten- or twenty-minute sermons have their place, but they cannot achieve anything like the biblical literacy envisaged here. Churches must develop more concerted adult educational programs that encourage participation and interactivity.[62] When Jesus discipled his followers and when Paul taught his churches, they used interactive methods.[63]

Churches that adhere to published lectionaries will find that current First Testament exposure is very brief and piecemeal, so we need new lectionaries that give significant attention to the First Testament and provide a flavor of whole books over a period of weeks. Public Bible reading is a skill to be learned; done well it can carry its own interpretation: done poorly it can alienate listeners. Readers often need support and practice to acquire the necessary confidence and skills.[64] Brief introductions to readings may provide the context and set the scene.

More insidious than the lure of the visual in Western culture is the pervasiveness of individualism. This has found its way into Bible reading and other practices that make up Christian spirituality, so that people are encouraged to seek personal revelations at the expense of corporate life.[65] There is a proper sense in which each person matters to God, and God seeks personal interaction with them, yet many models of Bible reading inculcate a search for a daily message from God to the individual; "Is there a promise, encouragement, or warning for me in this passage?" This needs to be supplemented by asking communal and social questions in an exploratory (rather than a didactic) way, such as "What might local churches learn from this story about God's people?" and "What insights into the world and society might be contained in this biblical book?"

Reading the Bible on a regular basis is a good practice because it builds familiarity, but it should be supplemented with aids that illuminate the ancient text, assist to see how it works, and help to wrestle with its challenges and contradictions.[66] Most important is reading the Bible with other people in small groups that allow for discussion and exploring the

---

62. See Knowles et al., *Adult Learner*.

63. After Eutychus' restoration from his fall, Paul's continued "conversing" until dawn with the believers in Troas (Acts 20:7-12); this was not a monologue sermon.

64. See Adler, *Sound of Scripture*.

65. This is assisted by the reading of the word "you" as in the singular, when it is often in the plural in the original languages. Perhaps we need to adopt a distinction like the Scottish plural, "yous," or a Southern "y'all"!

66. See Schlimm, *This Strange and Sacred Scripture*.

challenges acknowledged at the beginning of this book. Christian Bible readers would do well to find opportunities to develop conversations with Jewish people with an active faith.[67] We have much to learn from their love for the scriptures, and from their traditions that have kept their faith alive over centuries of marginalization, ostracism, and persecution by Christians.

Although the main focus of the First Testament is upon the story of God's people, we have seen that outsiders often figure in this story; indeed, that their response to God may put insiders to shame. This story serves God's mission to the whole of creation, and God's Spirit looks for surprising ways of opening eyes across the world. So Christian Bible readers would do well to find opportunities to develop conversations with people who have little interest in religion or who have been alienated from conventional churches. Simply telling friends that I have been writing this book has begun to open conversations about the Bible and environmental ethics.

A Literacy Agenda

In conclusion, here are several items that constitute a literacy agenda:

- I have argued for an interpretation of the First Testament that is sensitive to its literary character, and placed emphasis upon whole books rather than short extracts or "sound bites." Ways must be found to enable readers to grasp whole books, to see how whole books work from literary and theological perspectives. I have spent less time on historical perspectives, but they remain important.

- I have pointed to the genre diversity of the First Testament. Teachers and preachers often look for specific lessons to be learnt from the Bible, but reducing it to adroit alliterations or slick truisms does not do it justice. While lessons may be learnt from certain parts of the Bible, other parts are intended to provide food for thought, to stimulate questions, or to give voice to profound emotions.

---

67. In the early 1990s Textual Reasoning groups were set up by Jewish scholars, but then Christian and Muslim scholars were invited to contribute to the conversation. *Scriptural Reasoning* is now an international movement that promotes interfaith engagement and fosters interfaith engagement in schools.

FACILITATING ACCESS TO THE FIRST TESTAMENT

- I have also argued for the significance of the Torah in framing a Christian understanding of the First Testament. The canonical approach to First Testament theology is at least as important as a historical or time-line approach, and is vital for interpretation after Christendom.

- We should reverse the tendency to sanitize the Bible in church readings and personal Bible reading schemes; i.e., to cut short the more challenging passages, to avoid the puzzling parts, to select praise psalms rather than laments. There is a dishonesty about such selectivity, and it robs people of important spiritual resources.

- We must be alert to potential misunderstandings of the Bible, among children and adults. These must be identified and addressed in sensitive ways.

- An aspect of developing biblical literacy is enabling people to learn from previous failures. The Bible has been used to defend or support many evils from slavery and apartheid, to the abuse of women and children, to colonial oppression and war, to environmental exploitation and negligence. We should be teaching about these things; acknowledging past errors makes us more willing to be challenged about current interpretations.

- The churches' worst crimes have been perpetrated on the Jewish people. We must learn about and acknowledge what we have done; change our minds, acquire humility, and reach out to Jewish people. We have much to learn from their love of the scriptures and about how they may shape our lives.

Bibliography

Adler, Barbara Laughlin. *The Sound of Scripture: Reading the Bible Aloud—A Brief Guide for Lay Readers*. Minneapolis: Lutheran University Press, 2013.
Alexander, T. Desmond. "The Authorship of the Pentateuch." In *DOTP*, 61–72.
Allen, Leslie C. "First and Second Books of Chronicles." In *NIB*, Vol. III, 1999, 297–695.
Allison, Dale, C. *The New Moses: A Matthean Typology*. Edinburgh: T. & T. Clark, 1993.
Alter, Robert. *Ancient Israel: A Translation with Commentary. The Former Prophets: Joshua, Judges, Samuel, and Kings*. London: Norton, 2013.
———. *The Art of Biblical Narrative*. London: George Allen & Unwin, 1981.
———. *The Art of Biblical Poetry*. Edinburgh: T. & T. Clark, 1985.
Amit, Yairah. "'Am I Not More Devoted to You Than Ten Sons?' (1 Samuel 1.8): Male and Female Interpretation." In *A Feminist Companion to Samuel and Kings*, edited by Athalya Brenner, 68–76. Sheffield, UK: Sheffield Academic Press, 1994.
———. *Reading Biblical Narratives: Literary Criticism and the Hebrew Bible*. Minneapolis: Fortress, 2001.
Anderson, Craig Evan. "The Sword of Solomon: The Subversive Underbelly of Solomon's Judgment of the Two Prostitutes." In *Partners with God: Theological and Critical Readings of the Bible in Honor of Marvin A. Sweeney*, edited by Shelley L. Birdsong and Serge Frolov, 73–81. Claremont, CA: Claremont University Press, 2017.
Anderson, Gary A. *Christian Doctrine and the Old Testament: Theology in the Service of Exegesis*. Grand Rapids: Baker Academic, 2017.
Ansell, Nicholas. "This Is Her Body . . . : Judges 19 as a Call to Discernment." In *Tamar's Tears: Evangelical Engagements with Feminist Old Testament Hermeneutics*, edited by Andrew Sloane, 112–70. Eugene, OR: Pickwick, 2012.
Auerbach, Eric. *Mimesis: The Representation of Reality in Western Literature*. Princeton: Princeton University Press, 1968.
Bader-Saye, Scott. *Church and Israel after Christendom: The Politics of Election*. Reprint, Eugene, OR: Wipf & Stock, 1999.
Bartholomew, Craig G. "Biblical Theology." In *DTIB*, 84–90.
Bartholomew, Craig G., and David J. H. Beldman, eds. *Hearing the Old Testament: Listening for God's Address*. Grand Rapids: Eerdmans, 2012.
Bartholomew, Craig G., and Michael W. Goheen. *The Drama of Scripture: Finding Our Place in the Biblical Story*. Grand Rapids: Baker Academic, 2004.
Barton, Stephen C., and David Wilkinson, eds. *Reading Genesis after Darwin*. Oxford: Oxford University Press, 2009.

BIBLIOGRAPHY

Bates, Matthew W. *The Birth of the Trinity: Jesus, God and Spirit in New Testament & Early Christian Interpretations of the Old Testament*. Oxford: Oxford University Press, 2015.

———. *The Hermeneutics of the Apostolic Proclamation: The Center of Paul's Method of Scriptural Interpretation*. Waco, TX: Baylor University Press, 2012.

Bauckham, Richard. *Bible and Ecology*. London: SPCK, 2010.

———. "James and the Gentiles (Acts 15:13–21)." In *History, Literature, and Society in the Book of Acts*, edited by Ben Witherington III, 154–84. Cambridge: Cambridge University Press, 1996.

———. "Reading Scripture as a Coherent Story." In *The Art of Reading Scripture*, edited by Ellen F. Davis and Richard Hays, 38–53. Grand Rapids: Eerdmans, 2003.

Beale, Gregory K. *The Temple and the Church's Mission: A Biblical Theology of the Dwelling Place of God*. Downers Grove, IL: InterVarsity, 2004.

Becker, Adam, and Annette Yoshiko Reed, eds. *The Ways That Never Parted: Jews and Christians in Late Antiquity and the Early Middle Ages*. Minneapolis: Fortress, 2007.

Beldman, David. *Deserting the King: The Book of Judges*. Bellingham, WA: Lexham, 2017.

Benin, Stephen. *The Footprints of God: Divine Accommodation in Jewish and Christian Thought*. Albany, NY: State University of New York Press, 1993.

Berlin, Adele. *Poetics and Interpretation of Biblical Narrative*. Sheffield, UK: Almond, 1983.

Bimson, John J. *Redating the Exodus and Conquest*. JSOTSup 5. Sheffield, UK: JSOT, 1978.

Blenkinsopp, Joseph. *Creation, Un-creation, Re-creation: A Discursive Commentary on Genesis 1–11*. London: T. & T. Clark, 2011.

Block, Daniel I. *The Triumph of Grace: Literary and Theological Studies in Deuteronomy and Deuteronomic Themes*. Eugene, OR: Cascade, 2017.

Borgman, Paul. *David, Saul, & God: Rediscovering an Ancient Story*. Oxford: Oxford University Press, 2008.

Boyarin, Daniel. *Border Lines: The Partition of Judaeo-Christianity*. Philadelphia: University of Pennsylvania Press, 2004.

———. "Rethinking Jewish Christianity: An Argument for Dismantling a Dubious Category (to which is appended a correction of my *Border Lines*)." *Jewish Quarterly Review* 99.1 (2009) 7–36.

Boyd, Gregory A. *Cross Vision: How the Crucifixion of Jesus Makes Sense of Old Testament Violence*. Minneapolis: Fortress, 2017.

———. *The Crucifixion of the Warrior God: Interpreting the Old Testament's Violent Portraits of God in the Light of the Cross*. 2 vols. Minneapolis: Fortress, 2017.

Brenner, Athalya, ed. *A Feminist Companion to Judges*. Sheffield, UK: Sheffield Academic Press, 1993.

Brown, Jeanine K. *Scripture as Communication: Introducing Biblical Hermeneutics*. Grand Rapids: Baker Academic, 2007.

Brown, William P. *The Ethos of the Cosmos: The Genesis of Moral Imagination in the Bible*. Grand Rapids: Eerdmans, 1999.

———. *The Seven Pillars of Creation: The Bible, Science, and the Ecology of Wonder*. Oxford: Oxford University Press, 2010.

BIBLIOGRAPHY

Brueggemann, Walter. *Cadences of Home: Preaching among Exiles.* Louisville, KY: Westminster John Knox, 1997.

———. *David and His Theologian: Literary, Social and Theological Investigations of the Early Monarchy.* Edited by K. C. Hanson. Eugene, OR: Cascade, 2011.

———. *First and Second Samuel.* IBC. Louisville, KY: John Knox, 1990.

———. *From Whom No Secrets Are Hid: Introducing the Psalms.* Edited by Brent A. Strawn. Louisville, KY: Westminster John Knox, 2014.

———. *Ichabod towards Home: The Journey of God's Glory.* Grand Rapids: Eerdmans, 2002.

———. *A Pathway of Interpretation: The Old Testament for Pastors and Students.* Eugene, OR: Cascade, 2008.

———. *The Psalms and the Life of Faith.* Edited by Patrick D. Miller. Minneapolis: Fortress, 1995.

———. *A Social Reading of the Old Testament: Prophetic Approaches to Israel's Communal Life.* Edited by Patrick D Miller. Minneapolis: Fortress, 1994.

———. *The Theology of the Book of Jeremiah.* Old Testament Theology. Cambridge; Cambridge University Press, 2007.

———. *Theology of the Old Testament: Testimony, Dispute, Advocacy.* Minneapolis: Fortress, 1997.

———. *1 & 2 Kings.* SHBC. Macon, GA: Smyth & Helwys, 2000.

Brueggemann, Walter, and William H. Bellinger, Jr. *Psalms,* New Cambridge Bible Commentary. Cambridge: Cambridge University Press, 2014.

Brueggemann, Walter, and Todd Linafelt. *Introduction to the Old Testament: The Canon and Christian Imagination.* 2nd ed. Louisville, KY: Westminster John Knox, 2012.

Burge, Gary M. *Jesus and the Land: The New Testament Challenge to 'Holy Land' Theology.* London: SPCK, 2010.

Butler, Trent C. *Judges.* WBC. Grand Rapids: Zondervan, 2008.

Calvin, John. *Commentary on Genesis 1–23.* Translated by John King in 1847 from the original Latin (published 1554), compared with the French translation (published 1563). Loschberg, Germany: Jazzybee Verlag Jurgen Beck, 2016.

Carasik, Michael. *The Bible's Many Voices.* Lincoln, NE: University of Nebraska Press, 2014.

Cary, Phillip. *Augustine's Invention of the Inner Self: The Legacy of a Christian Platonist.* Oxford: Oxford University Press, 2000.

Chapman, Stephen B. *1 Samuel as Christian Scripture: A Theological Commentary.* Grand Rapids: Eerdmans, 2016.

Childs, Brevard S. *Biblical Theology of the Old and New Testaments: Theological Reflection on the Christian Bible.* London: SCM, 1992.

———. *Introduction to the Old Testament as Scripture.* London: SCM, 1979.

———. *Old Testament Theology in a Canonical Context.* London: SCM, 1985.

Cohn, Robert L. *2 Kings.* BO. Collegeville, MN: Liturgical, 2000.

Collins, John J. *Introduction to the Hebrew Bible.* 3rd ed. Minneapolis: Fortress, 2018.

Coloe, Mary L. *God Dwells with Us: Temple Symbolism in the Fourth Gospel.* Collegeville, MN: Liturgical, 2001.

Copan, Paul, and Matthew Flannagan. *Did God Really Command Genocide? Coming to Terms with the Justice of God.* Grand Rapids: Baker, 2014.

Cotter, David W. *Genesis.* BO. Collegeville, MN: Liturgical, 2003.

BIBLIOGRAPHY

Cotterell, Peter, and Max Turner. *Linguistics & Biblical Interpretation*. London: SPCK, 1989.
Creach, Jerome F. D. *Joshua*. IBC. Louisville, KY: Westminster John Knox, 2003.
———. *Violence in Scripture*. IRUSC. Louisville, KY: Westminster John Knox, 2013.
Crenshaw, James L. *Defending God: Biblical Responses to the Problem of Evil*. Oxford: Oxford University Press, 2005.
Crites, Stephen. "The Narrative Quality of Experience." *Journal of the American Academy of Religion* 39.3 (1971) 291–311.
Dalley, Stephanie. *The Mystery of the Hanging Garden of Babylon: An Elusive World Wonder Traced*. Oxford: Oxford University Press, 2013.
Davis, Ellen F. *Biblical Prophecy: Perspectives for Christian Theology, Discipleship, and Ministry*, IRUSC. Louisville, KY: Westminster John Knox, 2014.
———. "Critical Traditioning: Seeking an Inner Biblical Hermeneutic." In *The Art of Reading Scripture*, edited by Ellen F. Davis and Richard B. Hays, 163–97. Grand Rapids: Eerdmans, 2003.
———. *Opening Israel's Scriptures*. Oxford: Oxford University Press, 2019.
———. *Scripture, Culture, and Agriculture: An Agrarian Reading of the Bible*. Cambridge: Cambridge University Press, 2008.
Dawkins, Richard. *The God Delusion*. London: Bantam, 2006.
Day, John, ed. *In Search of Pre-Exilic Israel*. London: T. & T. Clark, 2004.
Dever, William G. *Beyond the Texts: An Archaeological Portrait of Ancient Judah and Israel*. Atlanta: SBL, 2017.
———. *What Did the Biblical Writers Know, and When Did They Know It? What Archaeology Can Tell Us about the Reality of Ancient Israel*. Grand Rapids: Eerdmans, 2001.
———. *Who Were the Early Israelites and Where Did They Come From?* Grand Rapids: Eerdmans, 2003.
Dillard, Raymond B., and Tremper Longman III. *Introduction to the Old Testament*. 2nd ed. Downers Grove, IL: InterVarsity, 2006.
Drane, John. *Introducing the Old Testament*. 4th ed. Oxford: Lion Hudson, 2019.
Draper, Andrew T. "The End of 'Mission': Christian Whiteness and the Decentering of White Identity." In *Can "White" People Be Saved? Triangulating Race, Theology, and Mission*, edited by Love L. Sechrest et al., 177–205. Downers Grove, IL: InterVarsity, 2018.
Duke, R. K. "Chronicles, Books of." In *DOTHB*, 161–81.
Dunn, James D. G. *The Parting of the Ways: Between Christianity and Judaism and the Significance for the Character of Christianity*. 2nd ed. London: SCM, 2011.
Earl, Douglas S. *The Joshua Delusion: Rethinking Genocide in the Bible*. Eugene, OR: Cascade, 2010.
Eichrodt, Walter. *Theology of the Old Testament*. 2 vols. Translated by John Baker. London: SCM, 1961.
Ellis, E. Earle. *Paul's Use of the Old Testament*. Grand Rapids: Baker, 1957.
Epp Weaver, Alain. *Inhabiting the Land: Thinking Theologically about the Palestinian-Israeli Conflict*. Eugene, OR: Cascade, 2018.
Fewell, Danna Nolan. "Judges." In *The Woman's Bible Commentary*, edited by Carol A. Newsom and Sharon H. Ringe, 67–77. Louisville, KY: Westminster John Knox, 1992.
———. "The Work of Biblical Narrative." In *OHBN*, 3–26.

Finkelstein, Israel, and Neil Asher Silberman. *The Bible Unearthed: Archaeology's New Vision of Ancient Israel and the Origin of Its Sacred Texts*. New York: Free Press, 2001.

Firth, David. "Asaph and the Sons of Korah." In *DOTWPW*, 24–27.

———. *Including the Stranger: Foreigners in the Former Prophets*. New Studies in Biblical Theology. Downers Grove, IL: Apollos, 2019.

Fishbane, Michael. *Biblical Interpretation in Ancient Israel*. Oxford: Clarendon, 1985.

———. *Biblical Text and Texture: A Literary Reading of Selected Texts*. Oxford: Oneworld, 1998.

Fokkelman, J. P. *Reading Biblical Narrative: An Introductory Guide*. Louisville, KY: Westminster John Knox, 1999.

———. *Reading Biblical Poetry: An Introductory Guide*. Louisville, KY: Westminster John Knox, 2001.

France, R. T. "Relationship between the Testaments." In *DTIB*, 666–72.

Franke, John R. *Ancient Christian Commentary on Scripture: Old Testament IV: Joshua, Judges, Ruth, 1–2 Samuel*. Downers Grove, IL: InterVarsity, 2005.

Fredricksen, Paula. *Augustine and the Jews: A Christian Defense of Jews and Judaism*. New Haven, CT: Yale University Press, 2010.

Fretheim, Terence E. "The Book of Genesis: Introduction, Commentary, and Reflections." In *NIB*, Vol. I, 1994, 319–674.

———. "Christology and the Old Testament." In *WKG*, 350–62.

———. *Creation Untamed: The Bible, God, and Natural Disasters*. Grand Rapids: Baker Academic, 2010.

———. "Divine Constancy and the Rejection of Saul's Kingship." In *WKG*, 267–73.

———. "Divine Dependence on the Human." In *WKG*, 25–39.

———. "God, Abraham, and the Abuse of Isaac." *Word & World* 15.1 (1995) 49–57.

———. *God and World in the Old Testament: A Relational Theology of Creation*. Nashville: Abingdon, 2005.

———. *Jeremiah*. SHBC. Macon, GA: Smyth & Helwys, 2002.

———. "Suffering God and Sovereign God in Exodus: A Collision of Images." In WKG, 104–123.

———. *The Suffering of God: An Old Testament Perspective*, OBT. Minneapolis: Fortress, 1984.

———. *What Kind of God? Collected Essays*. Edited by Michael J. Chan and Brent A. Strawn. Siphrut 14. Winona Lake, IN: Eisenbrauns, 2015.

———. "Theological Reflections on the Wrath of God." In *WKG*, 140–58.

Friedman, Richard Elliott. *The Disappearance of God: A Divine Mystery*. Boston: Little, Brown, 1995.

Frost, Michael, and Alan Hirsch. *The Shaping of Things to Come: Innovation and Mission for the 21st Century Church*. Peabody, MA: Henrickson, 2003.

Gilmour, Rachelle L. *Representing the Past: A Literary Analysis of Narrative Historiography in the Book of Samuel*. Leiden: Brill, 2011.

Goldenberg, David M. *Black and Slave: The Origins and History of the Curse of Ham*. Berlin: de Gruyter, 2017.

Goldingay, John. "Biblical Narrative and Systematic Theology." In *Between Two Horizons: Spanning New Testament Studies and Systematic Theology*, edited by Joel B. Green and Max Turner, 123–42. Grand Rapids: Eerdmans, 2000.

———. *Do We Need the New Testament? Letting the Old Testament Speak for Itself.* Downers Grove, IL: InterVarsity, 2015.

———. *Theological Diversity and the Authority of the Old Testament.* Grand Rapids: Eerdmans, 1987.

Gottwald, Norman K. *The Tribes of Yahweh: A Sociology of the Religion of Liberated Israel, 1250–1050 BCE.* Maryknoll, NY: Orbis, 1979.

Gowan, Donald. *Theology of the Prophetic Books: The Death and Resurrection of Israel.* Louisville, KY: Westminster John Knox, 1998.

Green, Barbara. *King Saul's Asking.* Collegeville, MN: Liturgical, 2003.

Green, Joel B. "Narrative Theology." In *DTIB*, 531–33.

Greenberg, Moshe. *Ezekiel 21–37: A New Translation with Introduction and Commentary.* AB. New York: Doubleday, 1997.

Greer, Jonathan S., John W. Hilber and John H. Walton, eds. *Behind the Scenes of the Old Testament: Cultural, Social and Historical Contexts.* Grand Rapids: Baker Academic, 2018.

Grohmann, Marianne. "Psalm 113 and the Song of Hannah (1 Samuel 2:1–10): A Paradigm for Intertextual Reading?" In *Reading the Bible Intertextually,* edited by Richard B. Hays, Stefan Alkier, and Leroy A. Huizenga, 119–35. Waco, TX: Baylor University Press, 2015.

Gros Louis, Kenneth R. R. "The Book of Judges." In *Literary Interpretations of Biblical Narratives,* edited by K. R. R. Gros Louis, with James S. Ackerman and Thayer S. Warshaw, 141–62. Nashville: Abingdon, 1974.

Gunn, David M. *The Fate of King Saul: An Interpretation of a Biblical Story.* JSOTSup 14. Sheffield, UK: JSOT, 1980.

———. *The Story of King David: Genre and Interpretation.* JSOTSup 6. Sheffield, UK: JSOT, 1978.

Halpern, Baruch. *David's Secret Demons: Messiah, Murder, Traitor, King.* Grand Rapids: Eerdmans, 2001.

Harvey, Graham. *Animism: Respecting the Living World.* 2nd ed. London: Hurst & Co., 2017.

Hauerwas, Stanley. *The Peaceable Kingdom: A Primer in Christian Ethics.* London: SCM, 1984.

Hawk, L. Daniel. *Joshua.* BO. Collegeville, MN: Liturgical, 2000.

———. "Joshua, Book of." In *DOTHB*, 563–75.

———. *Joshua in 3-D: A Commentary on Biblical Conquest and Manifest Destiny.* Eugene, OR: Cascade, 2010.

———. *The Violence of the Biblical God: Canonical Narrative and Christian Faith.* Grand Rapids: Eerdmans, 2019.

Hays, Richard B. *Echoes of Scripture in the Gospels.* Waco, TX: Baylor University Press, 2016.

———. *Echoes of Scripture in the Letters of Paul.* New Haven, CT: Yale University Press, 1989.

———. "Here We Have No Lasting City." In *The Epistle to the Hebrews and Christian Theology,* edited by Richard Bauckham, Daniel R. Driver, Trevor A. Hart, and Nathan MacDonald, 151–73. Grand Rapids: Eerdmans, 2009.

———. "On the Rebound: A Response to Critiques of *Echoes of Scripture in the Letters of Paul.*" In *Paul and the Scriptures of Israel,* edited by Craig A. Evans and James A. Sanders, 71–96. JSNTSup 83. Sheffield, UK: JSOT, 1993.

Heim, Knut Martin. *Like Grapes of Gold Set in Silver: An Interpretation of Proverbial Clusters in Proverbs 10:1—22:16*. Berlin: de Gruyter, 2001.

Heller, Roy L. *The Characters of Elijah and Elisha and the Deuteronomic Evaluation of Prophecy: Miracles and Manipulation*. LHBOTS 671. London: T. & T. Clark, 2018.

Hess, Richard S. "Kings, Book of." In *DTIB*, 422–25.

Ho, Peter C. W. *The Design of the Psalter: A Macrostructural Analysis*. Eugene, OR: Pickwick, 2019.

House, Paul R. *Old Testament Theology*. Downers Grove, IL: InterVarsity, 1998.

Howard, David M. Jr. *The Structure of Psalms 93-100*. Biblical and Judaic Studies 5. Winona Lake, IL: Eisenbrauns, 1997.

Howard-Brook, Wes. *Come Out, My People! God's Call Out of Empire in the Bible and Beyond*. Maryknoll, NY: Orbis, 2012.

———. *Empire Baptized: How the Church Embraced What Jesus Rejected (2nd-5th Centuries)*. Maryknoll, NY: Orbis, 2016.

Hubbard, Robert L. Jr. *Joshua*. NIVAC. Grand Rapids: Zondervan, 2009.

Hurtado, Larry W. "Monotheism." In *DTIB*, 519–21.

Iersel, Bas van, and Anton Weiler, eds. *Exodus: A Lasting Paradigm*. Concilium. Edinburgh: T. & T. Clark, 1987.

James, Peter. Review of W. G. Dever, *What Did the Biblical Writers Know? Palestine Exploration Quarterly* 134.2 (2002) 176–78.

James, Peter, and Peter van der Veen, eds. *Solomon & Shishak: Current Perspectives from Archaeology, Epigraphy, History and Chronology. Proceedings of the Third BICANE Colloquium held at Sidney Sussex College, Cambridge 26-27 March 2011*. Oxford: Archaeopress, 2015.

Janzen, J. Gerald. *Abraham and All the Families of the Earth*. International Theological Commentary. Grand Rapids: Eerdmans, 1993.

Jennings, Willie James. *The Christian Imagination: Theology and the Origins of Race*. New Haven, CT: Yale University Press, 2010.

Jobes, Karen H., and Moisés Silva. *Invitation to the Septuagint*. 2nd ed. Grand Rapids: Baker Academic, 2015.

Jobling, David. *1 Samuel*. BO. Collegeville, MN: Liturgical, 1998.

Joerstad, Mari. *The Hebrew Bible and Environmental Ethics: Humans, Nonhumans, and the Living Landscape*. Cambridge: Cambridge University Press, 2019.

Kelle, Brad E. *The Bible and Moral Injury: Reading Scripture alongside War's Unseen Wounds*. Nashville: Abingdon, 2020.

———. *Telling the Old Testament Story: God's Mission and God's People*. Nashville: Abingdon, 2017.

Keys, Gillian. *The Wages of Sin: A Reappraisal of the "Succession Narrative."* JSOTSup 221. Sheffield, UK: Sheffield Academic Press, 1996.

Kaufman, Thomas. *Luther's Jews: A Journey into Anti-Semitism*. Translated by Lesley Sharpe and Jeremy Noakes. Oxford: Oxford University Press, 2017.

Keesmaat, Sylvia C. "The Psalms in Romans and Galatians." In *The Psalms in the New Testament*, edited by Steve Moyise and Maarten J. J. Menken, 139–61. London: T. & T. Clark, 2004.

Kitchen, Kenneth A. *On the Reliability of the Old Testament*. Grand Rapids: Eerdmans, 2003.

Klein, Lillian R. *The Triumph of Irony in the Book of Judges*. JSOTSup 68. Sheffield, UK: Almond, 1988.

Knohl, Israel. *The Divine Symphony: The Bible's Many Voices.* Philadelphia: Jewish Publication Society, 2003.

Knowles, Malcolm S., Elwood F. Holton, and Richard A. Swanson. *The Adult Learner: The Definitive Classic in Adult Education and Human Resource Development.* 7th ed. London: Routledge, 2012.

Kreider, Alan. *The Patient Ferment of the Early Church: The Improbable Rise of Christianity in the Roman Empire.* Grand Rapids: Baker Academic, 2016.

Kugel, James L. *The Bible as It Was.* Cambridge: Belknap, 1997.

———. *The Great Shift: Encountering God in Biblical Times.* New York: Mariner, 2018.

———. *The Idea of Biblical Poetry: Parallelism and Its History.* New Haven, CT: Yale University Press, 1981.

Kuhn, Karl Allen. *Having Words with God: The Bible as Conversation.* Minneapolis: Fortress, 2008.

Lakoff, George, and Mark Johnson. *Metaphors We Live By.* 2nd ed. Chicago: University of Chicago Press, 2003.

Lalleman, Hetty. "Jeremiah, Judgement and Creation." *Tyndale Bulletin* 60.1 (2009) 15–24.

Lasine, Stuart. "Guest and Host in Judges 19: Lot's Hospitality in an Inverted World." *JSOT* 29 (1984) 37–59.

———. *Weighing Hearts: Character, Judgment, and the Ethics of Reading the Bible.* LHBOTS 568. London: T. & T. Clark, 2012.

Lasserre, Jean. *War and the Gospel.* Translated by Oliver Coburn. London: James Clarke, 1962.

Lemos, T. M. *Violence and Personhood in Ancient Israel and Comparative Contexts.* Oxford: Oxford University Press, 2017.

Levenson, Jon D. *The Death and Resurrection of the Beloved Son: The Transformation of Child Sacrifice in Judaism and Christianity.* New Haven, CT: Yale University Press, 1993.

Levinson, Bernard M. "Strategies for the Reinterpretation of Normative Texts within the Hebrew Bible." *International Journal of Legal Discourse* 3.1 (2018) 1–31.

Levy, Ian Christopher. *Introducing Medieval Biblical Interpretation: The Senses of Scripture in Premodern Exegesis.* Grand Rapids: Baker Academic, 2018.

Linafelt, Todd. "Poetry and Biblical Narrative." In *OHBN*, 84–92.

Lind, Millard C. *Yahweh Is a Warrior: The Theology of Warfare in Ancient Israel.* Scottdale, PA: Herald, 1980.

Lohfink, Gerhard. *Jesus of Nazareth: What He Wanted, Who He Was.* Translated by Linda Maloney. Collegeville, MN: Liturgical, 2015.

Lohfink, Norbert S.J. *The Covenant Never Revoked: Biblical Reflections on Christian-Jewish Dialogue.* Translated by John J. Scullion, S.J. New York: Paulist, 1991.

———. "Death at the River Frontier: Moses' Incomplete Mission and the Contours of the Bible." In *In the Shadow of Your Wings: New Readings of Great Texts from the Bible*, translated by Linda Maloney, 1–14. Collegeville, MN: Liturgical, 2003.

———. *The Inerrancy of Scripture and Other Essays.* Translated by R. A. Wilson. Berkeley, CA: BIBAL, 1992.

Long, V. Philips. *The Art of Biblical History.* Leicester, UK: Apollos, 1994.

———. *1 and 2 Samuel.* TOTC. Downers Grove, IL: InterVarsity, 2020.

Longenecker, Bruce. W., ed. *Narrative Dynamics in Paul: A Critical Assessment.* Louisville, KY: Westminster John Knox, 2002.

Longenecker, Richard N. *Biblical Exegesis in the Apostolic Period*. 2nd ed. Grand Rapids, Eerdmans, 1999.
Longman, Tremper, III. *How to Read Genesis*. Downers Grove, IL: InterVarsity, 2005.
Lucas, Ernest. *Can We Believe Genesis Today? The Bible and the Questions of Science*. 2nd ed. Leicester, UK: InterVarsity, 2001.
Mays, James L. *The Lord Reigns: A Theological Handbook to the Psalms*. Louisville, KY: Westminster John Knox, 1994.
Mbuvi, Amanda Beckenstein. *Belonging in Genesis: Biblical Israel and the Politics of Identity Formation*. Waco, TX: Baylor University Press, 2016.
McCann, J. Clinton. *Judges*. IBC. Louisville, KY: Westminster John Knox, 2002.
McConville, J. Gordon. *God and Earthly Power: An Old Testament Political Theology: Genesis–Kings*. LHBOTS 454. London: T. & T. Clark, 2006.
McConville, J. Gordon, and Stephen N. Williams. *Joshua*. THOTC. Grand Rapids: Eerdmans, 2010.
McDonald, Lee Martin. *The Biblical Canon: Its Origin, Transmission, and Authority*. 3rd ed. Grand Rapids: Baker Academic, 2007.
McEntire, Mark. *Portraits of a Mature God: Choices in Old Testament Theology*. Minneapolis: Fortress, 2013.
McKnight, Scot. *Reading Romans Backwards: A Gospel in Search of Peace in the Midst of the Empire*. London: SCM, 2019.
Miller, Alice. *The Untouched Key: Tracing Childhood Trauma in Creativity and Destructiveness*. New York: Doubleday, 1990.
Möller, Karl. "Rhetorical Criticism." In *DTIB*, 689–92.
Moberly, R. W. L. *The Theology of the Book of Genesis*. Cambridge: Cambridge University Press, 2009.
Morrison, Craig E. *2 Samuel*. BO. Collegeville, MN: Liturgical, 2013.
Motyer, Stephen. *Your Father the Devil? A New Approach to John and "the Jews."* Carlisle, UK: Paternoster, 1997.
Munayer, Salim J., and Lisa Loden, eds. *The Land Cries Out: Theology of the Land in the Israeli-Palestinian Context*. Eugene, OR: Cascade, 2012.
Murray, Stuart. *Post-Christendom: Church and Mission in a Strange New World*. 2nd ed. Eugene, OR: Cascade, 2018.
Nelson, Richard D. *Joshua: A Commentary*. OTL. Louisville, KY: Westminster John Knox, 1997.
———. *The Historical Books*. Interpreting Bible Texts. Nashville: Abingdon, 1998.
Noth, Martin. *The Deuteronomistic History*. JSOTSup 15. Translated by E. W. Nicholson. Sheffield, UK: JSOT, 1981
Nugent, John C. *The Politics of Yahweh: John Howard Yoder, The Old Testament, and the People of God*. Eugene, OR: Cascade, 2011.
Olson, Dennis T. "The Book of Judges: Introduction, Commentary, and Reflections." In *NIB*, Vol II, 1998, 721–946.
Otto, Eckhart. "Deuteronomy as the Legal Completion and Prophetic Finale of the Pentateuch." In *Paradigm Change in Pentateuchal Research*, edited by Matthias Armgardt, Benjamin Kilchör, Markus Zehnder, 179–88. Beihefte zur Zeitschrift für Altorientalische und Biblische Rechtsgeschichte 22. Wiesbaden: Harrassowitz Verlag, 2019.
Paynter, Helen. *God of Violence Yesterday: God of Love Today? Wrestling Honestly with the Old Testament*. Abingdon, UK: Bible Reading Fellowship, 2019.

———. Review of *Crucifixion of the Warrior God*, by Gregory Boyd. https://www.csbvbristol.org.uk/2019/04/25/crucifixion-of-the-warrior-god/.

———. *Telling Terror in Judges 19: Rape and Reparation for the Levite's wife*. Abingdon, UK: Taylor & Francis, 2019.

Pelikan, Jaroslav. *The Christian Tradition, Vol 1: The Emergence of the Catholic Tradition (100–600)*. Chicago: University of Chicago Press, 1961.

Pennington, Jonathan T. *Reading the Gospels Wisely: A Narrative and Theological Introduction*. Grand Rapids: Baker Academic, 2012.

Perkins, Pheme. "Gnosticism." In *EEC*, 465–70.

Perrin, Nicholas. *Jesus the Priest*. London: SPCK, 2018.

———. *Jesus the Temple*. London: SPCK, 2010.

Peterson, Brian Neil. *The Authors of the Deuteronomistic History: Locating a Tradition in Ancient Israel*. Minneapolis: Fortress, 2014.

Phillips, Gary. "The Commanding Faces of Biblical Stories." In *OHBN*, 583–97.

Pietersen, Lloyd. *Reading the Bible after Christendom*. Milton Keynes, UK: Paternoster, 2011.

Polzin, Robert. *David and the Deuteronomist: A Literary Study of the Deuteronomic History. Part Three: 2 Samuel*. Bloomington, IN: Indiana University Press, 1993.

———. *Moses and the Deuteronomist: A Literary Study of the Deuteronomic History. Part One: Deuteronomy, Joshua, Judges*. Bloomington, IN: Indiana University Press, 1980.

———. *Samuel and the Deuteronomist: A Literary Study of the Deuteronomic History. Part Two: 1 Samuel*. Bloomington, IN: Indiana University Press, 1989.

Preuss, Horst Dietrich. *Old Testament Theology*, 2 vols. Translated by Leo G. Perdue. Louisville, KY: Westminster John Knox, 1995–96.

Probst, Christopher J. *Demonizing the Jews: Luther and the Protestant Church in Nazi Germany*. Bloomington, IN: Indiana University Press, 2012.

Provan, Iain W. "Hearing the Historical Books." In *Hearing the Old Testament: Listening for God's Address*, edited by Craig G. Bartholomew and David J. H. Beldman, 254–76. Grand Rapids: Eerdmans, 2012.

———. *Seriously Dangerous Religion: What the Old Testament Really Says and Why It Matters*. Waco, TX: Baylor University Press, 2014.

Provan, Iain, V. Phillips Long, and Tremper Longman III. *A Biblical History of Israel*. Louisville, KY: Westminster John Knox, 2003.

von Rad, Gerhard. *Old Testament Theology*. 2 vols. Translated by D. M. G. Stalker. London: SCM, 1962–65.

Rendtorff, Rolf. *Canon and Theology: Overtures to an Old Testament Theology*. OBT. Minneapolis: Fortress, 1993.

Richter, Sandra L. "Deuteronomistic History." In *DOTHB*, 219–30.

———. *The Epic of Eden: A Christian Entry into the Old Testament*. Downers Grove, IL: InterVarsity, 2008.

Rohl, David. *A Test of Time: The Bible from Myth to History*. London: Century, 1995.

Römer, Thomas. *The So-Called Deuteronomistic History: A Sociological, Historical and Literary Introduction*. London: T. & T. Clark, 2007.

Rose, W. H. "Zerubbabel." In *DOTHB*, 1016–19.

Rost, Leonhard. *The Succession to the Throne of David*. Translated by Michael D. Rutter and David M. Gunn. Sheffield, UK: Almond, 1982. First published in German, Stuttgart: von W. Kohlhammer, 1926.

Rowlett, Lori L. *Joshua and the Rhetoric of Violence: A New Historicist Analysis.* JSOTSup 226. Sheffield, UK: Sheffield Academic Press, 1996.
Ryan, Jordan, and Matthew Schlimm. "Shedding Light: Conversation Starters for Churches." https://www.matthewschlimm.com/light.html.
Sacks, Jonathan. *Exodus: The Book of Redemption.* C&C. New Milford, CT: Magid, 2010.
———. *Genesis: The Book of Beginnings.* C&C. New Milford, CT: Magid, 2009.
Sanders, James A. *From Sacred Story to Sacred Text: Canon as Paradigm.* Philadelphia: Fortress, 1987.
Schama, Simon. *Belonging: The Story of the Jews, 1492–1900.* London: Bodley Head, 2017.
———. *The Story of the Jews, Vol. I, Finding the Words, 1000BCE–1492CE.* London: Bodley Head, 2013.
———. *The Story of the Jews.* (DVD) London: BBC Worldwide, 2013.
Schlimm, Matthew Richard. *From Fratricide to Forgiveness: The Language and Ethics of Anger in Genesis.* Siphrut 7. Winona Lake, IN: Eisenbrauns, 2011.
———. *This Strange and Sacred Scripture: Wrestling with the Old Testament and Its Oddities.* Grand Rapids: Baker Academic, 2015.
———. *70 Hebrew Words Every Christian Should Know.* Nashville: Abingdon, 2018.
Schneider, Tammi J. *Judges.* BO. Collegeville, MN: Liturgical, 2000.
Sechrest, Love. L. "Racism." In *DSE*, 655–57.
Sechrest, Love L., Johnny Ramírez-Johnson, and Amos Yong, eds. *Can "White" People Be Saved? Triangulating Race, Theology, and Mission.* Downers Grove, IL: InterVarsity, 2018.
Seibert, Eric A. *Subversive Scribes and the Solomonic Narrative: A Rereading of 1 Kings 1–11.* LHBOTS 436 London: T. & T. Clark, 2006.
Seitz, Christopher R. *Zion's Final Destiny: The Development of the Book of Isaiah: A Reassessment of Isaiah 36–39.* Minneapolis: Fortress, 1991.
Shalev, Elan. *American Zion: The Old Testament as a Political Text from the Revolution to the Civil War.* New Haven, CT: Yale University Press, 2013.
Smith, Daniel L. *The Religion of the Landless: The Social Context of the Babylonian Exile.* Bloomington, IN: Meyer-Stone, 1989.
Smith, Richard G. *The Fate of Justice and Righteousness during David's Reign: Narrative Ethics and Rereading the Court History according to 2 Samuel 8:15b—20:26.* LHBOTS 508. London: T. & T. Clark, 2009.
Smith-Christopher, Daniel. *A Biblical Theology of Exile.* OBT. Minneapolis: Fortress, 2002.
———. *Micah: A Commentary.* OTL. Louisville, KY: Westminster John Knox, 2015.
Soulen, R. Kendall, *The God of Israel and Christian Theology.* Minneapolis: Fortress, 1996.
Southgate, Christopher, ed. *God, Humanity and the Cosmos: A Textbook in Science and Religion.* 3rd ed. London: T. & T. Clark, 2011.
Sparks, Kenton L. "Gospel as Conquest: Mosaic Typology in Matthew 28:16–20." *CBQ* 68.4 (2006) 651–63.
———. "Propaganda." In *DOTHB*, 819–25.
———. *Sacred Word, Broken Word: Biblical Authority and the Dark Side of Scripture.* Grand Rapids: Eerdmans, 2011.
Spencer, F. Scott. *Salty Wives, Spirited Mothers, and Savvy Widows: Capable Women of Purpose and Persistence in Luke's Gospel.* Grand Rapids: Eerdmans, 2012.

Spina, Frank Anthony. *The Faith of the Outsider: Exclusion and Inclusion in the Biblical Story.* Grand Rapids: Eerdmans, 2005.
Stander, Hendrik F. "Marcion." In *EEC*, 715–17.
Stanley, Andy. *Aftermath Part 3: Not Difficult* (video). https://www.youtube.com/watch?v=pShxFTNRCWI/.
———. *Irresistible: Reclaiming the New That Jesus Unleashed for the World.* Grand Rapids: Zondervan, 2018.
Sternberg, Meir. *The Poetics of Biblical Narrative: Ideological Literature and the Drama of Reading.* Bloomington, IN: Indiana University Press, 1985.
Steussy, Marti J. *David: Biblical Portraits of Power.* Columbia: University of South Carolina Press, 1999.
———. *Samuel and His God.* Columbia: University of South Carolina Press, 2010.
Stone, Lawson G. "Ethical and Apologetic Tendencies in the Redaction of the Book of Joshua." *CBQ* 53.1 (1991) 25–36.
Strawn, Brent. *The Old Testament: A Concise Introduction.* New York; Routledge, 2020.
Swartley, "Sabbath." In *EEC*, 1007–8.
———. *Slavery, Sabbath, War & Women: Case Issues in Biblical Interpretation.* Scottdale, PA: Herald, 1985.
Sweeney, Marvin A. *Reading the Hebrew Bible after the Shoah: Engaging Holocaust Theology.* Minneapolis: Fortress, 2008.
———. *I & II Kings: A Commentary.* OTL. Louisville, KY: Westminster John Knox, 2007.
Thiselton, Anthony C. *Hermeneutics: An Introduction.* Grand Rapids: Eerdmans, 2009.
Trible, Phyllis. *Texts of Terror: Literary-Feminist Readings of Biblical Narratives.* Philadelphia: Fortress, 1984.
Trocmé, André. *Jesus and the Nonviolent Revolution.* Translated from French by Michael H. Shank and Marlin E. Miller. 1973. Reprint, Walden, NY: Plough, 2003.
Tuell, Steven S. *First and Second Chronicles.* IBC. Louisville, KY: John Knox, 2001.
Tull, Patricia K. *Inhabiting Eden: Christians, the Bible, and the Ecological Crisis.* Louisville, KY: Westminster John Knox, 2013.
Twelftree, Graham H. "Demon, Devil, Satan." In *DJG*, 163–72.
Van Dam, C. "Priestly Clothing." In *DOTP*, 643–46.
Walsh, Jerome T. *1 Kings.* BO. Collegeville, MN: Liturgical, 1996.
———. "The Organization of 2 Kings 3–11." *CBQ* 72 (2010) 238–54.
———. *Style and Structure in Biblical Hebrew Narrative.* Collegeville, MN: Liturgical, 2001.
Walton, John H. *Ancient Near Eastern Thought and the Old Testament: Introducing the Conceptual World of the Old Testament.* Grand Rapids: Baker, 2006.
Walton, John H., and J. Harvey Walton. *The Lost World of the Israelite Conquest: Covenant, Retribution, and the Fate of the Canaanites.* Downers Grove, IL: InterVarsity, 2017.
Webb, Barry G. *The Book of Judges.* NICOT. Grand Rapids: Eerdmans, 2012.
Webb, William J. *Slaves, Women & Homosexuals: Exploring the Hermeneutics of Cultural Analysis.* Downers Grove, IL: InterVarsity, 2001.
———. *Corporal Punishment in the Bible: A Redemptive-Movement Hermeneutic for Troubling Texts.* Downers Grove, IL: InterVarsity, 2011.
Webb, William J., and Gordon K. Oeste. *Bloody Brutal, and Barbaric? Wrestling with Troubling War Texts.* Downers Grove, IL: InterVarsity, 2019.

Wenham, Gordon J. "Genesis, Book of." In *DTIB*, 246–52.
———. *Genesis 1–15*. WBC. Waco, TX: Word, 1987.
———. *Genesis 16–50*. WBC. Waco, TX: Word, 1994.
———. *Story as Torah: Reading the Old Testament Ethically*. Edinburgh: T. & T. Clark, 2000.
Westbrook, April D. *"And He Will Take Your Daughters . . ." Woman Story and the Ethical Evaluation of Monarchy in the David Narrative*. LHBOTS 610. London: T. & T. Clark, 2015.
Wilken, Robert L. *John Chrysostom and the Jews: Rhetoric and Reality in the Late Fourth Century*. Berkeley, CA: University of California Press, 1983.
Williamson, H. G. M. "Isaiah: Book of." In *DOTP*, 364–78.
Wilson, Gerald H. *The Editing of the Hebrew Psalter*. Chico, CA: Scholars, 1985.
Wilson, Marvin R. *Our Father Abraham: Jewish Roots of the Christian Faith*. Grand Rapids: Eerdmans, 1989.
Wilson, Robert R. *Genealogy and History in the Biblical World*. New Haven, CT: Yale University Press, 1977.
Winter, Bruce W. *Seek the Welfare of the City: Christians as Benefactors and Citizens. First Century Christians in the Graeco-Roman World*. Grand Rapids: Eerdmans, 1994.
Woudstra, Marten H. *The Book of Joshua*. NICOT. Grand Rapids: Eerdmans, 1981.
Wright, Jacob L. *David, King of Israel, and Caleb in Biblical Memory*. New York: Cambridge University Press, 2014.
Wright, John W. "Genealogies." In *DOTP*, 345–50.
Wright, Tom. *Paul: A Biography*. London: SPCK, 2018.
Wright, N. T. *The Climax of the Covenant: Christ and the Law in Pauline Theology*. Edinburgh: T. & T. Clark, 1991.
———. "How Can the Bible be Authoritative?" *Vox Evangelica* 21 (1991) 7–32.
———. *The New Testament and the People of God: Christian Origins and the Question of God*, Vol. 1. London: SPCK, 1992.
———. *Paul and the Faithfulness of God: Christian Origins and the Question of God*, Vol. 4. London: SPCK, 2013.
Würthwein, Ernst. *The Text of the Old Testament: An Introduction to the Biblia Hebraica*. 3rd ed., revised and expanded by Alexander Achilles Fischer. Translated by Erroll F. Rhodes. Grand Rapids: Eerdmans, 2014.
Yoder, John Howard. *The Original Revolution: Essays on Christian Pacifism*. Scottdale, PA: Herald, 1980.
———. *The Politics of Jesus: Vicit Agnus Noster*. 2nd ed. Grand Rapids: Eerdmans, 1994.
———. "See How They Go with Their Face to the Sun." In *For the Nations: Essays Public & Evangelical*, 51–78. Grand Rapids: Eerdmans, 1997.
———. "Withdrawal and Diaspora: The Two Faces of Liberation." In *Freedom and Discipleship: Liberation Theology in an Anabaptist Perspective*, edited by Daniel S. Schipani, 76–84. Maryknoll, NY: Orbis, 1989.
Yoder Neufeld, Thomas R. *Put on the Armour of God: The Divine Warrior from Isaiah to Ephesians*. Sheffield, UK: Sheffield Academic Press, 1997.
Young, Davis A., and Ralph F. Stearley. *The Bible, Rocks and Time: Geological Evidence for the Age of the Earth*. Downers Grove, IL: IVP Academic, 2008.

Younger, K. Lawson Jr. *Ancient Conquest Accounts: A Study in Ancient Near Eastern and Biblical History Writing*. JSOTSup 98. Sheffield, UK: Sheffield Academic Press, 1990.

———. "Early Israel in Recent Biblical Scholarship." In *The Face of Old Testament Studies: A Survey of Contemporary Approaches*, edited by D. W. Baker and B. T. Arnold, 176–206. Grand Rapids: Baker, 1999.

———. *Judges and Ruth*. NIVAC. Grand Rapids: Zondervan, 2002.

Zenger, Erich. "The God of Exodus in the Message of the Prophets as Seen in Isaiah." In *Exodus: A Lasting Paradigm*, edited by Bas van Iersel and Anton Weiler, 22–33. Concilium. Edinburgh: T. & T. Clark, 1987.

www.ingramcontent.com/pod-product-compliance
Lightning Source LLC
Chambersburg PA
CBHW021649230426
43668CB00008B/567